WESTER
HOME PLANS

Over 200 Home Plans Specially Designed For

- California
- Pacific Northwest
- Rocky Mountains
- Texas & Western Plains
- Desert Southwest
- "Western" Lovers Everywhere

HOME PLANNERS, INC.

Published by Home Planners, Inc.
Editorial and Corporate Offices:
3275 West Ina Road, Suite 110
Tucson, Arizona 85741

Distribution Center:
29333 Lorie Lane
Wixom, Michigan 48393

Charles W. Talcott, Chairman
Rickard D. Bailey, President and Publisher
Cindy J. Coatsworth, Publications Manager
Paulette Mulvin, Editor
Paul D. Fitzgerald, Book Designer

Photo Credits
Front Cover: © Steve Whalen/Zephyr Pictures
Back Cover: ©Allen Maertz Photography.

First Printing, January 1992

10 9 8 7 6 5 4 3 2 1

Printed in the United States of America.

Library of Congress Catalog Card Number: 91-076715

ISBN: 0-918894-94-8

On the front cover: A beautiful example of Spanish Mission Style, our interpretation of the cover home, Design P3449, can be found on page 31.
Back Cover: This dramatic Santa Fe-Style home is our Design P3405. For more information about this design, see page 74.

Table Of Contents

Editor's Note

While no one particular style of home can be categorized as "Western Style," it is clear that homes built in the western regions of the country share some common denominators. All, for instance, abound with the freedom of form and spirit that defines the Western lifestyle. Relying on historical perspectives for detail, they combine a respect for classic models with a vision for comfortable, modern living. And they provide ample opportunity for indoor/outdoor livability. The homes on the following pages are superb examples of the best in Western design. From San Francisco Victorian to Santa Fe Pueblo, from Craftsman Bungalow to International Contemporary, they traverse the breadth of the West, both literally and figuratively, affording a full spectrum of the Western style for those who have come to know and love it.

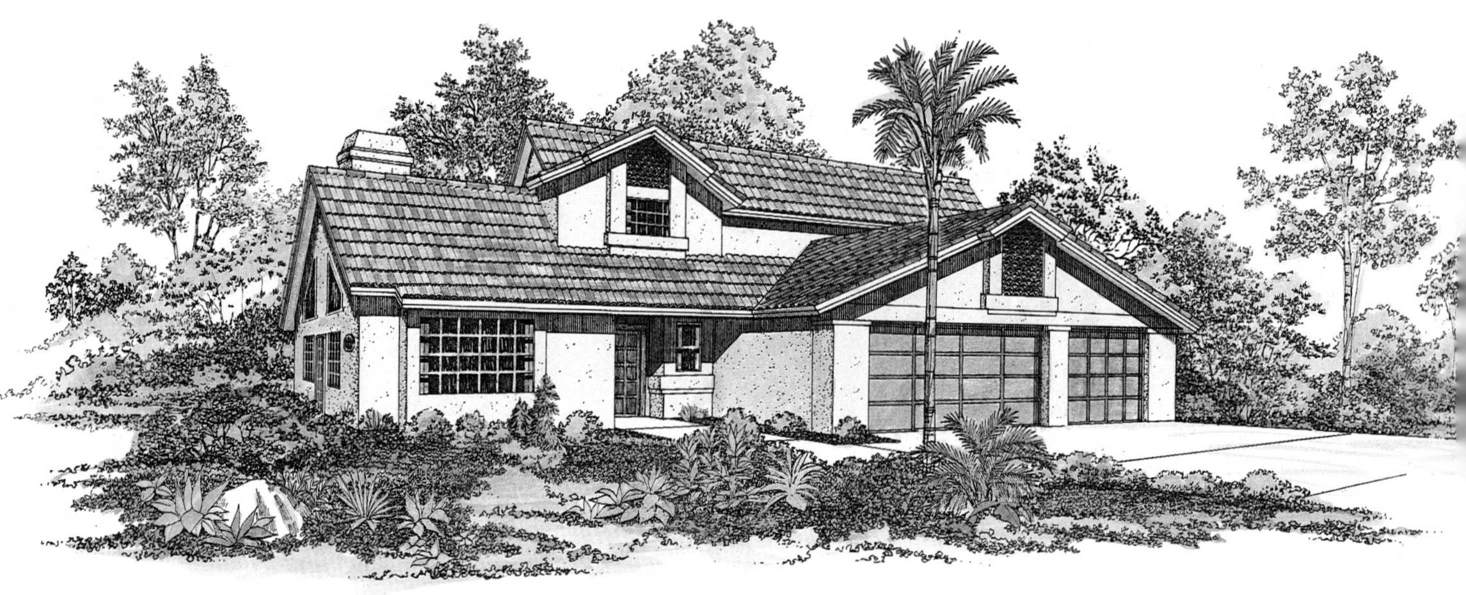

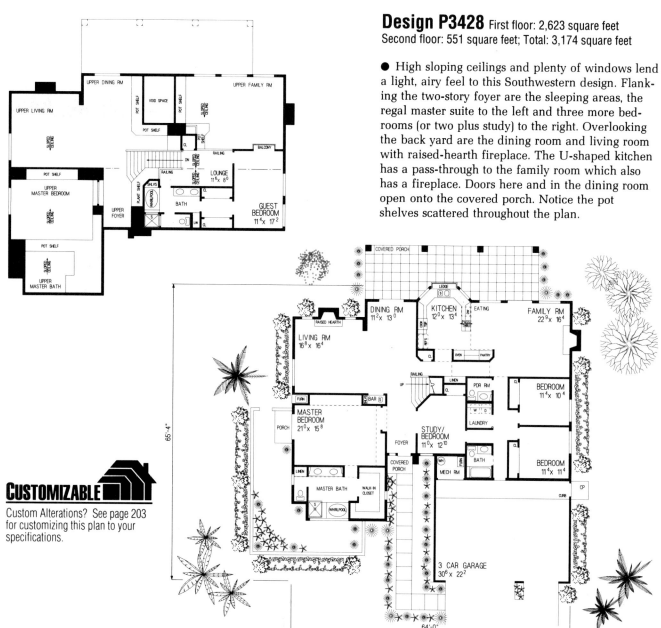

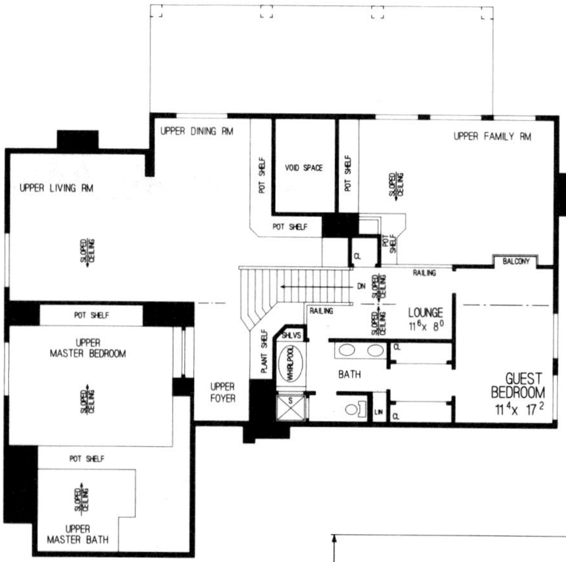

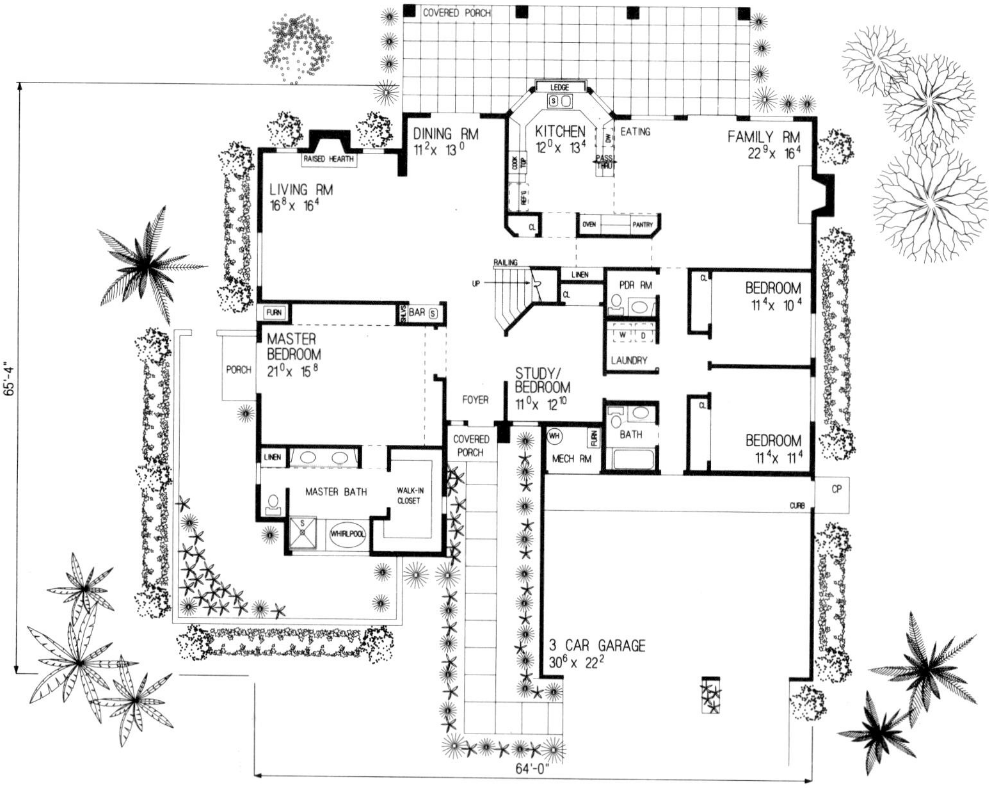

UPPER DINING RM
UPPER FAMILY RM
UPPER LIVING RM
POT SHELF
VOID SPACE
SLOPED CEILING
BALCONY
RAILING
DN
CL
LOUNGE 11^6 x 8^0
SHLVS
PLANT SHELF
WHIRLPOOL
BATH
LIN
GUEST BEDROOM 11^4 x 17^2
UPPER MASTER BEDROOM
UPPER FOYER
UPPER MASTER BATH

Design P3428 First floor: 2,623 square feet
Second floor: 551 square feet; Total: 3,174 square feet

● High sloping ceilings and plenty of windows lend a light, airy feel to this Southwestern design. Flanking the two-story foyer are the sleeping areas, the regal master suite to the left and three more bedrooms (or two plus study) to the right. Overlooking the back yard are the dining room and living room with raised-hearth fireplace. The U-shaped kitchen has a pass-through to the family room which also has a fireplace. Doors here and in the dining room open onto the covered porch. Notice the pot shelves scattered throughout the plan.

COVERED PORCH
LEDGE
DINING RM 11^2 x 13^0
KITCHEN 12^0 x 13^4
PASS THRU
EATING
FAMILY RM 22^9 x 16^4
RAISED HEARTH
LIVING RM 16^8 x 16^4
OVEN
PANTRY
CL
RAILING
UP
LINEN
PDR RM
BEDROOM 11^4 x 10^4
FURN
BAR
MASTER BEDROOM 21^0 x 15^8
PORCH
LAUNDRY
STUDY/ BEDROOM 11^0 x 12^{10}
FOYER
65'-4"
COVERED PORCH
WH
MECH RM
BATH
BEDROOM 11^4 x 11^4
LINEN
MASTER BATH
WALK-IN CLOSET
WHIRLPOOL
CP
CURB
3 CAR GARAGE 30^6 x 22^2
64'-0"

CUSTOMIZABLE

Custom Alterations? See page 203 for customizing this plan to your specifications.

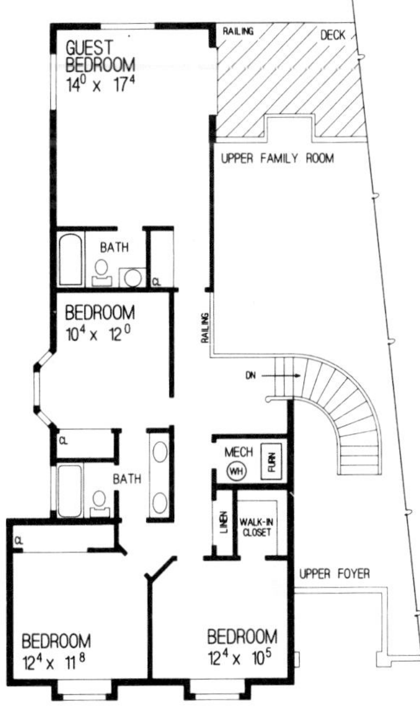

Design P3414

First Floor: 2,024 square feet
Second Floor: 1,144 square feet
Total: 3,168 square feet

Custom Alterations? See page 203 for customizing this plan to your specifications.

● Though seemingly compact from the exterior, this home allows for "wide-open-spaces" living. The two-story entry connects directly to a formal living/dining area, a fitting complement to the more casual family room and cozy breakfast room. Split-bedroom planning puts the master suite on the first floor for utmost privacy. Up the curved staircase are three family bedrooms, a guest room with deck, and two full baths.

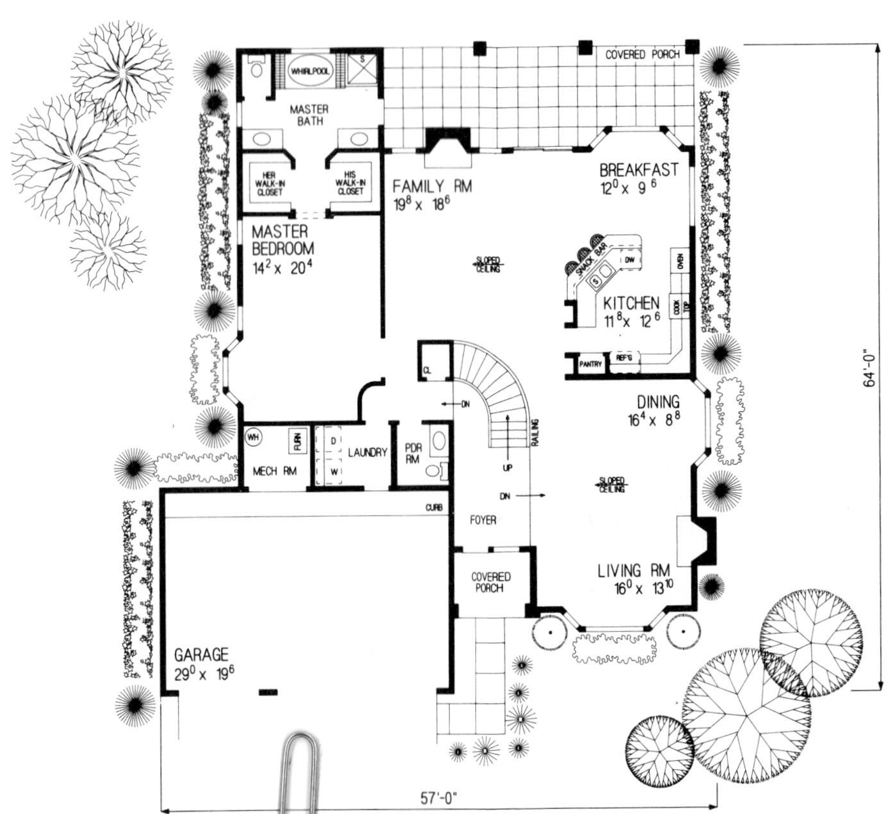

For more Spanish Eclectic designs, see pages 37-52.

Design P2236

Square Footage: 2,307

● Living in this Spanish adaptation truly will be fun for the whole family. It will matter very little whether the backdrop matches the mountains as shown or becomes the endless prairie, turns out to be the rolling farmland, or is the backdrop of suburbia, U.S.A. A family's flair for distinction will be satisfied by this picturesque exterior, while its requirements for everyday living will be gloriously catered to by its floor plan. The hub of the plan will be the kitchen-family room area. The beamed ceiling and raised hearth fireplace will contribute to the cozy, informal atmosphere. The separate dining room and the sunken living room function together formally. The master bedroom will enjoy its privacy from the three children's rooms located at the opposite end of the plan.

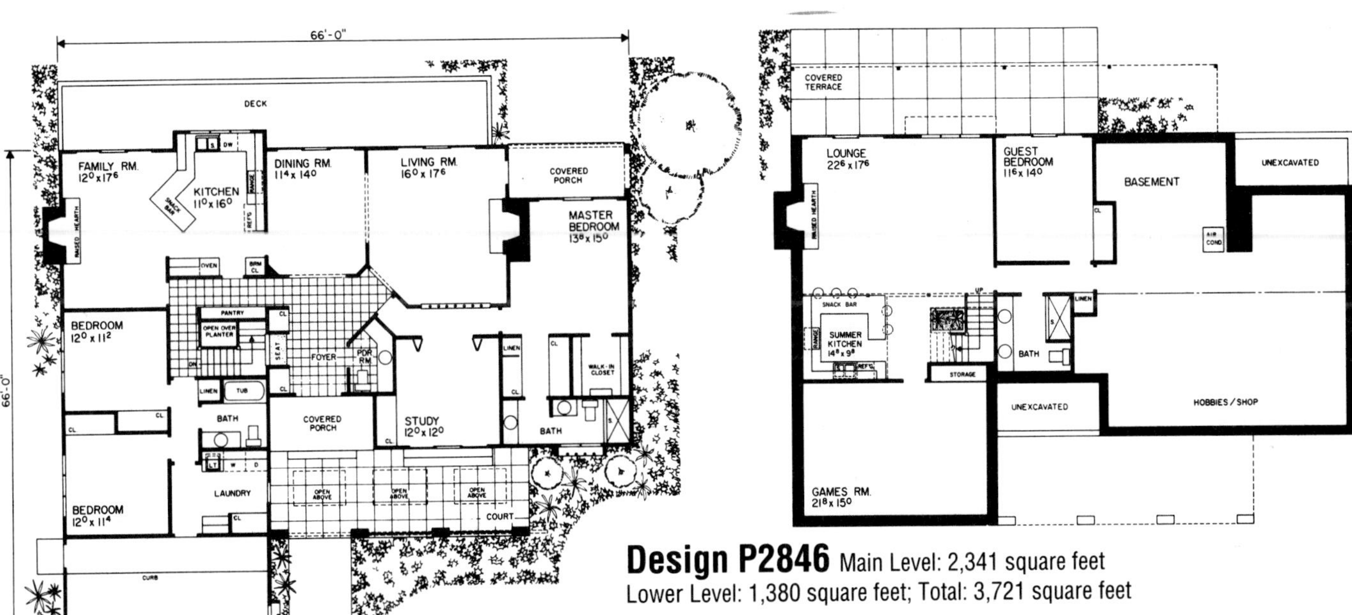

Design P2846 Main Level: 2,341 square feet
Lower Level: 1,380 square feet; Total: 3,721 square feet

● The street view of this Spanish design shows a beautifully designed one-story home, but now take a look at the rear elevation. This home has been designed to be built into a hill so the lower level can be opened to the sun. By so doing, the total livability is almost doubled. A unique feature of the lower level is the summer kitchen.

For more Spanish Colonial, Territorial and Rustic designs, see pages 53-70.

Design P2711

First Floor: 975 square feet
Second Floor: 1,024 square feet
Total: 1,999 square feet

L **D**

● Special features! A complete master suite with a private balcony plus two more bedrooms and a bath upstairs. The first floor has a study with a storage closet. A convenient snack bar is located between the kitchen and the dining room. The kitchen offers many built-in appliances. The gathering room (with fireplace) and dining room combination measures 31 feet wide. Note the extra curb space in the garage.

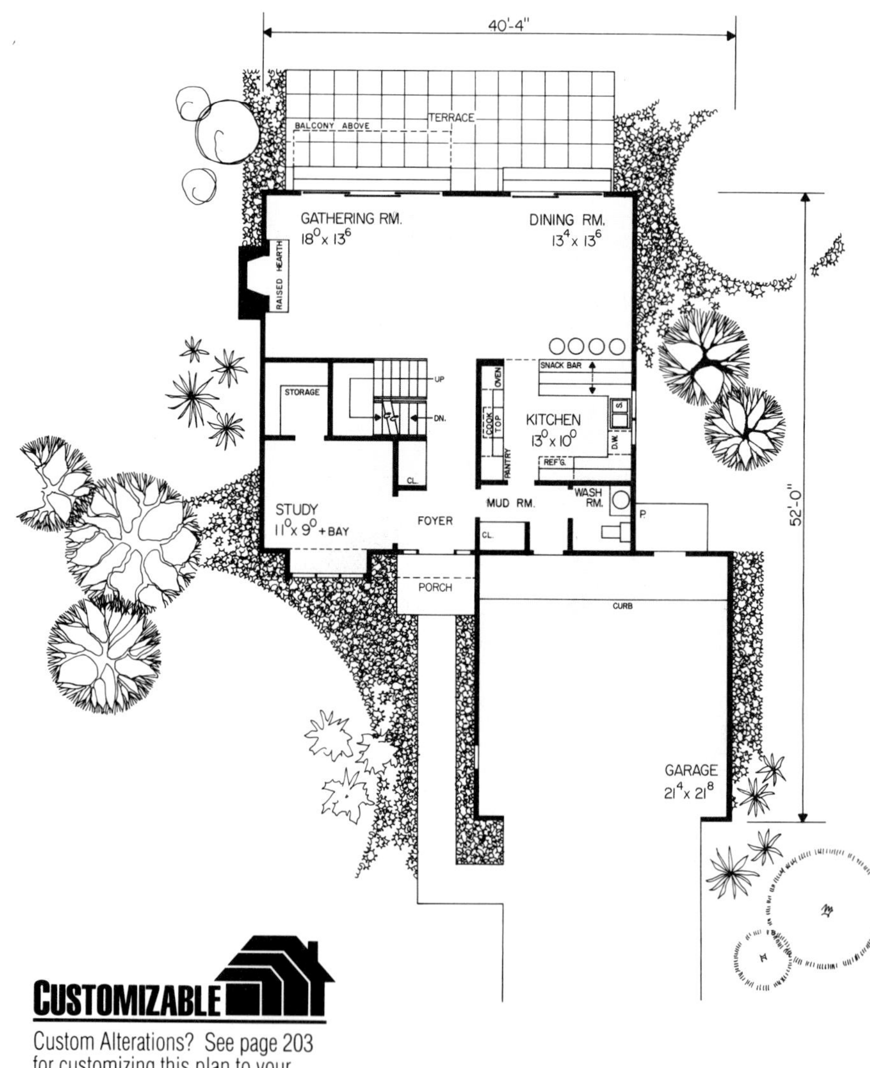

CUSTOMIZABLE

Custom Alterations? See page 203 for customizing this plan to your specifications.

Design P2937 Main Level: 1,096 square feet

Upper Level: 1,115 square feet; Lower Level: 1,104 square feet
Total: 3,315 square feet

L

● This contemporary multi-level home features an extended rear balcony that covers a rear patio, plus a master bedroom suite, complete with whirlpool and raised-hearth pass-thru. Two other bedrooms and a second bath are on the upper level.

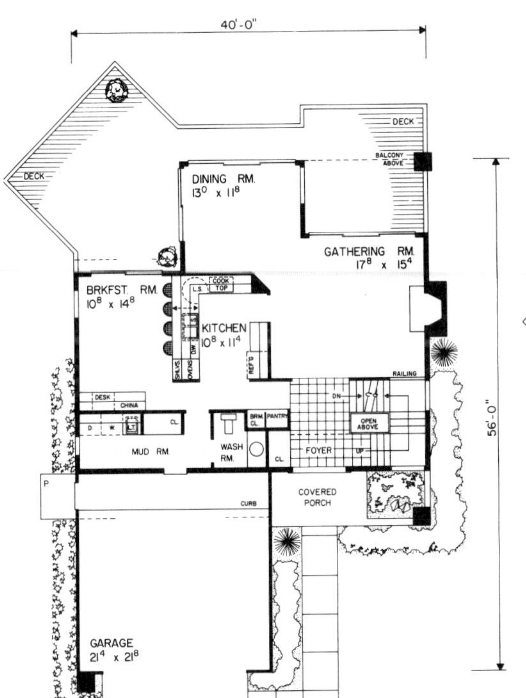

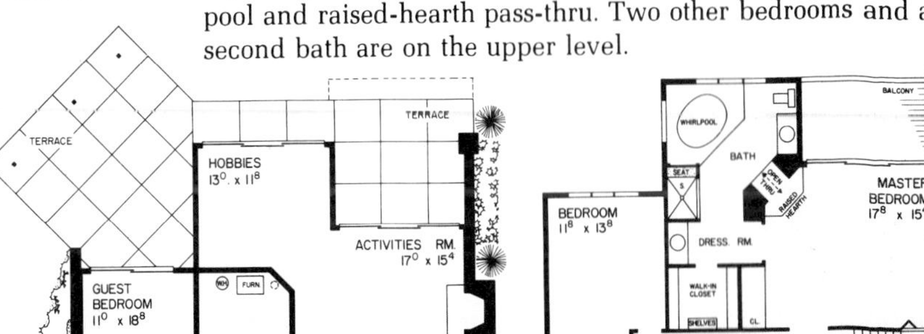

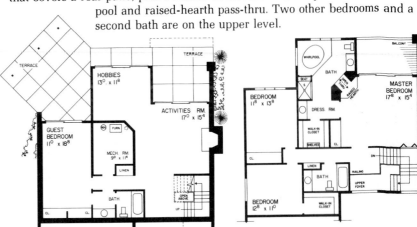

For more Pacific Wood Contemporary designs, see pages 111-128.

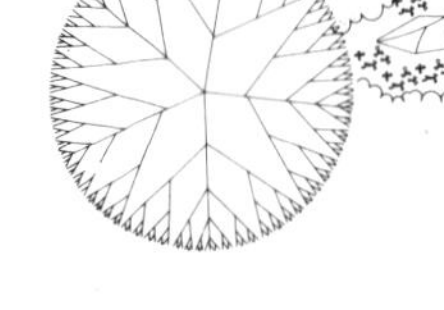

Design P3314

Square Footage: 1,951

● Formal living areas in this plan are joined by a three-bedroom sleeping wing. One bedroom, with foyer access, could function as a study. Two verandas and a screened porch enlarge the plan and enhance indoor/outdoor livability. Notice the abundant storage space.

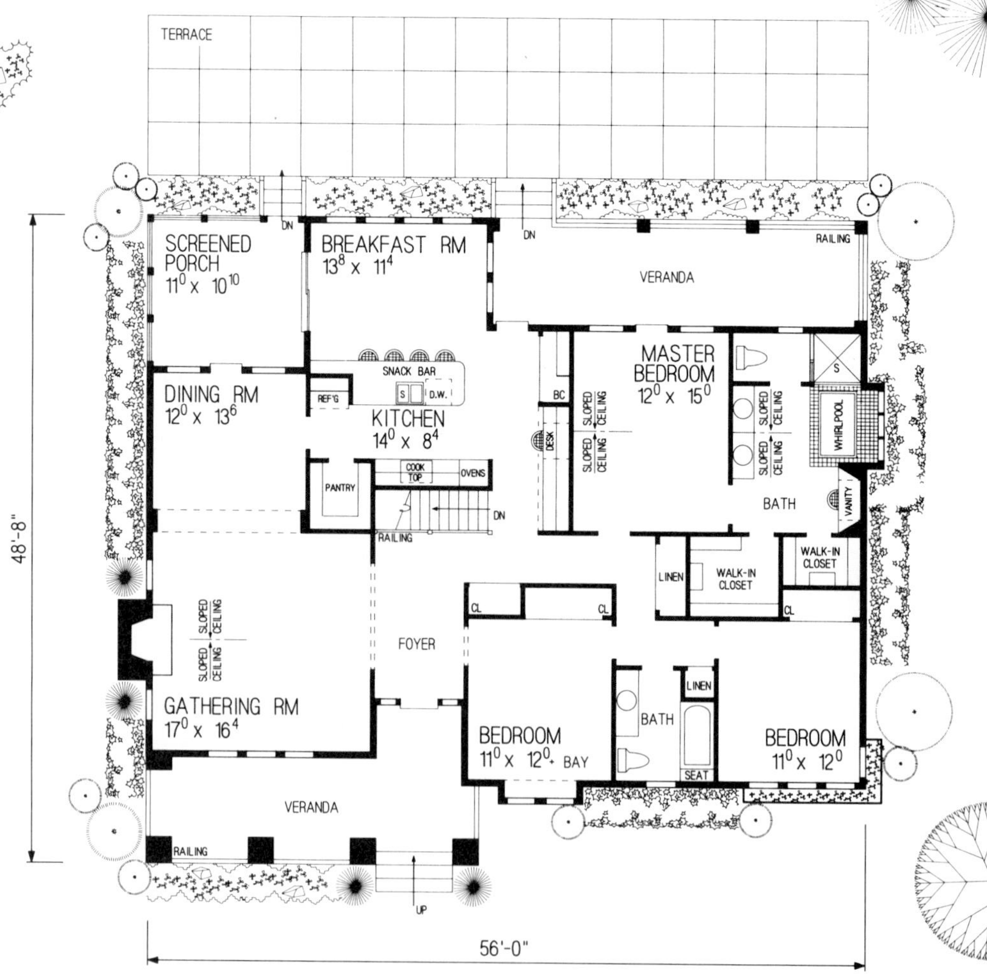

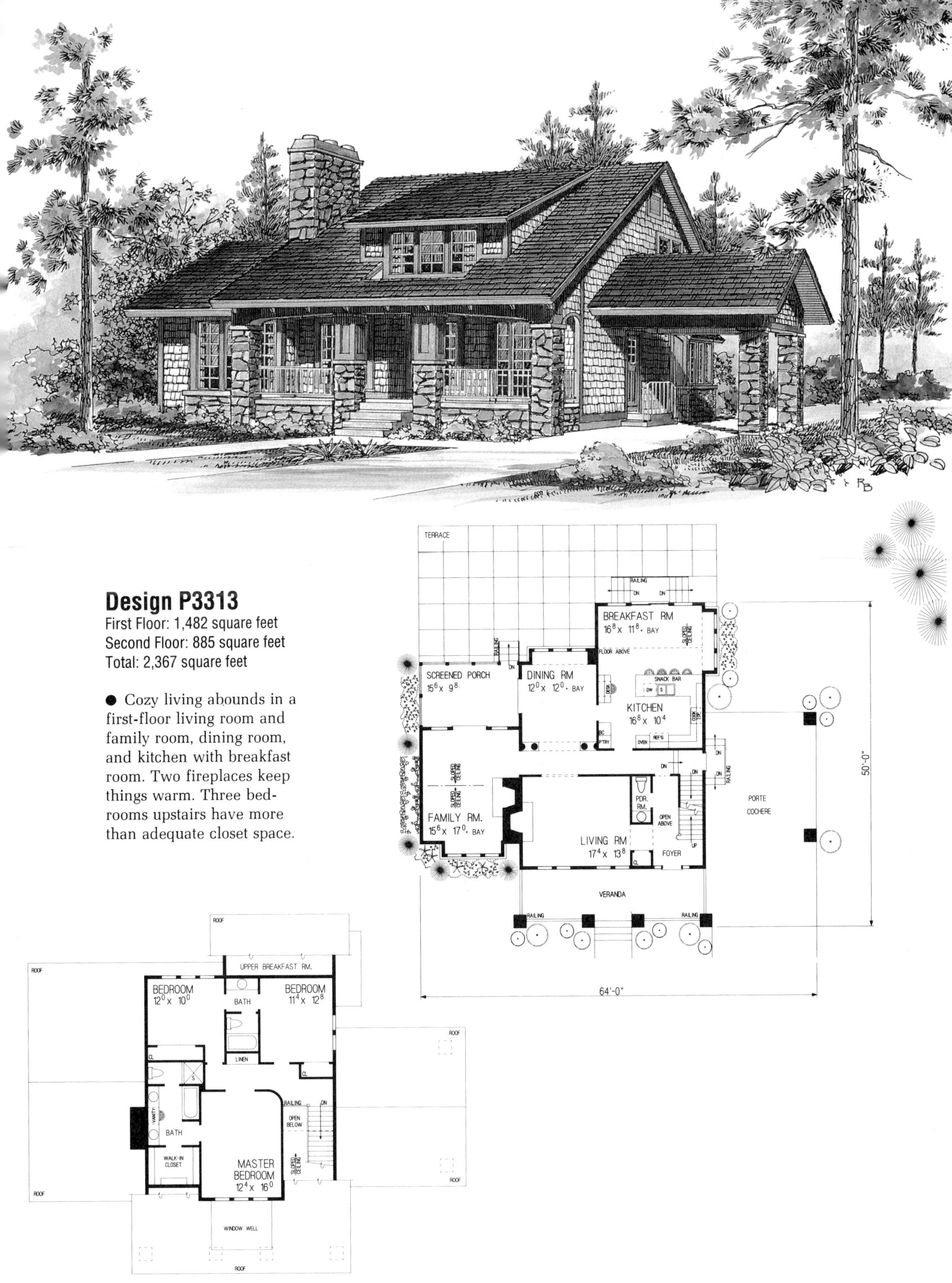

Design P3313

First Floor: 1,482 square feet
Second Floor: 885 square feet
Total: 2,367 square feet

● Cozy living abounds in a first-floor living room and family room, dining room, and kitchen with breakfast room. Two fireplaces keep things warm. Three bedrooms upstairs have more than adequate closet space.

For more California, Bungalow and International styles, see pages 97-110.

Design P2973

First Floor: 1,269 square feet
Second Floor: 1,227 square feet; Total: 2,496 square feet

L

● A most popular feature of the Victorian house has always been its covered porches. These finely detailed outdoor living spaces may be found on the front, the side, the rear or even in all three locations at once. The two designs on these two pages show just that. In addition to being an appealing exterior design feature, covered porches have their practical side, too. They provide wonderful indoor-outdoor living relationships. Imagine, sheltered outdoor living facilities for the various formal and informal living and dining areas of the plan. This home has a myriad of features to cater to the living requirements of the growing, active family.

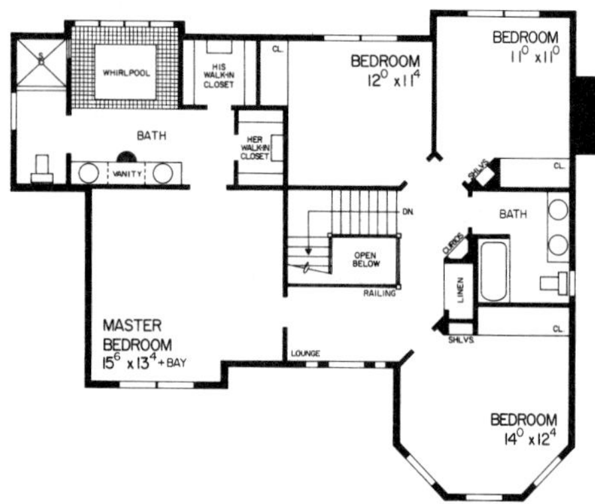

CUSTOMIZABLE

Custom Alterations? See page 203 for customizing this plan to your specifications.

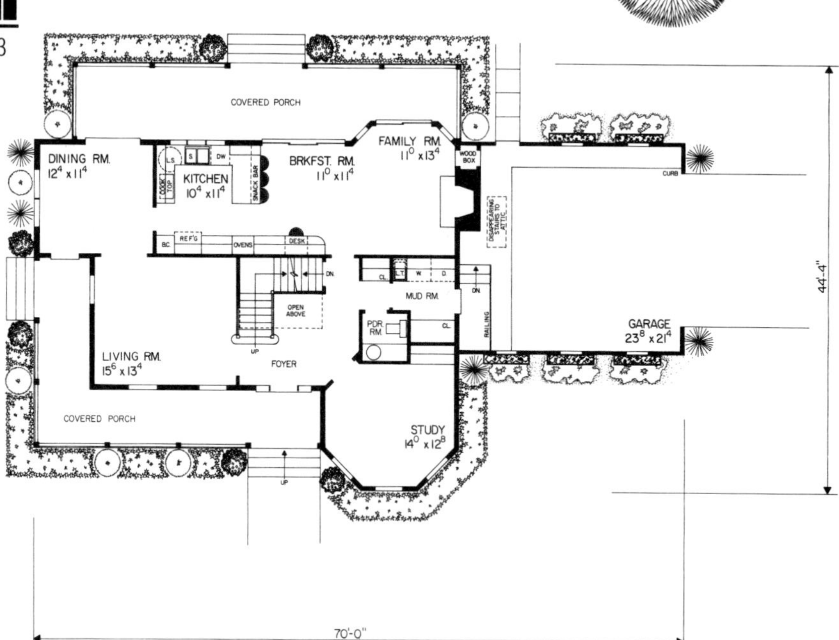

Design P2974

First Floor: 911 square feet; Second Floor: 861 square feet
Total: 1,772 square feet

L

● Victorian houses are well known for their orientation on narrow building sites. And when this occurs nothing is lost to captivating exterior styling. This house is but 38 feet wide. Its narrow width belies the tremendous amount of livability found inside. And, of course, the ubiquitous porch/veranda contributes mightily to style as well as livability. The efficient, U-shape kitchen is flanked by the informal breakfast room and formal dining room. The rear living area is spacious and functions in an exciting manner with the outdoor areas. Bonus recreational, hobby and storage space is offered by the basement and the attic.

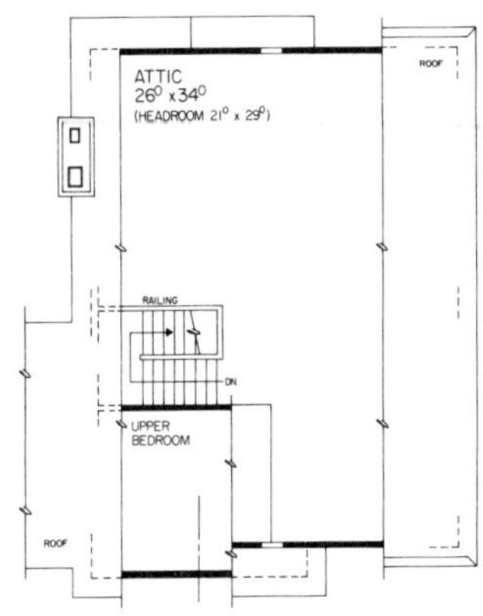

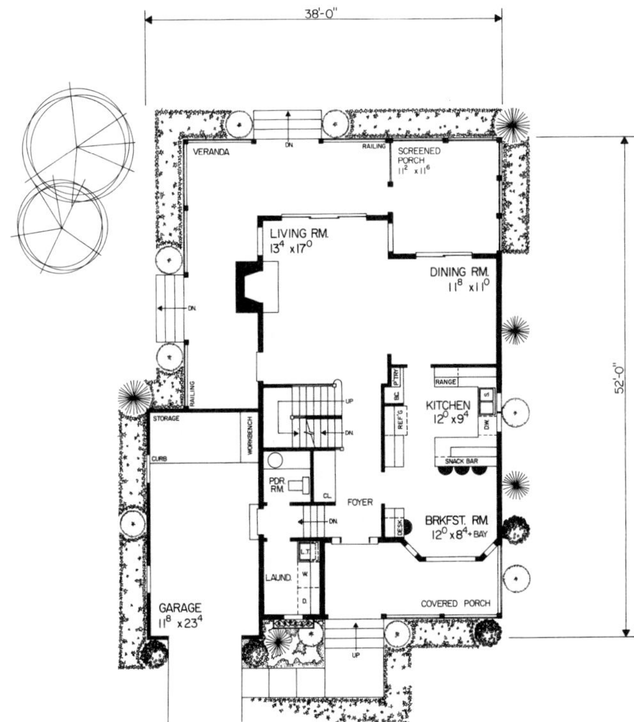

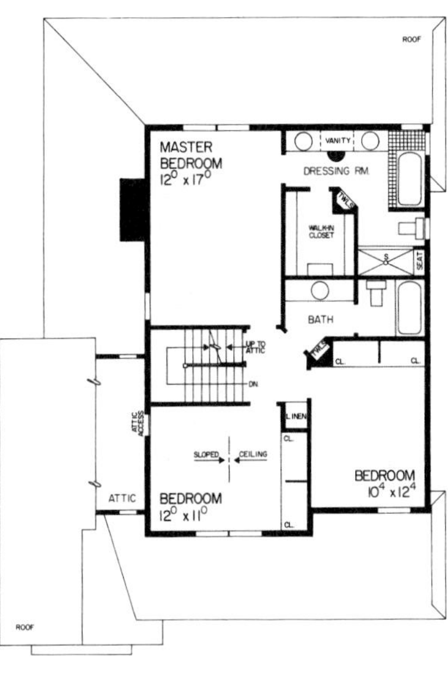

For more Victorian and Gothic designs, see pages 147-166.

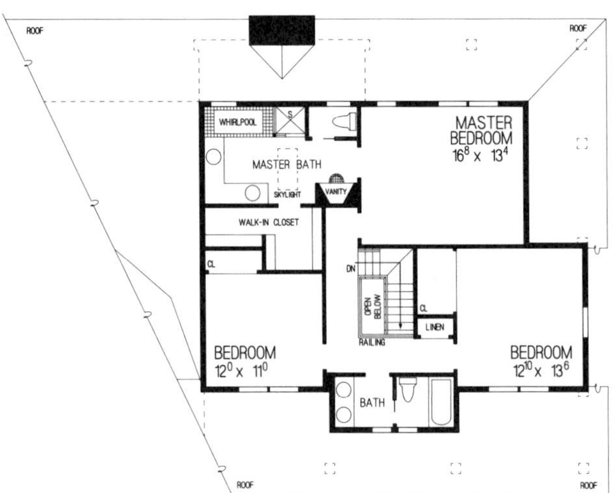

Design P3307

First Floor: 1,765 square feet
Second Floor: 1,105 square feet
Total: 2,870 square feet

L **D**

● A classic in its own right, this farmhouse design is sure to be on everyone's list of favorites. The facade says simple, country living, but the interior plan is practical and as modern as can be. Special features to appreciate include: three wide verandas, generous family room, study/guest room, well-appointed master suite, and raised-hearth fireplace.

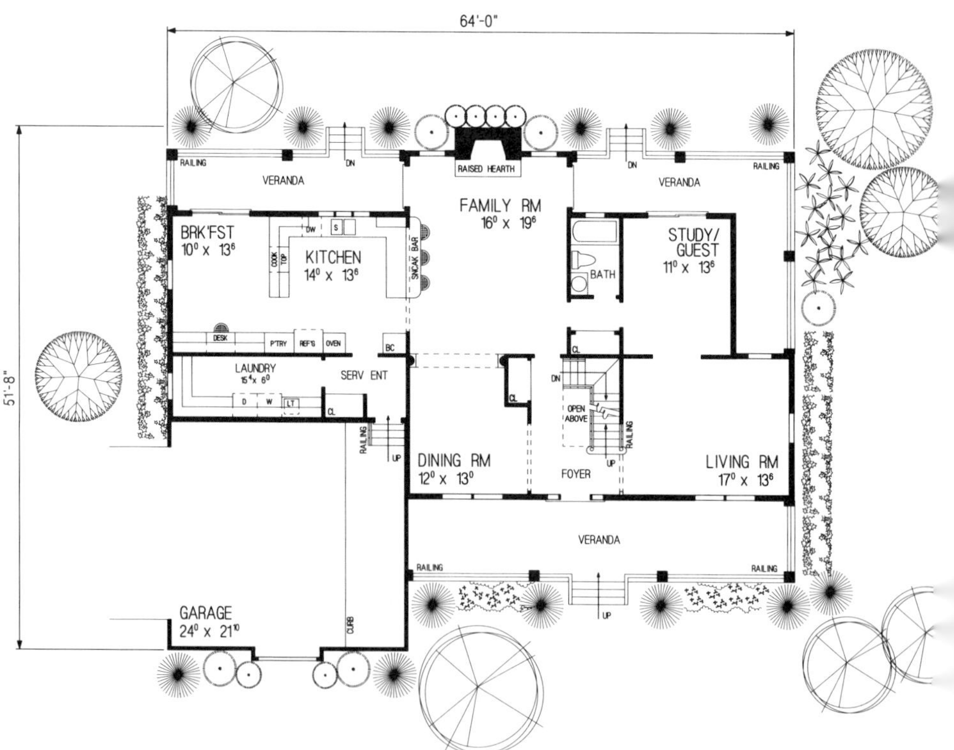

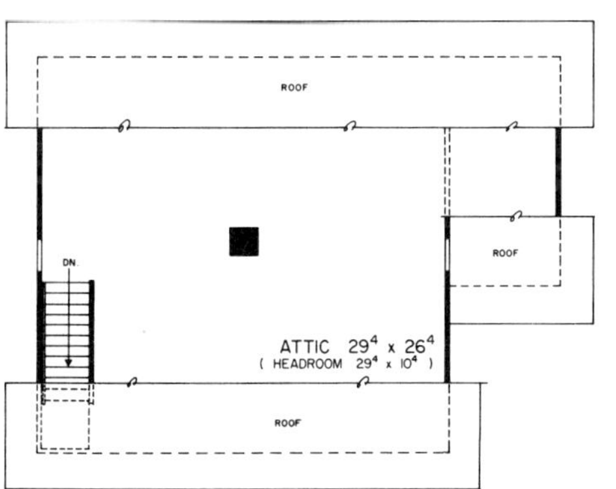

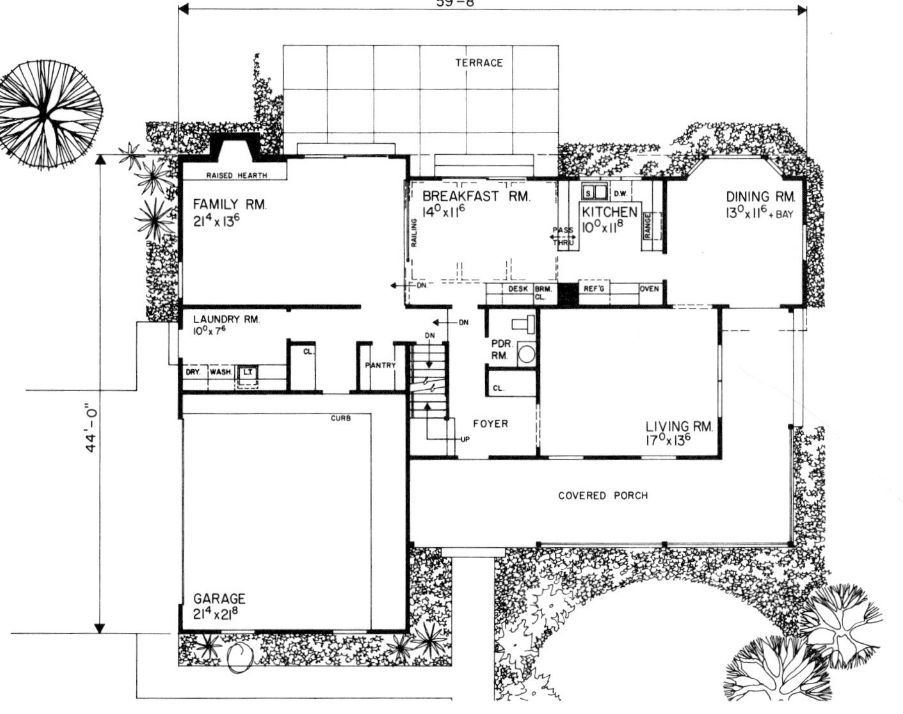

For more Western Farmhouses, see pages 167-178.

Design P2774

First Floor: 1,370 square feet
Second Floor: 969 square feet
Total: 2,339 square feet

L **D**

● A Farmhouse adaptation with all of the most up-to-date features expected in a new home. Beginning with the formal areas, this design offers pleasures for the entire family. There is the quiet, corner living room which has an opening to the sizable dining room. This room will have plenty of natural light from the delightful bay window which overlooks the rear yard. It is also conveniently located with the efficient, U-shaped kitchen just a step away. The kitchen features many built-ins with a pass-through to the beamed ceiling breakfast room. Sliding glass doors to the terrace are fine attractions in both the sunken family room and breakfast room. The service entrance to the garage has a storage closet on each side, plus there is a secondary entrance through the laundry area. Recreational activities and hobbies can be pursued in the basement area. Four bedrooms and two baths are on the second floor.

Custom Alterations? See page 203 for customizing this plan to your specifications.

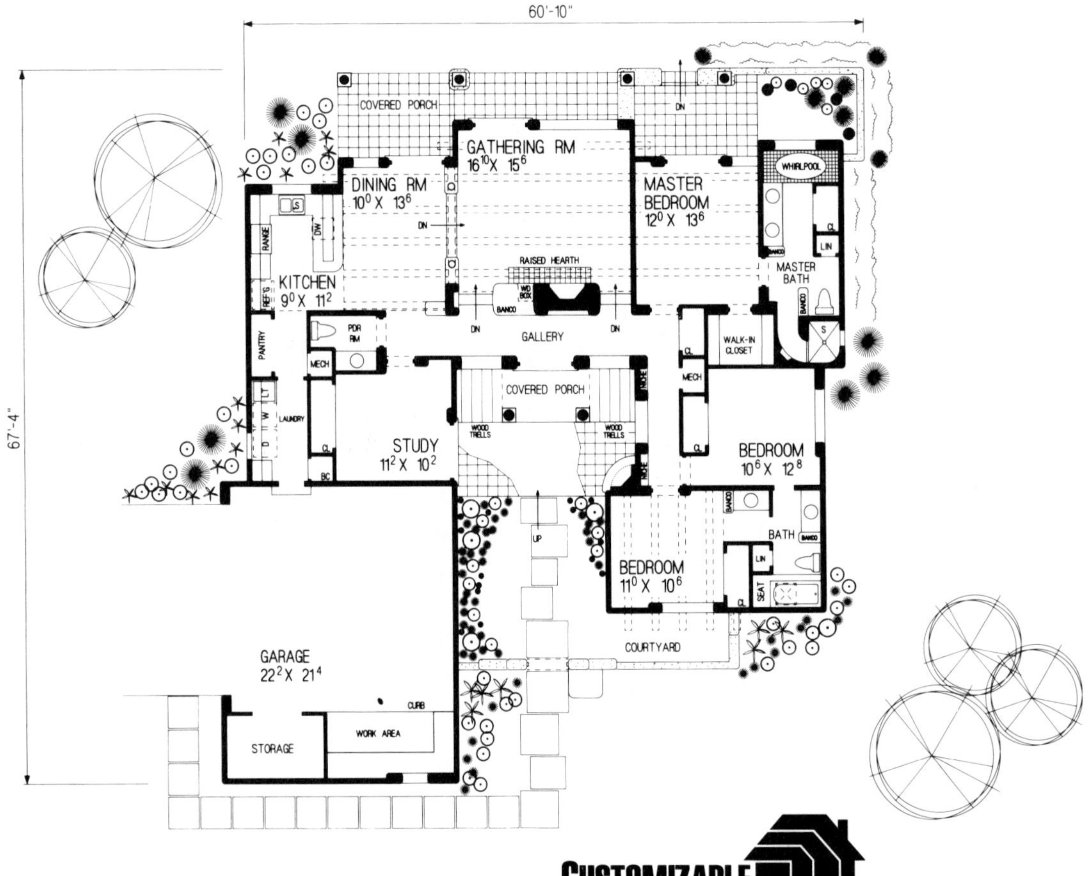

Custom Alterations? See page 203 for customizing this plan to your specifications.

Design P3431

Square Footage: 1,899

● Graceful curves welcome you into the courtyard of this Santa Fe home. Inside, a gallery directs traffic to the work zone on the left or the sleeping zone on the right. Straight ahead lies a sunken gathering room with beamed ceiling and raised-hearth fireplace. A large pantry offers extra storage space for kitchen items. The covered rear porch is accessible from the dining room, gathering room and secluded master bedroom. Luxury describes the feeling in the master bath with whirlpool tub, separate shower, double vanity and closet space. Two family bedrooms share a compartmented bath. The study could serve as a guest room, media room or home office.

Spanish Mission and Monterey

Spanish Mission

Among the most recognizable of all Southwestern-style homes, the Spanish Mission was developed in the spirit of mission churches established in the temperate climates of California. The first appearance of this style in residential California architecture was in the 1890s, but by 1900 it had spread to the Southwestern states of Arizona, New Mexico and western Texas. Between 1905 and 1920, it was a well-established style and was being built in scattered areas throughout the country.

The style reflects a peaceful era in California's history under Mexican rule. While earlier housing styles were likely to have interior courtyards which provided walled protection from invasion, the Spanish Mission-style home maintains exterior porches and balconies. The roof of such outdoor structures is often braced by square columns that join at the apex to form a rounded arch. One-story porches are common entry adornments and may extend completely across the full width of the facade.

The shape of the Spanish Mission-style home may be symmetrical—square or rectangular—or may use the square or rectangular shape as a base to which extensions are added, often in a seemingly asymmetrical fashion. Exterior walls are most often finished with smooth stucco.

Perhaps the most identifiable aspect of the Mission-style house is its red tile roof—common in the original mission churches. The roofs themselves are generally hipped with a low pitch, though gabled fronts may appear on the main roof or at the porch roof. A mission-styled dormer is not uncommon. Eaves are wide, overhanging and usually open.

Other significant components of this style include mission-like towers, a noticeable lack of exterior ornamentation and an occasional quatrefoil window—either glassed or open.

Monterey

Monterey-style homes were first built in the northern regions of California between 1925 and 1955. They were a return to the simpler architecture of Spanish Colonial times, with the earliest examples showing evidence of Spanish details. Later, as the style developed, characteristics of English Colonial homes began to appear.

The influence of Eastern Yankees on the northern portions of California allowed for an interesting mix of materials in the Monterey-style home. They are usually found with adobe or stucco exteriors with wood frames. In most cases, the first and second floors are composed of different materials—the first floor being built of brick and the second floor of wood.

The upper story often has a porch across the width of its facade or may sport a small balcony off an upstairs bedroom. The roofs of porches and balconies are supported by simple posts, often of hand-hewed wood.

Roofs are shallow and sometimes hipped but just as often are gabled. Common roof coverings are wood shingles or red tile.

Ornamentation is limited to paired windows and sometimes doors, both or either of which may have false shutters.

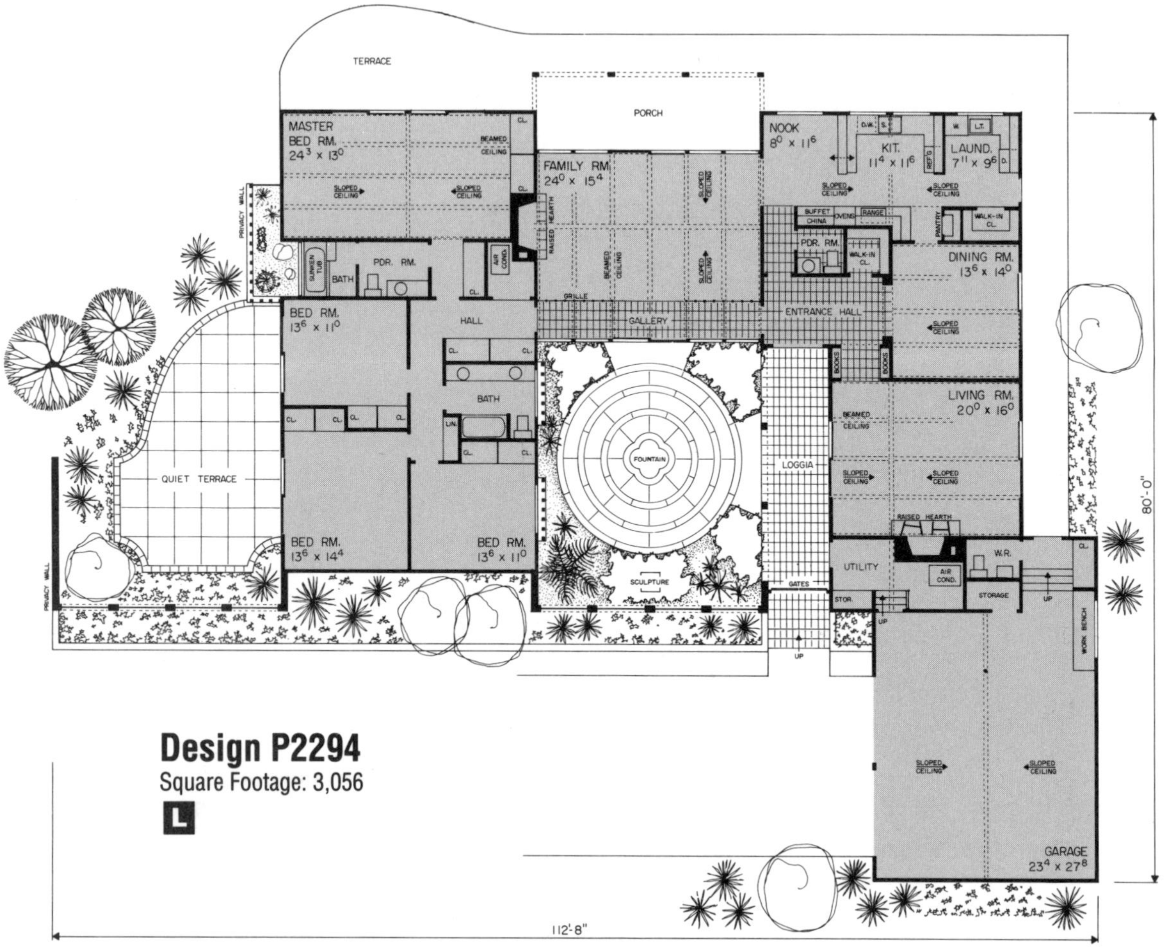

Design P2294

Square Footage: 3,056

L

● Here is a western ranch with an authentic Spanish flavor. Striking a note of distinction, the arched privacy walls provide a fine backdrop for the long, raised planter. The low-pitched roof features tile and has a wide overhang with exposed rafter tails. The interior is wonderfully zoned. The all-purpose family room is flanked by the sleeping wing and the living wing. Study each area carefully for the planning is excellent and the features are many. Indoor-outdoor integration is outstanding. At left — the spacious interior court. The covered passage to the double front doors is dramatic, indeed.

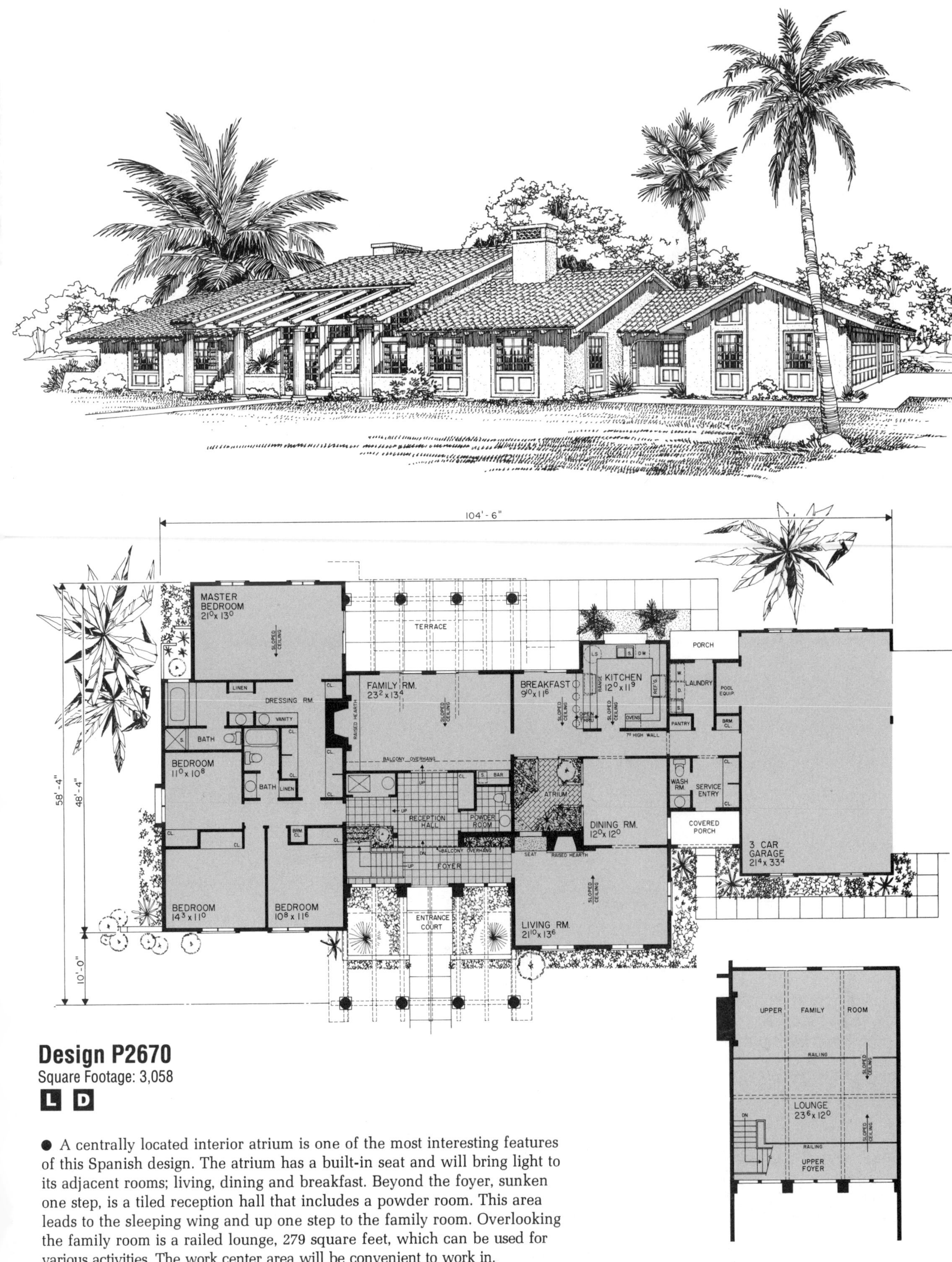

Design P2670

Square Footage: 3,058

L **D**

● A centrally located interior atrium is one of the most interesting features of this Spanish design. The atrium has a built-in seat and will bring light to its adjacent rooms; living, dining and breakfast. Beyond the foyer, sunken one step, is a tiled reception hall that includes a powder room. This area leads to the sleeping wing and up one step to the family room. Overlooking the family room is a railed lounge, 279 square feet, which can be used for various activities. The work center area will be convenient to work in.

Design P2850

Main Level: 1,530 square feet
Upper Level: 984 square feet
Lower Level: 951 square feet
Total: 3,465 square feet

L **D**

● Entering through the entry court of this Spanish design is very impressive. Down six steps from the foyer is the lower level, housing a bedroom and full bath, study and teenage activities room. Six steps up from the foyer is the upper-level bedroom area. The main level has the majority of the living areas: formal living and dining rooms, informal family room, kitchen with accompanying breakfast room and mud room consisting of laundry and wash room. This home even has a three-car garage.

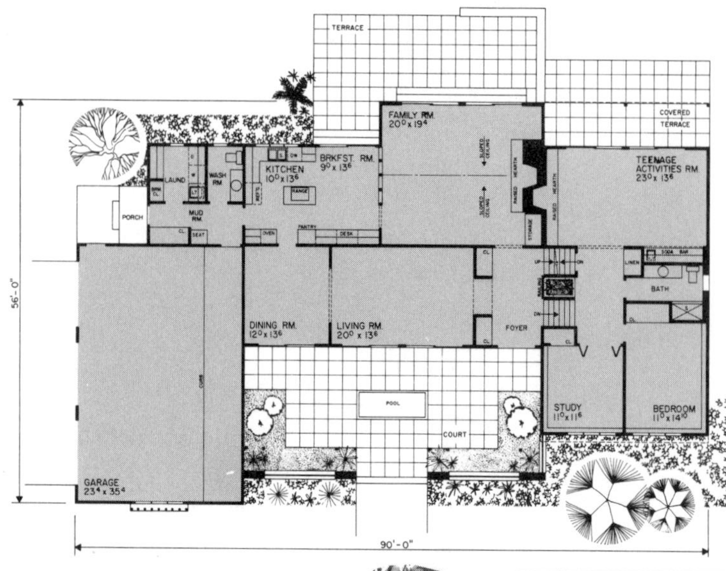

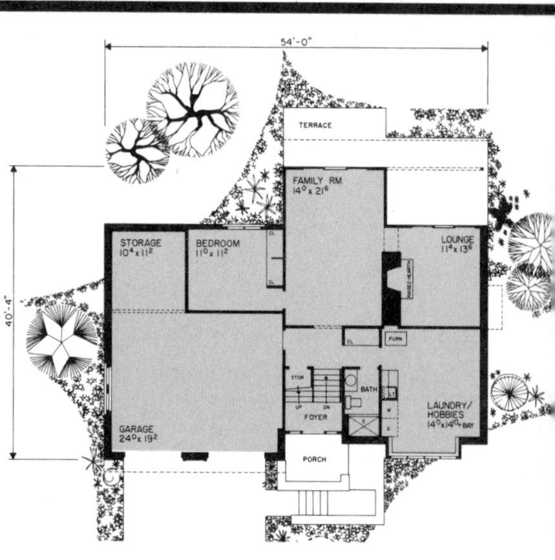

Design P2843

Upper Level: 1,861 square feet
Lower Level: 1,181 square feet
Total: 3,042 square feet

L

● Bi-level living will be enjoyed to its fullest in this Spanish- styled design. There is a lot of room for the various family activities. Informal living will take place on the lower level in the family room and lounge. The formal living and dining rooms, sharing a through-fireplace, are located on the upper level.

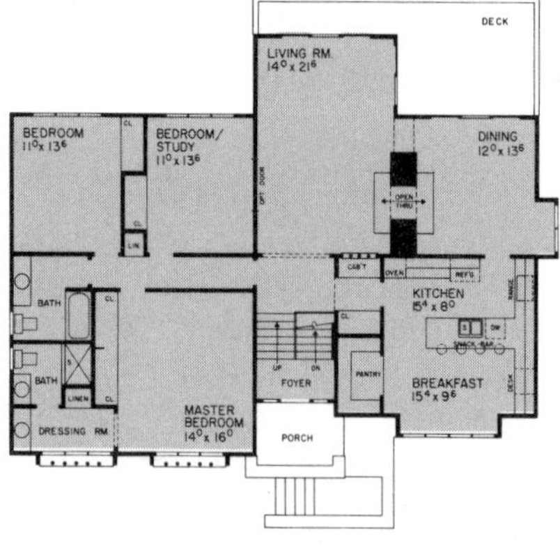

Design P2922

Square Footage: 3,505

● Loaded with custom features, this plan seems to have everything imaginable. There's an enormous sunken gathering room and cozy study. The country-style kitchen contains an efficient work area, as well as space for relaxing in the morning and sitting rooms. Two nice-sized bedrooms and a luxurious master suite round out the plan.

Design P2335

Square Footage: 2,674

● Surely a winner for those who have a liking for the architecture of the Far West. With or without the enclosure of the front court, this home with its stucco exterior, brightly colored roof tiles, and exposed rafter tails will be impressive, indeed. The floor plan reflects a wonderfully zoned interior. This results in a fine separation of functions which helps assure convenient living. The traffic patterns which flow from the spacious foyer are most efficient. Study them. While the sleeping wing is angled to the front line of the house, the sunken living room projects, at an angle, from the rear. Worthy of particular notice are such highlights as the two covered porches, the raised hearth fireplaces, the first floor laundry, the partial basement and the oversized garage with storage space.

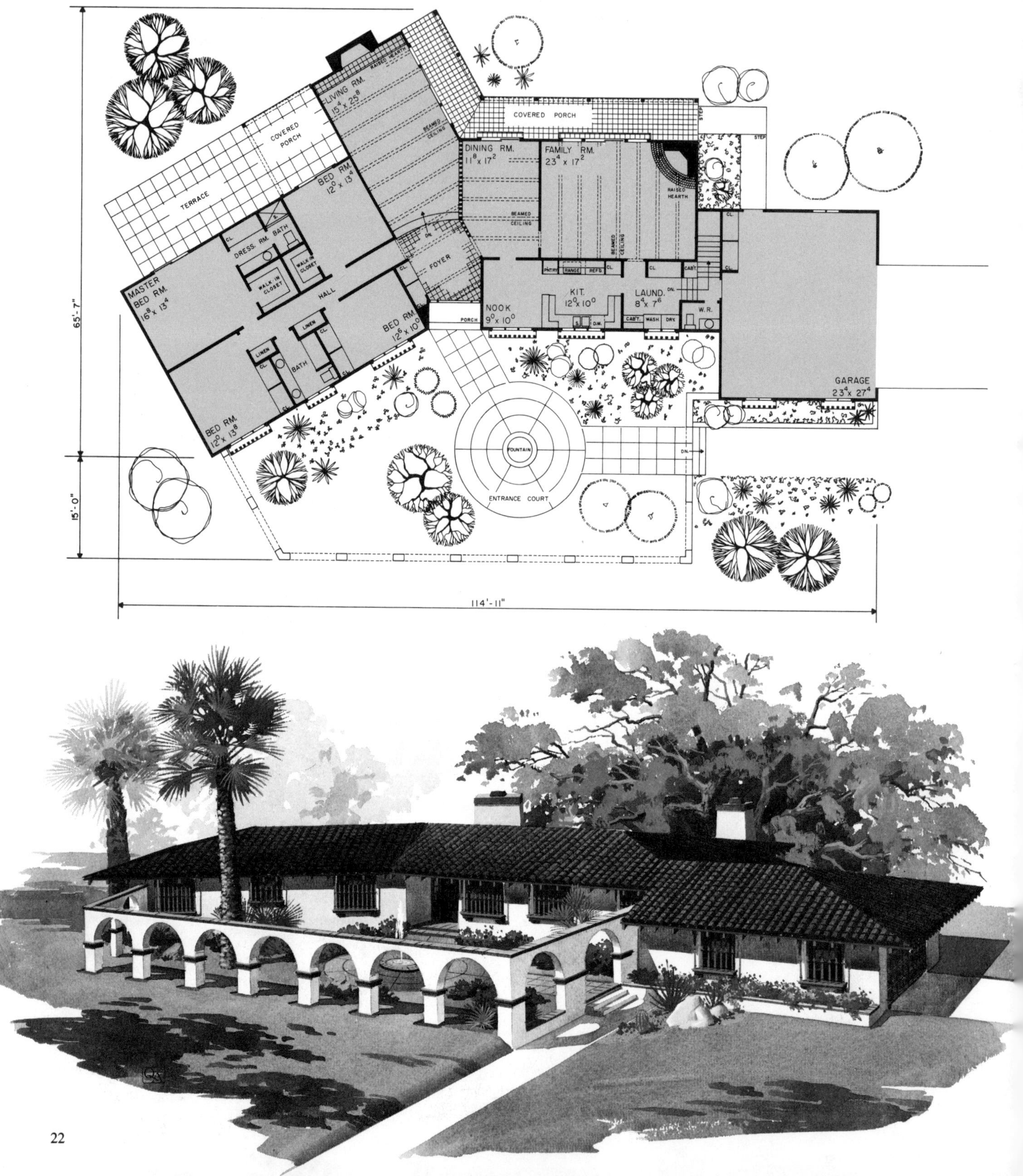

Design P2875

Square Footage: 1,913

L **D**

● This elegant Spanish design incorporates excellent indoor/outdoor living relationships for modern families who enjoy the sun. Note the overhead openings for rain and sun to fall upon a front garden, while a twin arched entry leads to the front porch and foyer. Inside, this floor plan features a modern kitchen with pass-through to a large gathering room with fireplace. Other features include a dining room, laundry room, a study off the foyer, plus three bedrooms including a master bedroom with its own whirlpool.

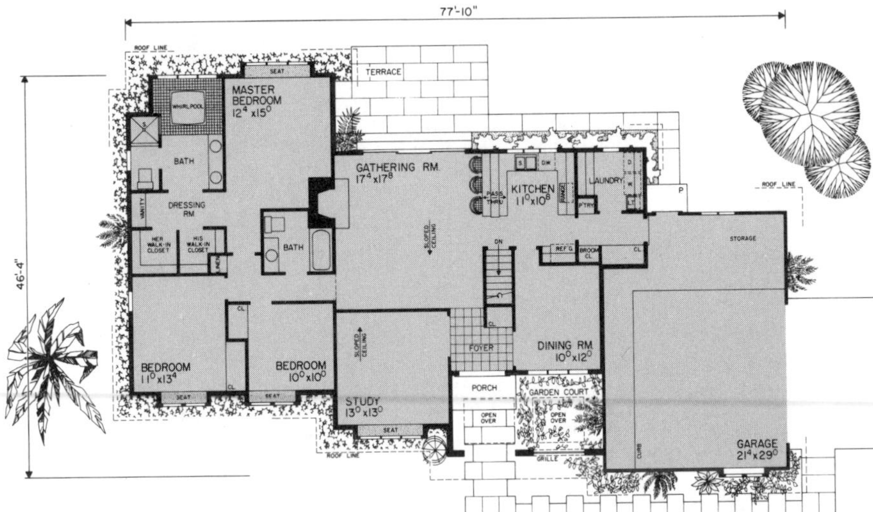

Design P2820

Square Footage: 2,261

L **D**

● A privacy wall around the courtyard with pool and trellised planter area is a gracious area by which to enter this one-story design. The Spanish flavor is accented by the grillework and the tiled roof. The front living room has sliding glass doors which open to the entrance court. The adjacent dining room features a bay window. Informal activities will be enjoyed in the rear family room with sloped, beamed ceiling, raised-hearth fireplace, sliding glass doors to the terrace and a snack bar. The sleeping wing can remain quiet away from the plan's activity centers.

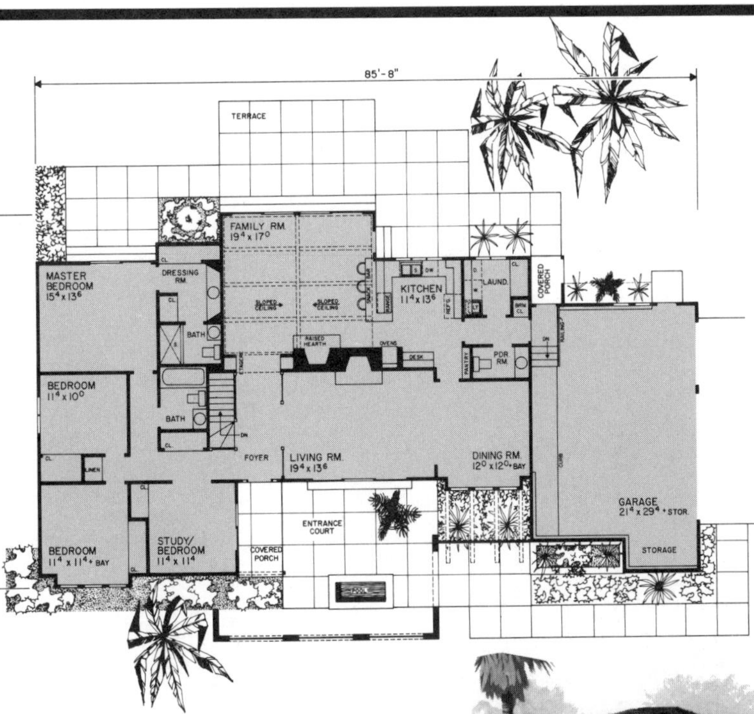

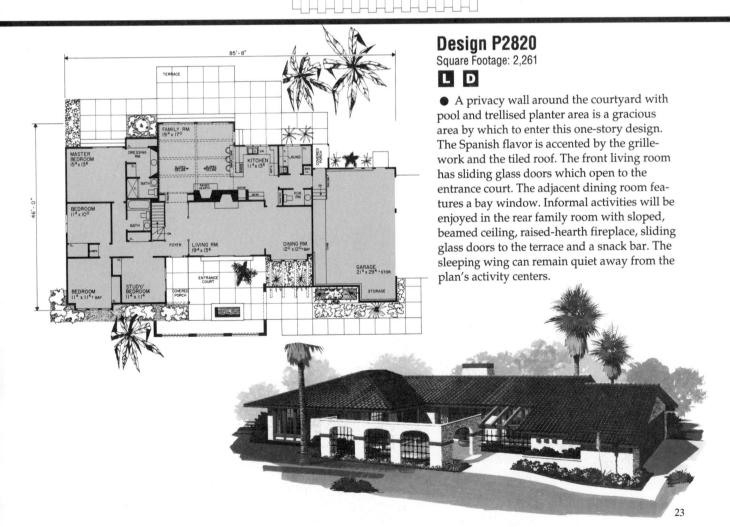

Design P3448

First Floor: 2,504 square feet
Second Floor: 1,673 square feet
Total: 4,168 square feet

● Spacious rooms are the rule in this home. A sunken living room stretches for a full 25 feet. The family room with fireplace is impressive in size, and even the kitchen abounds in space with a separate eating area (with coffered ceiling), a snack bar, island cook top, and a walk-in pantry. The first-floor master suite contains His and Hers walk-in closets, a three-way fireplace, whirlpool, and double bowl vanity. Three bedrooms upstairs share a compartmented bath. Back on the first floor, a fifth bedroom with private bath is perfect for guest quarters.

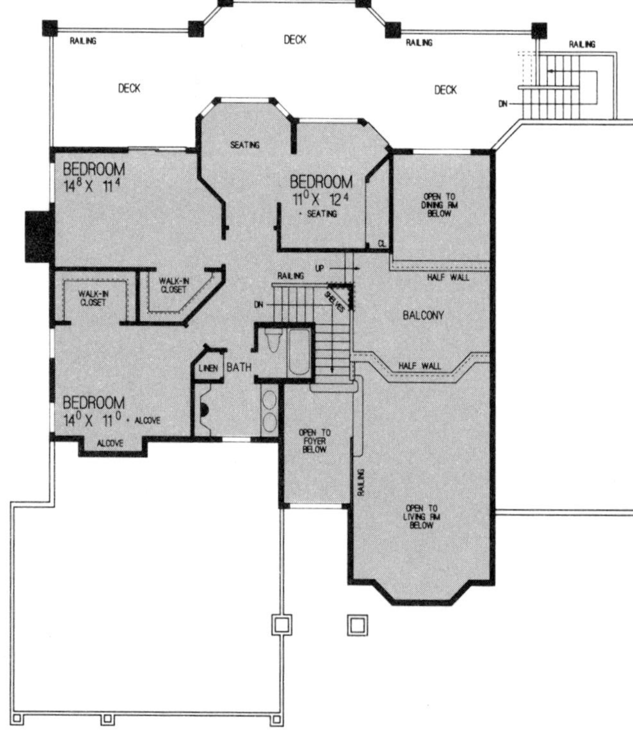

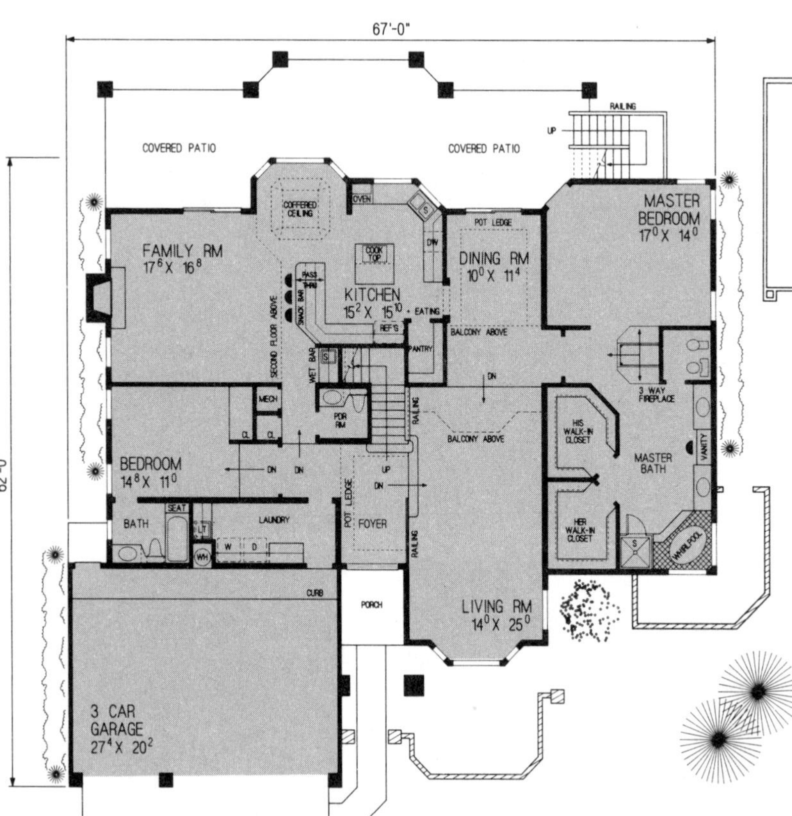

Custom Alterations? See page 203 for customizing this plan to your specifications.

Design P3447

First Floor: 2,296 square feet
Second Floor: 1,027 square feet
Total: 3,323 square feet

Custom Alterations? See page 203 for customizing this plan to your specifications.

● Family activities of all types have a distinct place in this home. The first floor contains a game room, along with a living room/dining room combination with sloped ceiling and a family room with fireplace. The spacious, angled kitchen includes a snack bar, walk-in pantry, and adjacent breakfast area with a bay. A covered patio in the back makes for pleasant outside dining in any weather. An elegant staircase is accented by a niche and art gallery. The master bedroom features a private deck, two closets and a lavish bath. Two additional bedrooms share a full bath.

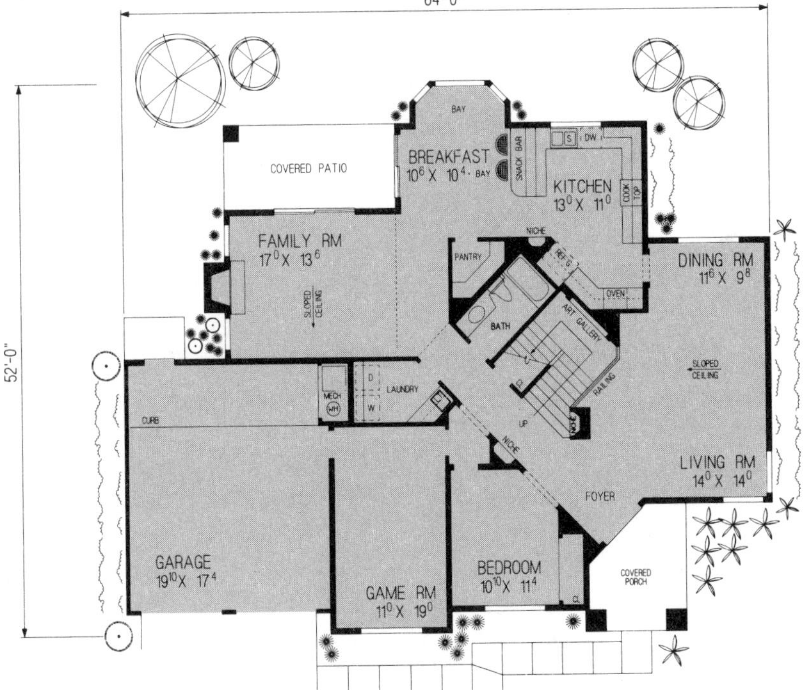

Design P3323

First Floor: 1,923 square feet
Second Floor: 838 square feet
Total: 2,751 square feet

● This two-story southwestern home was designed to make living patterns as pleasant as they can be. Take a step down from the foyer and go where your mood takes you: a gathering room with fireplace and an alcove for reading or quiet conversations, a media room for enjoying the latest technology, or to the dining room with sliding glass doors to the terrace. The kitchen has an island range and eating space. Also on the first floor is a large master suite including a sitting area with terrace access, walk-in closet and whirlpool. An elegant spiral staircase leads to two family bedrooms sharing a full bath and a guest bedroom with private bath.

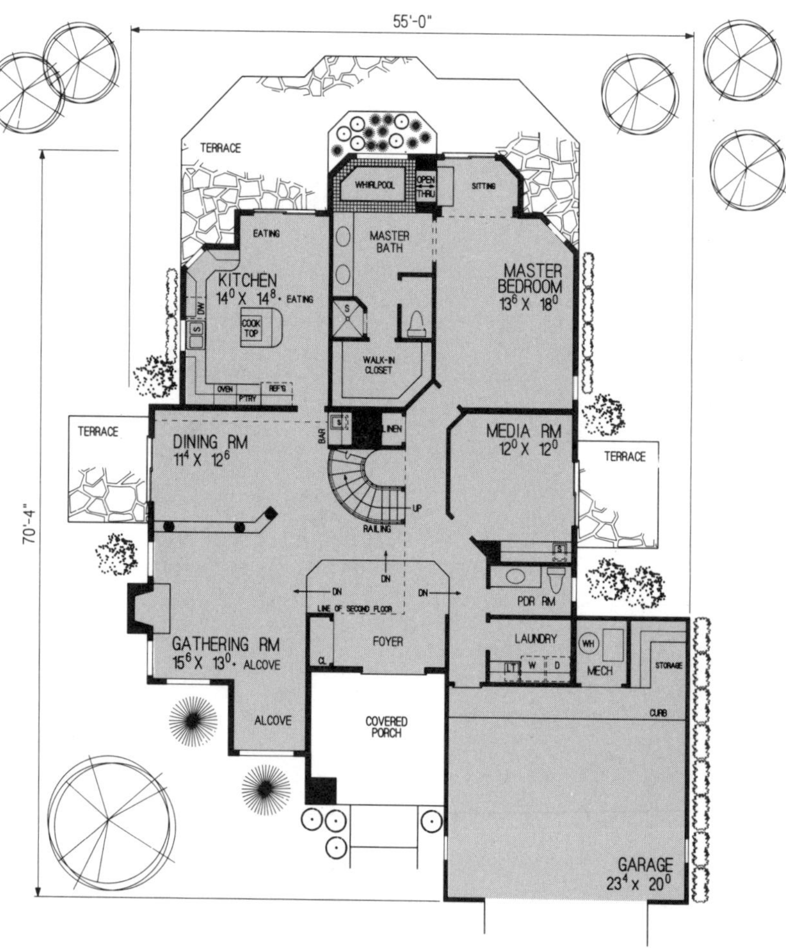

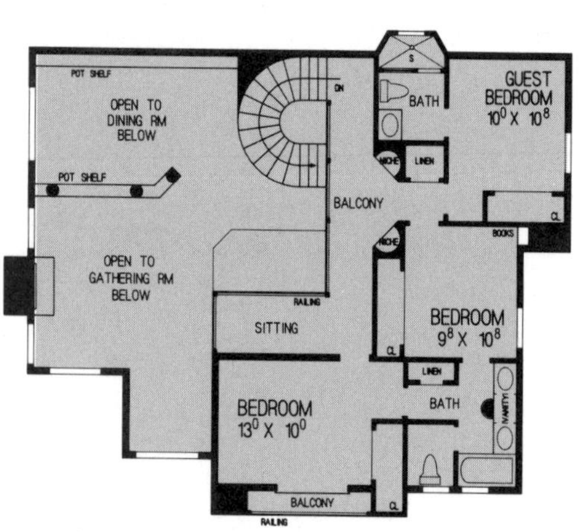

CUSTOMIZABLE

Custom Alterations? See page 203 for customizing this plan to your specifications.

Design P3409

First Floor: 1,481 square feet
Second Floor: 1,287 square feet
Total: 2,768 square feet

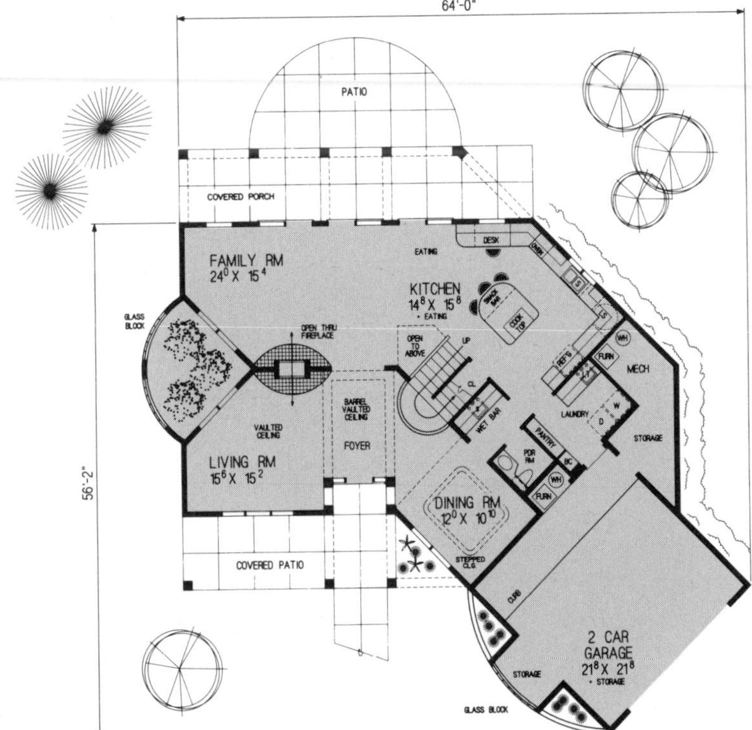

● Glass block walls and a foyer with barrel vaulted ceiling create an interesting exterior. Covered porches to the front and rear provide for excellent indoor/outdoor living relationships. Inside, a large planter and through-fireplace enhance the living room and family room. The dining room has a stepped ceiling. A desk, eating area and snack bar are special features in the kitchen. The master suite features a large walk-in closet, bath with double bowl vanity and separate tub and shower, and a private deck. Three additional bedrooms share a full bath.

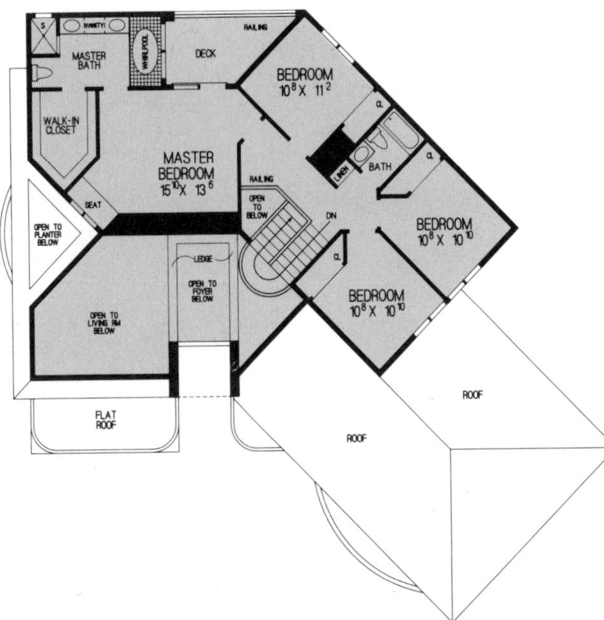

Design P3408

Square Footage: 2,940

● Interesting angles make for interesting rooms. The sleeping zone features two large bedrooms with unique shapes and a master suite with spectacular bath. A laundry placed nearby is both convenient and economical, located adjacent to a full bath. The central kitchen offers a desk and built-in breakfast table. Meals can also be enjoyed in the adjacent eating area, formal dining room with stepped ceiling, or outside on the rear patio. A planter and glass block wall separate the living room and family room, which is warmed by a fireplace.

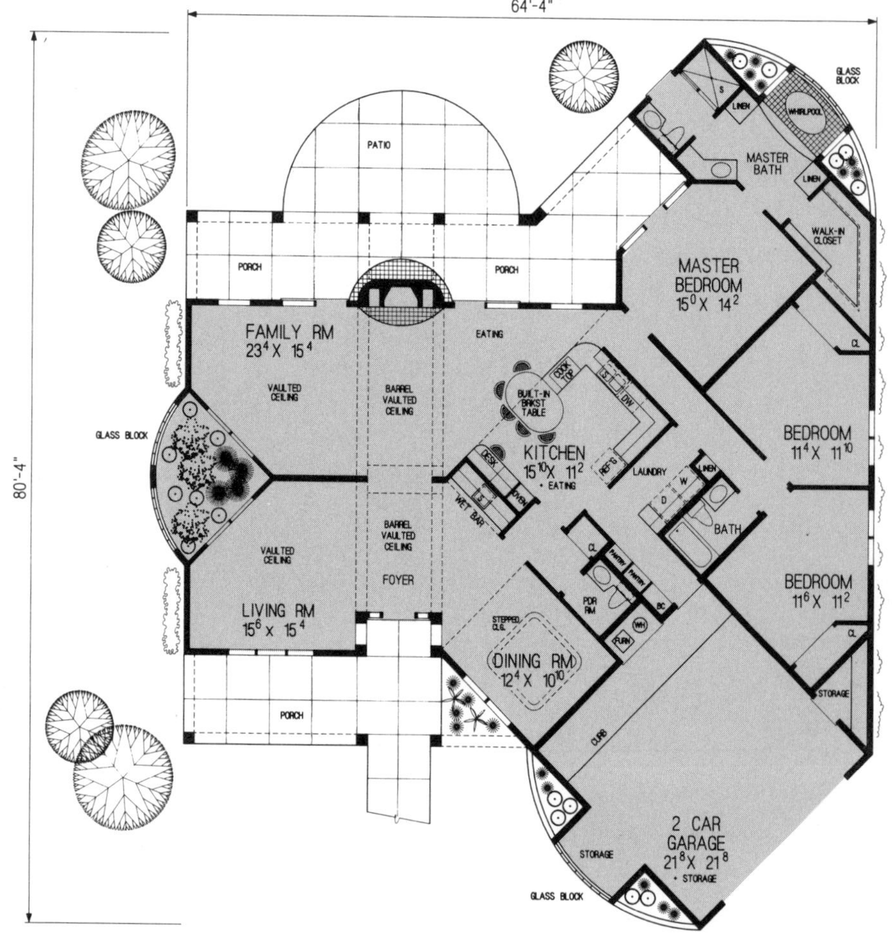

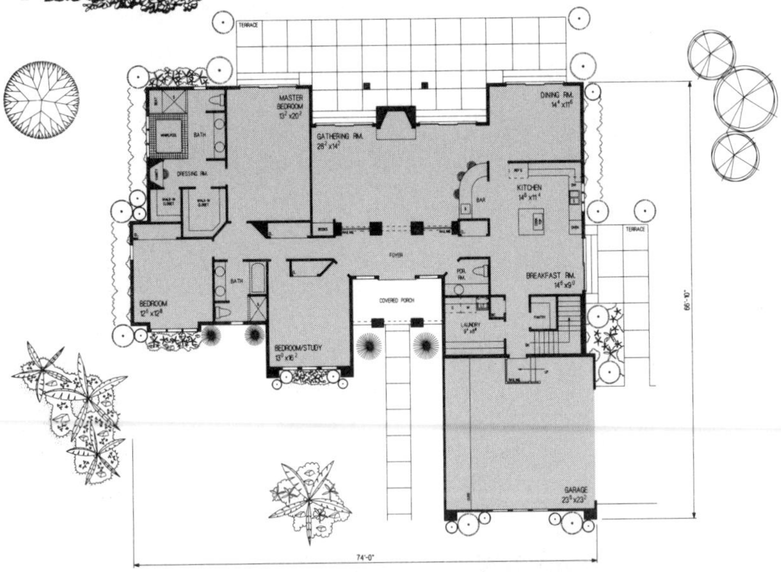

Design P2950

Square Footage: 2,559

● A natural desert dweller, this stucco, tile-roofed beauty is equally comfortable in any clime. Inside, there's a well-planned design. Common living areas — gathering room, formal dining room, and breakfast room — are offset by a quiet study that could be used as a bedroom or guest room. A master suite features two walk-in closets, a double vanity, and whirlpool spa. The two-car garage has a service entrance; close by is an adequate laundry area and a pantry. Notice the warming hearth in the gathering room and the snack bar area for casual dining.

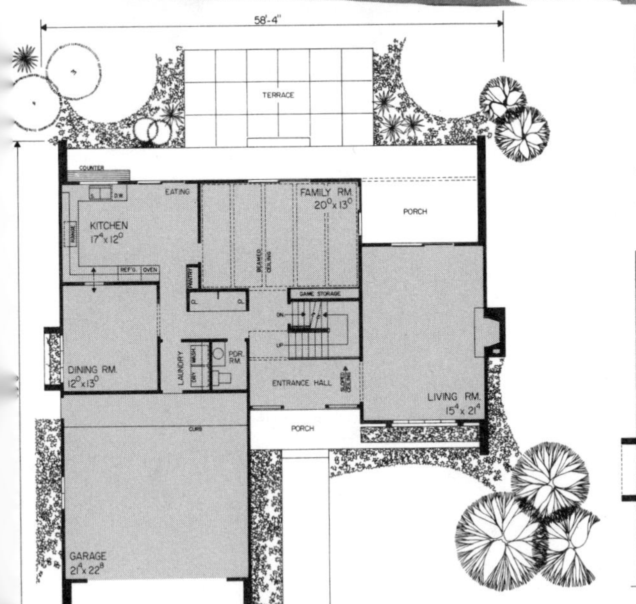

Design P2390

First Floor: 1,368 square feet
Second Floor: 1,428 square feet; Total: 2,796 square feet

D

● If yours is a large family and you like the architecture of the Far West, don't look further. Particularly if you envision building on a modest sized lot. Projecting the garage to the front contributes to the drama of this two-story. Its stucco exterior is beautifully enhanced by the clay tiles of the varying roof surfaces. The focal point, of course, is the five bedroom, three bath second floor. Four bedrooms have access to the outdoor balcony.

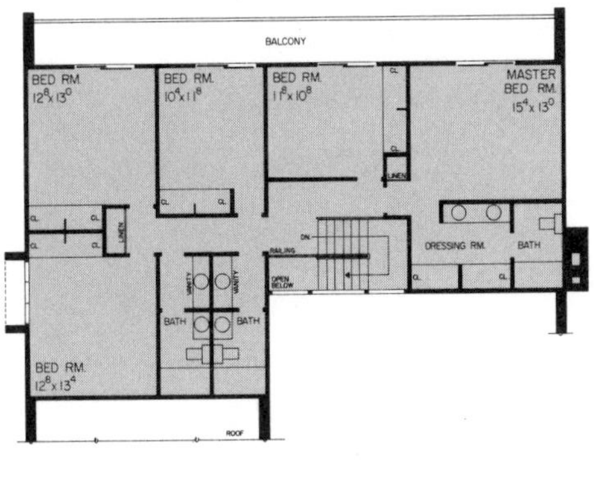

Design P3425

First Floor: 1,776 square feet
Second Floor: 1,035 square feet
Total: 2,811 square feet

Custom Alterations? See page 203 for customizing this plan to your specifications.

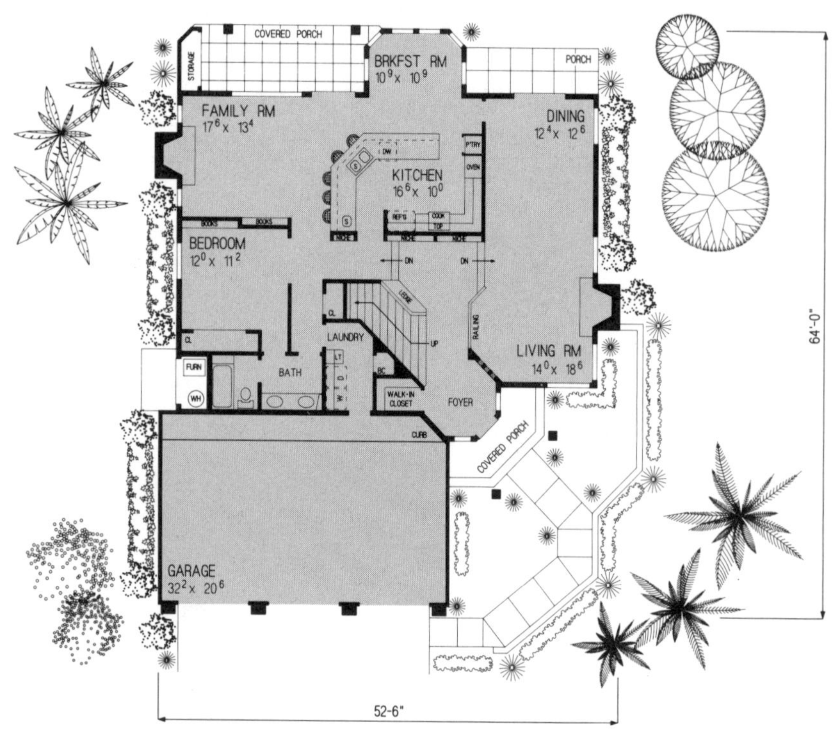

● Here's a two-story Spanish design with an appealing, angled exterior. Inside is an interesting floor plan containing rooms with a variety of shapes. Formal areas are to the right of the entry tower: a living room with fireplace and large dining room. The kitchen has loads of counter space and is complemented by a bumped-out breakfast room. Note the second fireplace in the family room and the first floor bedroom. Three second-floor bedrooms include a master suite with balcony and large bath.

Design P3449

First Floor: 1,336 square feet
Second Floor: 1,186 square feet
Total: 2,522 square feet

● This design is featured on the front cover. A covered porch leads inside to a wide, tiled foyer. A curving staircase makes an elegant expression in the open space including the living and dining rooms with two-story ceilings. A through-fireplace warms the nook and family room with wet bar and glass shelves. The nook also includes planters on two sides. Just above, light spills into the whirlpool in the master bath with dual vanities and walk-in closet. The master bedroom includes a sitting area, two more closets, and access to a private covered deck. Two family bedrooms share a full bath with dual vanities.

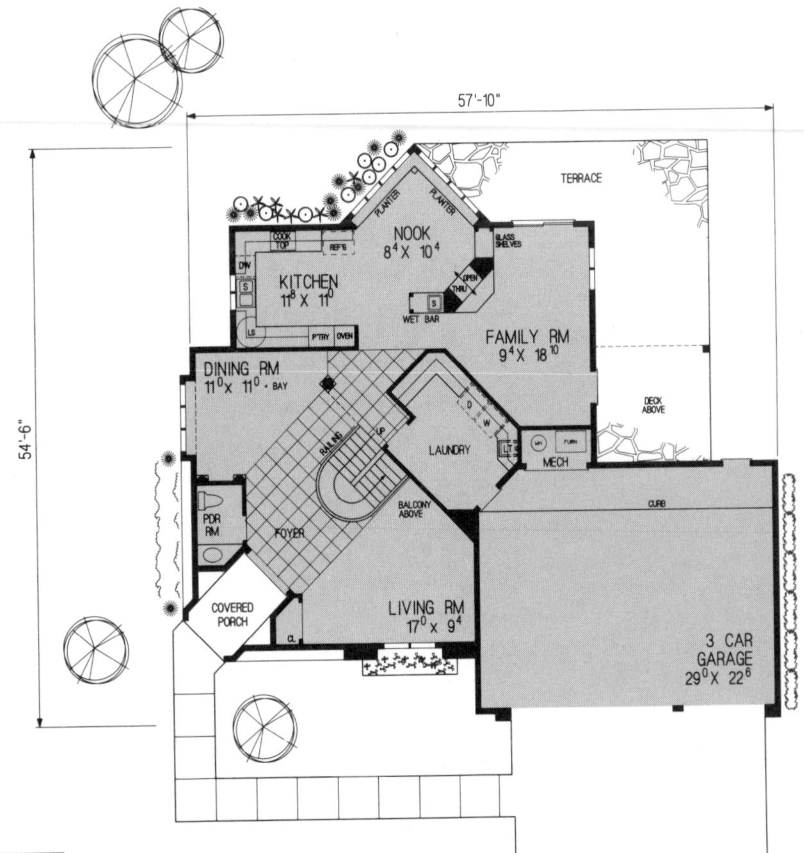

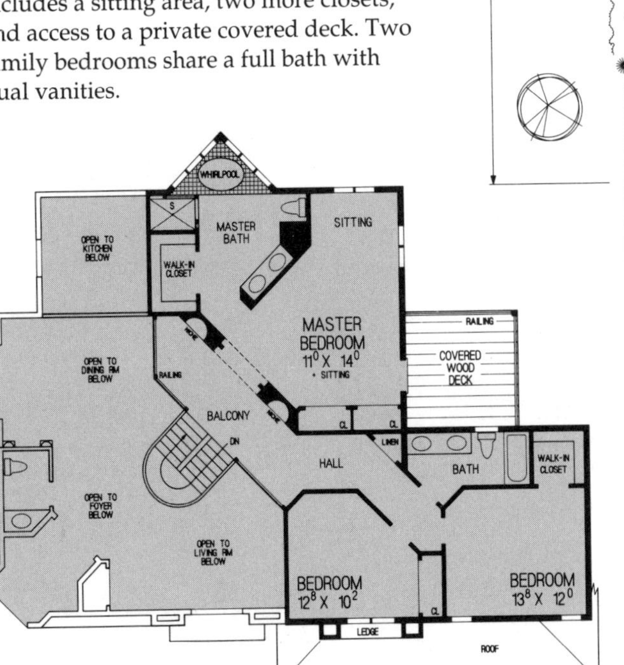

Custom Alterations? See page 203 for customizing this plan to your specifications.

Design P3440

Square Footage: 2,300

● Pack 'em in! There's plenty of room for everyone in this three-, or optional four-bedroom home. The expansive gathering room welcomes family and guests with a through-fireplace to the dining room, an audio/visual center, and a door to the outside. The kitchen includes a wide pantry, a snack bar, and a separate eating area. Included in the master suite: two walk-in closets, shower, whirlpool tub and seat, dual vanities, and linen storage.

Custom Alterations? See page 203 for customizing this plan to your specifications.

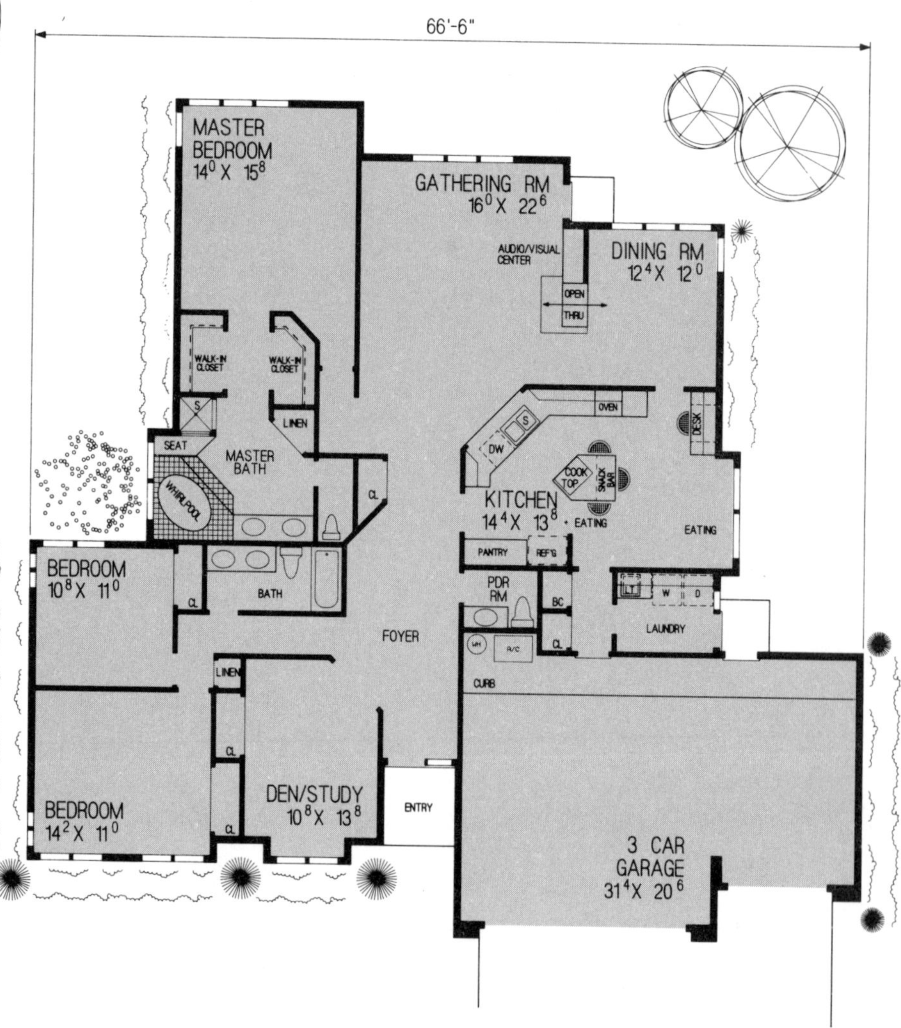

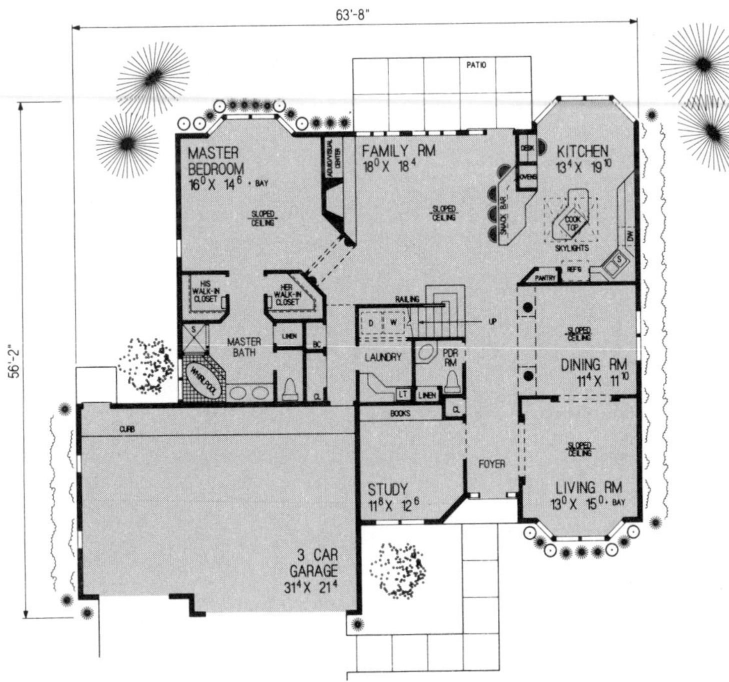

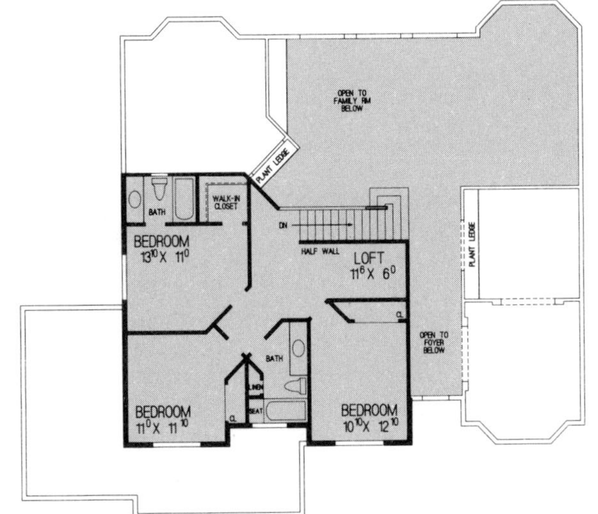

Design P3441

First Floor: 2,022 square feet
Second Floor: 845 square feet
Total: 2,867 square feet

● Special details make the difference between a house and a home. A snack bar, audio/visual center and a fireplace make the family room livable. A desk, island cook top, bay, and skylights enhance the kitchen area. The dining room features two columns and a plant ledge. The first-floor master suite includes His and Hers walk-in closets, a spacious bath, and a bay window. On the second floor, one bedroom features a walk-in closet and private bath, while two additional bedrooms share a full bath.

Custom Alterations? See page 203 for customizing this plan to your specifications.

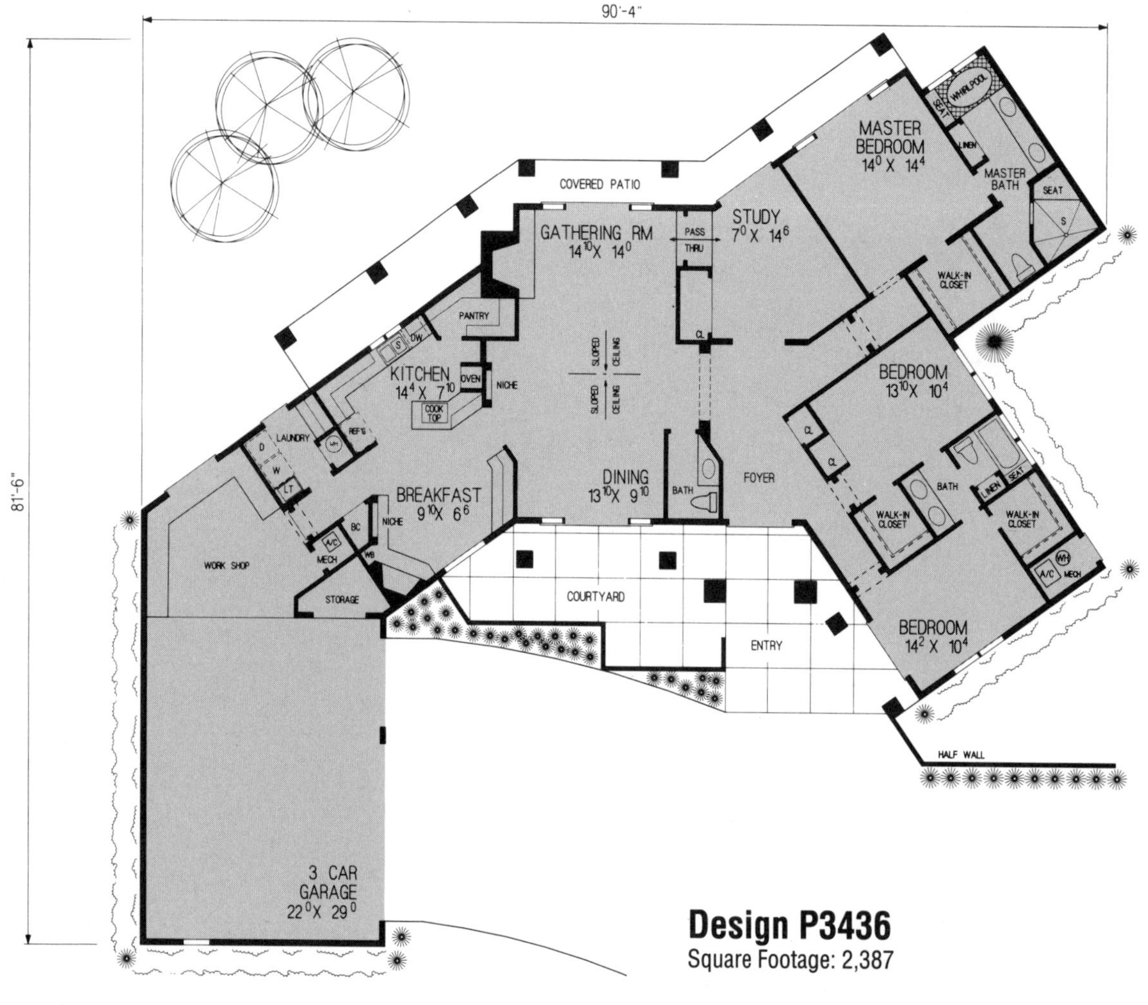

90'-4"

81'-6"

COVERED PATIO

GATHERING RM 14^{10} X 14^{0}

PASS THRU

STUDY 7^{0} X 14^{6}

MASTER BEDROOM 14^{0} X 14^{4}

WHIRLPOOL

SEAT

LINEN

MASTER BATH

SEAT

WALK-IN CLOSET

PANTRY

KITCHEN 14^{4} X 7^{10}

DW

OVEN

NICHE

COOK TOP

REF'G

SLOPED CEILING

SLOPED CEILING

CL

BEDROOM 13^{10} X 10^{4}

LAUNDRY

BREAKFAST 9^{10} X 6^{6}

DINING 13^{10} X 9^{10}

BATH

FOYER

CL

CL

WALK-IN CLOSET

BATH

LINEN

SEAT

WALK-IN CLOSET

WORK SHOP

MECH

BC

NICHE

WB

A/C

STORAGE

COURTYARD

ENTRY

BEDROOM 14^{2} X 10^{4}

A/C

MECH

HALF WALL

3 CAR GARAGE 22^{0} X 29^{0}

Design P3436

Square Footage: 2,387

● An expansive gathering room/dining area with sloped ceiling makes a grand impression. The kitchen includes a large pantry and adjoining breakfast area with fireplace. A courtyard in the front can be reached through the dining room or front bedroom, while a covered rear patio is accessible through the gathering room, study, or master bedroom. Each of the three bedrooms includes a walk-in closet and convenient access to a full bath.

Custom Alterations? See page 203 for customizing this plan to your specifications.

CUSTOMIZABLE

Custom Alterations? See page 203 for customizing this plan to your specifications.

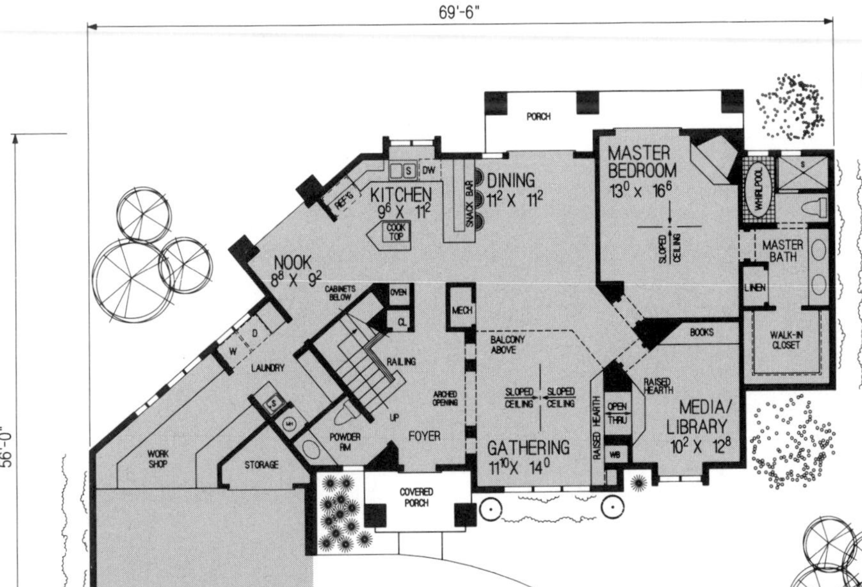

Design P3437

First Floor: 1,522 square feet
Second Floor: 730 square feet
Total: 2,252 square feet

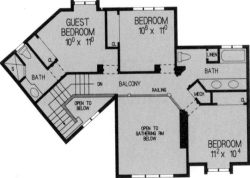

● This two-story Spanish Mission-style home has character inside and out. The first-floor master suite features a fireplace and gracious bath with walk-in closet, whirlpool, shower, dual vanities, and linen storage. A second fireplace serves both the gathering room and media room or library. The kitchen with island cook top includes a snack bar and an adjoining breakfast nook. Three bedrooms and two full baths occupy the second floor.

Design P2801

First Floor: 1,172 square feet
Second Floor: 884 square feet
Total: 2,056 square feet
L **D**

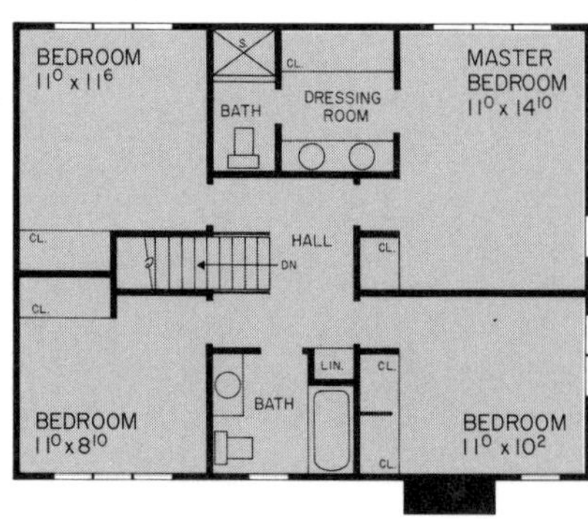

● Built-ins in the breakfast room for china and pantry goods are certainly features to be mentioned up-front. A second china cabinet is located adjacent to the formal dining room, across from the stairs to the second floor. The great room will be just that. It is sunken two steps, has a beamed ceiling, the beauty of a fireplace and two sets of sliding glass doors to a front and rear courtyard. The built-in wet bar and fireplace are the features of the family room. The foyer of this Spanish design is very spacious and houses a powder room. Laundry facilities are within the mud room. Four bedrooms and two baths are on the second floor. Don't miss the two enclosed courtyards.

Spanish Eclectic

Between 1915 and 1940, a new style of Southwestern dwelling emerged with freer form and substance than any up until that time. The Panama-California Exposition of 1915 inspired architects of the day to place more emphasis on Spanish rather than local details. Because of this, they chose to christen the new style Spanish Colonial Revival—a style which enjoyed its zenith during the 1920s and 1930s.

Modern creations in the Spanish Eclectic style do indeed mimic the characteristics of Spanish architecture—low-pitched roofs with little or no eave overhang that are finished in red tile. The roof tiles may be Mission (which are half-cylinders placed with every other one curved side down) or Spanish tiles (which are S-shaped).

Roof patterns include five types:

Side-gabled roof. Gables open to the sides of the home. The main house itself may have winged extensions with lower-gabled roofs also opening to the sides. Multi-level Spanish Eclectic homes lend themselves easily to this roof type.

Cross-gabled roof. The most common type of roof in the Spanish Eclectic, it occurs on an L-shaped one- or two-story home which may or may not have wings with lower-gabled roofs.

Combined hipped and gabled roofs. This type is usually found on a two-story rectangular plan and exemplifies influences of the diverse roof patterns found in historic Spanish villages.

Flat roof. Though not very common, some Spanish Eclectic homes include a flat roof, often with shed roofs over entries or over bumped-out windows. Walls that extend up above the roof line are common in flat-roofed Spanish Eclectic-style homes.

Ornamentation is derived from several different cultures: Moorish, Byzantine, Gothic and Renaissance. The Spanish Eclectic home is notable for its smooth stucco surfaces and for decorative arches above the main entry door or a prominent window. Exterior doors are often elegantly wrought in heavily carved wood with decorative metal, have surrounds of tile work or stone and may be adorned with wooden columns or pilasters. Doors to exterior balconies or porches are often paired and have multi-paned glass. Decorative grilles are common at windows and doors and may be used as railing for second-story balconies or ground-level terraces. Round or square towers are often found and may be ornamented with elaborate Spanish tiles, as may chimney tops. Partially enclosed patios and garden courtyards complement exterior spaces of the home. These exterior spaces may be enhanced with fountains, covered walkways and arbors. Decorative tilework on chimneys and tiled vents are also seen. In many cases, the facade is quite plain and unadorned but opens to an interior courtyard.

Though the style does occur in scattered suburban patches throughout the country, it is most strongly represented in areas first colonized by Spain: California, Arizona, New Mexico, Texas and Florida.

Design P3344

Square Footage: 3,054

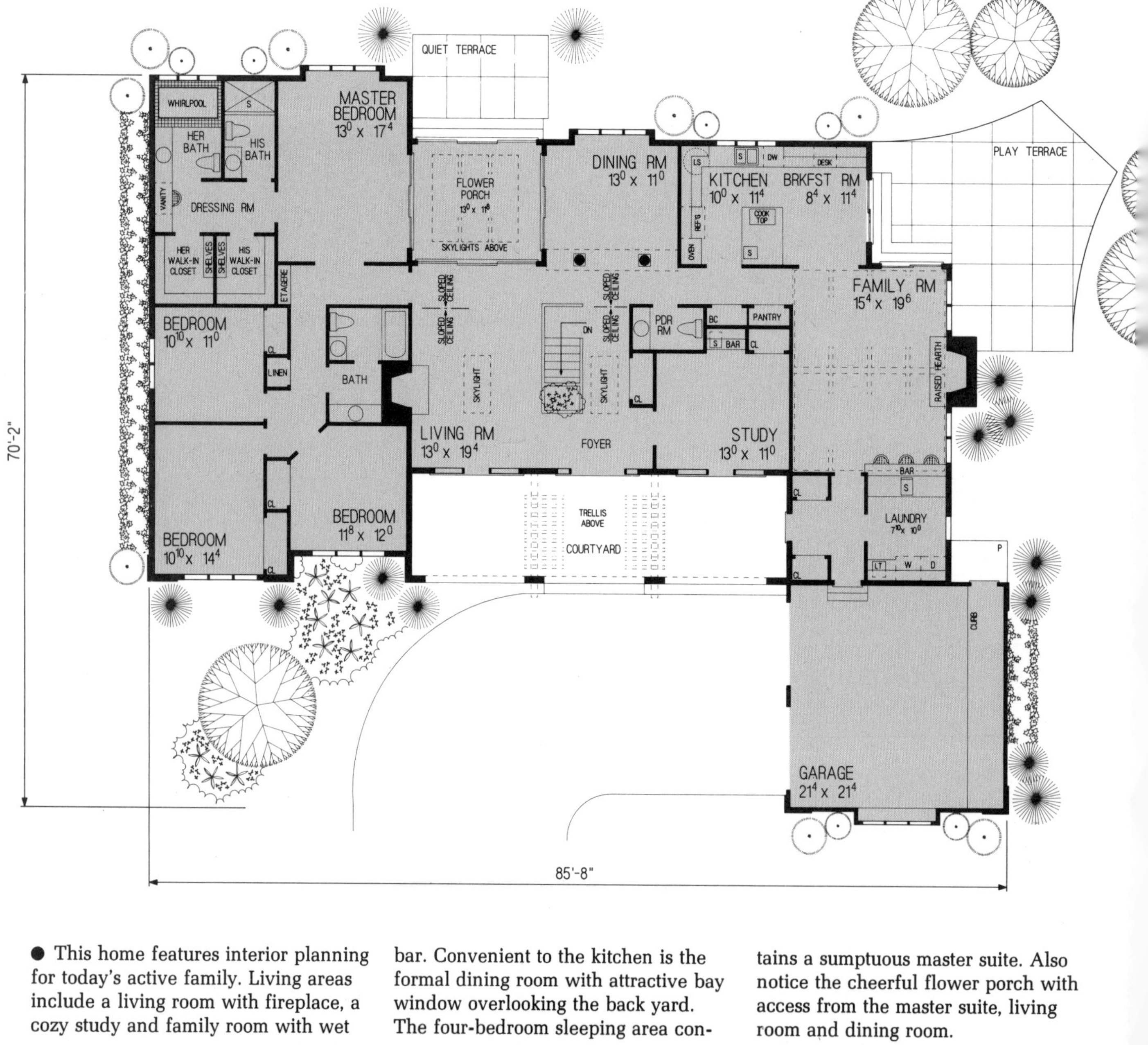

QUIET TERRACE

MASTER BEDROOM 13^0 x 17^4

WHIRLPOOL

HER BATH

HIS BATH

DRESSING RM

VANITY

HER WALK-IN CLOSET

HIS WALK-IN CLOSET

SHELVES

ETAGERE

FLOWER PORCH 13^0 x 11^8

SKYLIGHTS ABOVE

DINING RM 13^0 x 11^0

KITCHEN 10^0 x 11^4

BRKFST RM 8^4 x 11^4

DW

DESK

COOK TOP

REF'G

OVEN

PLAY TERRACE

FAMILY RM 15^4 x 19^6

RAISED HEARTH

BEDROOM 10^{10} x 11^0

LINEN

BATH

SLOPED CEILING

SKYLIGHT

DN

PDR RM

PANTRY

BAR

LIVING RM 13^0 x 19^4

FOYER

STUDY 13^0 x 11^0

LAUNDRY 7^{10} x 10^0

BEDROOM 11^8 x 12^0

BEDROOM 10^{10} x 14^4

TRELLIS ABOVE

COURTYARD

CURB

GARAGE 21^4 x 21^4

70'-2"

85'-8"

● This home features interior planning for today's active family. Living areas include a living room with fireplace, a cozy study and family room with wet bar. Convenient to the kitchen is the formal dining room with attractive bay window overlooking the back yard. The four-bedroom sleeping area contains a sumptuous master suite. Also notice the cheerful flower porch with access from the master suite, living room and dining room.

● This design is carefully zoned for utmost livability. The entry foyer routes traffic to all areas of the house. To the rear is the living room/dining room combination with built-in china cabinet. To the left, the kitchen is open to the breakfast room and family room with fireplace. The master bedroom is on the right and features a whirlpool and a private porch. Upstairs are three more bedrooms and an outdoor balcony.

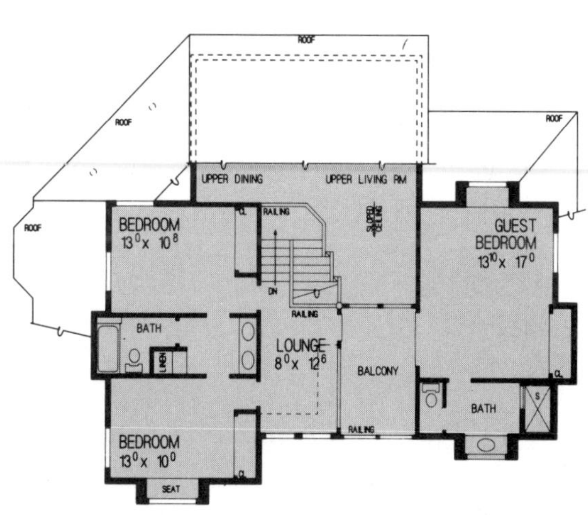

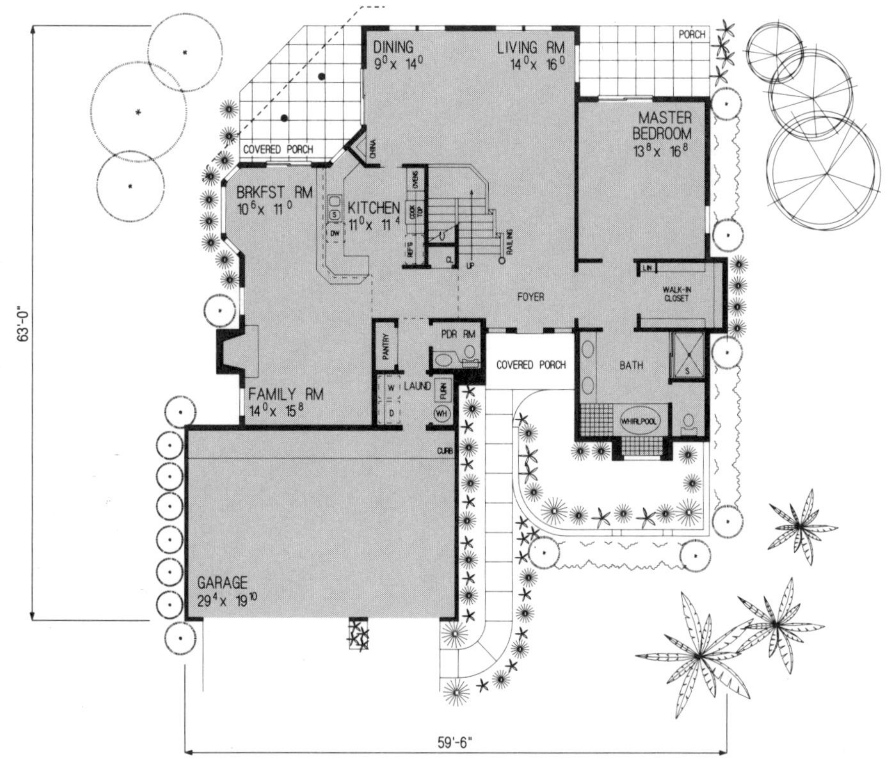

Design P3426

First Floor: 1,859 square feet
Second Floor: 969 square feet
Total: 2,828 square feet

Custom Alterations? See page 203 for customizing this plan to your specifications.

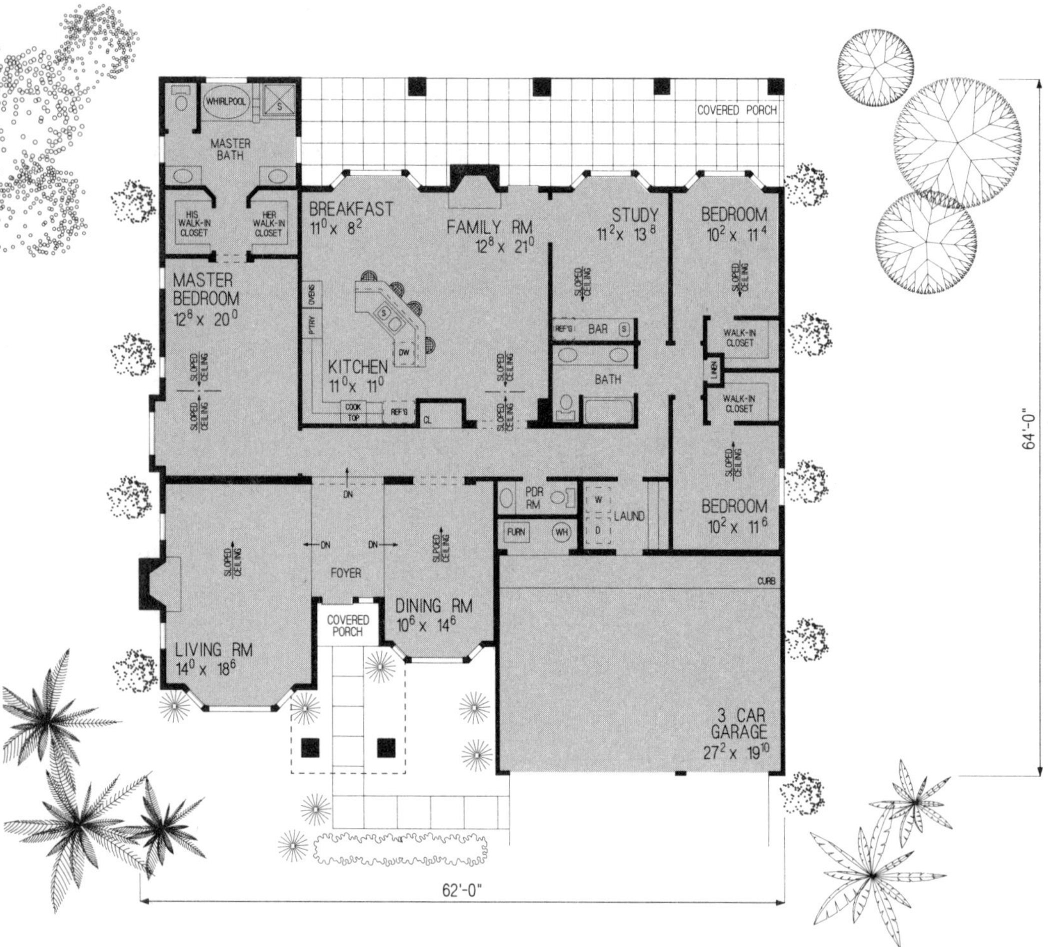

Design P3413

Square Footage: 2,517

● Though distinctly Southwest in design, this home has some features that are universally appealing. Note, for instance, the central gallery, perpendicular to the raised entry hall, and running almost the entire width of the house. An L-shaped, angled kitchen serves the breakfast room and family room in equal fashion. Sleeping areas are found in four bedrooms including an optional study and exquisite master suite.

Custom Alterations? See page 203 for customizing this plan to your specifications.

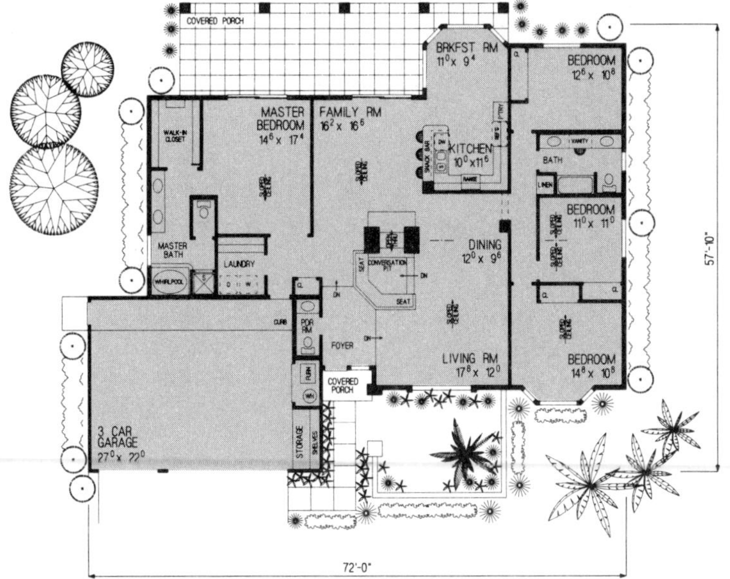

Design P3430

Square Footage: 2,394

● This dramatic design benefits from open planning. The centerpiece of the living area is a sunken conversation pit which shares a through-fireplace with the family room. The living room and dining room share space beneath a sloped ceiling. The open kitchen features a snack bar and breakfast room and conveniently serves all living areas. Split zoning in the sleeping area places the private master suite to the left of the plan and three more bedrooms, including one with a bay window, to the right.

Custom Alterations? See page 203 for customizing this plan to your specifications.

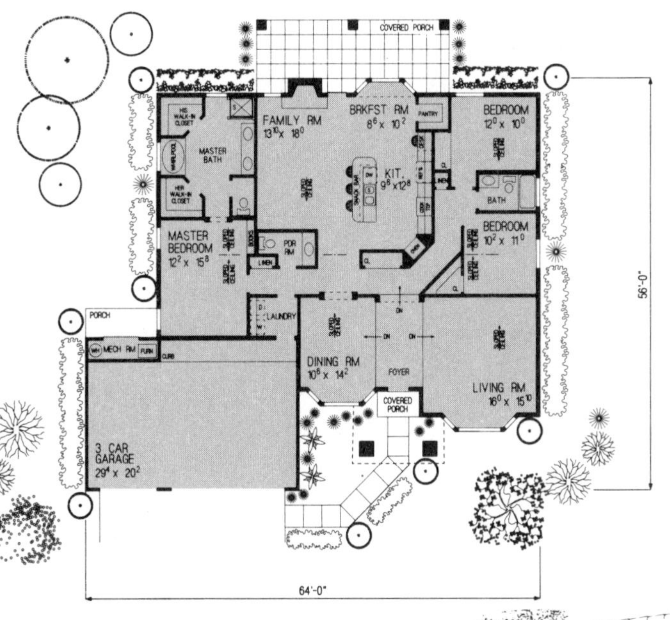

Design P3412

Square Footage: 2,150

● Although typically Southwestern in design, this home will bring style to any neighborhood. Huge bay windows flood the front living and dining rooms with plenty of natural light. An amenity-filled kitchen with attached family room will be the main gathering area, where the family works and relaxes together. Notice the fireplace, the island snack bar and walk-in pantry. A split sleeping zone separates the master suite with luxurious bath from the two family bedrooms. Also notice the covered porch off the family room.

Custom Alterations? See page 203 for customizing this plan to your specifications.

Design P3421

Square Footage: 2,145

● Split-bedroom planning makes the most of a one-story design. In this case the master suite is on the opposite side of the house from two family bedrooms. Gourmets can rejoice at the abundant work space in the U-shaped kitchen and will appreciate the natural light afforded by the large bay window in the breakfast room. A formal living room has a sunken conversation area with a cozy fireplace as its focus. The rear covered porch can be reached through sliding glass doors in the family room.

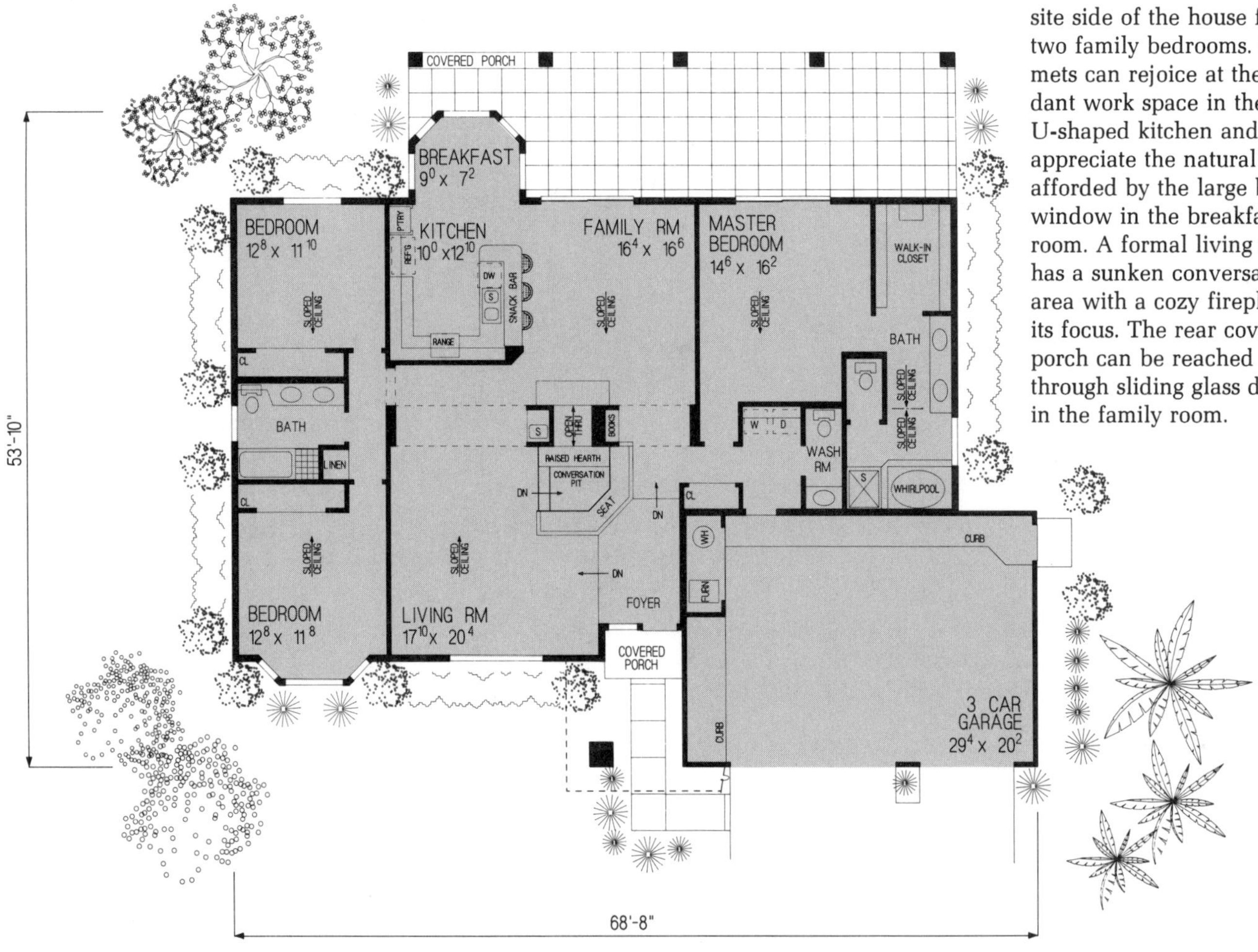

COVERED PORCH
BREAKFAST 9^{0} x 7^{2}
BEDROOM 12^{8} x 11^{10}
KITCHEN 10^{0} x 12^{10}
FAMILY RM 16^{4} x 16^{6}
MASTER BEDROOM 14^{6} x 16^{2}
WALK-IN CLOSET
BATH
WASH RM
WHIRLPOOL
RAISED HEARTH
CONVERSATION PIT
LIVING RM 17^{10} x 20^{4}
BEDROOM 12^{8} x 11^{8}
FOYER
COVERED PORCH
3 CAR GARAGE 29^{4} x 20^{2}
53'-10"
68'-8"

Custom Alterations? See page 203 for customizing this plan to your specifications.

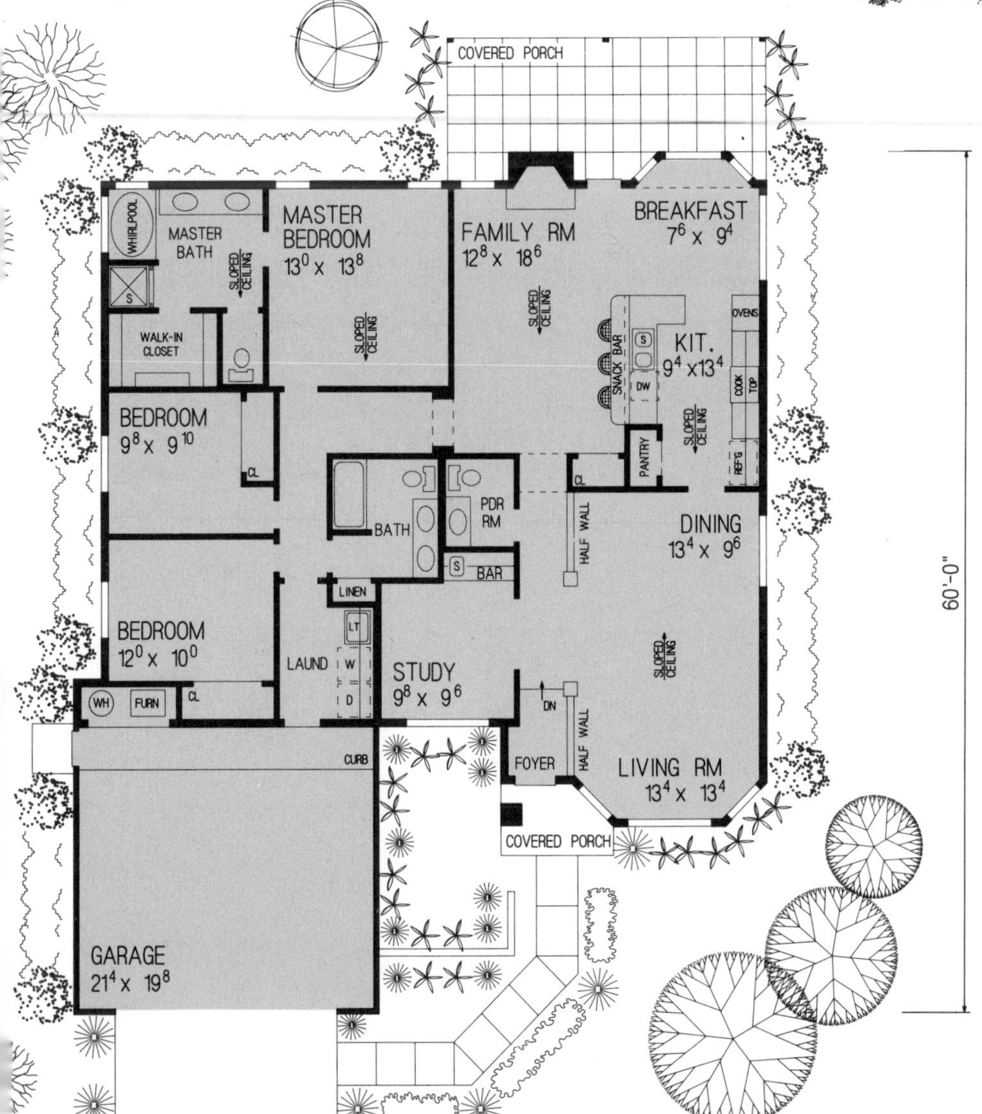

Design P3422

Square Footage: 1,932

● An enclosed entry garden greets visitors to this charming Southwestern home. Inside, the foyer is flanked by formal and informal living areas — a living room and dining room to the right and a cozy study to the left. To the rear, a large family room, breakfast room and open kitchen have access to a covered porch and overlook the back yard. Notice the fireplace and bay window. The three-bedroom sleeping area includes a master with a spacious bath with whirlpool.

Custom Alterations? See page 203 for customizing this plan to your specifications.

Design P3416

Square Footage: 1,375

● Here's a Southwestern design that will be economical to build and a pleasure to occupy. The front door opens into a spacious living room with corner fireplace and dining room with coffered ceiling. The nearby kitchen serves both easily. A few steps away is the cozy media room with built-in space for audio/visual equipment. Down the hall are two bedrooms and two baths; the master features a whirlpool. A guest room is found around the entry court and includes a fireplace and sloped ceiling.

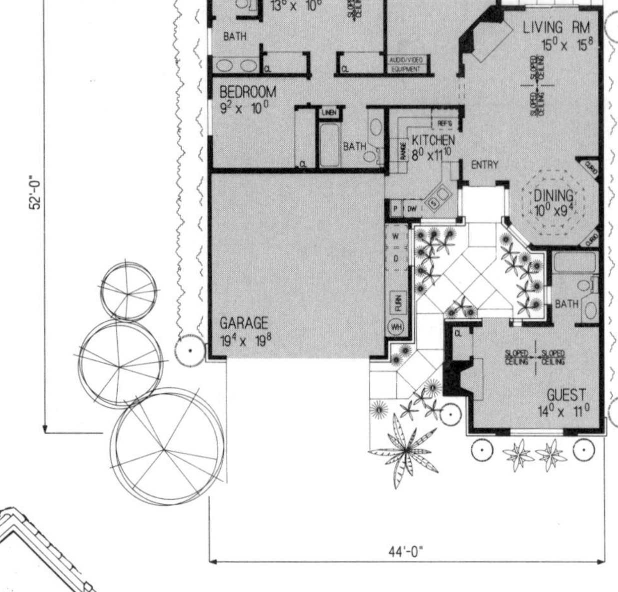

Custom Alterations? See page 203 for customizing this plan to your specifications.

Design P3419

Square Footage: 1,965

● This attractive, multi-gabled exterior houses a compact, livable interior. The entry foyer effectively routes traffic to all areas: left to the family room and kitchen, straight back to the dining room and living room, and right to the four-bedroom sleeping area. The spacious family room provides an informal gathering space while the living and dining rooms are perfect for formal occasions. The highlight of the sleeping area is the master bedroom with its whirlpool, walk-in closet and view of the back yard.

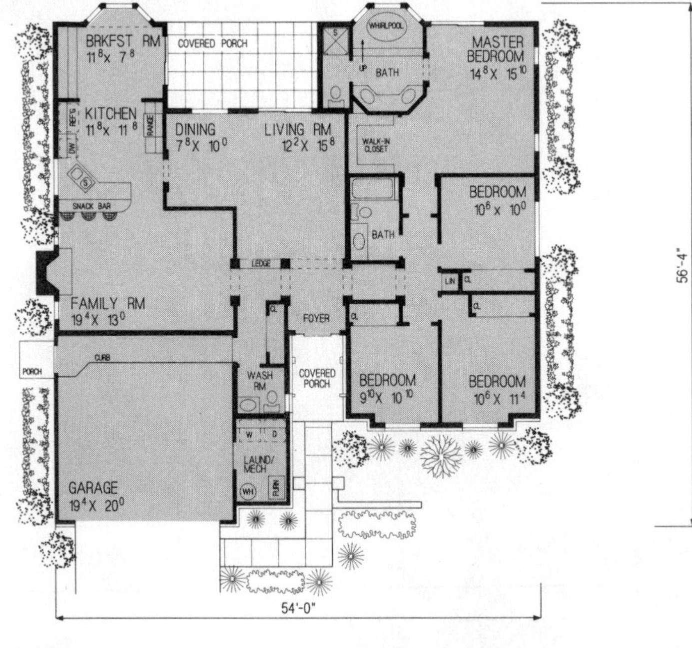

Custom Alterations? See page 203 for customizing this plan to your specifications.

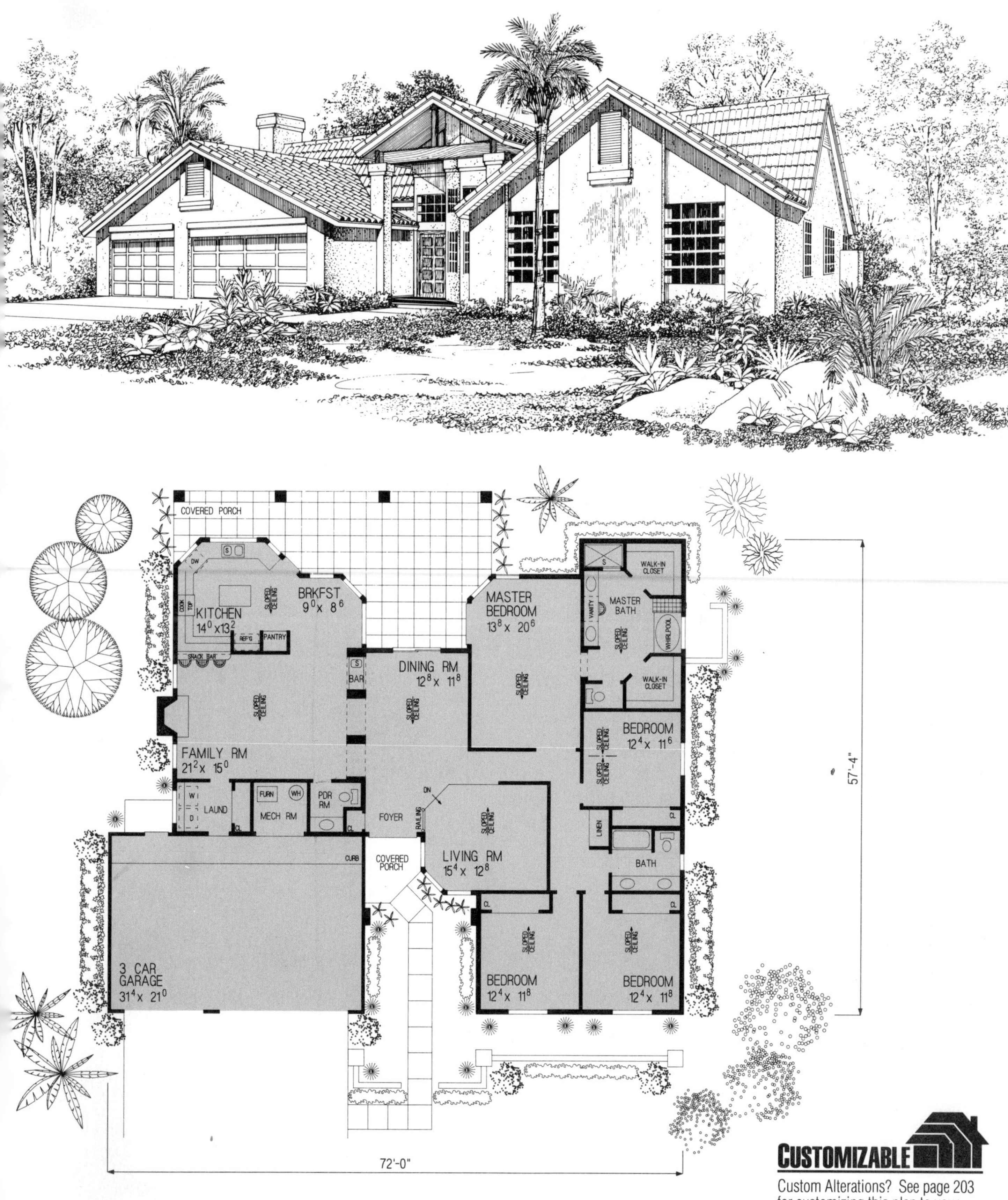

CUSTOMIZABLE

Custom Alterations? See page 203 for customizing this plan to your specifications.

Design P3423 Square Footage: 2,577

● This spacious Southwestern home will be a pleasure to come home to. Immediately off the foyer are the dining room and step-down living room with bay window. The highlight of the four-bedroom sleeping area is the master suite with porch access and a whirlpool for soaking away the day's worries. The informal living area features an enormous family room with fireplace and bay-windowed kitchen and breakfast room. Notice the snack bar pass-through to the family room.

Design P3411

Square Footage: 2,441

● You'll love the entry to this Southwestern home — it creates a dramatic first impression and leads beautifully to the formal living and dining rooms. Beyond, look for an open family room and dining area in the same proximity as the kitchen. Sliding glass doors here open to a backyard patio. Take your choice of four bedrooms or five, depending on how you wish to use the optional room. The huge master suite is not to be missed.

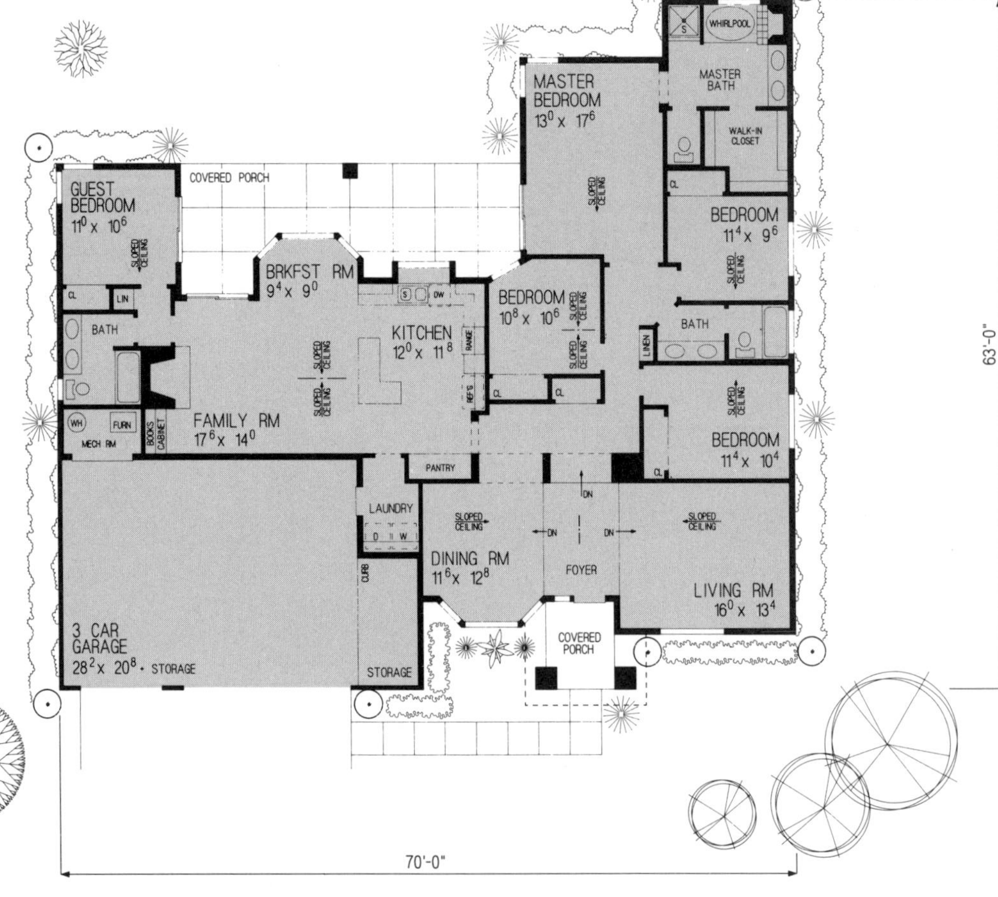

Custom Alterations? See page 203 for customizing this plan to your specifications.

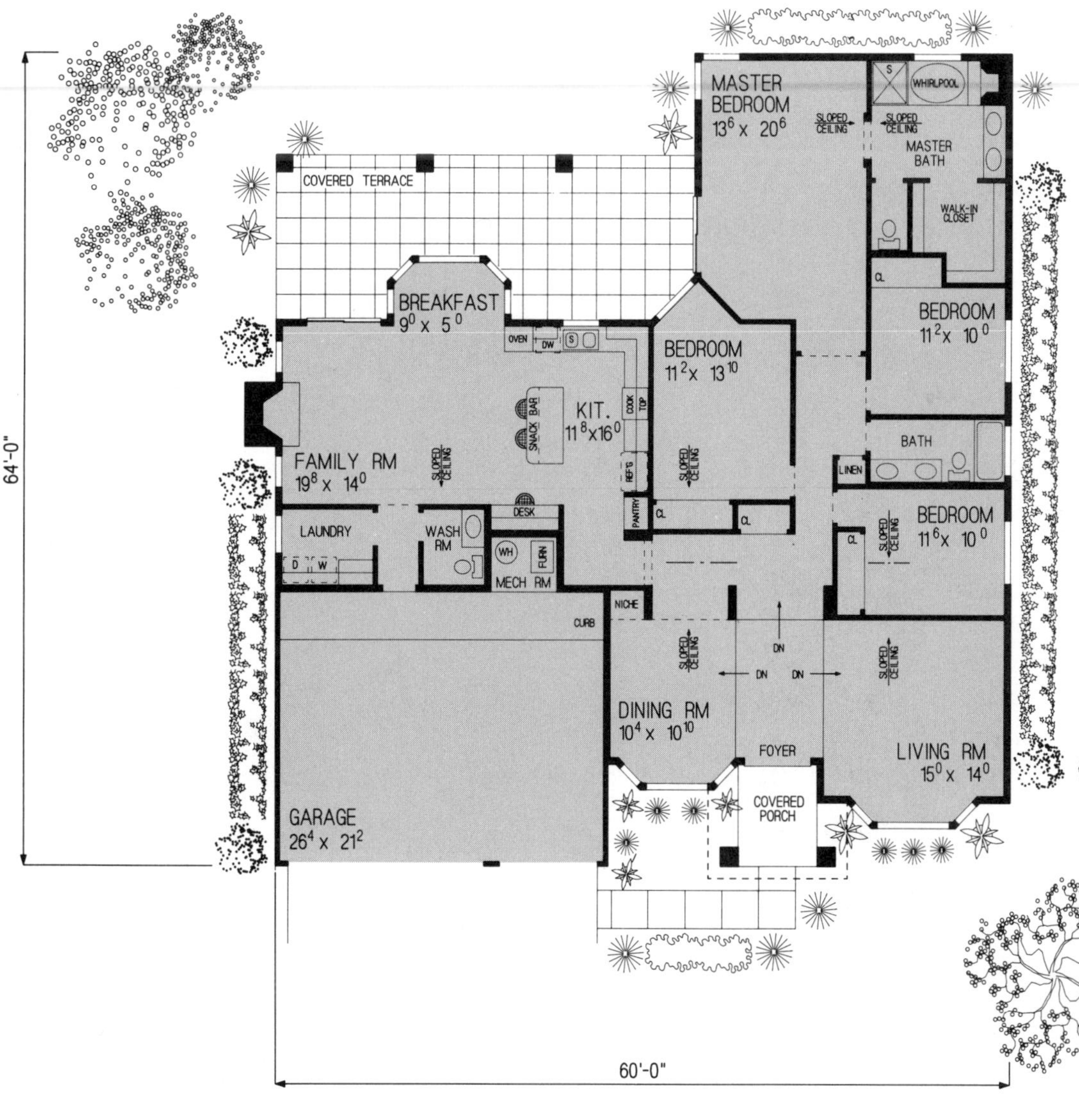

MASTER BEDROOM 13^6 x 20^6
SLOPED CEILING
S
WHIRLPOOL
MASTER BATH
WALK-IN CLOSET
CL
COVERED TERRACE
BREAKFAST 9^0 x 5^0
OVEN
DW
S
BEDROOM 11^2x 13^{10}
BEDROOM 11^2x 10^0
KIT. 11^8x16^0
SNACK BAR
COOK TOP
REF'G
PANTRY
FAMILY RM 19^8 x 14^0
BATH
LINEN
BEDROOM 11^6x 10^0
LAUNDRY
D W
WASH RM
WH
FURN
DESK
MECH RM
NICHE
CURB
DN
DINING RM 10^4 x 10^{10}
FOYER
LIVING RM 15^0 x 14^0
COVERED PORCH
GARAGE 26^4 x 21^2
64'-0"
60'-0"

Design P3415

Square Footage: 2,406

● Relax and enjoy the open floor plan of this lovely one-story. Its family room with fireplace and space for eating are a suitable complement to the formal living and dining rooms to the front of the house. There are four bedrooms, or three if you choose to make one a den, and 2½ baths. Don't miss the large pantry and convenient laundry area.

CUSTOMIZABLE

Custom Alterations? See page 203 for customizing this plan to your specifications.

Design P3424 First Floor: 1,625 square feet
Second Floor: 982 square feet; Total: 2,607 square feet

Custom Alterations? See page 203 for customizing this plan to your specifications.

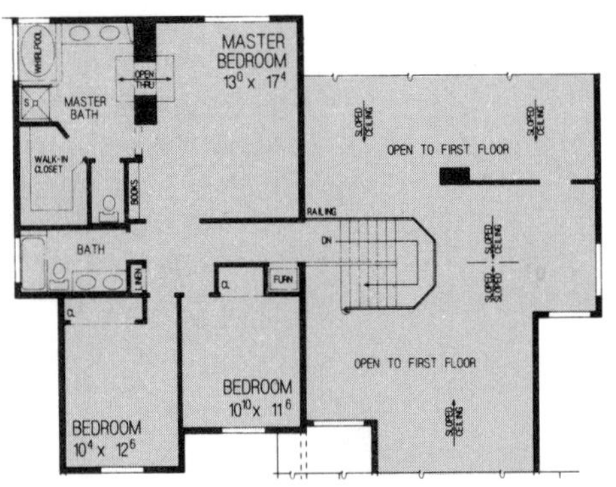

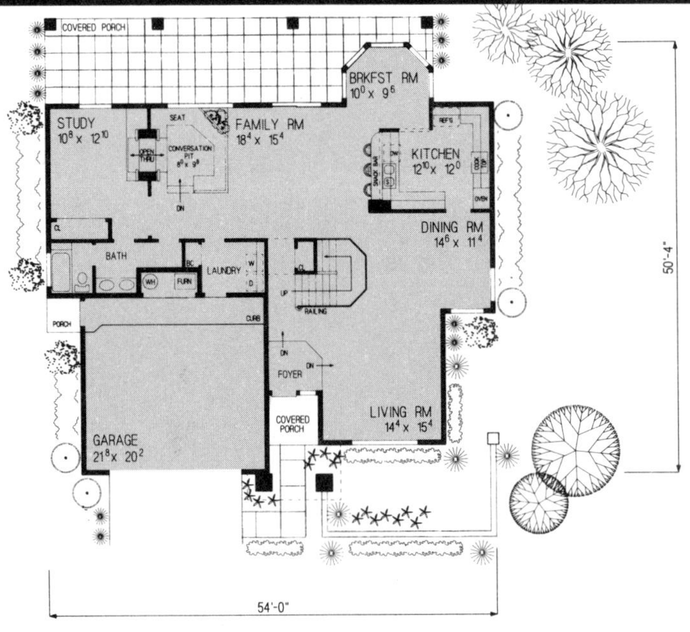

CUSTOMIZABLE

Custom Alterations? See page 203 for customizing this plan to your specifications.

Design P3417 First Floor: 875 square feet Second Floor: 731 square feet; Total: 1,606 square feet

● Perfect for a starter home, this plan provides both formal and informal living areas. There's a living room with bay window and adjacent dining area. Open to the kitchen, the spacious family room is large enough to accommodate an informal eating area. The second floor boasts a balcony lounge overlooking the family room, master bedroom with bay window and two smaller family bedrooms.

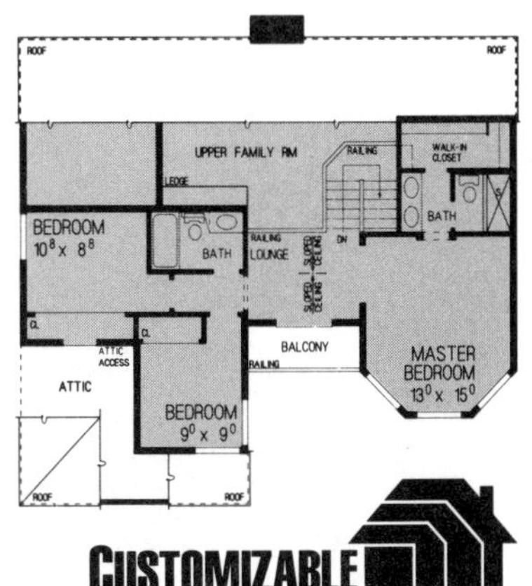

CUSTOMIZABLE

Custom Alterations? See page 203 for customizing this plan to your specifications.

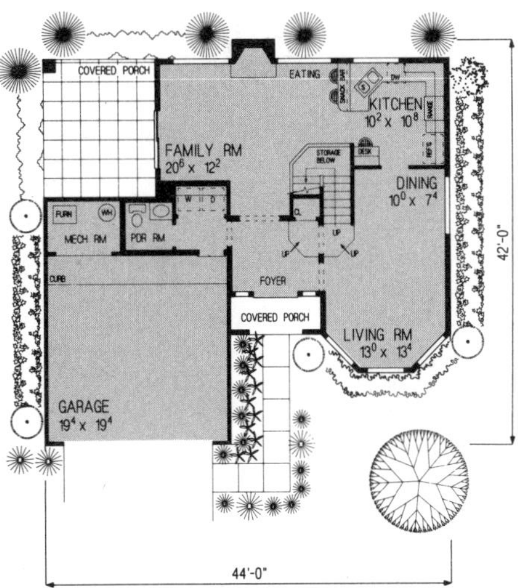

● You'll find plenty about this Spanish design that will convince you that this is *the* home for your family. Enjoy indoor/outdoor living in the gigantic family room with covered porch access and a sunken conversation area sharing a through fireplace with the study. An L-shaped kitchen has an attached, glass-surrounded breakfast room and is conveniently located next to the formal dining room/living room combination. Besides the opulent master suite on the second floor, there are two family bedrooms and a full bath.

Design P3418

First Floor: 1,283 square feet
Second Floor: 552 square feet
Total: 1,835 square feet

● This home is ideal for the economically minded who don't want to sacrifice livability. The entry foyer opens directly into the two-story living room with fireplace. To the right, the kitchen with peninsula cooktop and snack bar conveniently serves both the breakfast room and the formal dining room. Also on this level, the master bedroom boasts an enormous bath with a whirlpool and His and Hers walk-in closets. Three other bedrooms are located upstairs to ensure peace and quiet. Also notice the abundant storage space in the attic.

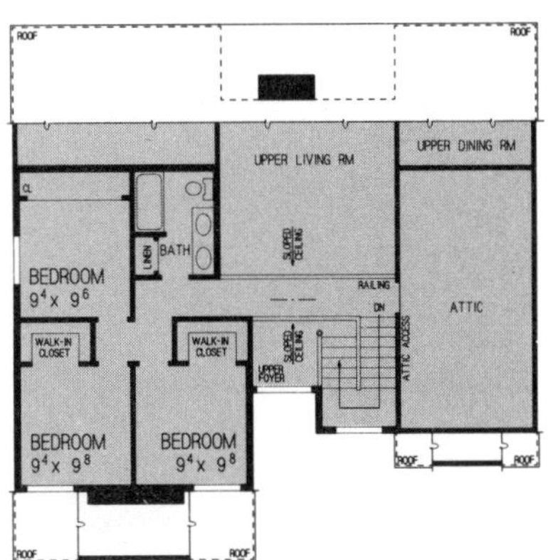

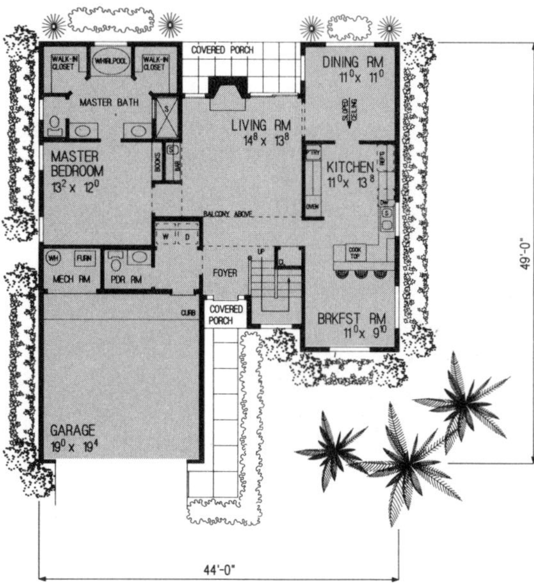

Custom Alterations? See page 203 for customizing this plan to your specifications.

Design P3427 First Floor: 1,574 square feet
Second Floor: 1,177 square feet; Total: 2,751 square feet

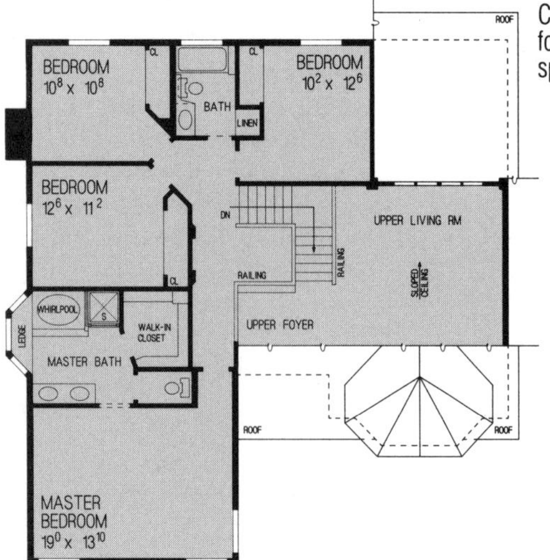

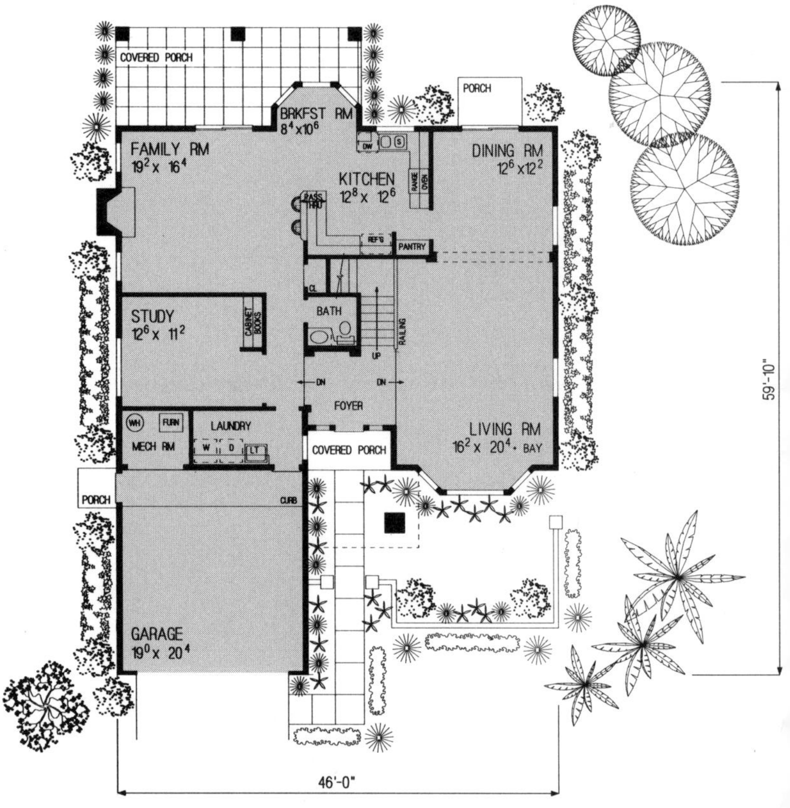

● Varying rooflines and unusual window treatments will make this home a standout anywhere. The transom-lit foyer opens onto a cozy study and a spacious living room with dramatic bay window. To the rear, the kitchen easily serves the dining room and the bay-windowed breakfast room. The family room features a large fireplace. Upstairs are four bedrooms including a master with whirlpool bath.

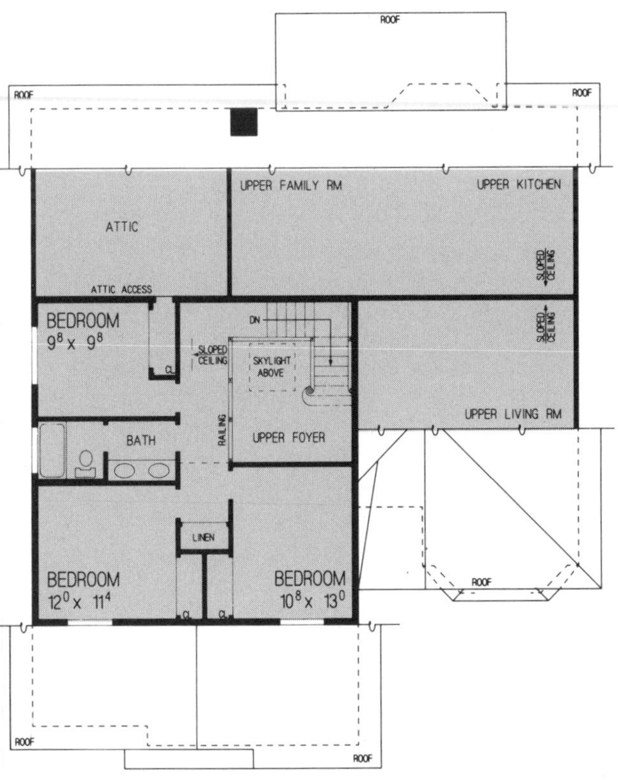

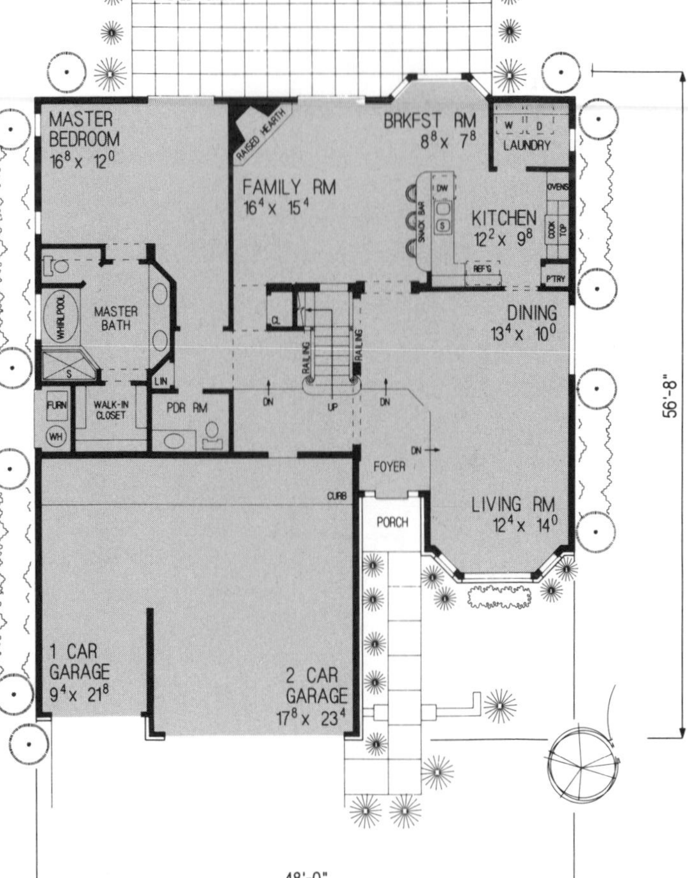

Design P3420

First Floor: 1,617 square feet
Second Floor: 658 square feet; Total: 2,275 square feet

● Here is a moderate-sized house with a wealth of amenities typical of much larger homes. Interesting window treatments include two bay windows, one in the living room and one in the breakfast room. In the kitchen there's a snack bar pass-through to the family room which boasts a corner raised-hearth fireplace. Also on this level, the master suite features a large bath with whirlpool and access to the rear covered porch. Upstairs are three more bedrooms and a shared bath. Notice the attic storage space.

Custom Alterations? See page 203 for customizing this plan to your specifications.

Design P2948

Square Footage: 1,830

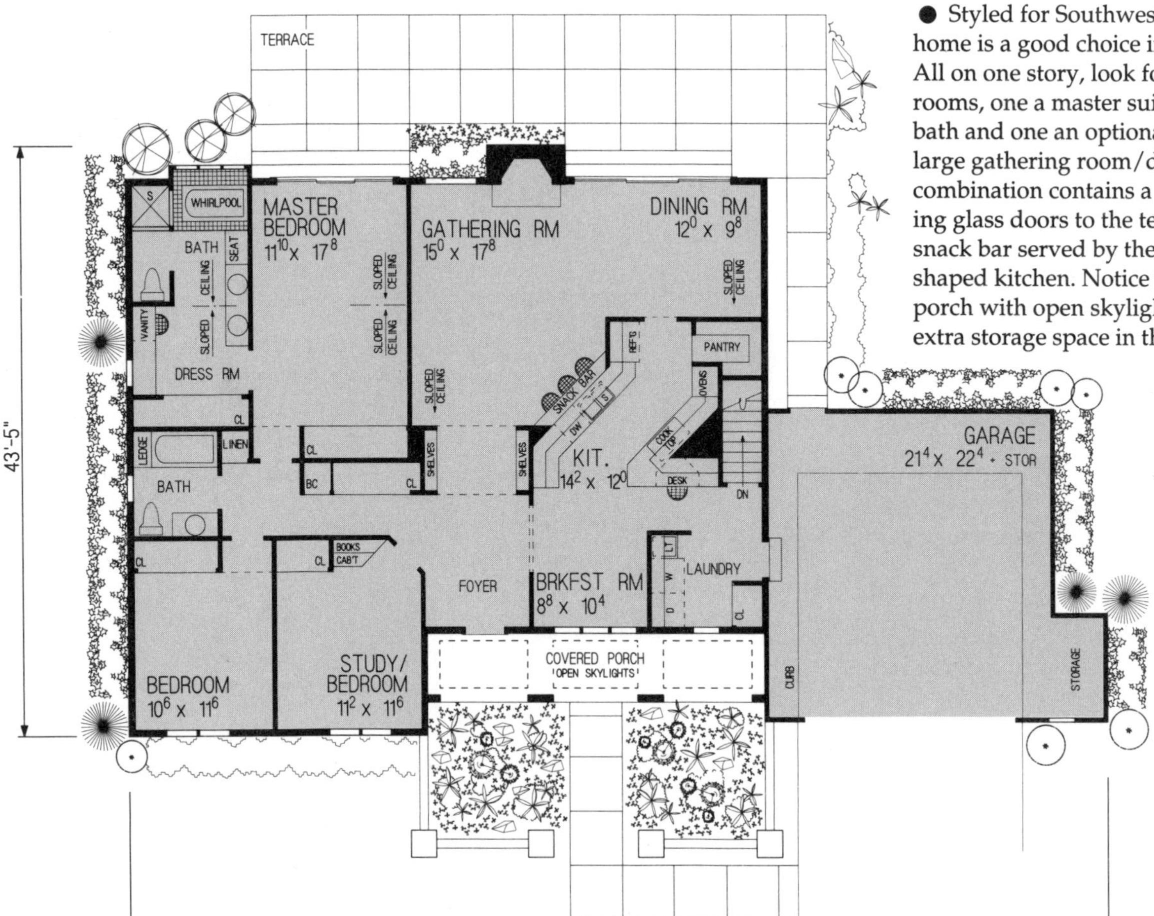

● Styled for Southwest living, this home is a good choice in any region. All on one story, look for three bedrooms, one a master suite with deluxe bath and one an optional study. The large gathering room/dining room combination contains a fireplace, sliding glass doors to the terrace, and a snack bar served by the uniquely shaped kitchen. Notice the covered porch with open skylights and the extra storage space in the garage.

CUSTOMIZABLE

Custom Alterations? See page 203 for customizing this plan to your specifications.

Spanish Colonial, Territorial and Rustic

Spanish Colonial

The Spanish settlement of the New World occurred during a period roughly from 1600 to 1850 and encompassed the vast area of land we now know as Texas, New Mexico, Arizona and California from San Diego north to San Francisco. The homes of the colonization borrowed from local dwellings, particularly churches, these being the predominant structures in the early settlements. Builders used available materials (mostly adobe) and tended to keep the homes utilitarian with little attention to the fine detail that would later adorn Southwestern-style homes.

Spanish Colonial homes are perhaps best identified as one-story thick adobe or wood frame dwellings with a low-pitched or flat roof. It is most appropriate to think of them as a line of independent rooms laid end to end and connected by an exterior corridor or porch. Although today most of the rooms are connected with inner doors, early examples often contained rooms that had their own exterior doors and were entirely self-contained. This method of building represented a practical approach to home improvement—rooms were added as wealth increased and families grew. Additions were made either in an in-line pattern or were turned to cause the formation of an L- or U-shaped structure. Larger homes of the wealthier landowners might enclose an inner courtyard. U-shaped, L-shaped and inner-courtyard homes are common in most modern renditions.

A distinguishing characteristic of these homes is their lack of ornamentation. What little decorative detailing may occur is generally reminiscent of Greek Revival style (a carry-over from patterns occurring in the East), although when balconies are added the structure begins to resemble Monterey style.

Territorial

When the home is a single story and has a flat roof with fired brick covering the roof parapet, it is considered Territorial style. These homes feature finished Doric columns that are milled, sanded and painted as well as canales, or drain spouts, that are also mill-sawn.

Territorial style developed later in the 1800s due to Anglo influences after New Mexico became a territory of the United States. Other developments occurring in this Territorial period include a move away from the "in-line" pattern of the Spanish Colonial style to more of a center-hall style. The availability of mill-sawn beams which were longer and stronger than hand-hewn beams allowed this dramatic development. Also, because of the decreased threat of Indian attack, homes in the Territorial mode employed larger windows than their predecessors—often windows with sashes that could be opened in good weather.

Rustic

Combining elements of both Spanish Colonial and Territorial homes, Rustic versions retain the low, in-line or L- and U-shaped configurations but contain decorative components devised from coarser materials. Common elements include roughened timbers, hand-hewn materials, and ironwork hinges and ornamentation on heavy wooden doors. Exposed weathered beams often add quite an authentic touch.

CUSTOMIZABLE

Custom Alterations? See page 203 for customizing this plan to your specifications.

Design P3400 Square Footage: 2,784

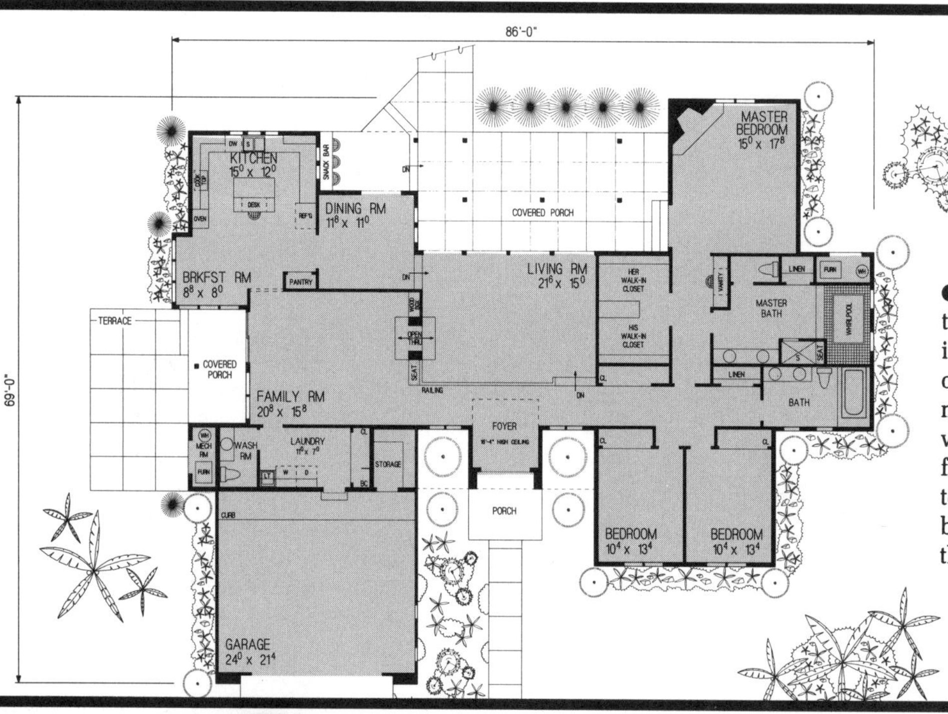

Design P3401

Square Footage: 2,850

● This Southwestern design caters to families who enjoy outdoor living and entertaining. Doors open onto shaded terraces from the master bedroom and living room, while a sliding glass door in the family room accesses a smaller terrace. Also notice the outdoor bar with pass-through window to the kitchen.

CUSTOMIZABLE

Custom Alterations? See page 203 for customizing this plan to your specifications.

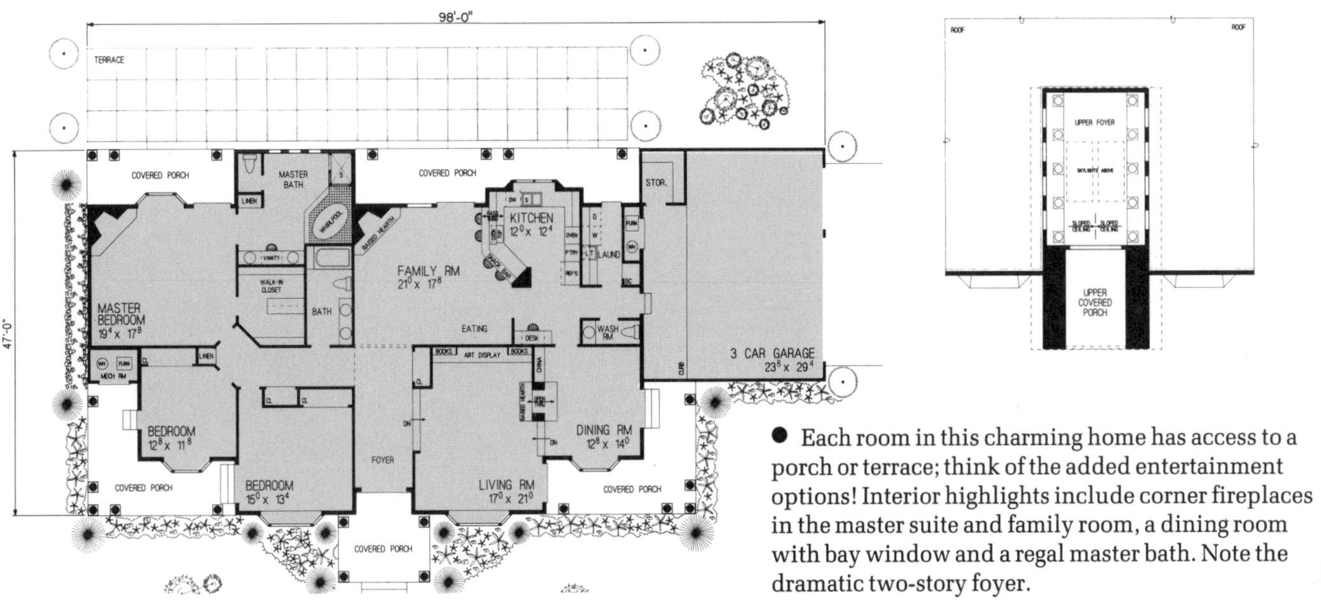

● Each room in this charming home has access to a porch or terrace; think of the added entertainment options! Interior highlights include corner fireplaces in the master suite and family room, a dining room with bay window and a regal master bath. Note the dramatic two-story foyer.

CUSTOMIZABLE

Custom Alterations? See page 203 for customizing this plan to your specifications.

Design P3402

Square Footage: 3,212

● This one-story pairs the customary tile and stucco of Spanish design with a livable floor plan. The sunken living room with its open-hearth fireplace promises to be a cozy gathering place. For more casual occasions, there's a family room with fireplace off the entry foyer. Also noteworthy: a sizable kitchen and a sumptuous master suite.

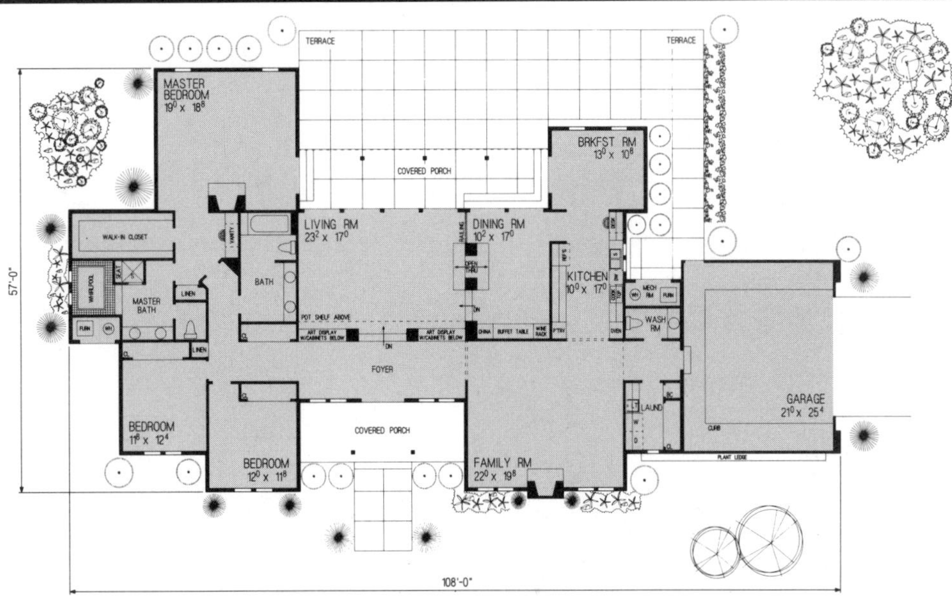

Design P3435

First Floor: 1,946 square feet
Second Floor: 986 square feet
Total: 2,932 square feet

● Here's a grand Spanish Mission home designed for family living. Enter at the angled foyer which contains a curved staircase to the second floor. Family bedrooms are here along with a spacious guest suite. The master bedroom is found on the first floor and has a private patio and whirlpool overlooking an enclosed garden area. Besides a living room and dining room connected by a through-fireplace, there is a family room with casual eating space. There is also a library with large closet. You'll appreciate the abundant built-ins and interesting shapes throughout this home.

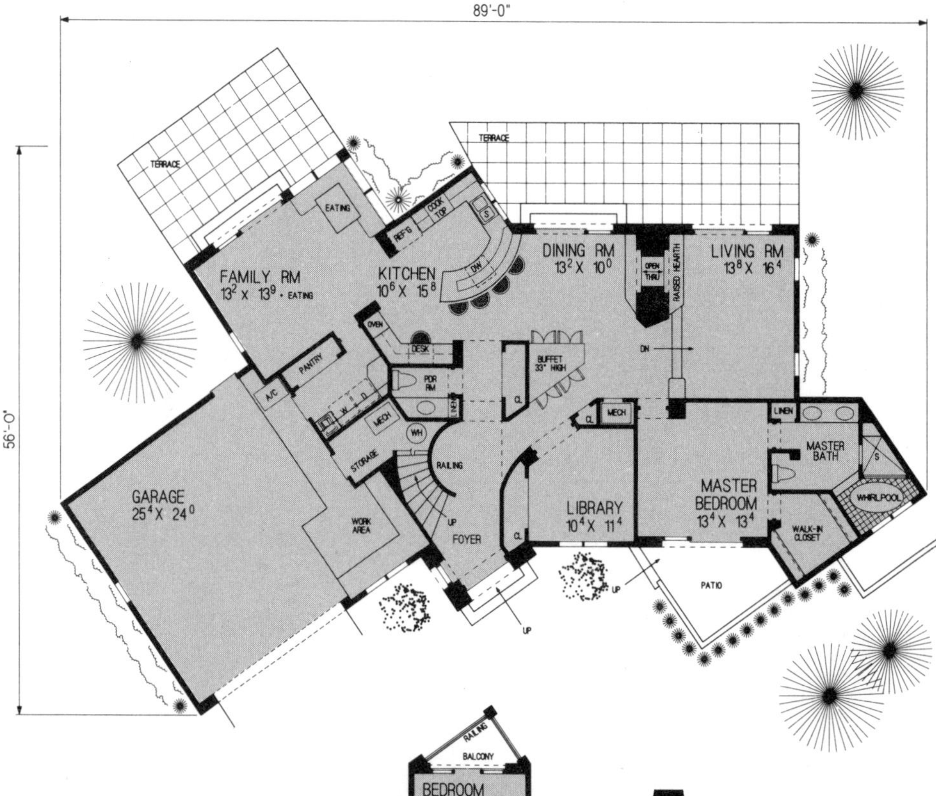

89'-0"

56'-0"

Custom Alterations? See page 203 for customizing this plan to your specifications.

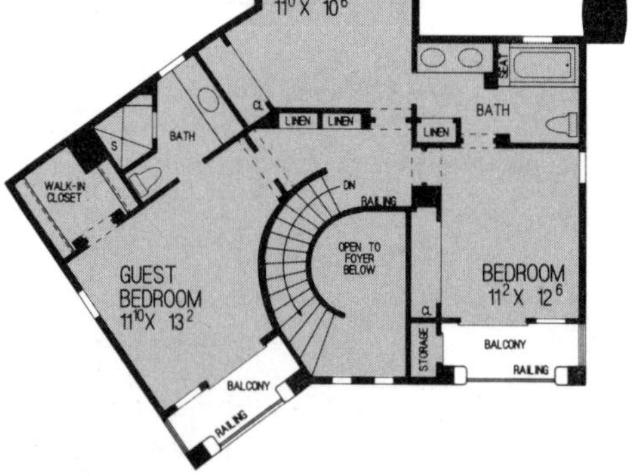

Design P2315

First Floor: 1,415 square feet
Second Floor: 1,101 square feet
Total: 2,516 square feet

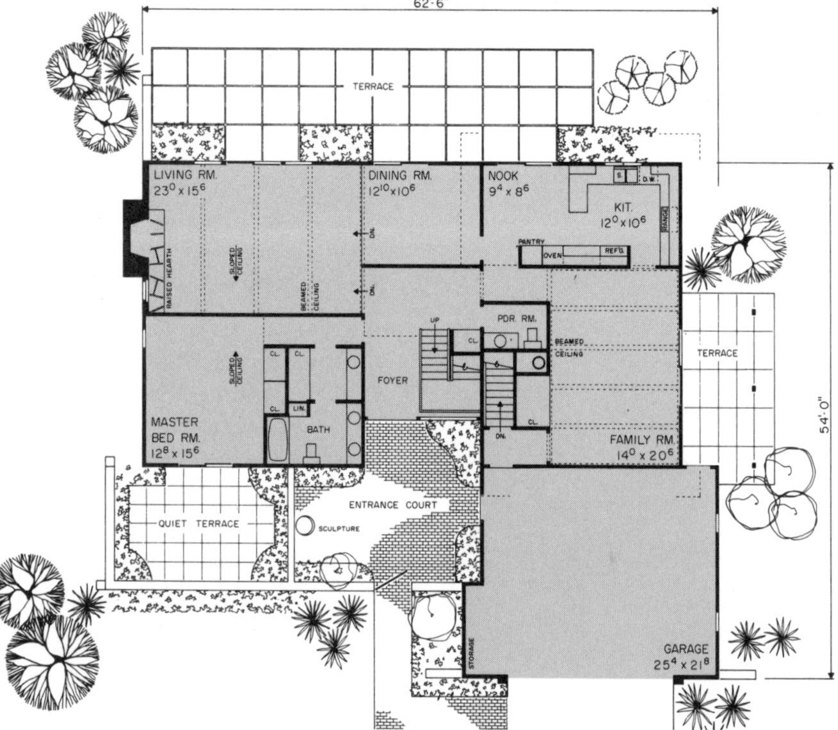

● This refreshing two-story has just enough individuality - both inside and out - to assure its own full measure of distinction. Sliding glass doors provide the living, dining and family rooms with direct access to their own terrace areas. You can look down into the foyer and the dining room from the second floor.

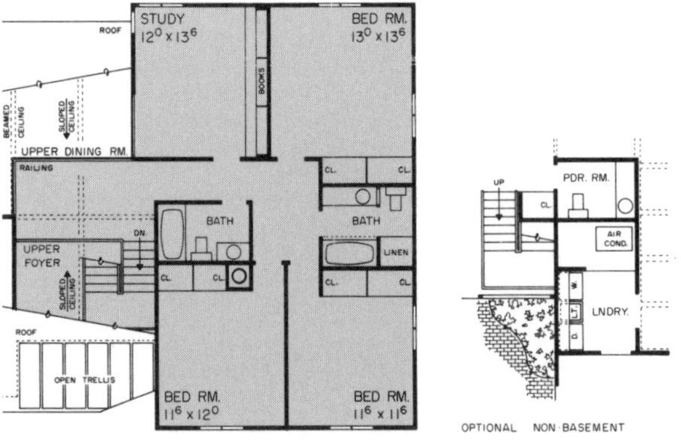

Design P2252

First Floor: 1,810 square feet
Second Floor: 1,033 square feet; Total: 2,843 square feet

Design P2741

Square Footage: 1,842

● Here is another example of what 1,800 square feet can deliver in comfort and convenience. The setting reminds one of the sun country of Arizona. However, this design would surely be an attractive and refreshing addition to any region. The covered front porch with its adjacent open trellis area shelters the center entry. From here traffic flows efficiently to the sleeping, living and kitchen zones. There is much to recommend each area. The sleeping with its fine bath and closet facilities; the living with its spaciousness, fireplace and adjacent dining room; the kitchen with its handy nook, excellent storage, nearby laundry and extra washroom.

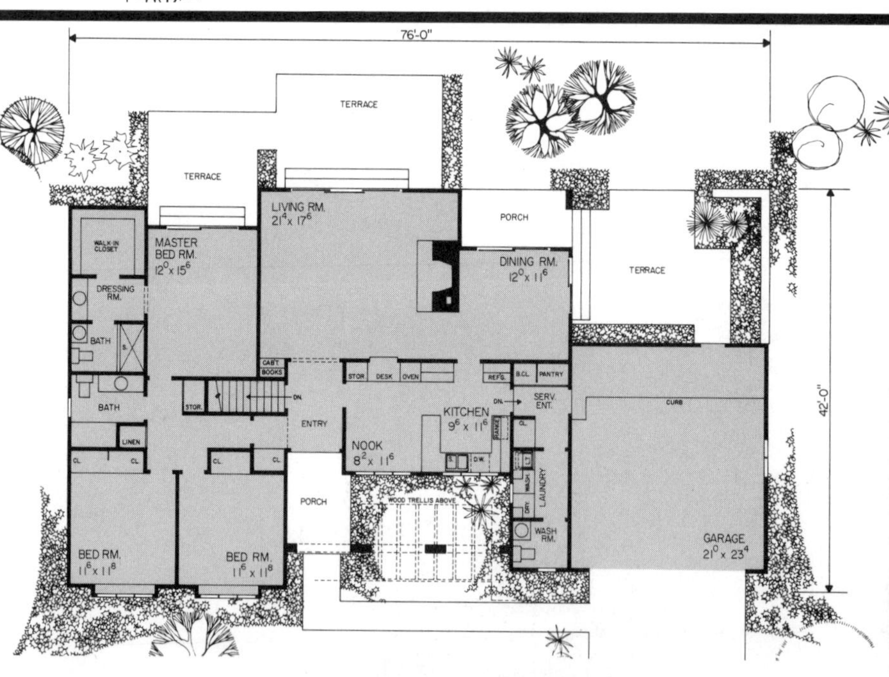

Design P2232

Square Footage: 1,776

● This appealing design definitely has its roots deep in the Spanish Southwest. Its exterior characteristics offer a unique charm that is unmatched. Take note of the elegantly arched front porch with its heavy beamed ceiling. It sets this design apart from the rest. The interior distinction to this home is the center foyer that routes traffic effectively to the main zones of the house. Upon entering, a nice sized living room is a few steps down. An efficient kitchen with adjacent dining room will be enjoyed. Close to the kitchen is a roomy family room. It has a snack bar. Take a few steps down the hall to the two bedrooms and a master bedroom. Notice that both the master bedroom and family room have sliding glass doors that provide access to the terrace.

71'-4"
38'-10"
TERRACE
BED RM. 14⁰ x 11⁶
BATH
MASTER BED RM. 12⁸ x 15⁰
FAMILY RM. 13⁰ x 17⁴
WALK-IN CL.
WOOD BOX
LINEN
BATH
AIR COND.
SNACK BAR
CHINA BUFFET
STOR.
OVENS
BED RM. 10⁸ x 11⁶
FOYER
DINING RM. 9⁴ x 10⁴
KIT. 15⁰ x 10⁴
PANTRY
UTILITY RM.
COVERED PORCH
LIVING RM. 19⁰ x 13⁸
GARAGE 20⁰ x 25⁰

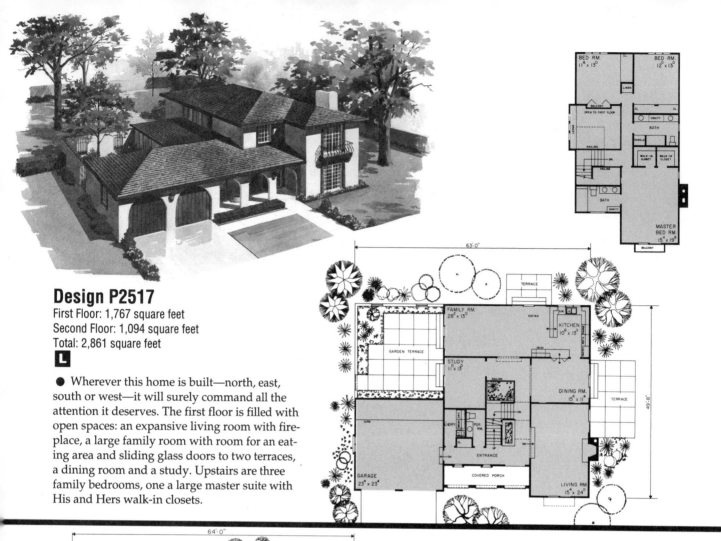

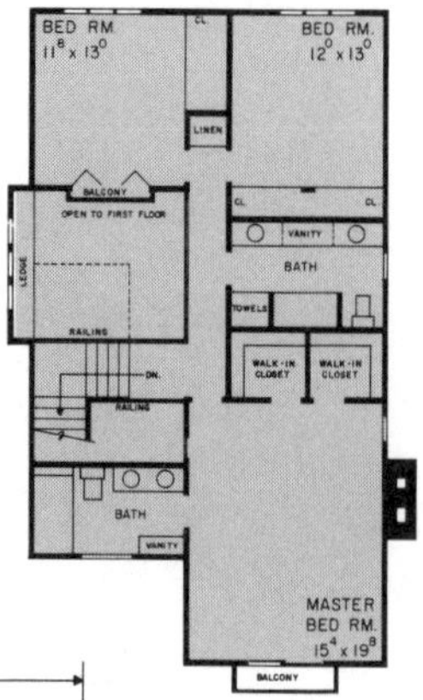

Design P2517

First Floor: 1,767 square feet
Second Floor: 1,094 square feet
Total: 2,861 square feet

L

● Wherever this home is built—north, east, south or west—it will surely command all the attention it deserves. The first floor is filled with open spaces: an expansive living room with fireplace, a large family room with room for an eating area and sliding glass doors to two terraces, a dining room and a study. Upstairs are three family bedrooms, one a large master suite with His and Hers walk-in closets.

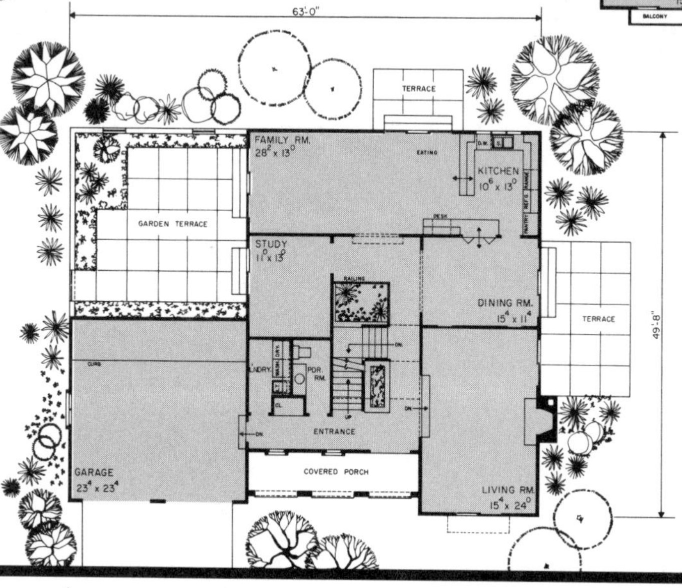

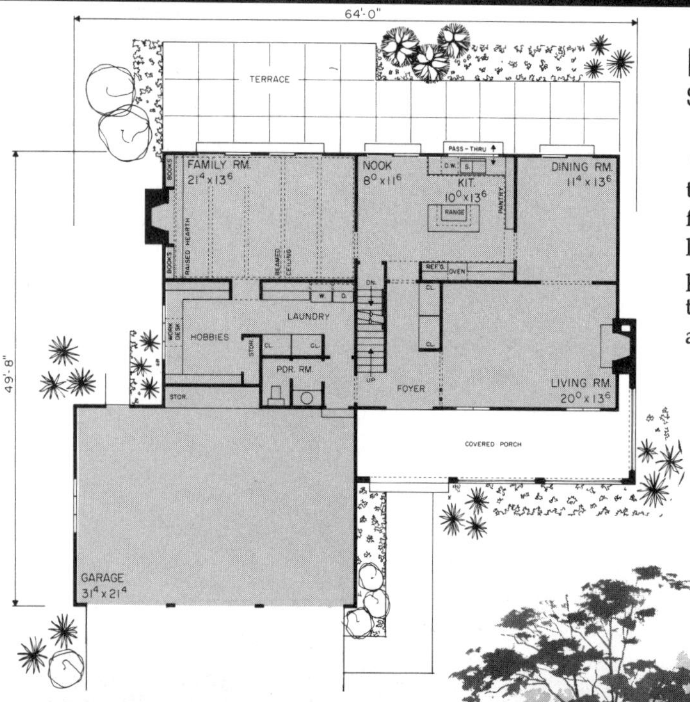

Design P2323

First Floor: 1,430 square feet
Second Floor: 1,172 square feet; Total: 2,602 square feet

● Planned to accommodate large families, this home contains five bedrooms and two baths on the second floor. The first floor also has a great deal of living space. The formal living room and the informal family room (each with a fireplace) are both very spacious. An island range in the kitchen two eating areas, a large hobby room with built-ins and an adjacent laundry are features you won't want to miss.

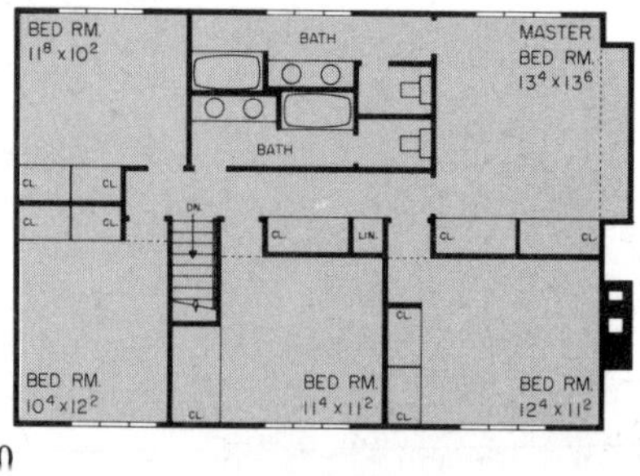

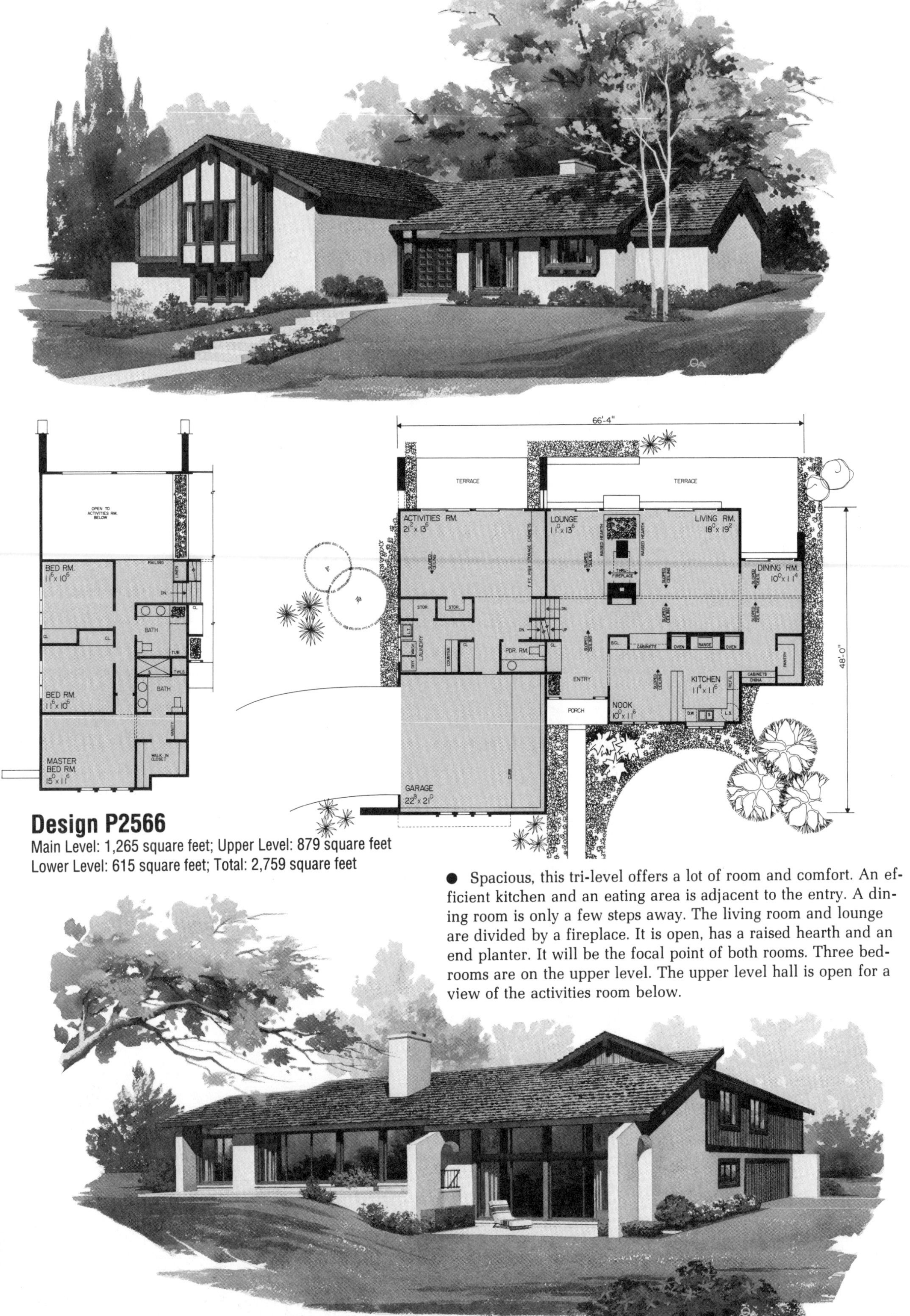

Design P2566

Main Level: 1,265 square feet; Upper Level: 879 square feet
Lower Level: 615 square feet; Total: 2,759 square feet

● Spacious, this tri-level offers a lot of room and comfort. An efficient kitchen and an eating area is adjacent to the entry. A dining room is only a few steps away. The living room and lounge are divided by a fireplace. It is open, has a raised hearth and an end planter. It will be the focal point of both rooms. Three bedrooms are on the upper level. The upper level hall is open for a view of the activities room below.

Custom Alterations? See page 203 for customizing this plan to your specifications.

Design P2804

Square Footage: 1,674

L D

● Stuccoed arches, multi-paned windows and a gracefully sloped roof accent the exterior of this Spanish-inspired design. The sleeping area includes two, or optional three, bedrooms. The interior kitchen will efficiently serve the dining room, covered dining porch and breakfast room with great ease. The gathering room, an impressive 16 x 20 feet, features a fireplace. Special details include a bay window in the front bedroom, snack bar and desk in the breakfast room, and extra storage space in the garage.

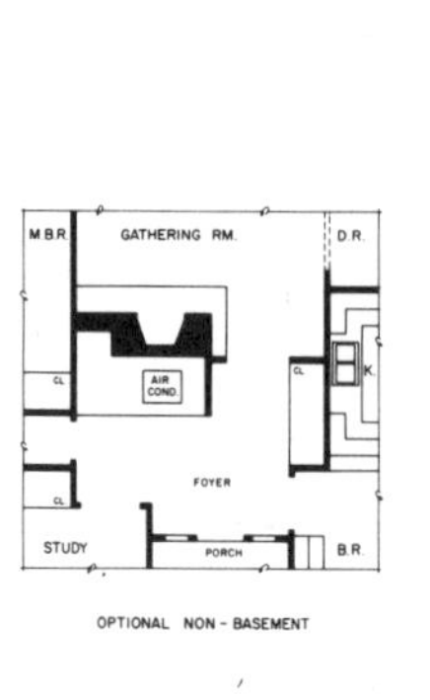

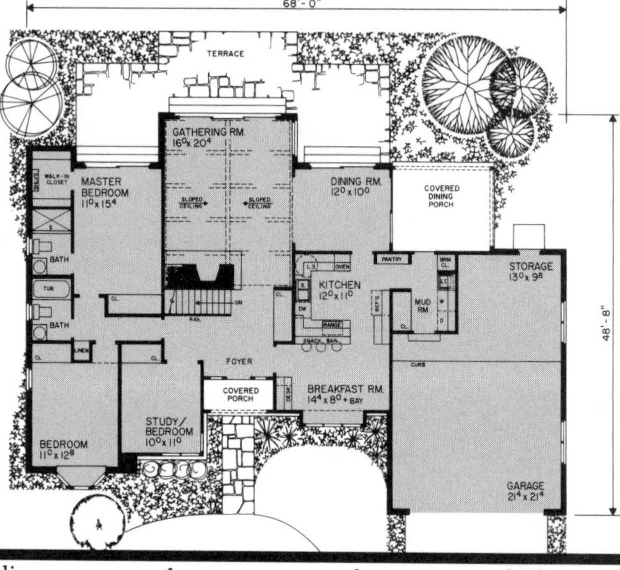

Design P2677

Square Footage: 1,634

● Notice the difference in these plan's livability. Design P2200 has a shared living dining room overlooking the backyard and a front master bedroom with a side terrace where Design P2677 has a separate front dining room, family room with access to the rear terrace and a rear master bedroom with an adjacent covered porch. Both designs have two additional bedrooms besides the master bedroom. Access to the basement varies in each plan.

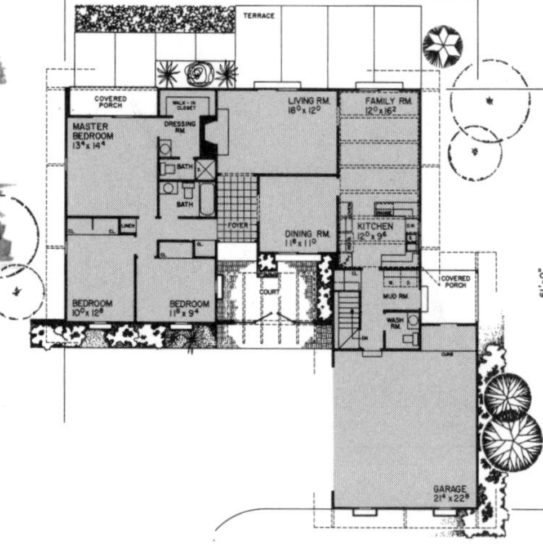

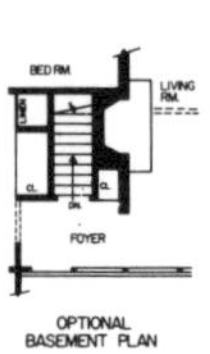

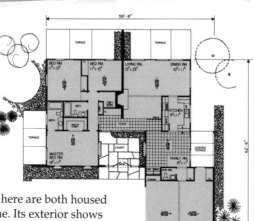

Design P2200

Square Footage: 1,695

● The two plans featured here are both housed in this L-shaped ranch home. Its exterior shows a Spanish influence by utilizing a stucco exterior finish, grilled windows and an arched entryway. Beyond the arched entryway is the private front court which leads to the tiled foyer. Interior livability has been well planned in both designs.

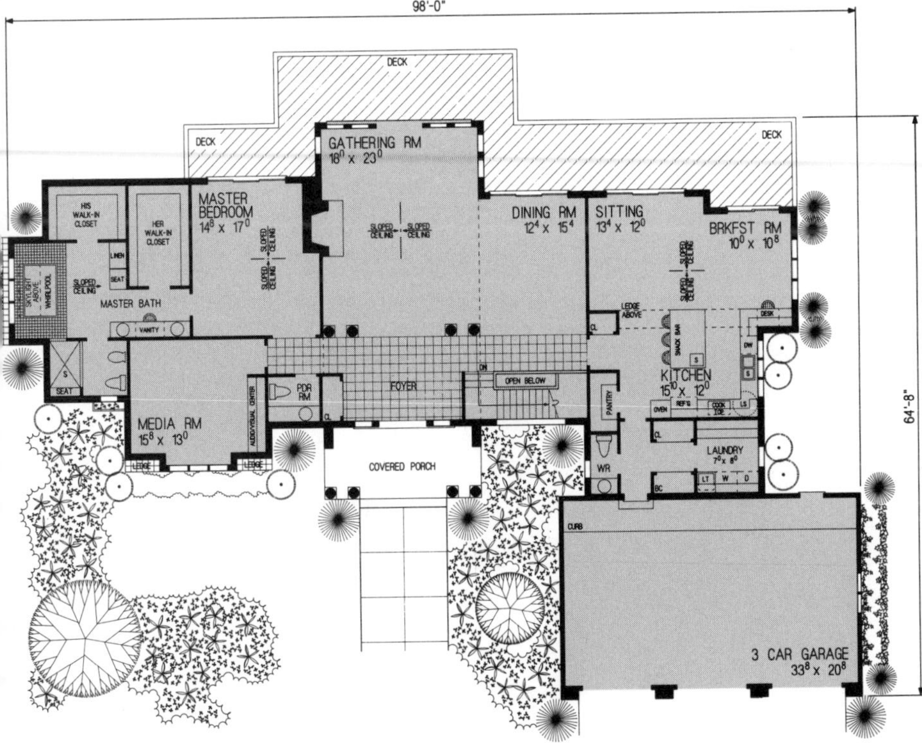

Design P3311

Main Level: 2,662 square feet
Lower Level: 1,548 square feet
Total: 4,210 square feet

● Here's a hillside haven for family living with plenty of room to entertain in style. Enter the main level from a dramatic columned portico that leads to a large entry hall. The gathering room is straight back and adjoins a formal dining area. A true gourmet kitchen with plenty of room for casual eating and conversation is nearby. The abundantly appointed master suite on this level is complemented by a luxurious bath. Note the media room to the front of the house. On the lower level are two more bedrooms, a full bath, a large activity area with fireplace and a convenient summer kitchen.

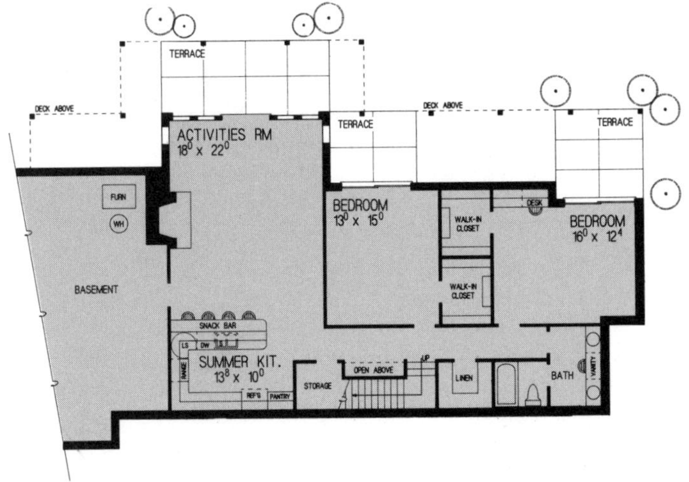

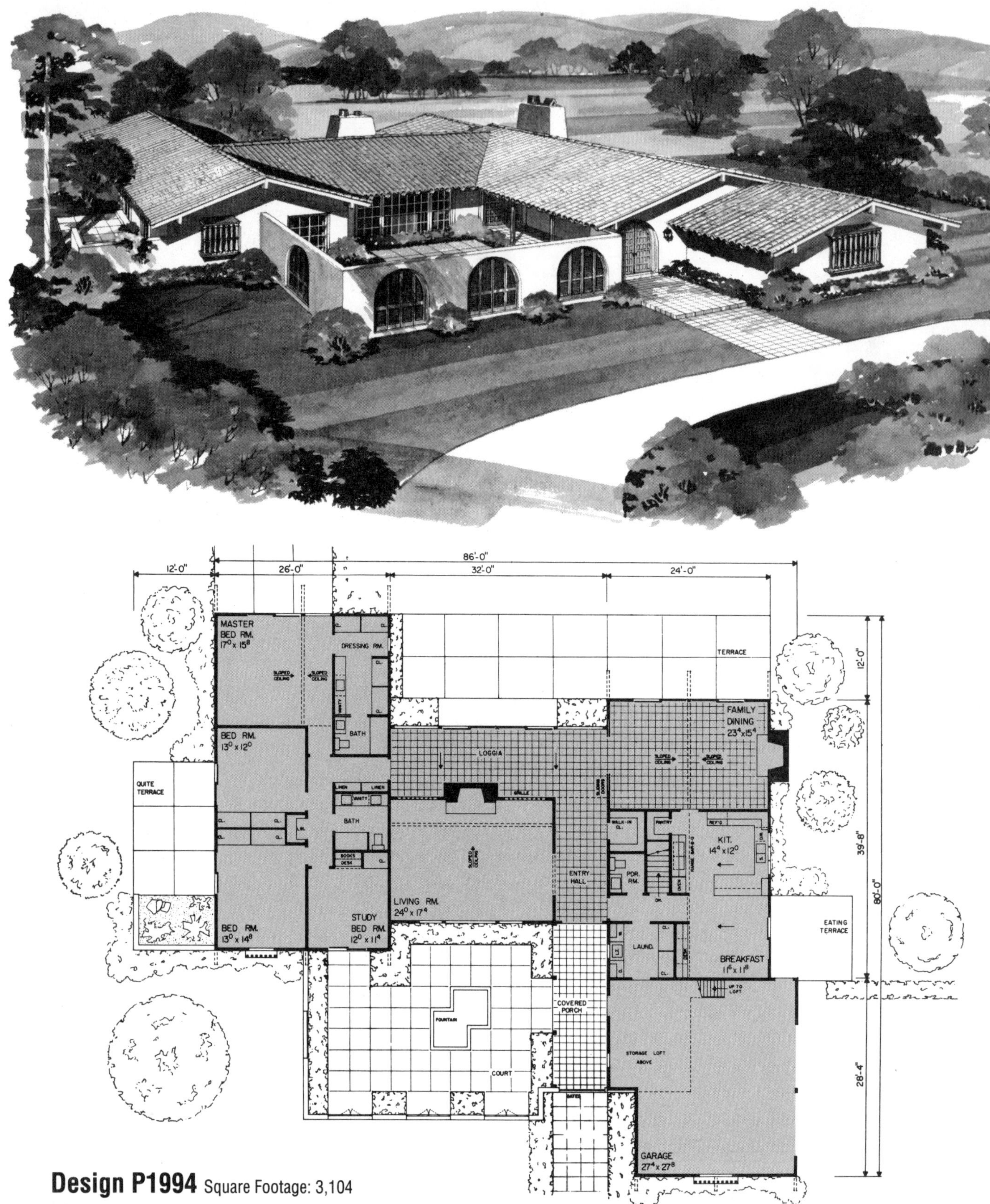

Design P1994 Square Footage: 3,104

● The Spanish flavor of the old Southwest is delightfully captured by this sprawling ranch house. Its L-shape and high privacy wall go together to form a wide open interior court. This will be a great place to hold those formal and/or informal garden parties. The plan itself is wonderfully zoned. The center portion of the house is comprised of the big, private living room with sloped ceiling. Traffic patterns will noiselessly skirt this formal area. The two wings—the sleeping and informal living—are connected by the well-lighted and spacious loggia. In the sleeping wing, observe the size of the various rooms and the fine storage. In the informal living wing, note the big family room and breakfast room that family members will enjoy.

Design P2143 Main Level: 832 square feet; Upper Level:864 square feet; Lower Level: 864 square feet; Total: 2,560 square feet

● Here the Spanish Southwest comes to life in the form of an enchanting multi-level home. There is much to rave about. The architectural detailing is delightful, indeed. The entrance courtyard, the twin balconies and the roof treatment are particularly noteworthy. Functioning at the rear of the house are the covered patio and the balcony with its lower patio. Well zoned, the upper level has three bedrooms and two baths; the main level has its formal living and dining rooms to the rear and kitchen area looking onto the courtyard; the lower level features the family room, study and laundry. Be sure to notice the extra wash room and the third full bath. There are two fireplaces each with a raised hearth. A dramatic house wherever built!

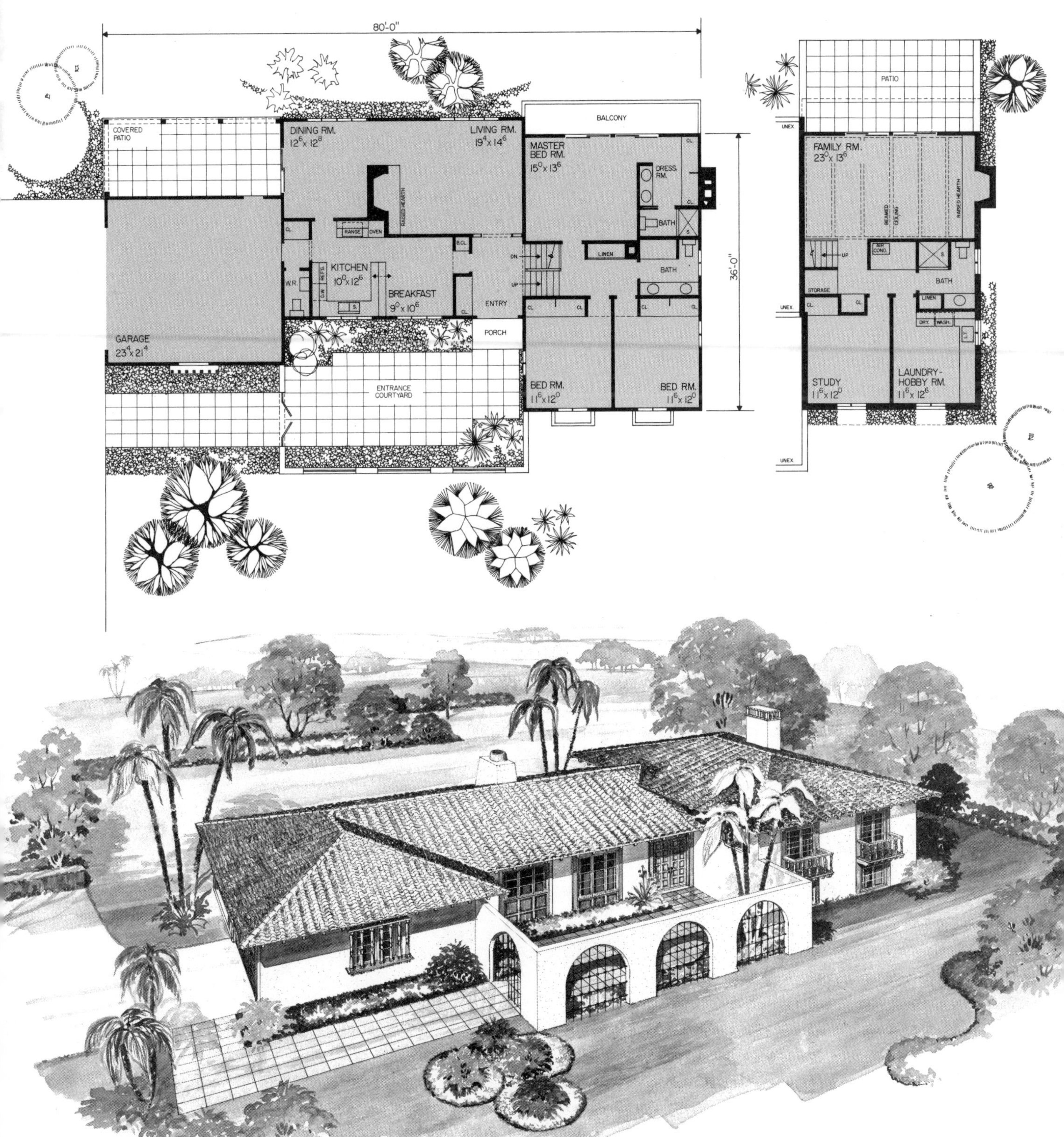

● Echoing design themes of old Spain, this history house distills the essence of country houses built by rancheros in Early California. Yet its floor plan provides all the comfort and convenience essential to our contemporary living. Among its charming features is a secluded court, or patio; a greenhouse tucked in behind the garage; a covered rear porch; a low-pitched wide overhanging roof with exposed rafter tails; sloping beamed ceilings. Contributing to the authenticity of the design are the two sets of panelled doors. The covered walk to the front doors provides a sheltered area adjacent to the court. Once inside, the feeling of space continues to impress.

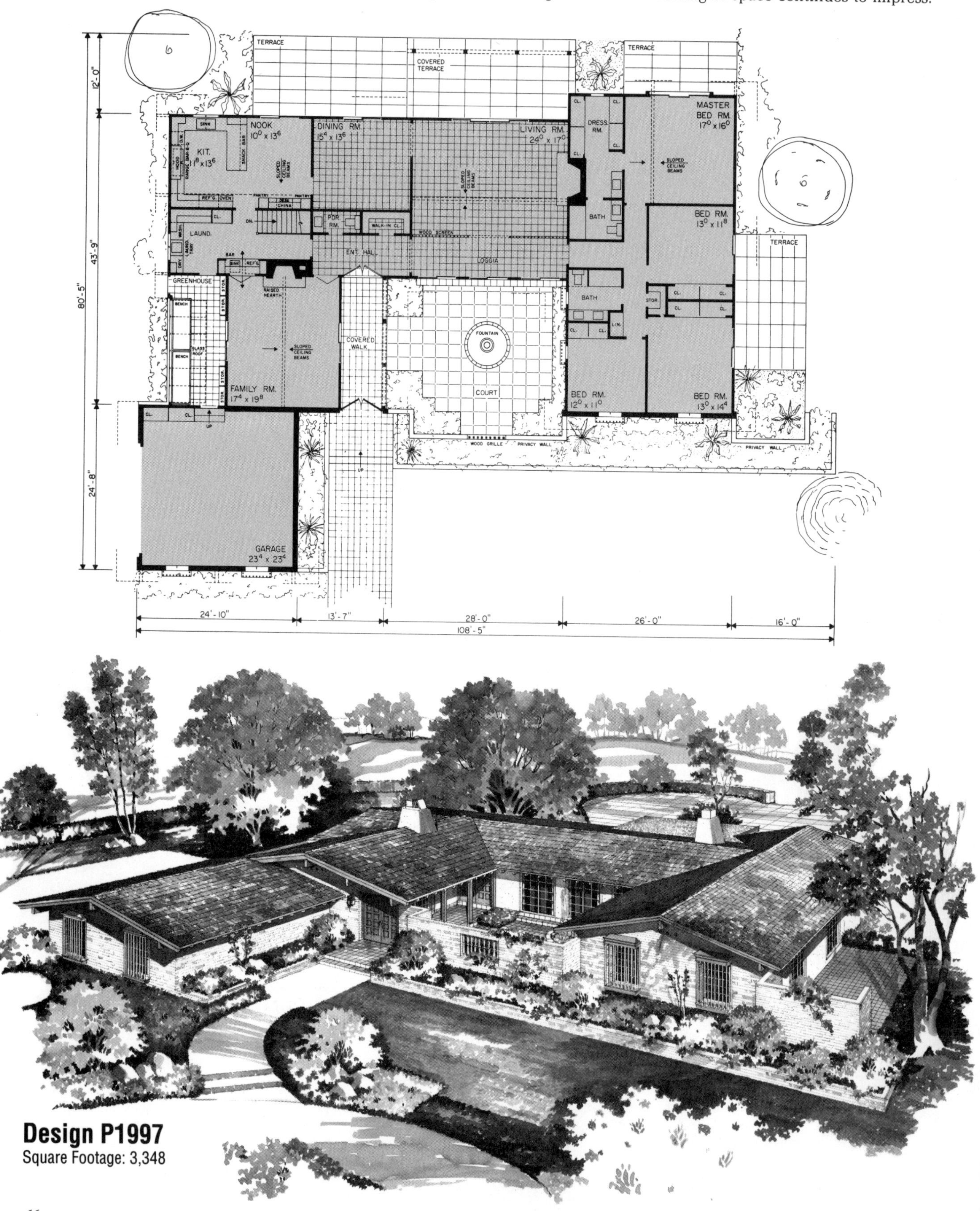

Design P1997
Square Footage: 3,348

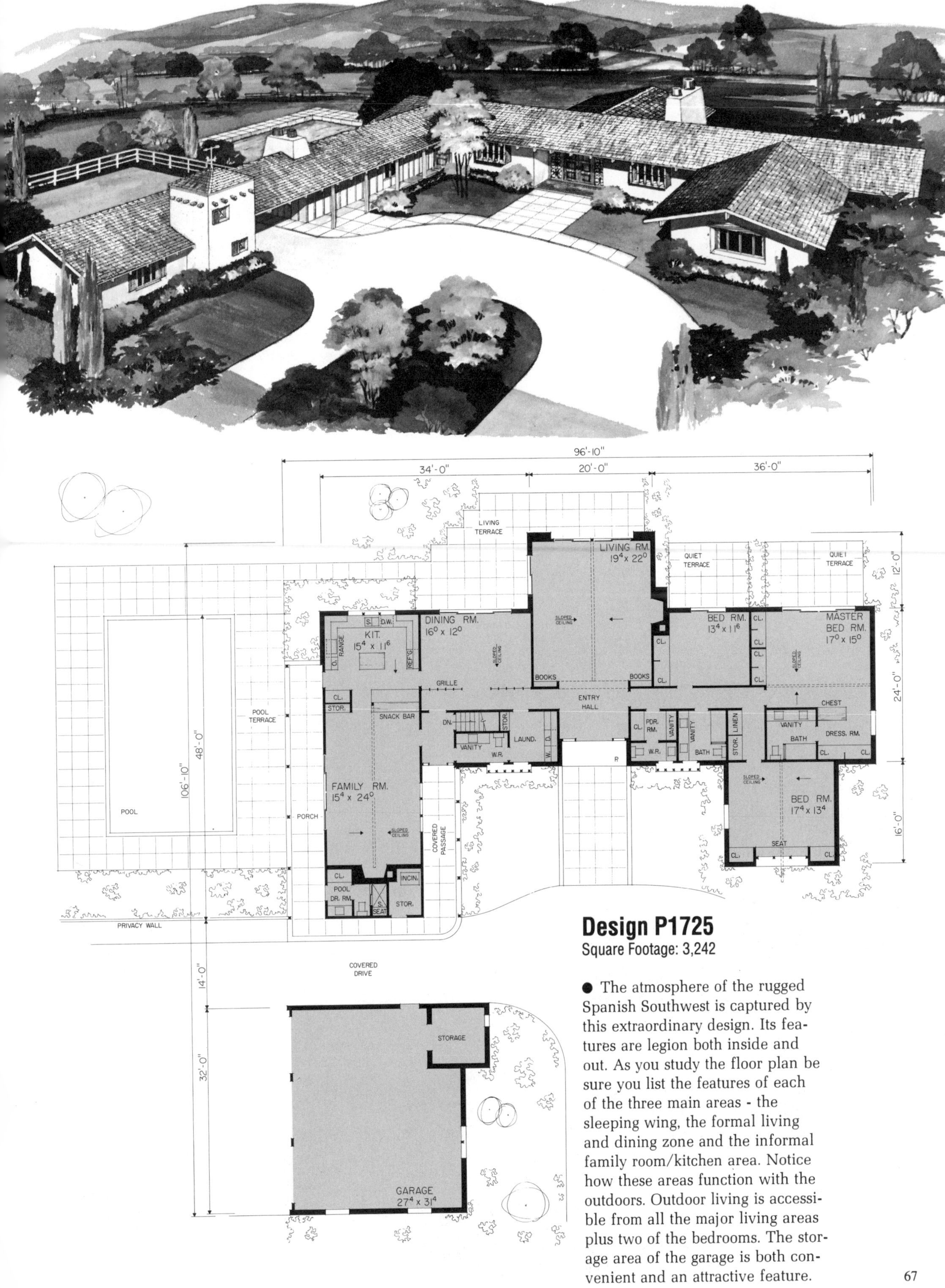

Design P1725

Square Footage: 3,242

● The atmosphere of the rugged Spanish Southwest is captured by this extraordinary design. Its features are legion both inside and out. As you study the floor plan be sure you list the features of each of the three main areas - the sleeping wing, the formal living and dining zone and the informal family room/kitchen area. Notice how these areas function with the outdoors. Outdoor living is accessible from all the major living areas plus two of the bedrooms. The storage area of the garage is both convenient and an attractive feature.

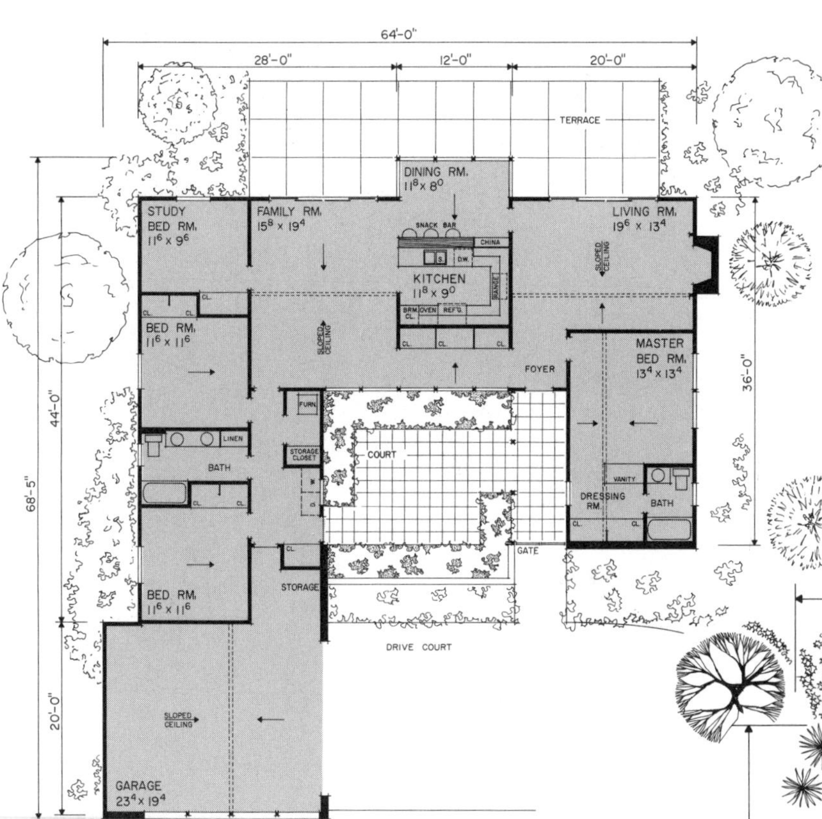

Design P1726

Square Footage: 1,910

● The U-shaped plan has long been honored for its excellent zoning. As the floor plan for this fine Spanish adaptation illustrates, it not only provides separation between parents' area and children's wing, but also it places a buffer area in the center. This makes the kitchen the "control center" for the home - handy to the family room, living room and the dining alcove.

Design P2743

Square Footage: 1,892

● Placing the attached garage at the front cuts down on the size of a site required for this design. It also represents an appealing design factor. The privacy wall and overhead trellis provide a pleasant front courtyard. Inside, the gathering room satisfies the family's more gregarious instincts, while there is always the study nearby to serve as a more peaceful haven. The separate dining room and the nook offer dining flexibility. The two full baths highlight the economical back-to-back plumbing feature.

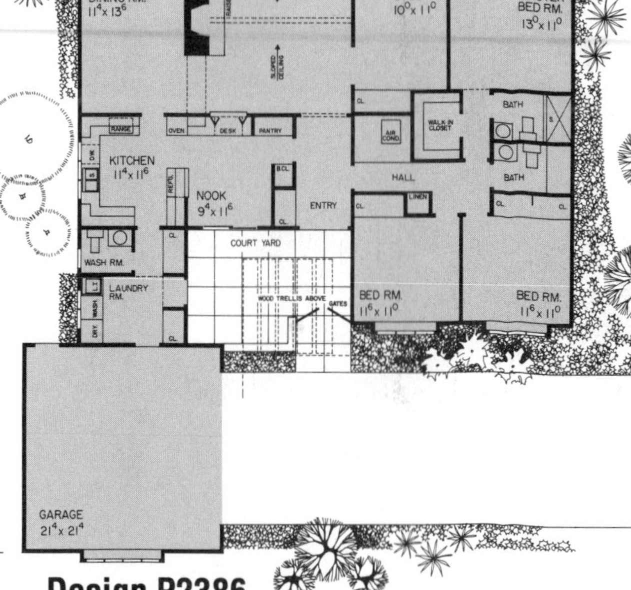

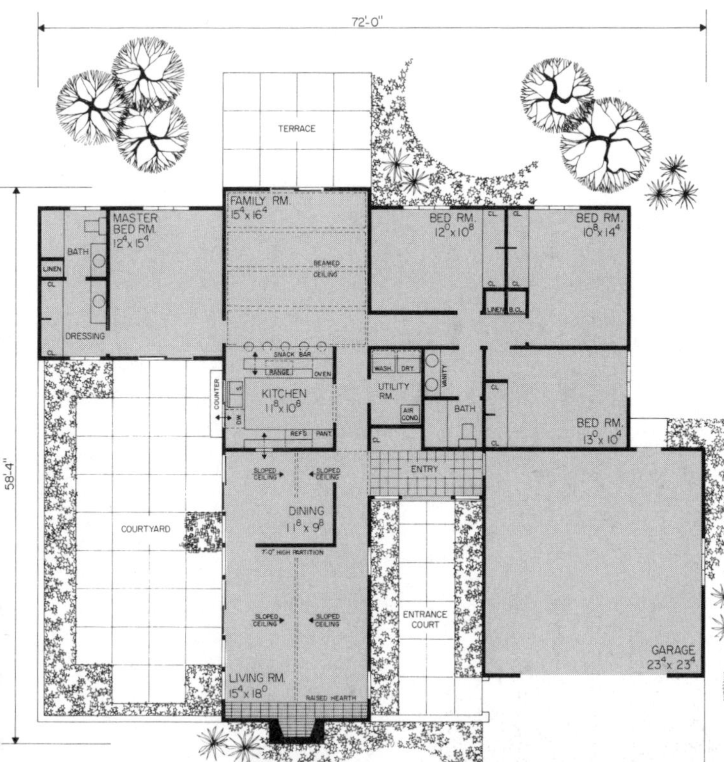

Design P2386

Square Footage: 1,994

L

● This distinctive home may look like the Far West, but don't let that inhibit you from enjoying the great livability it has to offer. Wherever built, you will experience a satisfying sense of pride in ownership. Imagine, an entrance court in addition to a large side courtyard! A central core is made up of the living, dining and family rooms, plus the kitchen. Each functions with an outdoor living area. The younger generation has its sleeping zone separated from the master bedroom. The location of the attached garage provides direct access to the front entry. Don't miss the vanity, utility room with laundry equipment, snack bar or raised hearth fireplace. Note three pass-thrus from the kitchen.

Design P2214 First Floor: 3,011 square feet
Second Floor: 2,297 square feet; Total: 5,308 square feet

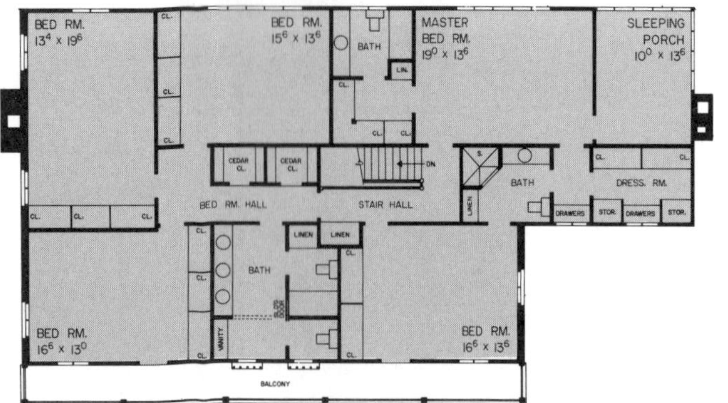

● A Spanish hacienda with all the appeal and all the comforts one would want in a new home. This is a house that looks big and really is big. Measuring 100 feet across the front with various appendages and roof planes, this design gives the appearance of a cluster of units. The house represents over 5,000 square feet of livability, excluding the garage. There are five bedrooms on the second floor plus a sixth bedroom and a study on the first floor. The master bedroom features two full baths and a sleeping porch. The living room is 27 feet long and if you wanted more space you could do away with the plant area. Or, maybe you'd prefer to make this a music area. A full house can be seated in the 18 foot dining room. Kitchen is nearby for ease in serving. Certainly a great house for the large, active family.

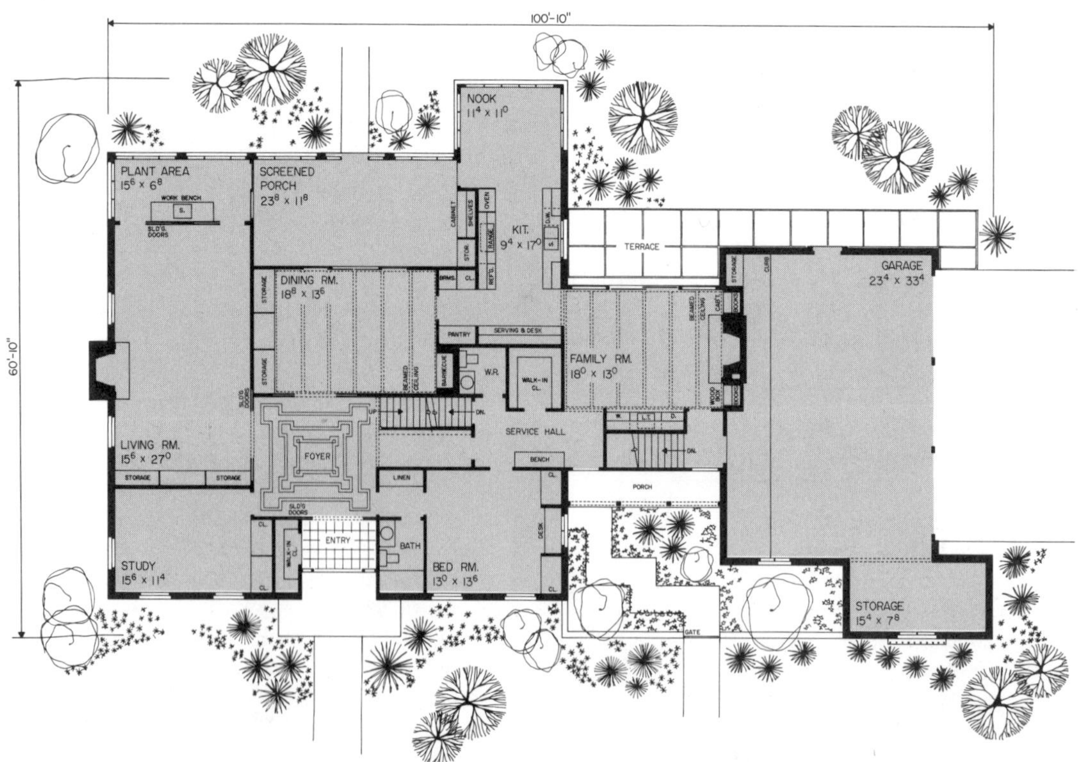

Modern Santa Fe or Pueblo Style

Distinctive in nature, the Santa Fe home was first inspired by local buildings in the Southwest and brings together the finest elements of flat-roofed Spanish Colonial design and the primitive dwellings of the Native American Pueblos. The style first saw prominence in California but quickly spread to Arizona and New Mexico where it is most popular today. The finest examples are located in Albuquerque and Santa Fe where, because of local building restrictions and historical preservation codes, some original dwellings can be found.

Santa Fe homes have some of the most unique and quaint features of any of the Southwestern styles. They generally imitate the mud houses of the Native American Pueblo culture, using adobe or stucco over wood frame or adobe brick as their main building material.

Walls may slope inward and have surfaces of rough textured adobe or stucco that is often earth-toned or white in color. Common are the projecting wood beams, called vigas, that extend through the walls. Though today vigas are mostly ornamental, their history is quite interesting. While adobe mud was available for house walls, other building materials in the desert Southwest were scarce and difficult to come by and there was little timber for beams. Homes were built with the vigas, or beams, crossing the width of the house as a support for smaller poles known as lattias. The roof was then completed with mud. Hence the width of a house was largely determined by the length of available vigas. The length of a room and the total number of rooms could be increased simply by adding more vigas. Newcomers often used existing beams from abandoned houses to build their new homes, since the beams were precut and available. Often the vigas were longer than the width of the house, creating the charming effect of projecting beams that is so cherished in Pueblo-style homes today.

Roofs of Modern Santa Fe homes are almost always flat and often feature a parapeted wall above the roof line. Walls and roof parapets are characterized by irregular, rounded edges, imitating the rain- and wind-weathered edges on the original dwellings of this style. Corners where walls join are likewise rounded or blunted as are window and door surrounds.

Because the earliest examples of the Santa Fe style were built during a period when threat of Indian attack was common, these homes were often built fortress-like with a completely enclosed interior courtyard. Later, as settlements grew and Indian attacks decreased, portals, or covered patios, were added to the exteriors. Both conventions are common and delightful elements of the Modern Santa Fe home.

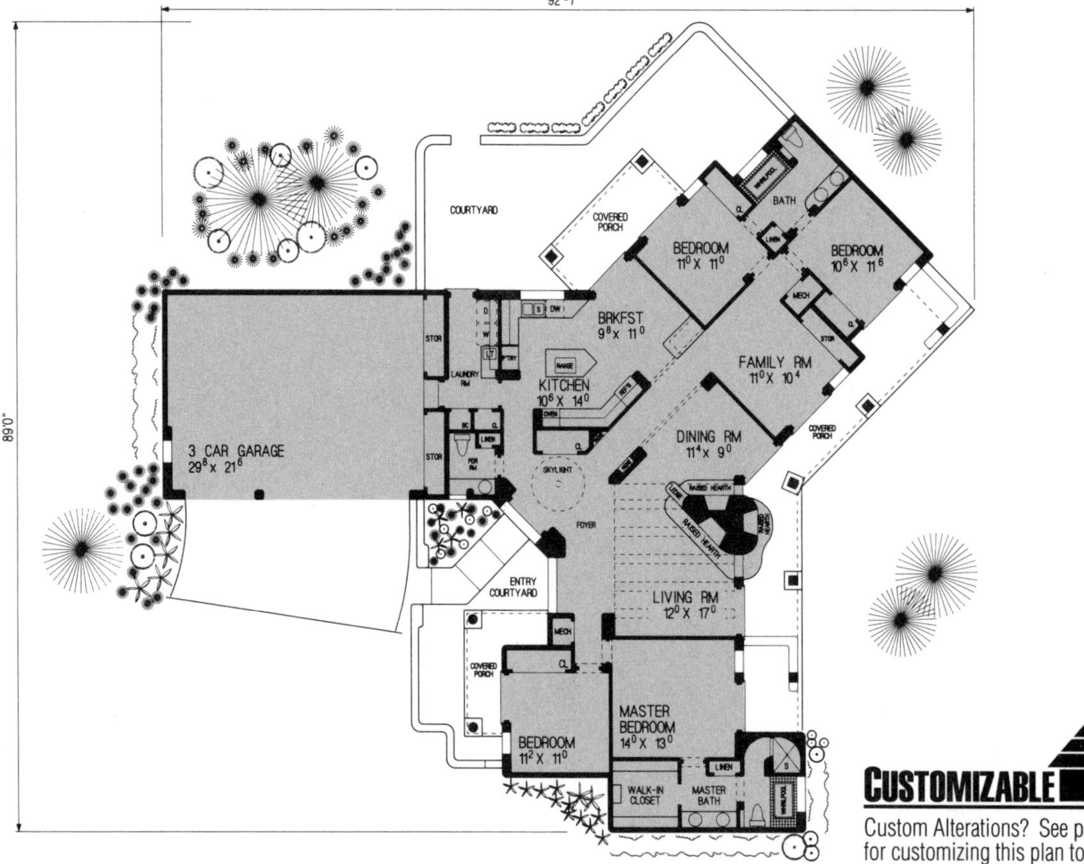

CUSTOMIZABLE

Custom Alterations? See page 203 for customizing this plan to your specifications.

Design P3433

Square Footage: 2,350

● Santa Fe styling creates interesting angles in this one-story home. A grand entrance leads through a courtyard into the foyer with circular skylight, closet space and niches, and convenient powder room. Turn right to the master suite with deluxe bath and a bedroom close at hand, perfect for a nursery, home office or exercise room. Two more family bedrooms are placed quietly in the far wing of the house. Fireplaces in the living room, dining room and covered porch create various shapes. Make note of the island range in the kitchen, extra storage in the garage, and covered porches on two sides.

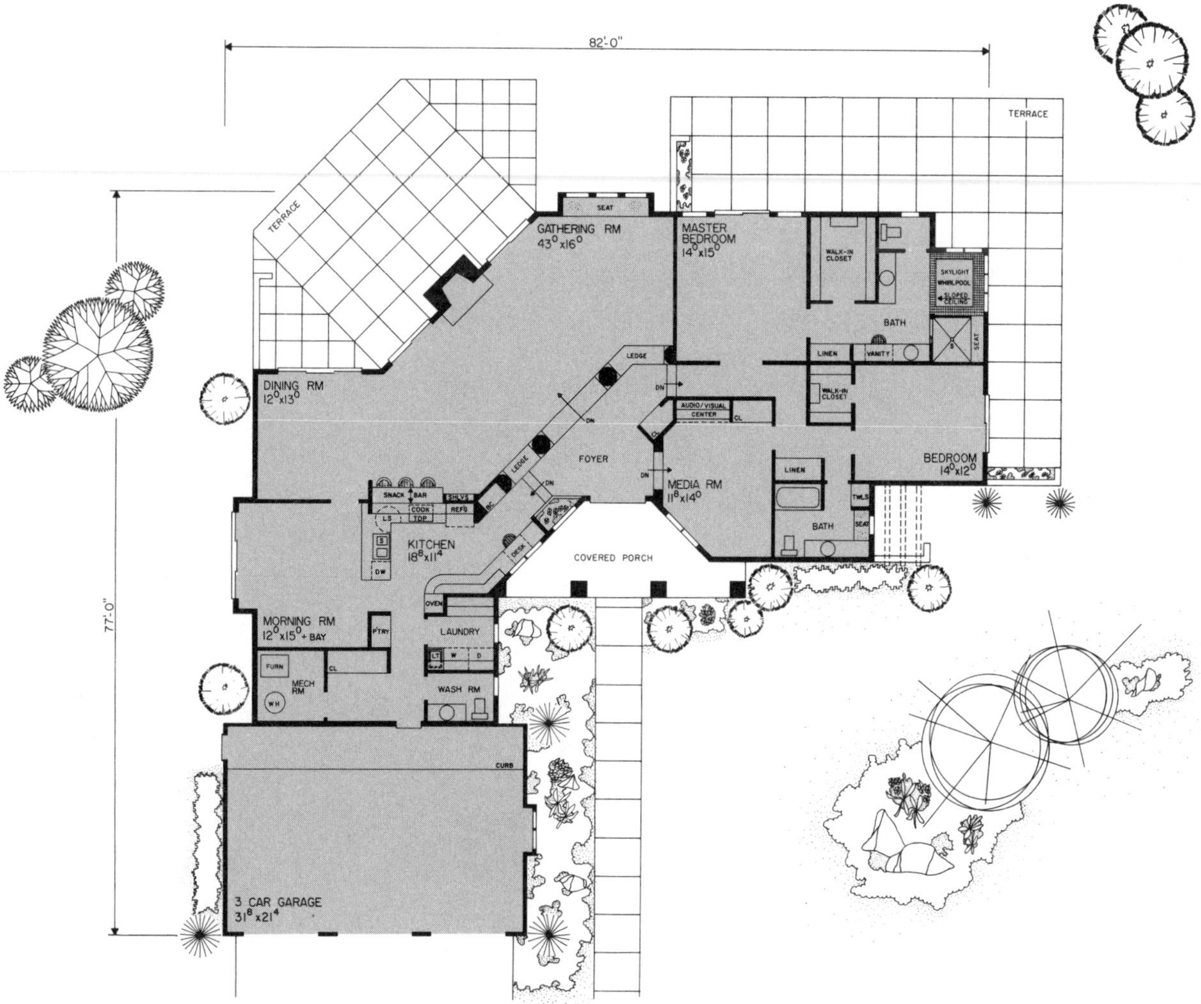

82'-0"

77'-0"

TERRACE

GATHERING RM
43^0x16^0

SEAT

MASTER BEDROOM
14^0x15^0

WALK-IN CLOSET

SKYLIGHT
WHIRLPOOL
SLOPED CEILING

BATH

LINEN

VANITY

SEAT

DINING RM
12^0x13^0

LEDGE

AUDIO/VISUAL CENTER

CL

WALK-IN CLOSET

FOYER

DN

MEDIA RM
11^8x14^0

LINEN

BEDROOM
14^0x12^0

SNACK BAR

SHLVS

COOK TOP

REFG

LS

KITCHEN
18^6x11^4

DW

DESK

BATH

TWLS

COVERED PORCH

OVEN

MORNING RM
12^0x15^0+ BAY

PTRY

LAUNDRY

FURN

MECH RM

WH

CL

WASH RM

CURB

3 CAR GARAGE
31^8x21^4

Design P2949

Square Footage: 2,922

D

● Spanish and western influences take center stage in a long, low stucco design. You'll enjoy the Texas-sized gathering room that opens to a formal dining area and has a snack bar through to the kitchen. More casual dining is accommodated in the nook. A luxurious master suite is graced by plenty of closet space and a soothing whirlpool spa. Besides another bedroom and full bath, there is a media room that could easily double as a third bedroom or guest room.

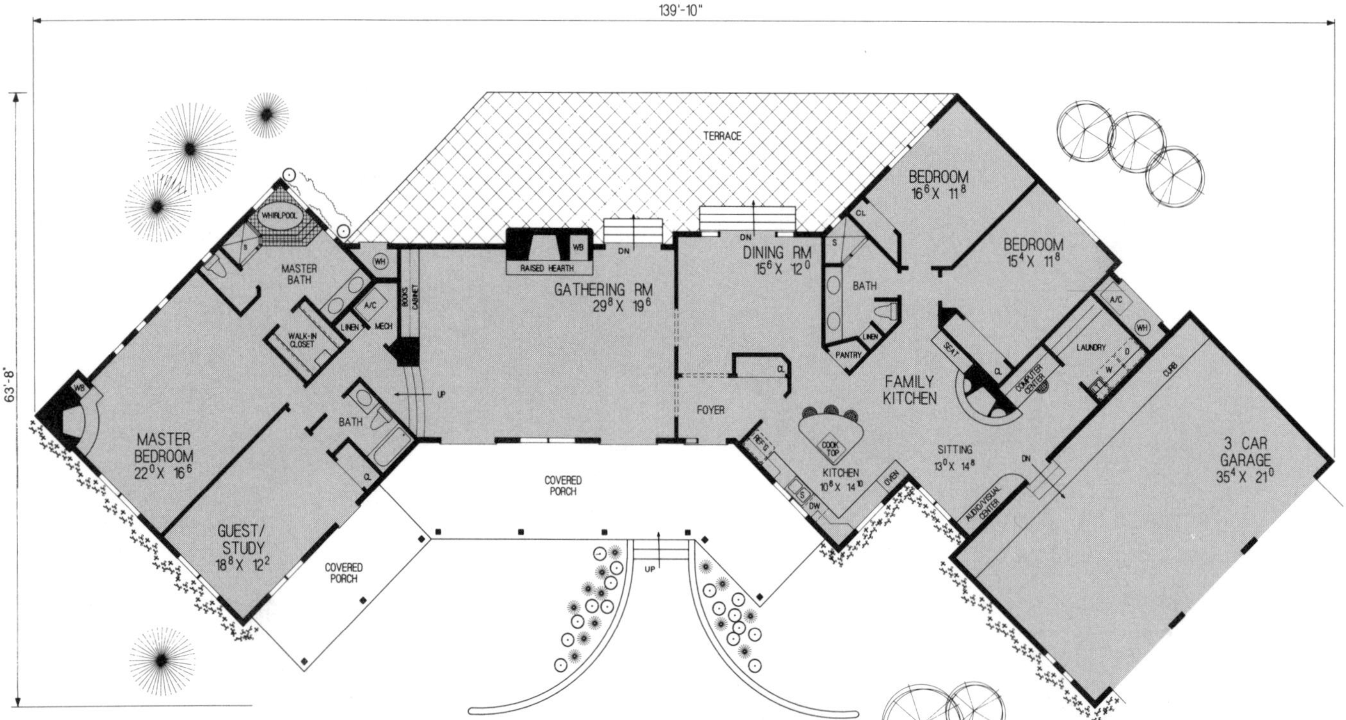

139'-10"

63'-8"

TERRACE

BEDROOM
16^6 X 11^8

BEDROOM
15^4 X 11^8

WHIRLPOOL

MASTER BATH

WALK-IN CLOSET

LINEN

MECH

A/C

WH

RAISED HEARTH

WB

DN

GATHERING RM
29^8 X 19^6

DINING RM
15^6 X 12^0

BATH

PANTRY

LINEN

CL

SEAT

FAMILY KITCHEN

COMPUTER CENTER

LAUNDRY

CURB

MASTER BEDROOM
22^0 X 16^6

BATH

UP

FOYER

COOK TOP

KITCHEN
10^8 X 14^{10}

OVEN

DW

REF'G

SITTING
13^0 X 14^8

AUDIO/VISUAL CENTER

3 CAR GARAGE
35^4 X 21^0

GUEST/ STUDY
18^8 X 12^2

COVERED PORCH

COVERED PORCH

CUSTOMIZABLE

Custom Alterations? See page 203 for customizing this plan to your specifications.

Design P3405

Square Footage: 3,144

● In classic Santa Fe style, this home strikes a beautiful combination of historic exterior detailing and open floor planning on the inside. A covered porch running the width of the facade leads to an entry foyer that connects to a huge gathering room with fireplace and formal dining room. The family kitchen allows special space for casual gatherings. The right wing of the home holds two family bedrooms and full bath. The left wing is devoted to the master suite and guest room or study. Built-ins abound throughout the house.

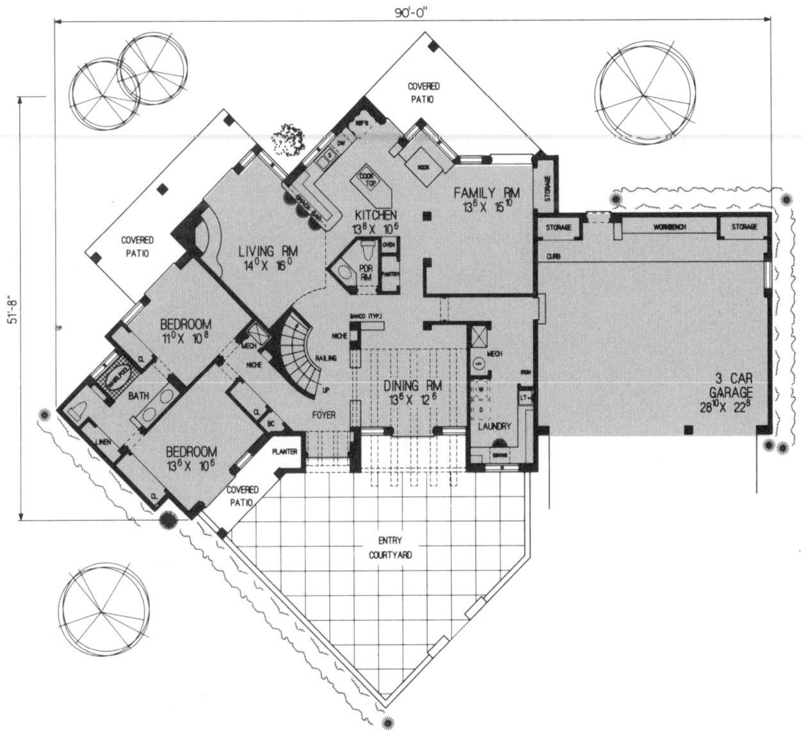

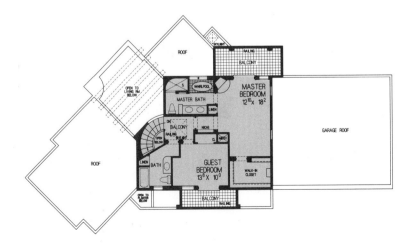

Design P3432

First Floor: 1,966 square feet
Second Floor: 831 square feet
Total: 2,797 square feet

● Unique in nature, this two-story Santa Fe-style home is as practical as it is lovely. The facade is elegantly enhanced by a large entry court, overlooked by windows in the dining room and a covered patio from one of two family bedrooms. The entry foyer leads to living areas at the back of the plan: a living room with corner fireplace and a family room connected to the kitchen via a built-in eating nook. Upstairs, the master suite features a grand bath and large walk-in closet. The guest bedroom has a private bath. Every room in this home has its own outdoor area.

Custom Alterations? See page 203 for customizing this plan to your specifications.

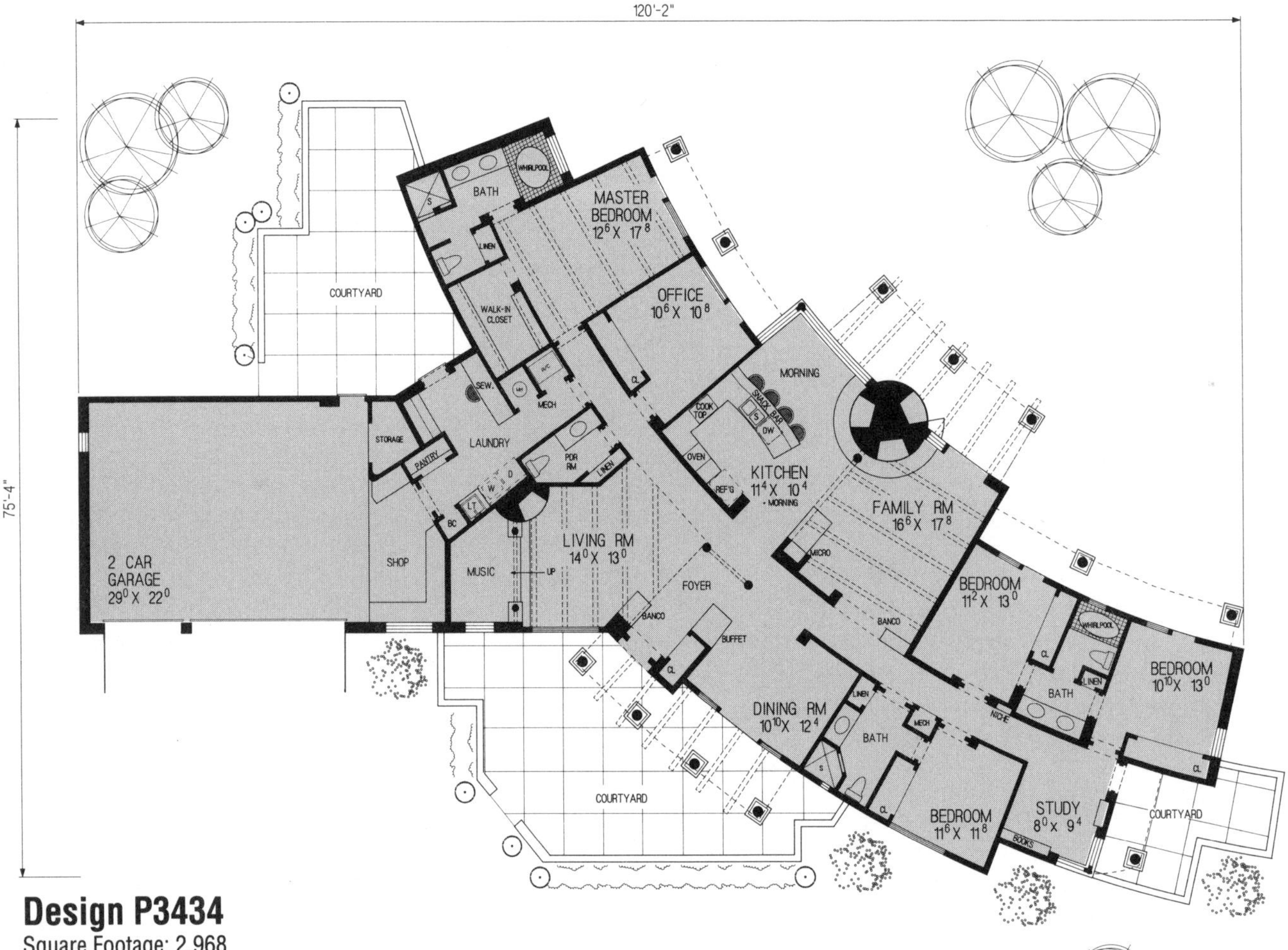

120'-2"
75'-4"
COURTYARD
BATH
WHIRLPOOL
MASTER BEDROOM 12⁶ X 17⁸
LINEN
WALK-IN CLOSET
OFFICE 10⁶ X 10⁸
CL
MORNING
COOK TOP
SNACK BAR
DW
SEW.
MECH
STORAGE
PANTRY
LAUNDRY
PDR RM
LINEN
OVEN
REF'G
KITCHEN 11⁴ X 10⁴ + MORNING
FAMILY RM 16⁶ X 17⁸
MICRO
2 CAR GARAGE 29⁰ X 22⁰
SHOP
BC
MUSIC
UP
LIVING RM 14⁰ X 13⁰
FOYER
BANCO
BUFFET
BEDROOM 11² X 13⁰
BANCO
WHIRLPOOL
CL
LINEN
BEDROOM 10¹⁰ X 13⁰
BATH
NICHE
DINING RM 10¹⁰ X 12⁴
LINEN
MECH
BATH
CL
COURTYARD
BEDROOM 11⁶ X 11⁸
STUDY 8⁰ X 9⁴
BOOKS
COURTYARD

Design P3434

Square Footage: 2,968

● An in-line floor plan follows the tradition of the original Santa Fe-style homes. The slight curve to the overall configuration lends an interesting touch. From the front courtyard, the plan opens to a formal living room and dining room complemented by a family room and kitchen with morning room. The master bedroom is found to one side of the plan while family bedrooms share space at the opposite end. There's also a huge office and a study area for private times. With 3½ baths, a workshop garage, full laundry/sewing area, and three courtyards, this plan adds up to great livability.

Custom Alterations? See page 203 for customizing this plan to your specifications.

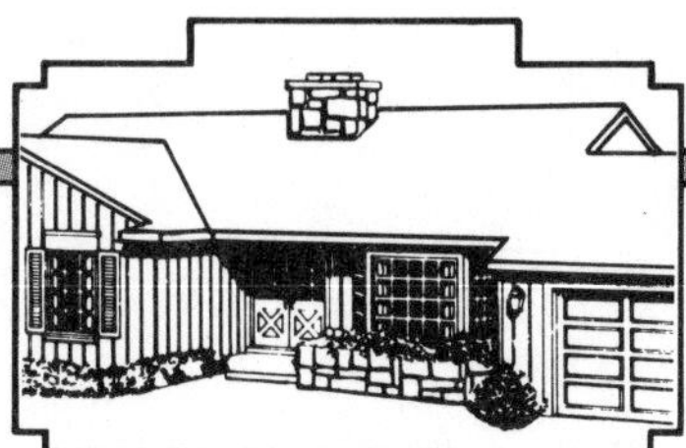

Western Ranch Homes

First developed in the 1930s, the one-story Western Ranch saw prominence in the 1940s and became one of the most popular designs in all regions of the country throughout the 1950s and 1960s. The basically stable economy and general prosperity of these two decades allowed for a mass movement of families to suburban areas where they purchased larger lots. This permitted the building of homes with a rambling, sprawling nature. It also allowed for garages to be built directly onto the home, a convention that persists in most new housing today.

The basic characteristics of the Western Ranch house borrow from Spanish Colonial design with some modern components. Most are asymmetrical in design with a low-pitched roof that may be hipped, cross-gabled or side-gabled. There is usually moderate or even wide eave overhang that is boxed or left open and, in more rustic versions, rafters are exposed.

The most common building material for these homes is wood— both vertical and horizontal—or brick cladding. It is not unusual to see the two materials used in combination to beautiful effect. Stonework accents are also quite appealing. Stucco and stucco with wood are often seen in areas of the Southwest.

What limited ornamentation is in evidence is traditional in nature. Most common are decorative wood or iron porch supports, false shutters and perhaps some rustic-looking window trim. Shake roofs, wooden porch and terrace rails and other wood trim are all details that complement the Western Ranch. Horizontal bands of windows and simple double-hung windows predominate with an occasional picture window in the main living areas. The presence of private patios or terraces, usually found to the rear of the house, corresponds to the courtyard feature found in Spanish Colonial homes.

While the vast majority of Western Ranch homes are one-story, some more recent variations have expanded their living space to 1½- story or one-story with a walk-out basement. These new configurations take nothing away from the low-slung appeal of the Western Ranch and add much in terms of livability: split-sleeping arrangements, second-floor lounges, basement hobby and game rooms and increased storage.

Design P2906 First Floor: 2,121 square feet
Second Floor: 913 square feet; Total: 3,034 square feet

D

● This striking Contemporary with Spanish good looks offers outstanding living for lifestyles of today. A three-car garage opens to a mudroom, laundry, and washroom to keep the rest of the house clean. An efficient, spacious kitchen opens to a spacious dining room, with pass-thru also leading to a family room. The family room and adjoining master bedroom suite overlook a backyard terrace. Just off the master bedroom is a sizable study that opens to a foyer. Steps just off the foyer make upstairs access quick and easy. The center point of this modern Contemporary is a living room that faces a front courtyard and a lounge above the living room. Three second-story bedrooms and an upper foyer join the upstairs lounge.

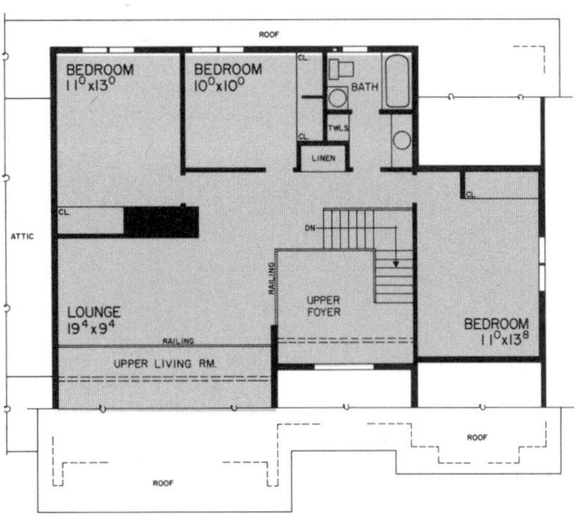

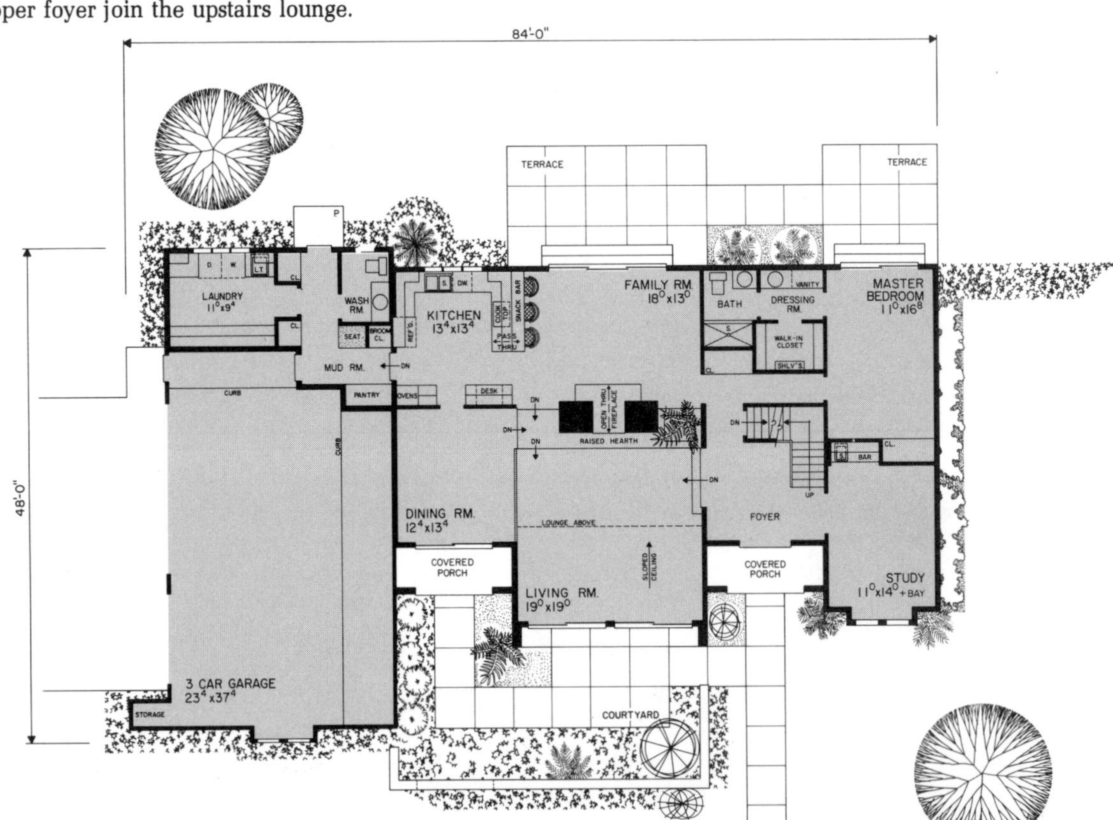

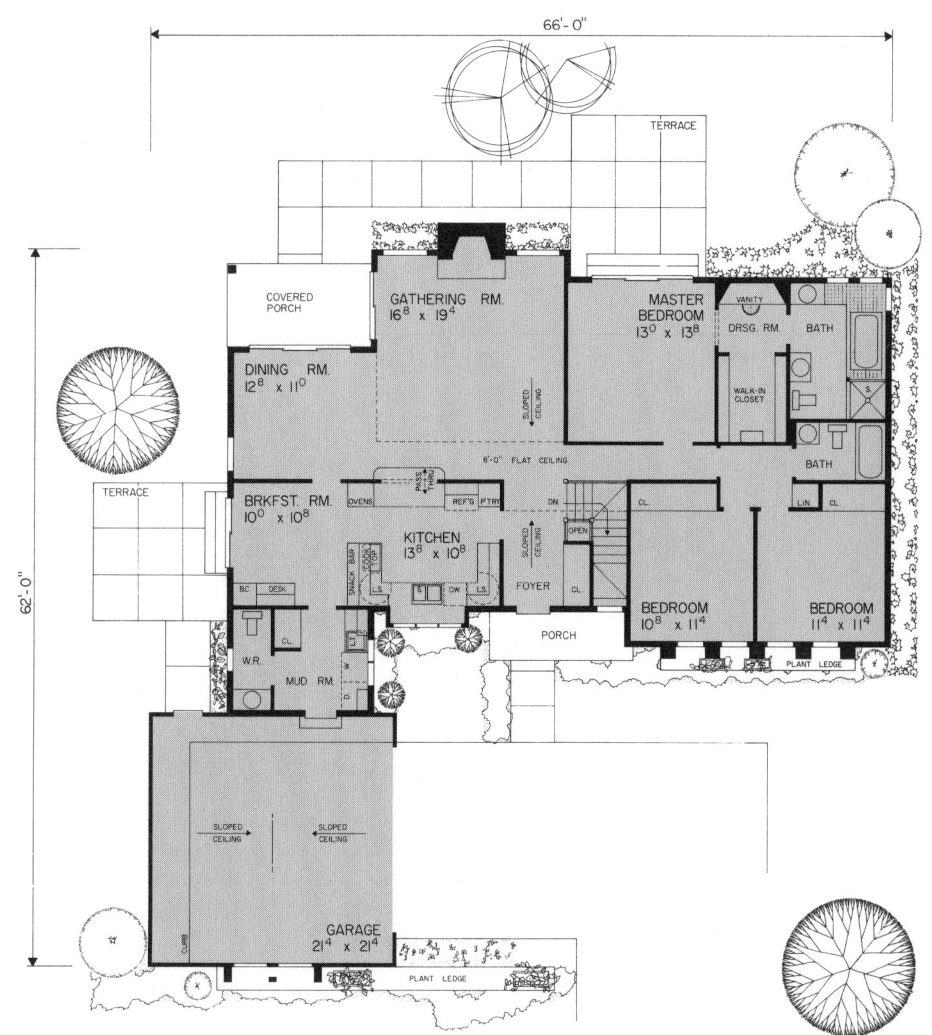

Design P2912

Square Footage: 1,864

● This modern design with smart Spanish styling incorporates careful zoning by room functions with lifestyle comfort. All three bedrooms, including a master bedroom suite, are isolated at one end of the one-story home for privacy and out of traffic patterns. Entry to a breakfast room and kitchen is possible through a mud room off the garage. That's good news for people carrying groceries from car to kitchen or people with muddy shoes during inclement weather. The modern kitchen includes a snack bar and cook top with multiple access to breakfast room, side foyer, and pass-thru to hallway. There's also a nearby formal dining room. A large rear gathering room features sloped ceiling and its own fireplace. Note the two-car garage and built-in plant ledge in front. Gabled end window treatment plus varied roof lines further enhance the striking appearance of this efficient design.

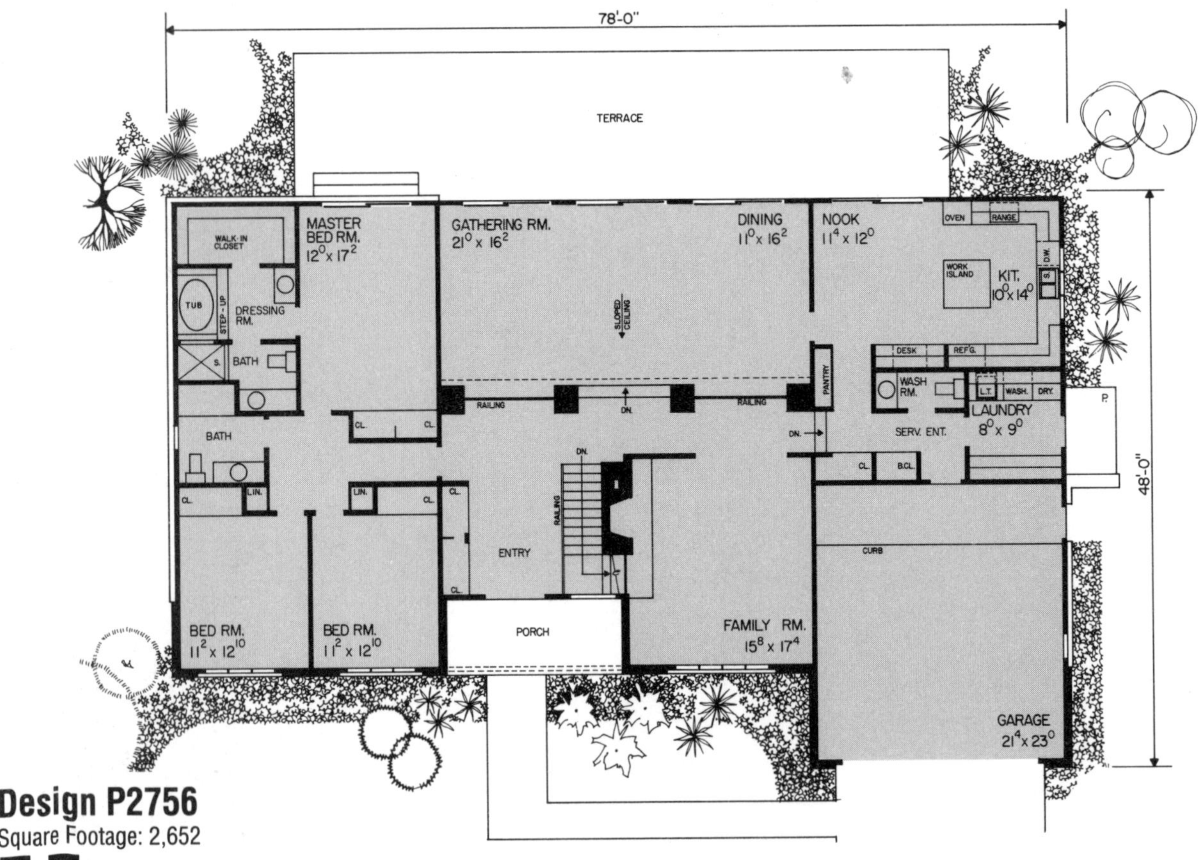

Design P2756

Square Footage: 2,652

L **D**

● This one-story, contemporary design is bound to serve your family well. It will assure the best in contemporary living with its many fine features. Notice the bath with tub and stall shower, dressing room and walk-in closet featured with the master bedroom. Two more family bedrooms are adjacent. The sunken gathering room/dining room is highlighted by the sloped ceiling and sliding glass doors to the large, rear terrace. This formal area is a full 32' x 16'. Imagine the great furniture placement that can be done in this area. In addition to the gathering room, there is an informal family room with a fireplace. You will enjoy the efficient kitchen and get much use out of the work island, pantry and built-in desk. Note the service entrance with washroom and laundry.

Design P2866

Square Footage: 2,371

● An extra living unit has been built into the design of this home. It would make an excellent "mother-in-law" suite. Should you choose not to develop this area as indicated, maybe you might use it as two more bedrooms, a guest suite or even as hobby and game rooms. Whatever its final use, it will complement the rest of this home. The main house also deserves mention. The focal point will be the large gathering room. Its features include a skylight, sloped ceiling, centered fireplace flanked on both sides by sliding glass doors and adjacent is a dining room on one side, study on the other. The work center is clustered together. Three bedrooms and two baths make up the private area. Note the outdoor areas: court with privacy wall, two covered porches and a large terrace.

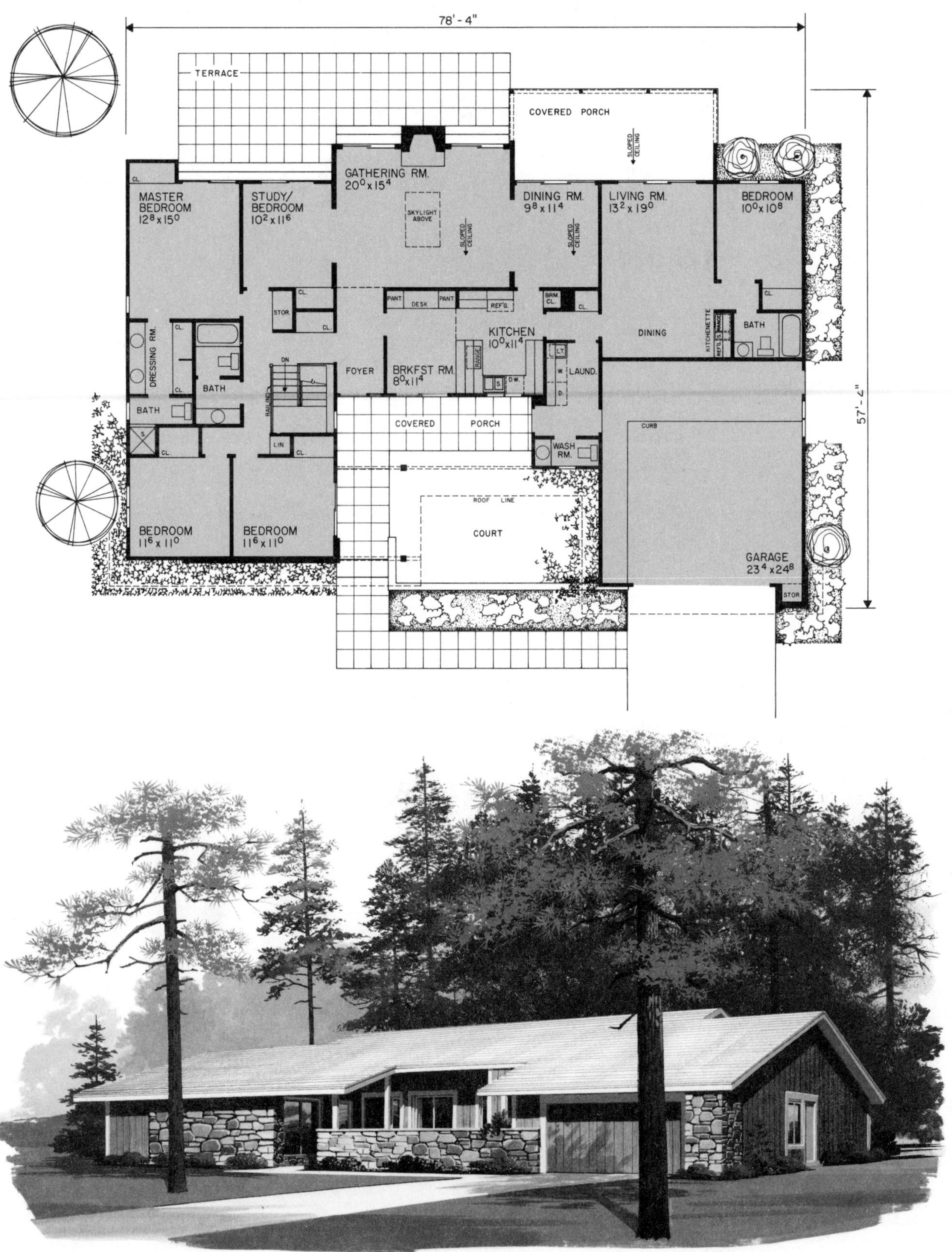

Design P2765

Square Footage: 3,365

D

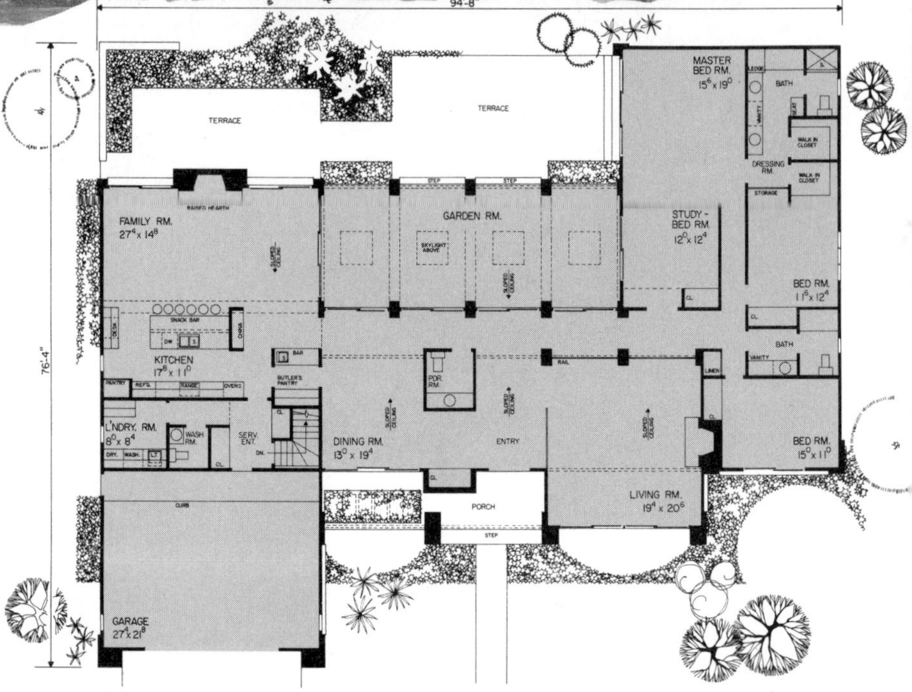

● This three (optional four) bedroom contemporary is a most appealing design. It offers living patterns that will add new dimensions to your everyday routine. The sloped ceilings in the family room, dining room and living room add much spaciousness to this home. The efficient kitchen has many fine features including the island snack bar and work center, built-in desk, china cabinet and wet bar. Adjacent to the kitchen is a laundry room, washroom and stairs to the basement. Formal and informal living will each have its own area. A raised hearth fireplace and sliding glass doors to the rear terrace in the informal family room. Another fireplace in the front formal living room. You will enjoy all that nature light in the garden room from the skylights in the sloped ceiling.

Design P2764

Square Footage: 2,946

● If uniqueness is what you seek, this home will be ideal. Notice the large, gated-in entry court, vertical paned windows and contrasting exterior materials. The entry/dining area has a built-in planter with a skylight above. The living and family rooms both have an attractive sloped ceiling. They share a raised-hearth, through-fireplace and both have access to the large wraparound terrace. The kitchen/nook area also has access to the terrace and features a snack bar, built-in desk and large butler's pantry.

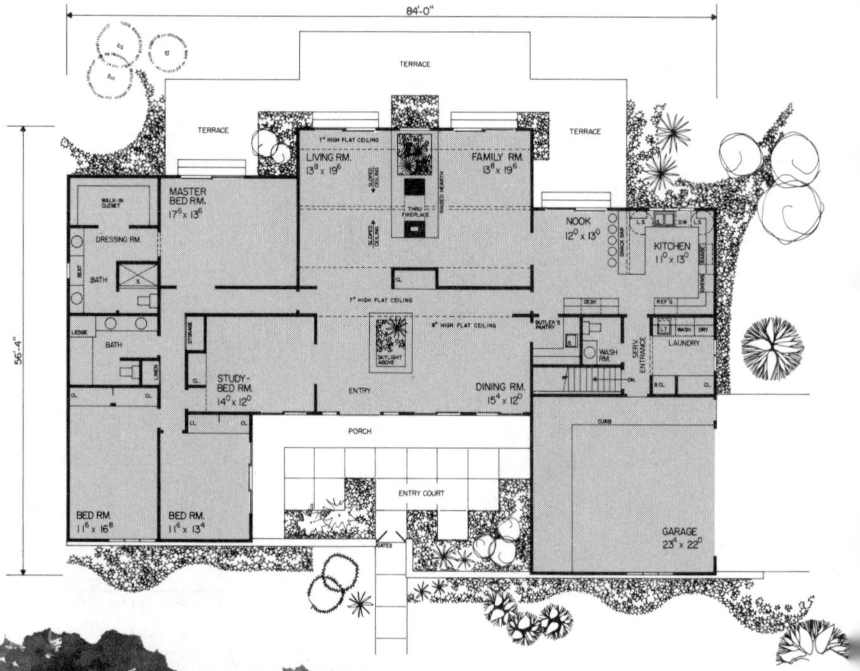

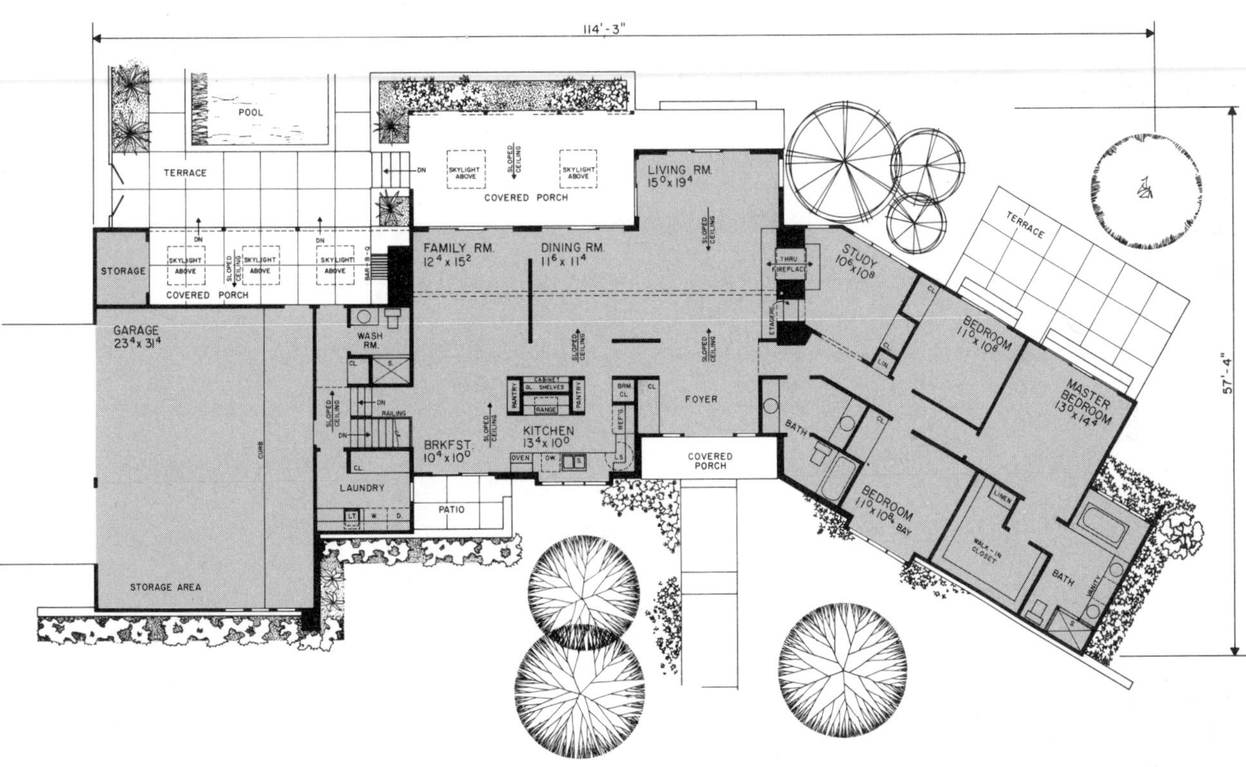

Design P2819

Square Footage: 2,459

● Indoor-outdoor living will be enjoyed to the fullest in this rambling one-story contemporary plan. Each of the rear rooms in this design, excluding the study, has access to a terrace or porch. Even the front breakfast room has access to a private dining patio. The covered porch off the living areas, family, dining and living rooms, has a sloped ceiling and skylights. A built-in barbecue unit and a storage room will be found on the second covered porch. Inside, the plan offers exceptional living patterns for various activities. Notice the thru-fireplace that the living room shares with the study. A built-in etagere is nearby. The three-car garage has an extra storage area.

Design P2256
Square Footage: 2,632

● This refreshing contemporary home has a unique exterior that is enhanced by a great floor plan. The central focus is the large living room with raised-hearth fireplace. To the right is the formal dining room and island kitchen with informal eating space. To the left are three family bedrooms — the master has a gigantic walk-in closet. All are tied together with a long hallway. Don't miss the wide terrace at the rear of the plan.

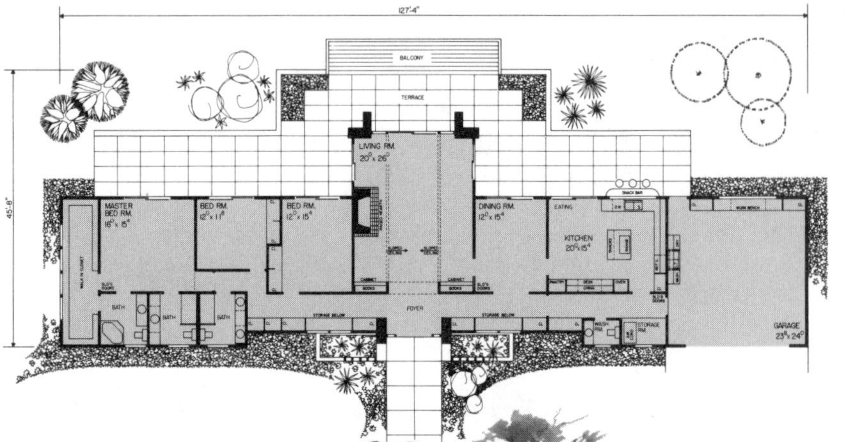

Design P2534
Square Footage: 3,262

L

● The angular wings of this ranch home contribute to its distinctive design. The spacious entrance hall gives way to a large gathering room — the heart of the home. Flanking this all purpose area are a more private study on the right and a formal dining room on the left. The kitchen adjoins the dining room and includes informal eating space. Three bedrooms are found in the right-hand wing. The master bedroom has a private terrace and His and Hers walk-in closets.

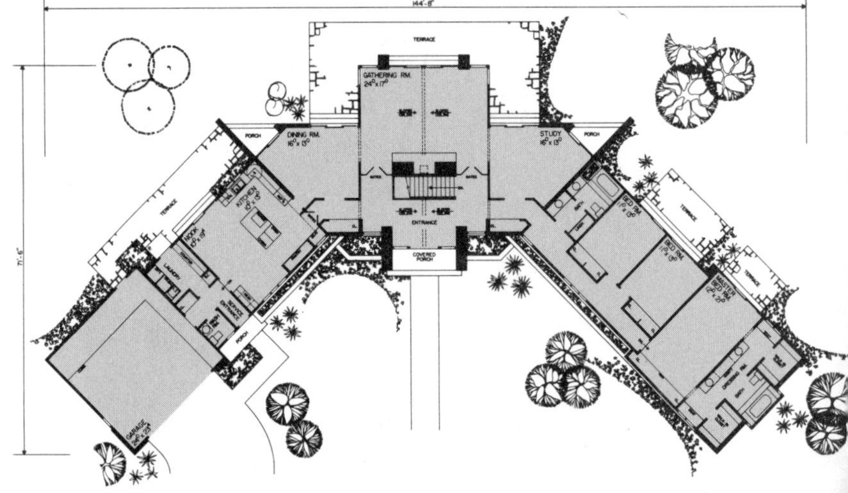

Design P1928

Square Footage: 3,272

● You'll find this contemporary home is worthy of your consideration if you're looking for a house of distinction. The dramatic exterior is a surefire stopper. Even the most casual passer-by will take a second look. Interesting roof surfaces, massive brick chimney wall, recessed entrance, raised planters and garden wall are among the features that spell design distinction. And yet, the exterior is only part of the story this home has to tell. Its interior is no less unique. Consider the sunken living room, sloping, beamed ceiling of the family room, wonderful kitchen/laundry area, four-bedroom sleeping area with all those closets, bath facilities and sliding doors.

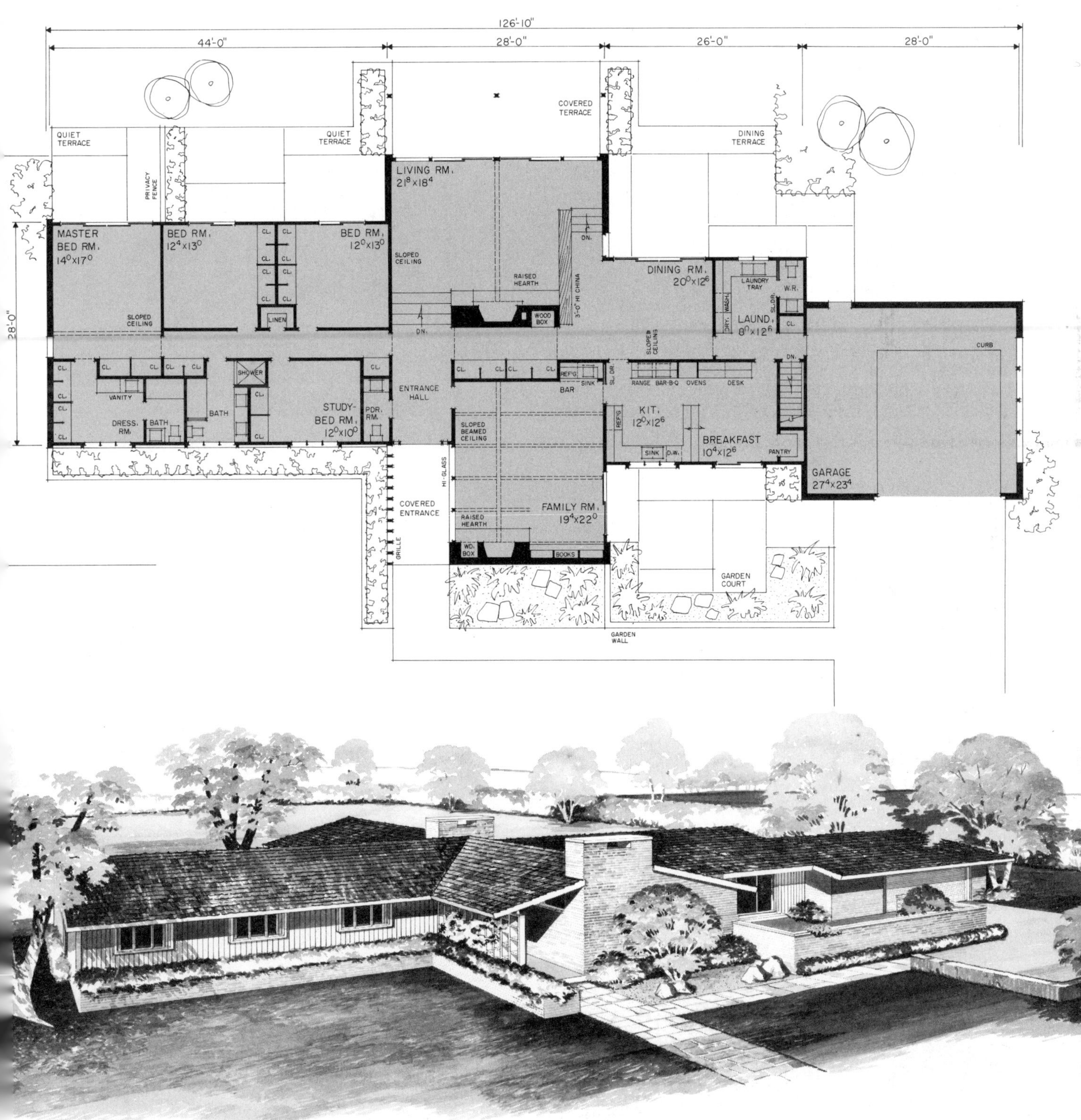

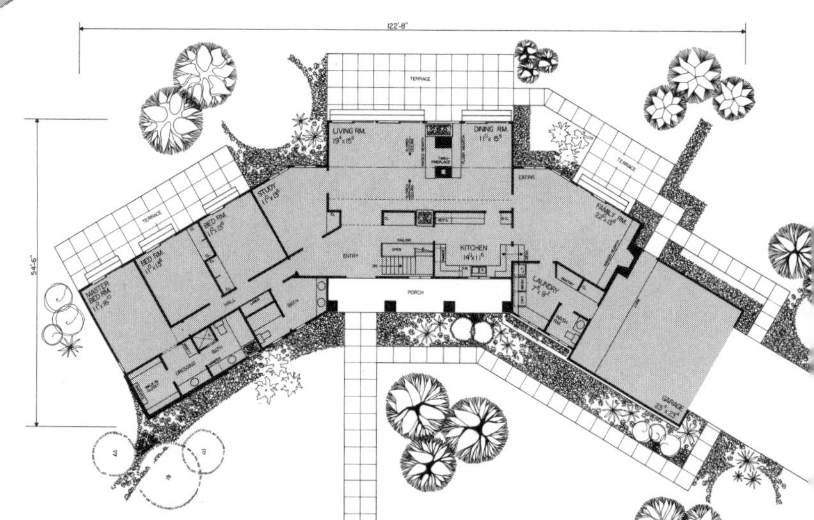

Design P2595

Square Footage: 2,653

● A winged design puts everything in the right place. At the center, formal living and dining rooms with sloped ceiling share one fireplace for added charm. Sliding glass doors in both rooms open onto the main terrace. In the right wing, there is a spacious family room with another raised-hearth fireplace, built-in desk, dining area and adjoining smaller terrace. A study, the master suite and family bedrooms (all bedrooms having access to a third terrace) plus baths are in the left wing. Notice the open staircase leading to the basement.

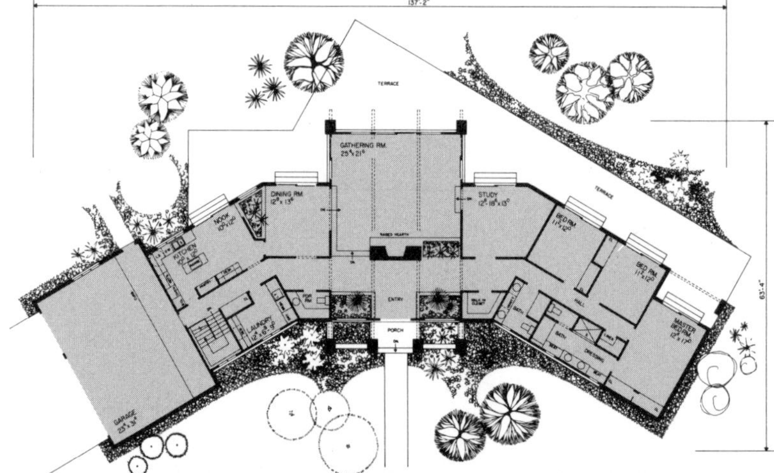

Design P2720

Square Footage: 3,130

● A raised-hearth fireplace lights up the sunken gathering room at the center of this home. For more living space, a well-located study and formal dining room each have direct access to the gathering room. The kitchen boasts all the right features: island range, pantry, built-in desk and separate breakfast nook. Bedrooms include a master suite with double closets, dressing room and private bath. Don't miss the extra curb area in the garage.

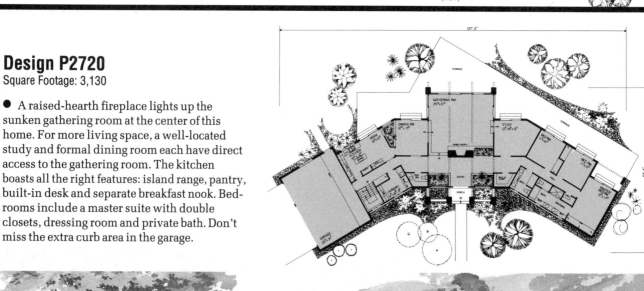

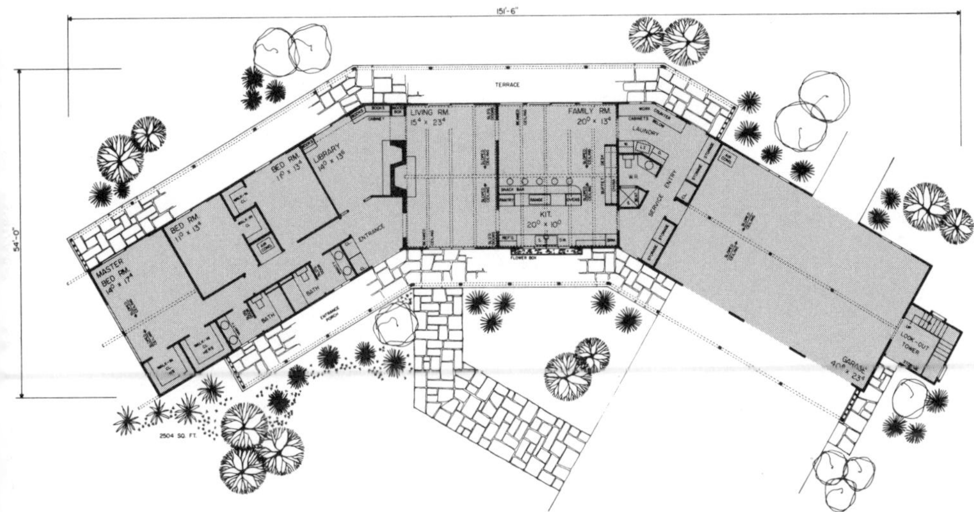

Design P2258

Square Footage: 2,504

● Here's a real Western Ranch House with all the appeal of its forebears. As for the livability offered by this angular design, the old days of the rugged west never had anything like this.

Design P2317

Square Footage: 3,161

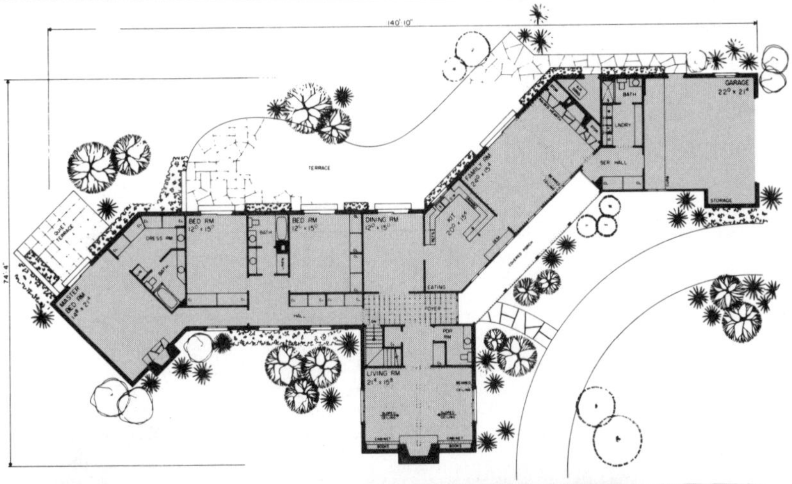

● Here's a rambling English manor with a full measure of individuality. The formal living room with sloping beamed ceiling and fireplace flanked by bookshelves and cabinets is offset by an informal family room. The kitchen separates this room from the formal dining room. Three bedrooms include a large master suite with private terrace. Don't miss the huge main terrace and the three full baths.

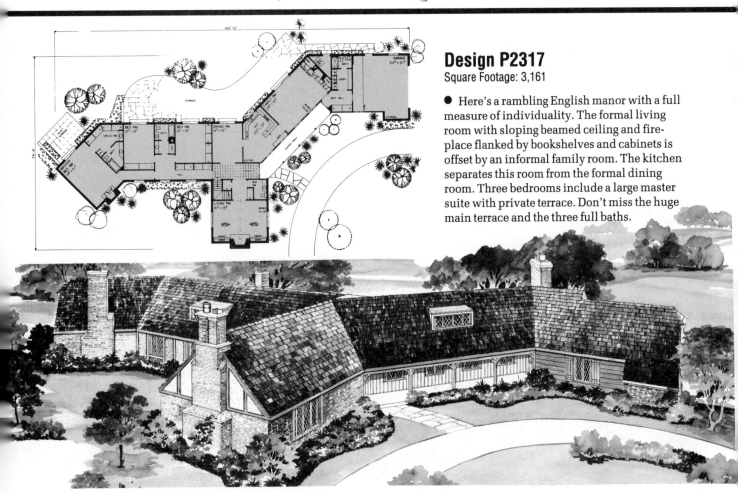

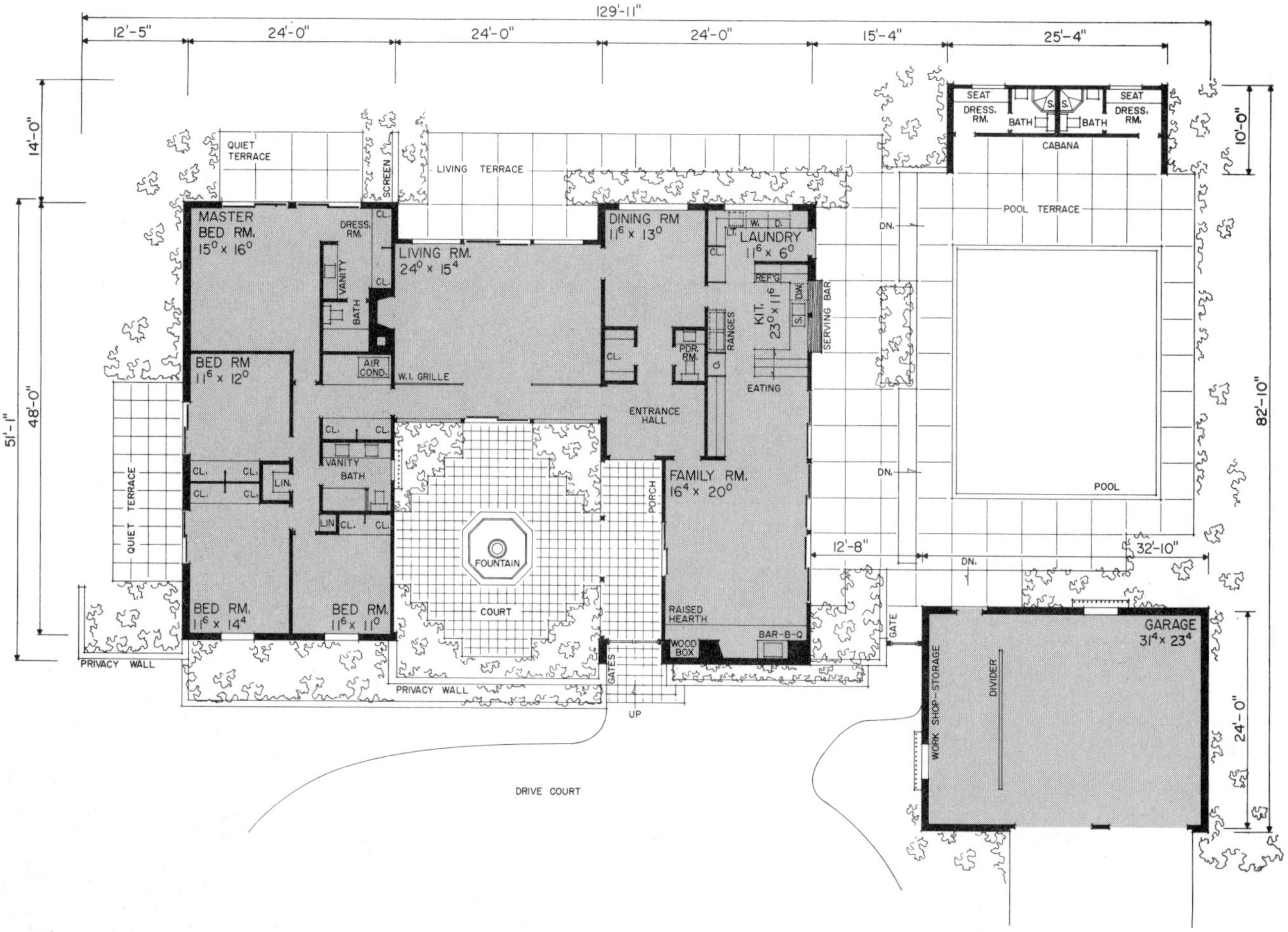

Design P1756 Square Footage: 2,736

● Reminiscent of the West and impressive, indeed. If you are after something that is luxurious in both its appearance and its livability this design should receive your consideration. This rambling ranch house, which encloses a spacious and dramatic flower court, is designed for comfort and privacy indoors and out. Study the outdoor areas. Notice the seclusion each of them provides. Three bedrooms, plus a master suite with dressing room and bath form a private bedroom wing. Formal and informal living areas serve ideally for various types of entertaining. There is excellent circulation of traffic throughout the house. The kitchen is handy to the formal dining room and the informal family room. Don't miss raised hearth fireplace.

Design P2251

Square Footage: 3,112

● It will not matter at all where this distinctive ranch home is built. Whether located in the south, east, north or west the exterior design appeal will be breathtakingly distinctive and the interior livability will be delightfully different. The irregular shape is enhanced by the low-pitched, wide overhanging roof. Two wings project to help form an appealing entrance court from the main living area of the house. Variations in grade result in the garage being on a lower level. The plan reflects an interesting study in zoning and a fine indoor-outdoor relationship of the various areas.

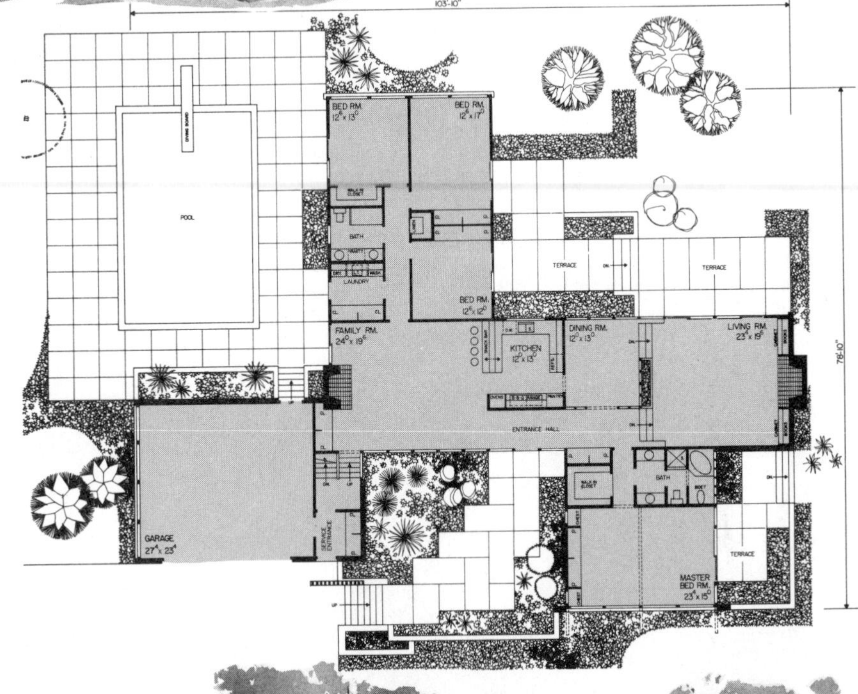

Design P2504

Main Level: 1,918 square feet
Lower Level: 1,910 square feet
Total: 3,828 square feet

● A front court area welcomes guests on their way to the double front doors. These doors, flanked by floor-to-ceiling glass panels, are sheltered by the porch. Adjacent to this area are the sliding glass doors of the breakfast nook which can enjoy to the fullest the beauty of the front yard. This design has taken advantage of the sloping site to open up the lower level. In this case, the lower level has virtually the same glass treatment as its corresponding room above.

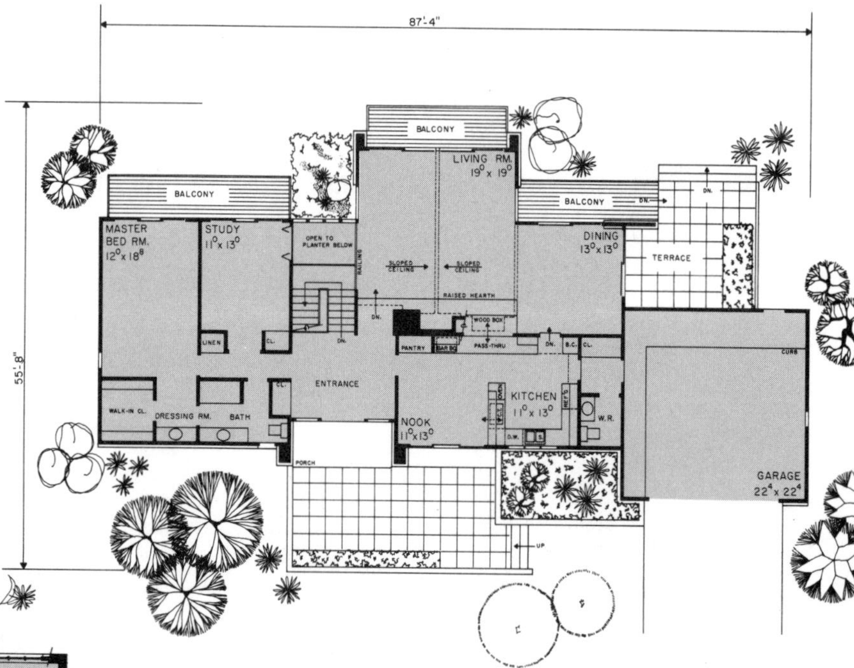

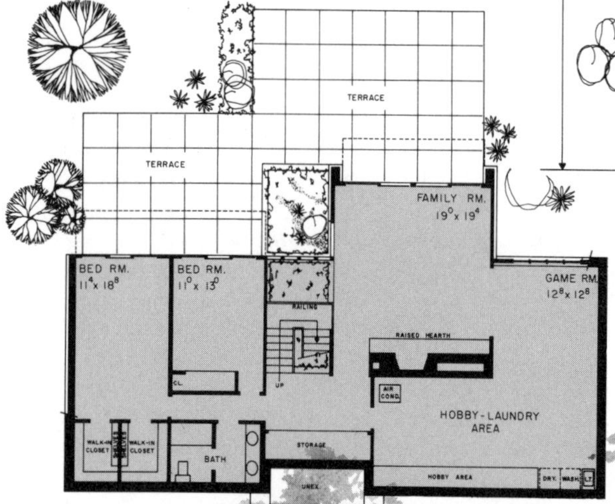

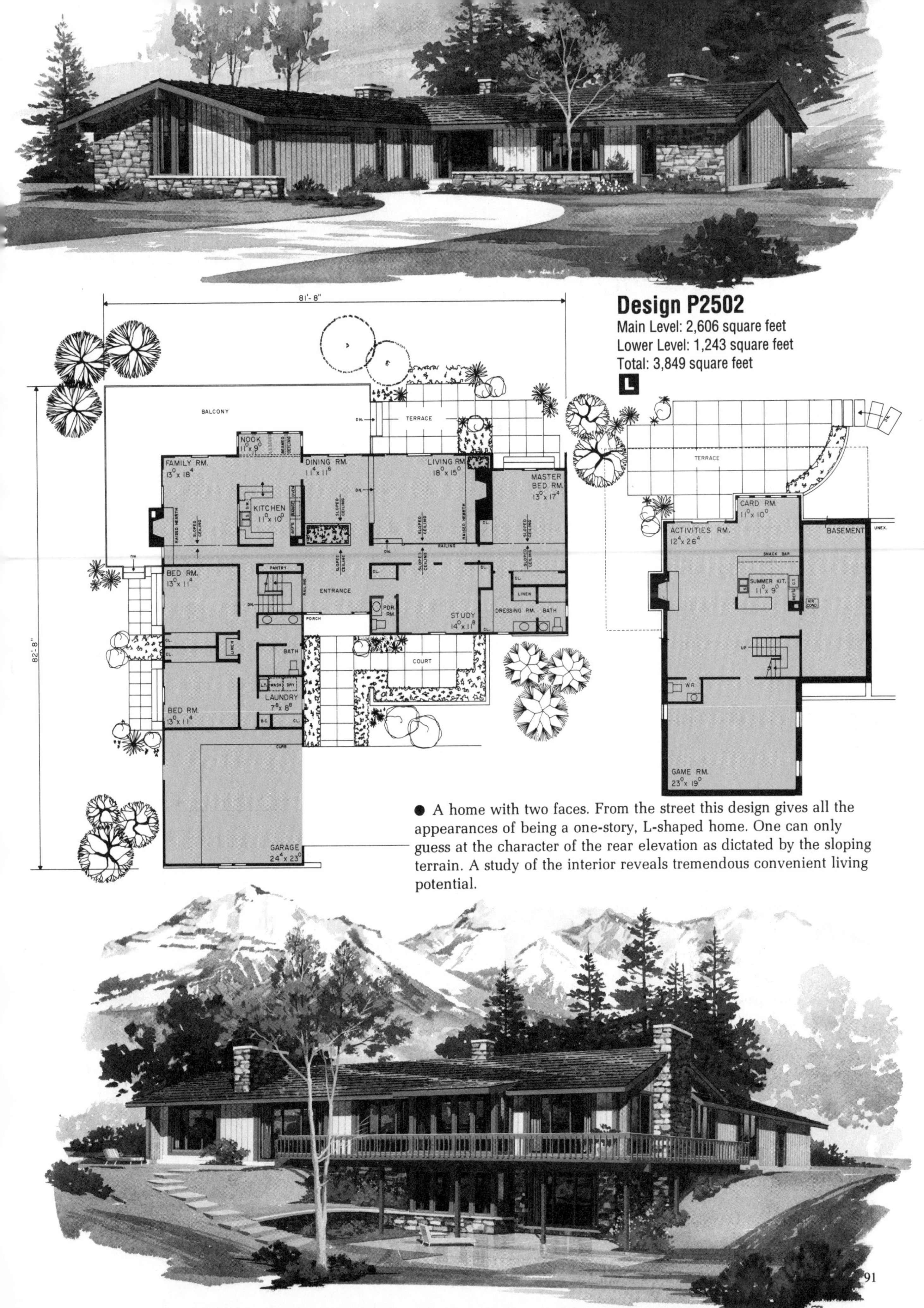

Design P2502

Main Level: 2,606 square feet
Lower Level: 1,243 square feet
Total: 3,849 square feet

L

● A home with two faces. From the street this design gives all the appearances of being a one-story, L-shaped home. One can only guess at the character of the rear elevation as dictated by the sloping terrain. A study of the interior reveals tremendous convenient living potential.

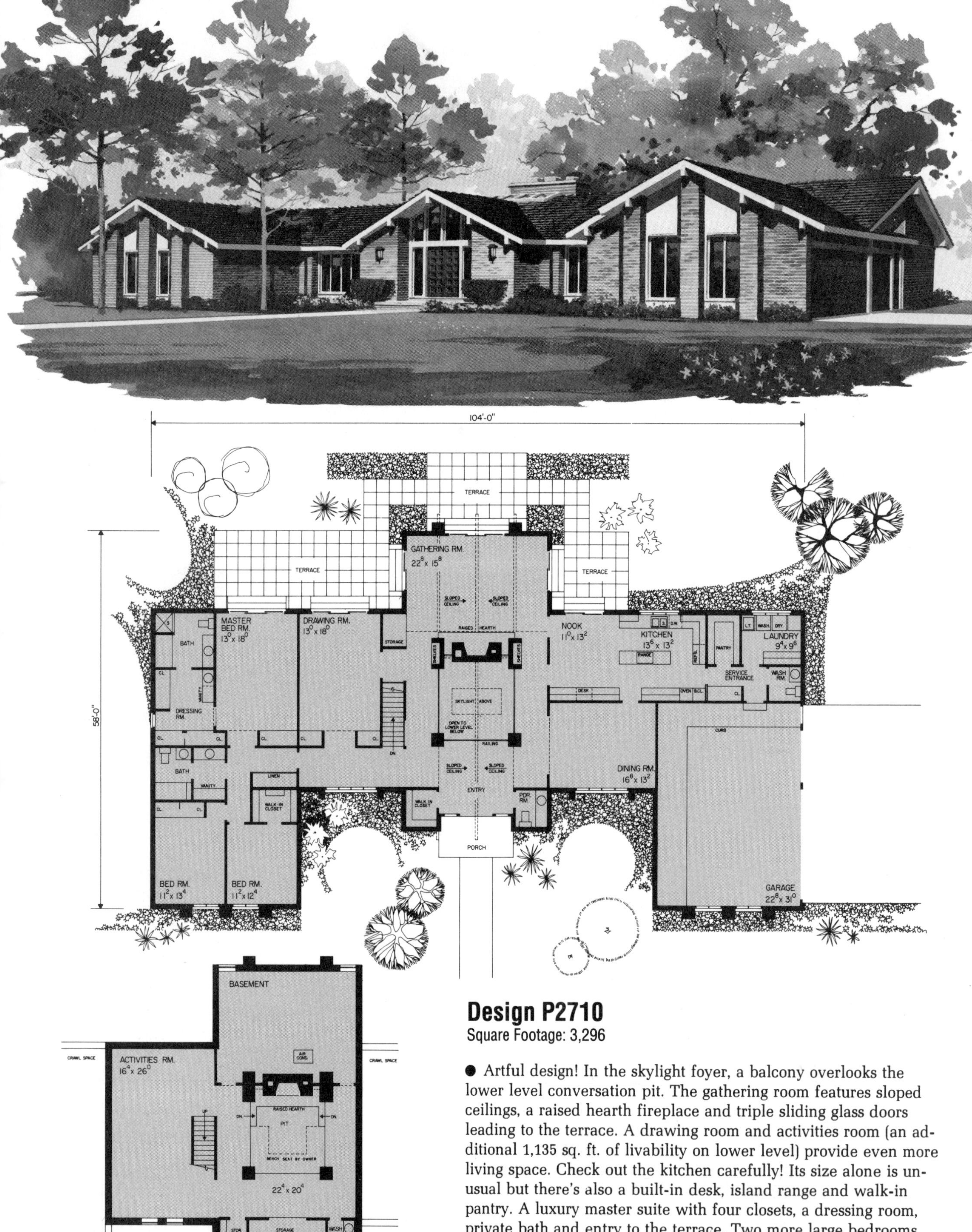

Design P2710

Square Footage: 3,296

● Artful design! In the skylight foyer, a balcony overlooks the lower level conversation pit. The gathering room features sloped ceilings, a raised hearth fireplace and triple sliding glass doors leading to the terrace. A drawing room and activities room (an additional 1,135 sq. ft. of livability on lower level) provide even more living space. Check out the kitchen carefully! Its size alone is unusual but there's also a built-in desk, island range and walk-in pantry. A luxury master suite with four closets, a dressing room, private bath and entry to the terrace. Two more large bedrooms. This is a glamourous home. Its unique design makes you proud when guests arrive. And its spacious qualities make family life a joy. The storage facilities in this plan are particularly noteworthy.

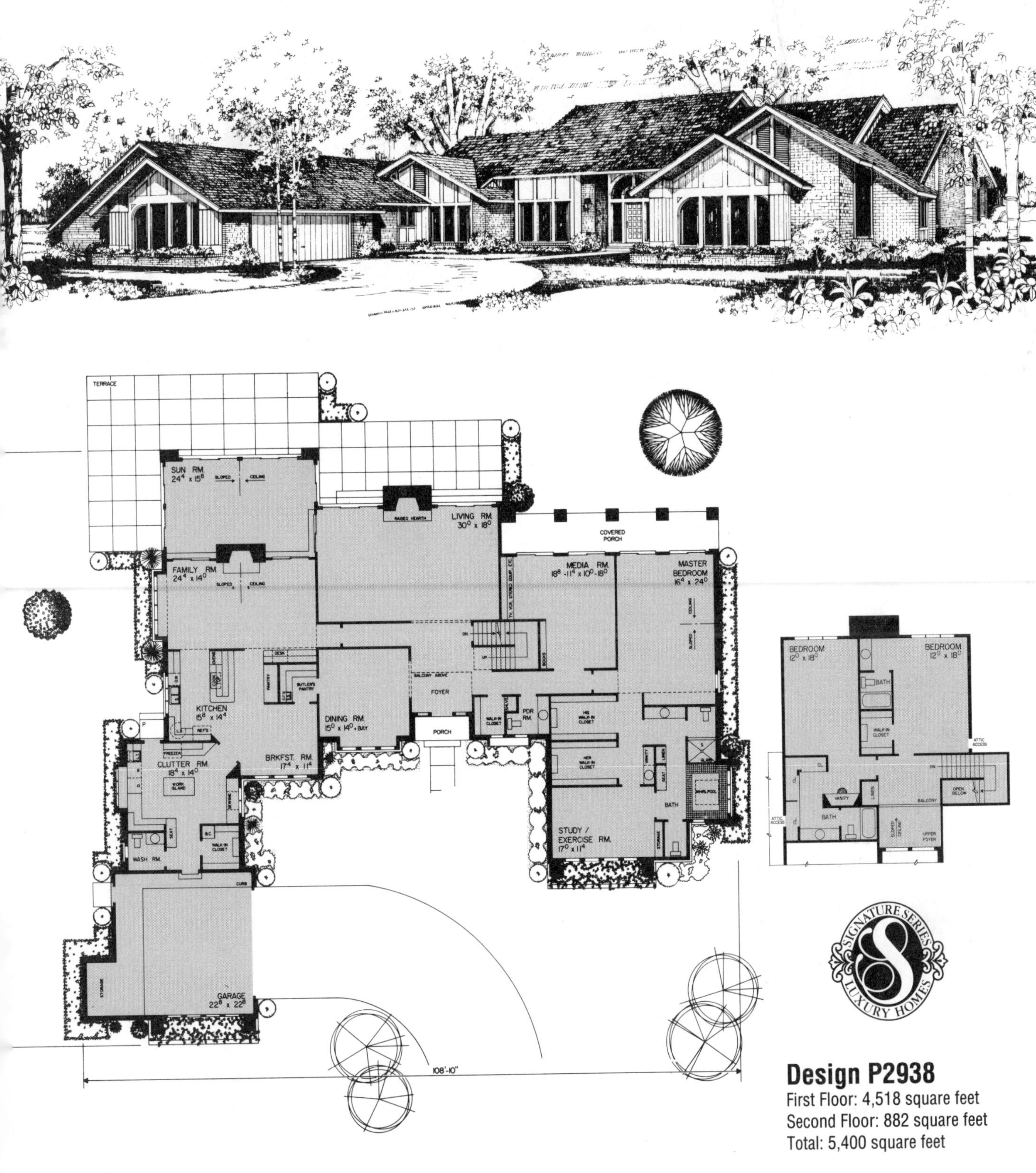

Design P2938

First Floor: 4,518 square feet
Second Floor: 882 square feet
Total: 5,400 square feet

● A semi-circular fanlight and side-lights grace the entrance of this striking contemporary. The lofty foyer, with balcony above, leads to an elegant, two-story living room with fireplace. The family room, housing a second fireplace, leads to a glorious sunroom; both have dramatic sloped ceilings. The kitchen and breakfast room are conveniently located for access to the informal family room or to the formal dining room via the butler's pantry. The large adjoining clutter room with work island offers limitless possibilities for the seamstress, hobbyist, or indoor gardener. An executive-sized, first-floor master suite offers privacy and relaxation; the bath with whirlpool tub and dressing area with twin walk-in closets open to a study that could double as an exercise room. Two second-floor bedrooms with private baths and walk-in closets round out the livability in this gracious home.

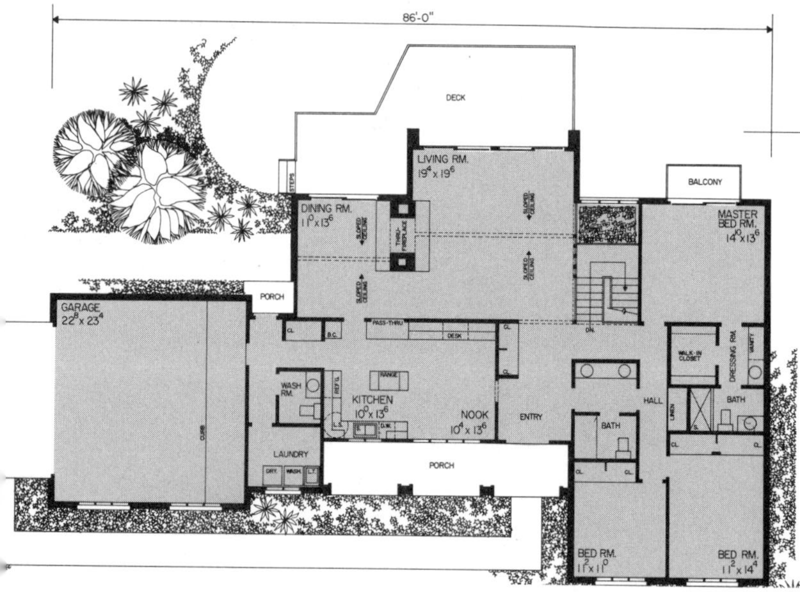

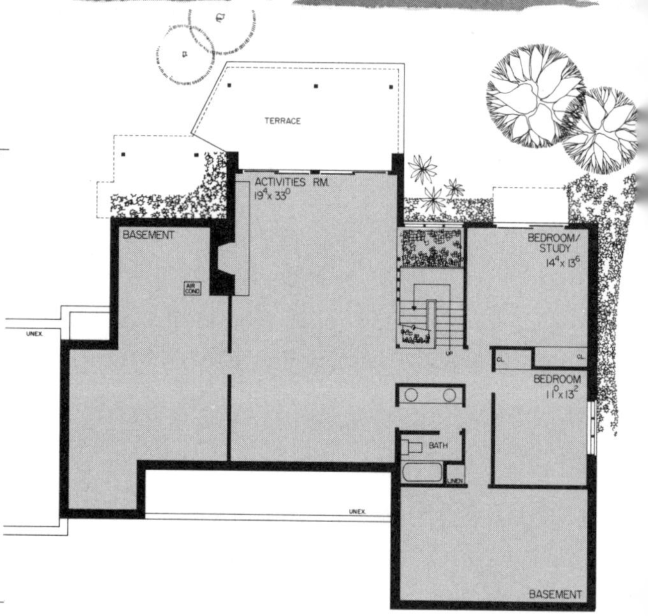

● This hillside home gives all the appearances of being a one-story ranch home; and what a delightful one at that! Should the contours of your property slope to the rear, this plan permits the exposing of the lower level. This results in the activities room and bedroom/study gaining direct access to outdoor living. Certainly a most desirable aspect for active, outdoor family living. The large and growing family will be admirably served with five bedrooms and three baths. An extra washroom and separate laundry add to the convenient living potential.

Design P2549

Main Level: 2,260 square feet
Lower Level: 1,406 square feet
Total: 3,666 square feet

Design P2920 First Floor: 3.067 square feet

Second Floor: 648 square feet; Total: 3,715 square feet

L **D**

● Utilizing the same floor plan as Design P2921, This contemporary design also has a great deal to offer. Study the living areas. A fireplace opens up to both the living room and country kitchen. Privacy is the key word when describing the sleeping areas. The first floor master bedroom is away from the traffic of the house and features a dressing/exercise room, whirlpool tub, shower and a spacious walk-in closet. Two more bedrooms and a full bath are on the second floor. The three-car garage is arranged so that the owners have use of a double-garage with an attached single on reserve for guests.

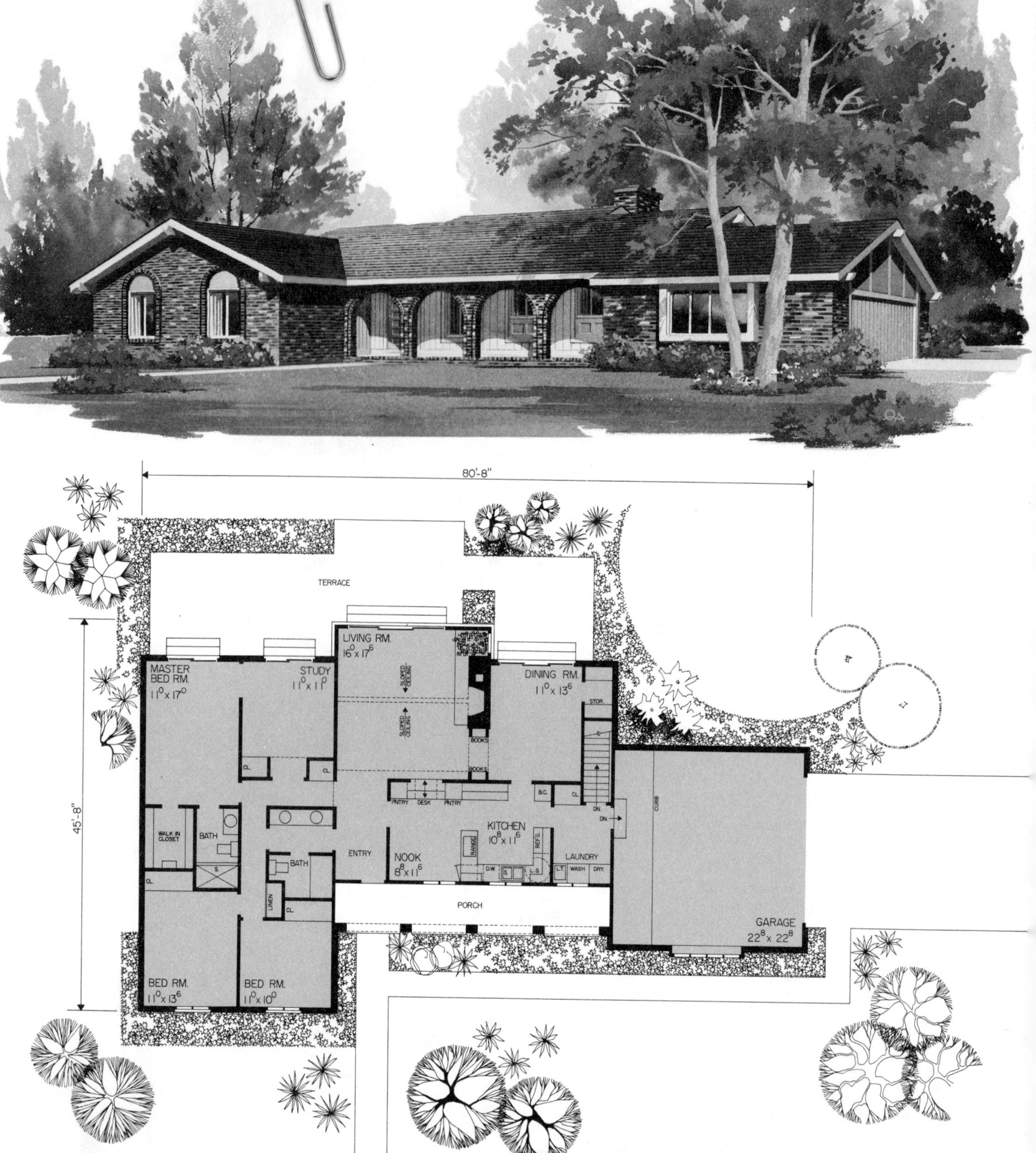

Design P2557

Square Footage: 1,955

● This eye-catching design with a flavor of the Spanish Southwest will be as interesting to live in as it will be to look at. The character of the exterior is set by the wide overhanging roof with its exposed beams; the massive arched pillars; the arching of the brick over the windows; the panelled door and the horizontal siding that contrasts with the brick. The master bedroom/study suite is a focal point of the interior. However, if necessary, the study could become the fourth bedroom. The living and dining rooms are large and are separated by a massive raised hearth fireplace. Don't miss the planter, the book niches and the china storage. The breakfast nook and the laundry flank the U-shaped kitchen. Notice the twin pantries, the built-in planning desk and the pass thru. That's a big lazy susan to the right of the kitchen sink. Notice the twin lavatories in the big main bath.

Craftsman, International and Contemporary Style

Craftsman

The architectural inspiration of two California brothers, Charles Sumner Greene and Henry Mather Greene, blossomed into what we know today as the Craftsman and its one-story version known as the Bungalow, a forerunner of the modern ranch style. In 1903, these two brothers designed a very simple Craftsman-style Bungalow and continued over the next several years to develop the style. The idea was furthered through popular home magazines of the day and soon vast numbers of pattern books appeared containing plans for the Craftsman Bungalows.

Perhaps the most recognizable feature of Craftsman homes is a wide front porch which includes distinctive porch supports that are usually short and square. These supports may connect to solid piers above the line of the porch floor or may continue on their own to ground level. Common materials for these supports are stone, stucco, brick and shingle.

Craftsman roofs are low-pitched and mostly gabled and may have a peak or flair at the roof line owing to Oriental influences. Like homes in the Spanish Eclectic mode, the roofs appear in four styles. Front- and side-gabled are the most common with cross-gabled being next. Hipped roofs are not common but do sometimes appear on both one- and two-story versions. Rafter ends are exposed and there may be false beams under the gables. Eave overhangs are almost always wide.

The most common exterior material for Craftsman and Bungalow styles is wood clapboard with wood shingles being second in popularity. Stone, brick, concrete block and stucco are also used and it is common to see a variety of these materials used in combination.

Ornamentation is generally fairly simple. Dormer windows sometimes occur and some decorative work may be in evidence at the exposed rafter ends and at corner braces. Stone chimneys flanked by two small, high windows and additional stickwork at the gables or even Tudor-like half-timbering are other decorative details sometimes found.

International and Contemporary Style

In the years between World War I and World War II, a group of European architects created home designs that were radically different from any previously seen. This avant-garde style developed into what came to be called International style.

Distinguishing characteristics of International style include a multi-leveled flat roof devoid of a ledge at the roof line, large sections of flush-set windows, smooth wall surfaces (often of stark white stucco), little or no ornamentation and an asymmetrical facade. Rounded corners, flat-topped cylindrical towers and cantilevered projections are also common.

After World War II, the style gained wider popularity as it developed into a less harsh version known as Contemporary style. It featured either a flat or gabled roof and a wider variety of exterior materials including wood, brick and stone. The flat-roofed types are more similar to International style and are labeled American International. The gable-roofed types take design characteristics from Craftsman and Prairie styles.

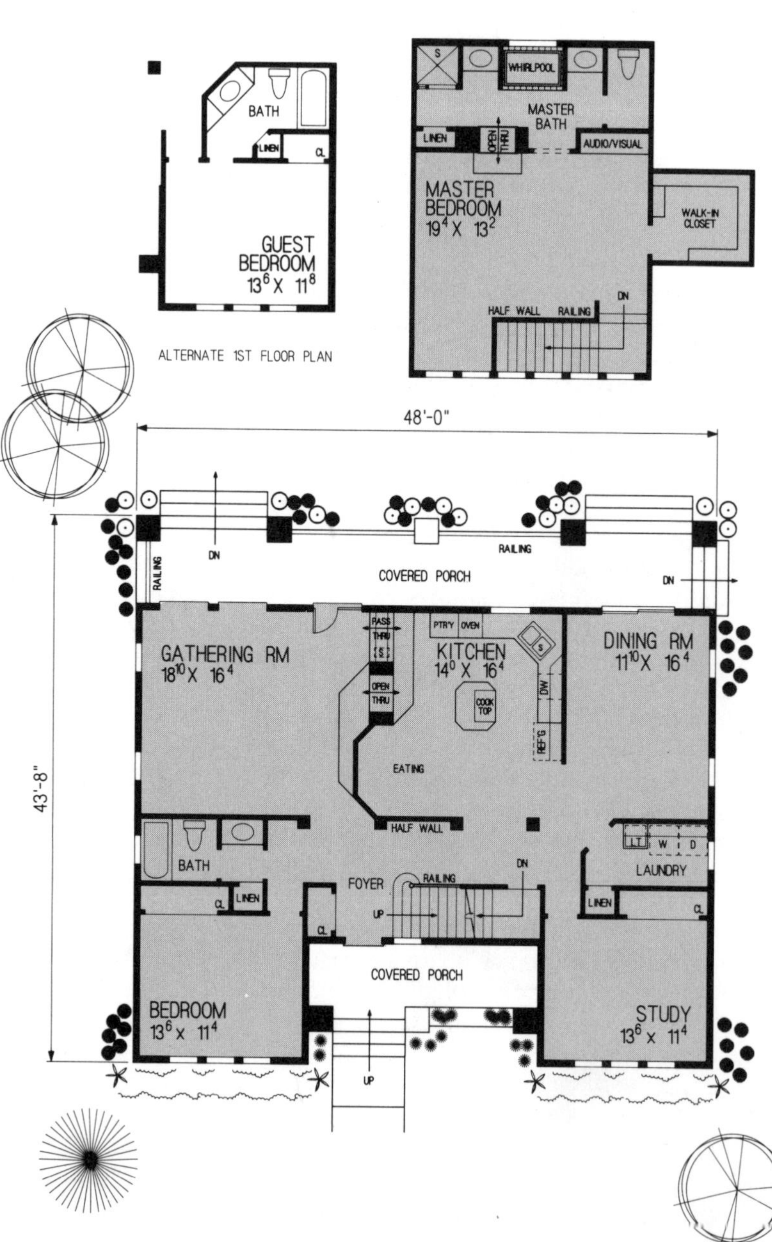

Design P3318

First Floor: 1,557 square feet
Second Floor: 540 square feet
Total: 2,097 square feet

● Details make the difference in this darling two-bedroom (or three-bedroom if you choose) bungalow. From covered front porch to covered rear porch, there's a fine floor plan. Living areas are to the rear: a gathering room with through-fireplace and pass-through counter to the kitchen and a formal dining room with porch access. To the front of the plan are a family bedroom and bath and a study. The study can also be planned as a guest bedroom with bath. Upstairs is the master bedroom with through-fireplace to the bath and a gigantic walk-in closet.

Custom Alterations? See page 203 for customizing this plan to your specifications.

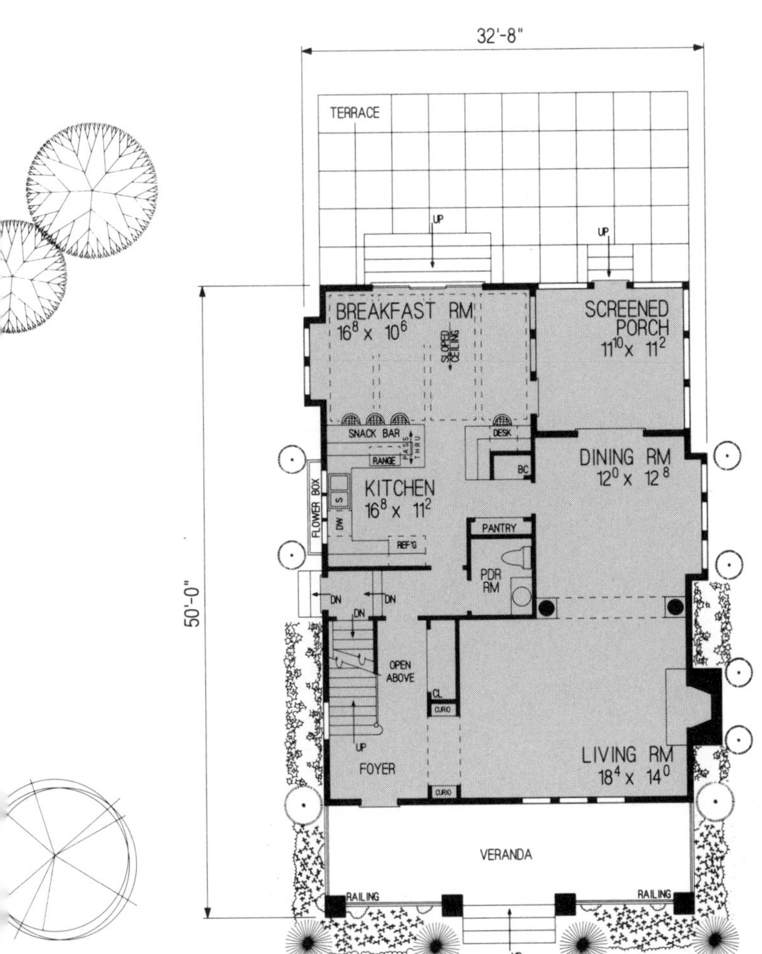

Design P3316

First Floor: 1,111 square feet
Second Floor: 886 square feet
Total: 1,997 square feet

● Don't be fooled by a small-looking exterior. This plan offers three bedrooms and plenty of living space. Notice that the screened porch leads to a rear terrace with access to the breakfast room. A living room/dining room combination adds spaciousness to the first floor.

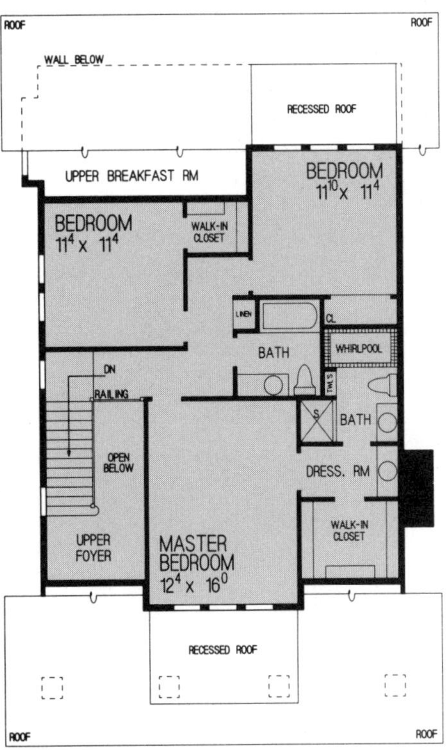

Design P3319

Square Footage: 2,274

● This attractive bungalow design separates the master suite from family bedrooms and puts casual living to the back in a family room. The formal living and dining areas are centrally located and have access to a rear terrace, as does the master suite. The kitchen sits between formal and informal living areas. The two family bedrooms are found to the front of the plan. A home office or study opens off the front foyer and the master suite.

Custom Alterations? See page 203 for customizing this plan to your specifications.

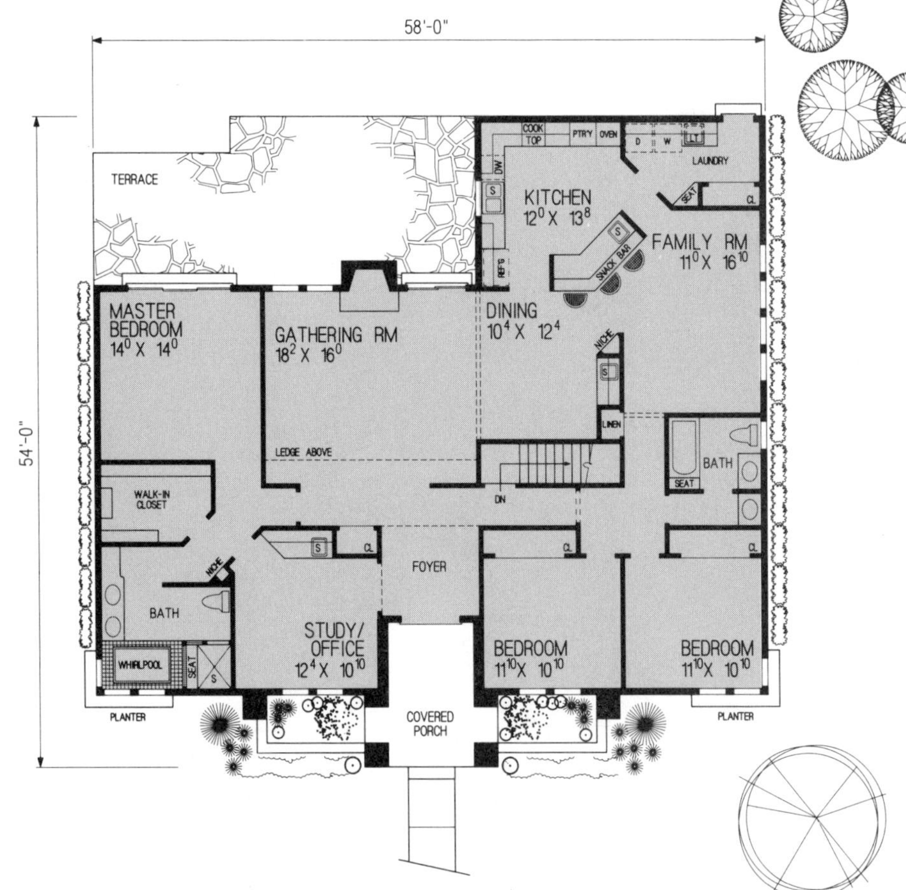

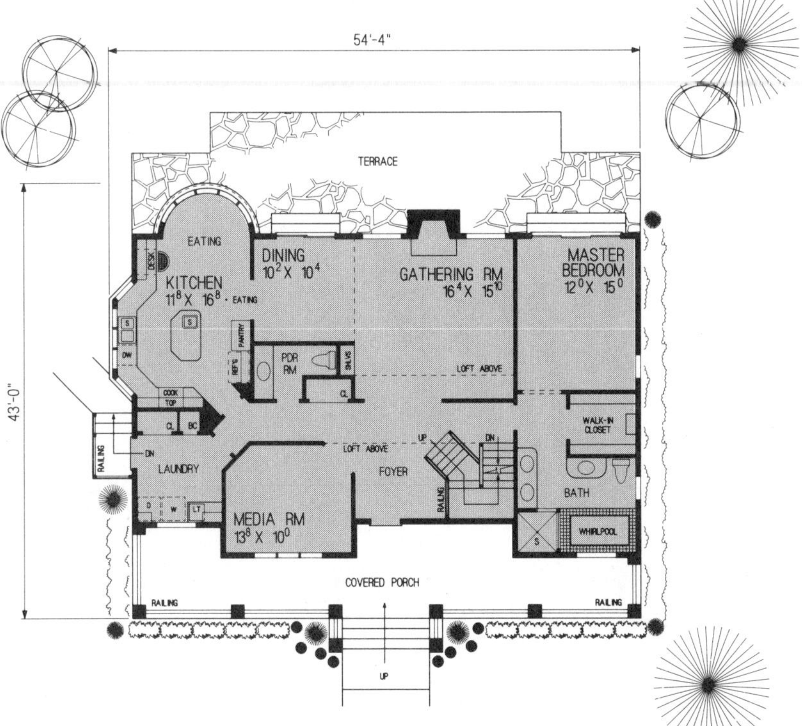

Design P3321

First Floor: 1,705 square feet
Second Floor: 572 square feet
Total: 2,277 square feet

● Cozy and completely functional, this 1½-story bungalow has many amenities not often found in homes its size. The covered porch at the front opens at the entry to a foyer with angled staircase. To the left is a media room, to the rear the gathering room with fireplace. Attached to the gathering room is a formal dining room with rear terrace access. The kitchen features a curved casual eating area and island work station. The right side of the first floor is dominated by the master suite. It has access to the rear terrace and a luxurious bath. Upstairs are two family bedrooms connected by a loft area overlooking the gathering room and foyer.

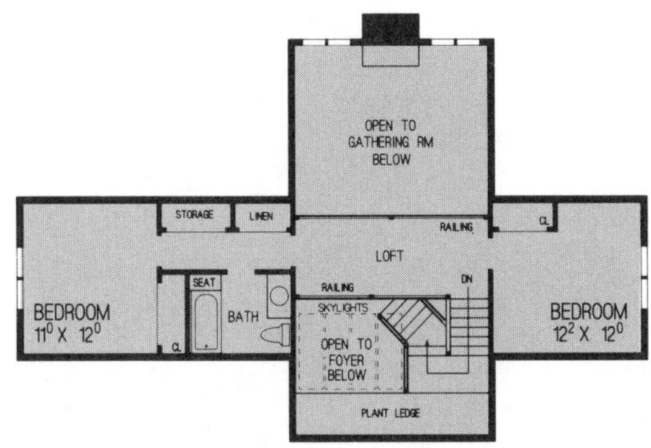

Custom Alterations? See page 203 for customizing this plan to your specifications.

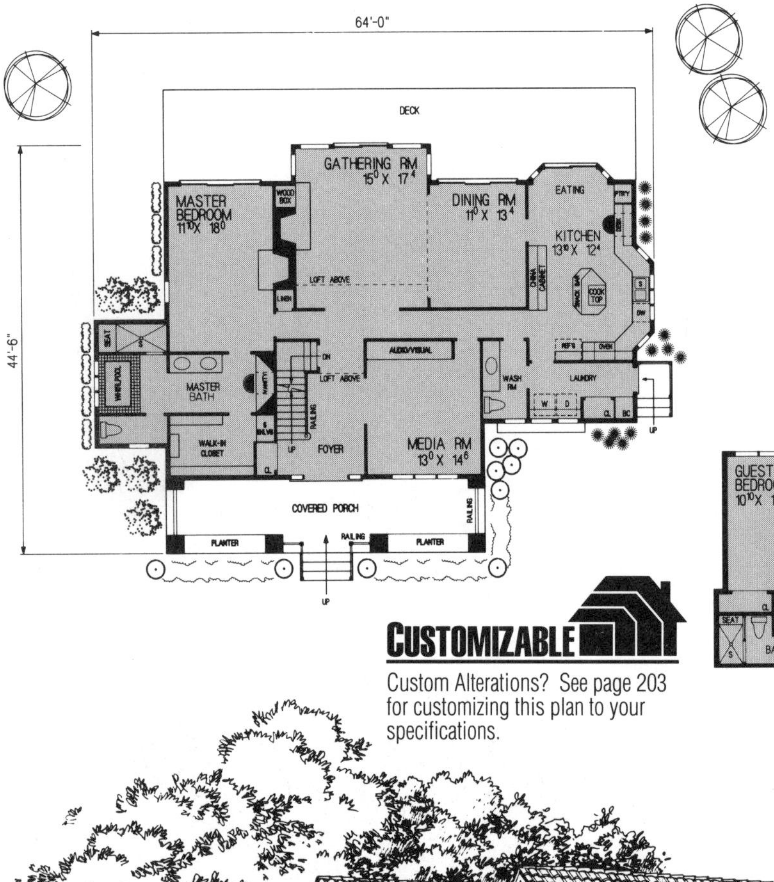

Design P3322 First Floor: 1,860 square feet Second Floor: 935 square feet; Total: 2,795 square feet

● This cleverly designed Southwestern-style home takes its cue from the California Craftsman and Bungalow styles that have seen such an increase in popularity lately. Nonetheless, it is suited to just about any climate. Its convenient floor plan includes living and working areas on the first floor in addition to a master suite. The second floor holds two family bedrooms and a guest bedroom. Note the abundance of window area to the rear of the plan.

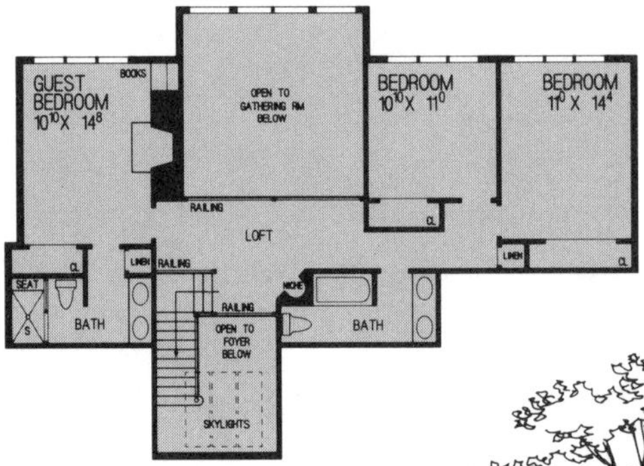

CUSTOMIZABLE

Custom Alterations? See page 203 for customizing this plan to your specifications.

Design P2896

Upper Level: 1,856 square feet; Lower Level: 1,454 square feet; Total: 3,310 square feet

● This design is very inviting with its contemporary appeal. A large kitchen with an adjacent snack bar makes light meals a breeze. The adjoining breakfast room offers a scenic view through sliding glass doors. Notice the sloped ceiling in the dining and gathering rooms. A fireplace in the gathering room adds a cozy air. An interesting feature is the master bedroom's easy access to the study. Also, take note of the sliding doors in the master bedroom which lead to a private balcony. On the lower level, a large activities room will be a frequently used spot by family members. The fireplace and wet bar add a nice touch for entertaining friends. Also, notice the sliding glass doors which lead to the terrace. Take note of the two or optional three bedrooms - the choice is yours.

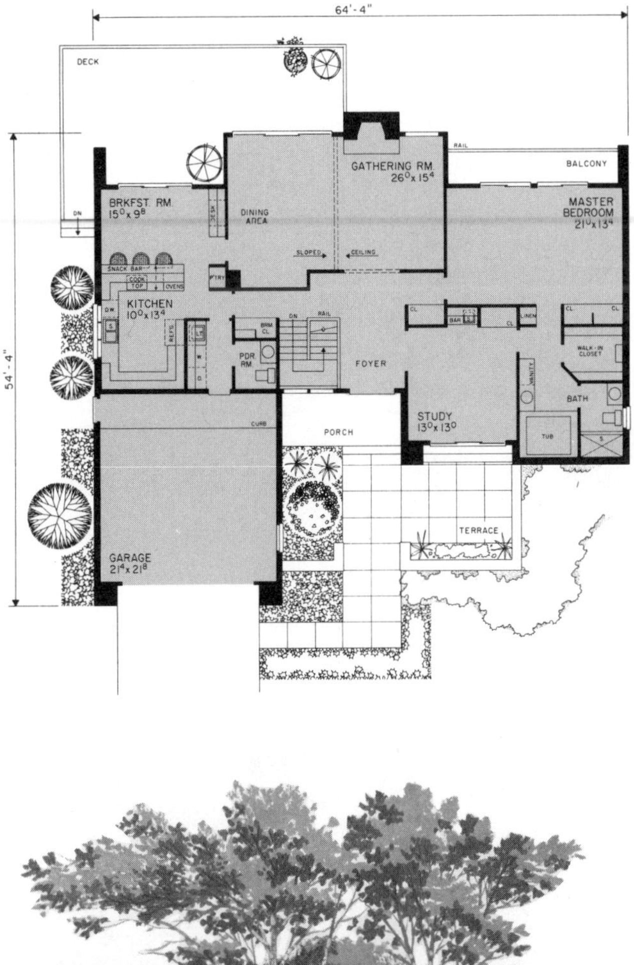

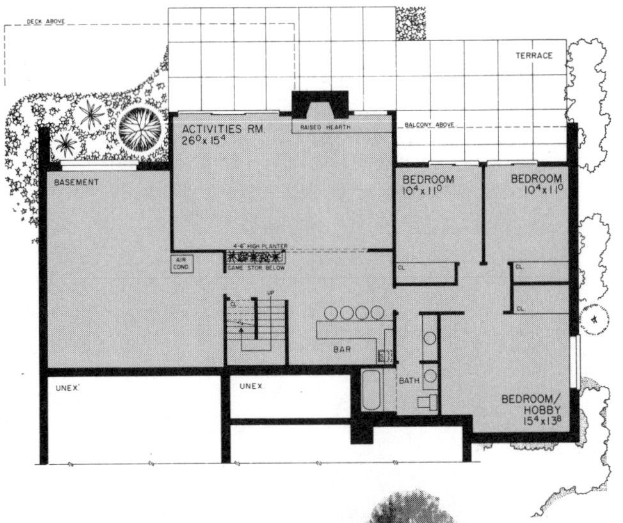

Design P2893

Main Level: 1,297 square feet; Upper Level: 1,256 square feet
Lower Level: 654 square feet; Total: 3,207 square feet

D

● Here is a contemporary split-level with a lot of appeal. Up a few steps you will find three bedrooms and a bath. Also, a master bedroom suite with an oversized tub, shower, walk-in closet and sliding glass doors to a balcony. A sunken living room is on the main level, where it shares with the dining room a through- fireplace, sloped ceiling and skylights. A spacious kitchen and breakfast room are nearby. The lower level has a large family room with sliding glass doors to the lower terrace, a wet bar and a fireplace.

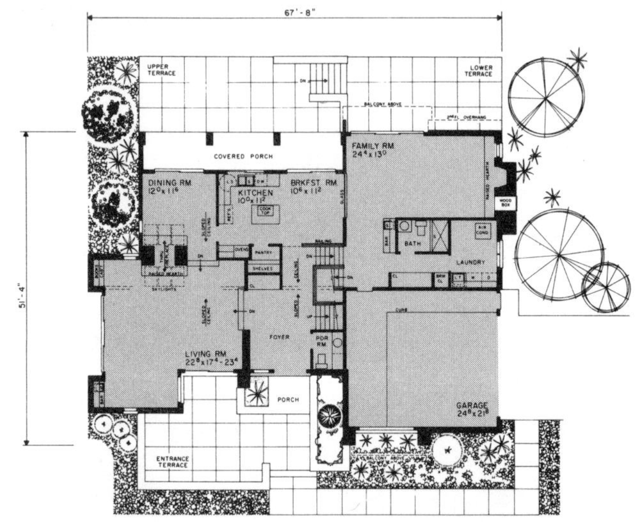

Design P2135

Square Footage: 2,495 (Excluding Atrium)

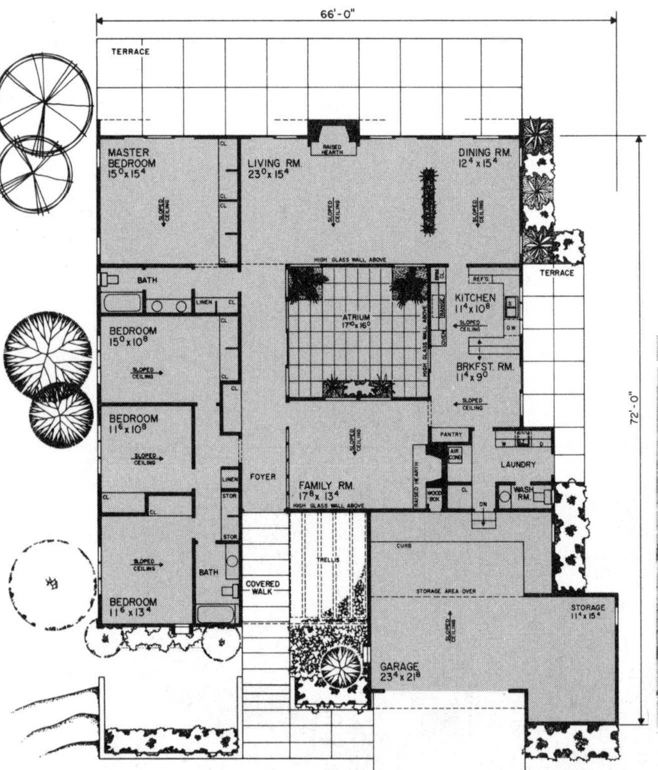

● The proud occupants of this contemporary home will forever be thrilled at their choice of such a distinguished exterior and such a practical and exciting floor plan. Inside there is a feeling of spaciousness created by the sloping ceilings. The uniqueness of this design is further enhanced by the atrium. Open to the sky, this outdoor area can be en-joyed from all parts of the house. The sleeping zone has four bedrooms, two baths and plenty of closets. The informal living zone has a fine kitchen and breakfast room. The large living/dining area contains a raised-hearth fireplace.

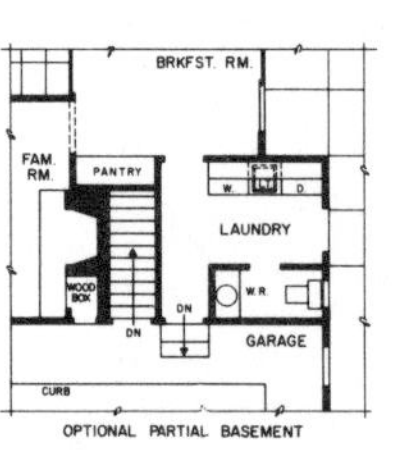

Design P2856 Upper Level: 1,801 square feet
Lower Level: 2,170 square feet; Total: 3,971 square feet

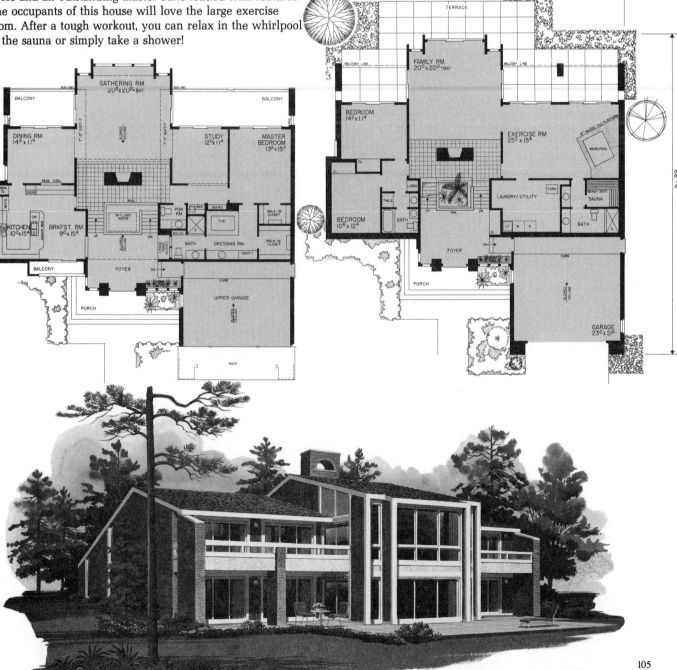

● This attractive, contemporary bi-level will overwhelm you with its features: two balconies, an open staircase with planter below, two lower level bedrooms, six sets of sliding glass doors and an outstanding master suite loaded with features. The occupants of this house will love the large exercise room. After a tough workout, you can relax in the whirlpool or the sauna or simply take a shower!

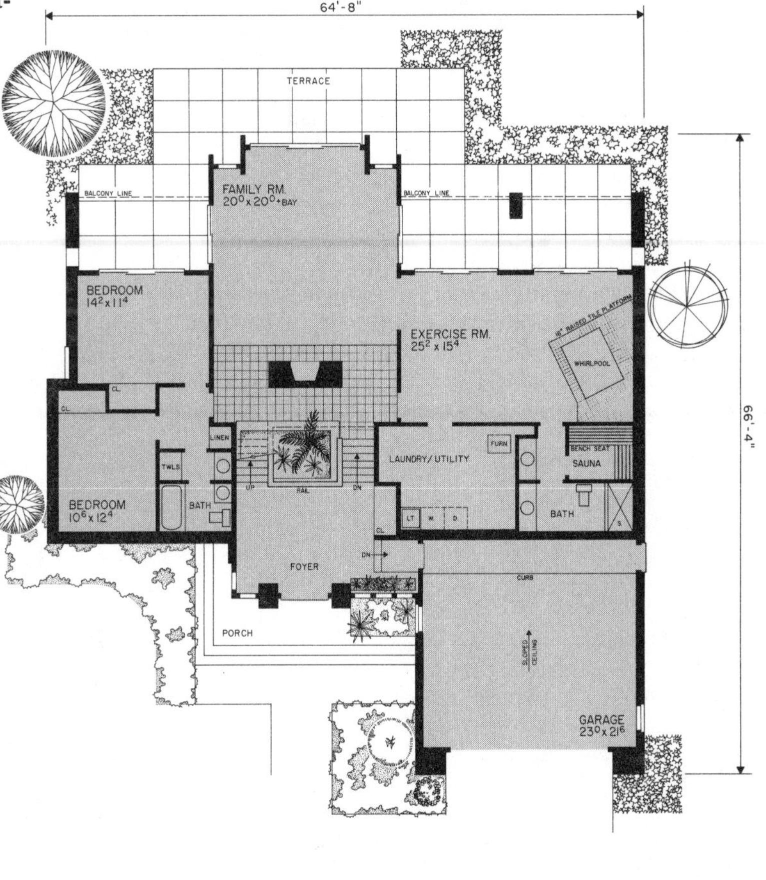

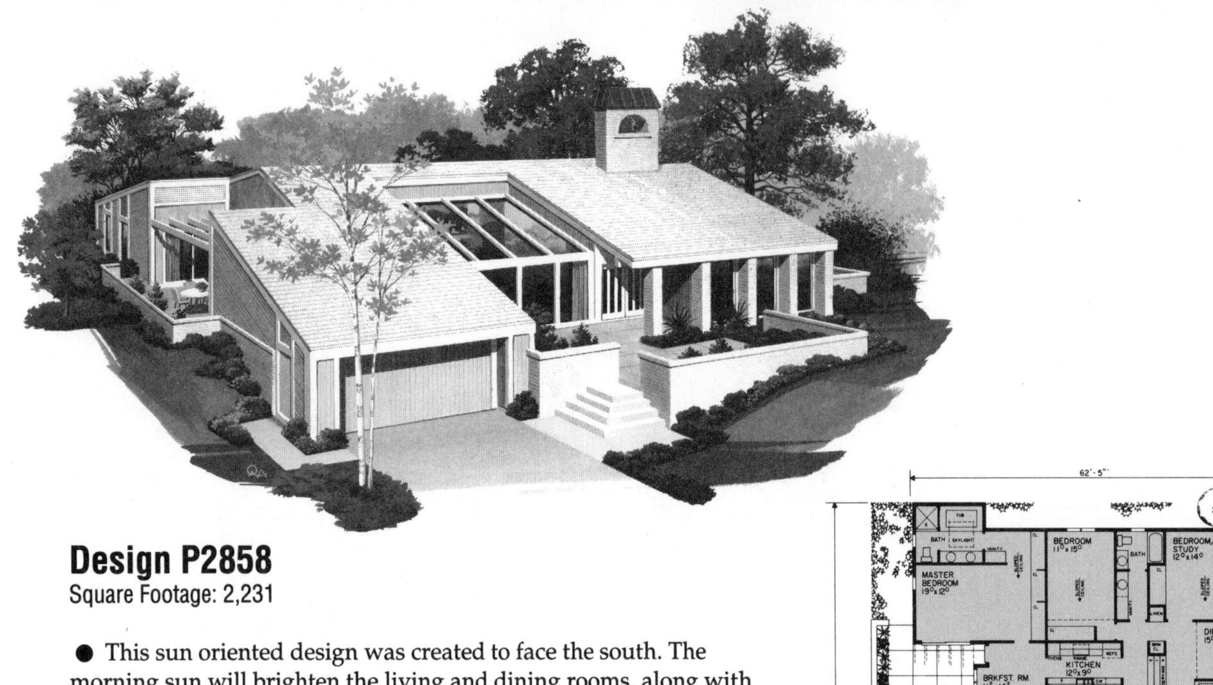

Design P2858

Square Footage: 2,231

● This sun oriented design was created to face the south. The morning sun will brighten the living and dining rooms, along with the adjacent terrace. Sun enters the garden room by way of the glass roof and walls. In the winter, the solar heat gain from the garden room should provide relief from high energy bills. Solar shades allow you to adjust the amount of light that you want to enter in the warmer months. The kitchen has a snack bar and a serving counter to the dining room. The breakfast room with laundry area is also convenient to the kitchen. Three bedrooms are on the northern wall. The master bedroom has a large tub and a separate shower with a four-foot-square skylight above. When this design is oriented toward the sun, it should prove to be energy efficient and a joy to live in.

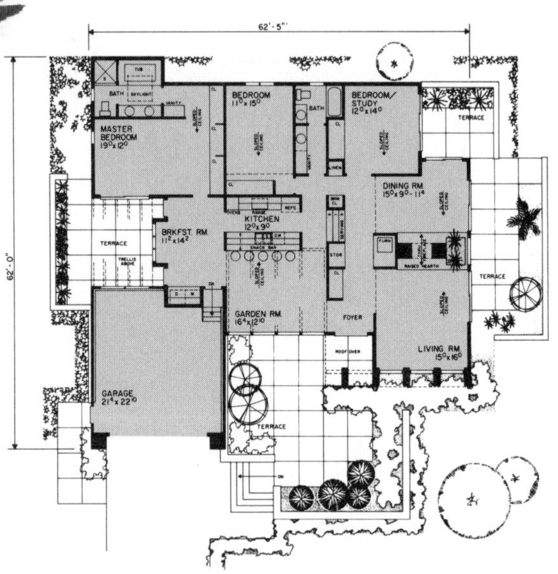

Design P2881

Square Footage: 2,770

● Energy-efficiency was a major consideration in this contemporary design. It was planned for a south-facing lot in temperate zones. Note the variety of outdoor living areas and the centrally located kitchen. Three bedrooms dominate the back of the house, including a master suite with a private terrace. There are two fireplaces: one in the living room and one in the family room.

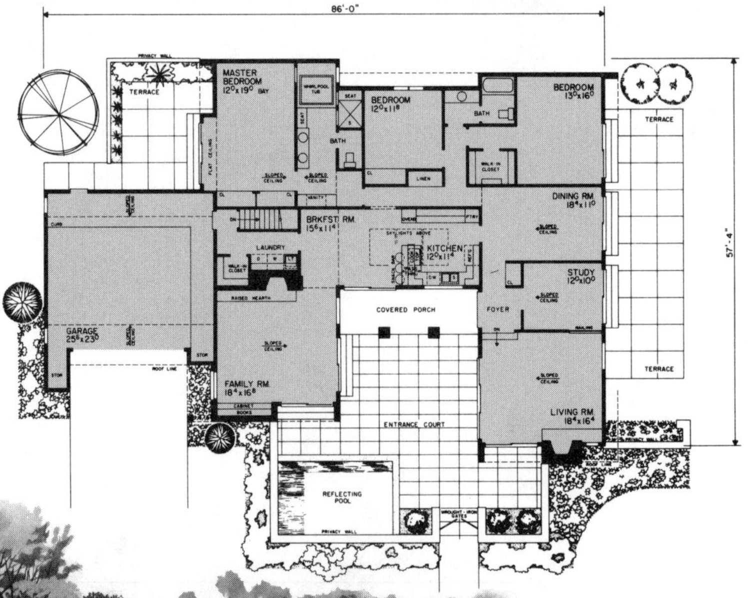

Design P2894

Upper Level: 1,490 square feet
Lower Level: 1,357 square feet; Total: 2,847 square feet

● Contemporary, bi-level living will be enjoyed by all members of the family. Upon entering the foyer, complimented by skylights, stairs will lead you to the upper and lower levels. Up a few steps, you will find yourself in the large gathering room. The fireplace, sloped ceiling and the size of this room will make this a favorite spot. To the left is a study/bedroom with a full bath and walk-in closet. Notice the efficient kitchen and breakfast room with nearby wet bar. The lower level houses two bedrooms and a bath to one side; and a master bedroom suite to the other. Centered is a large activity room with raised-hearth fireplace. It will be enjoyed by all. Note - all of the rear rooms on both levels have easy access to the outdoors for excellent indoor-outdoor livability.

Design P3403

First Floor: 2,240 square feet
Second Floor: 660 square feet
Total: 2,900 square feet

L **D**

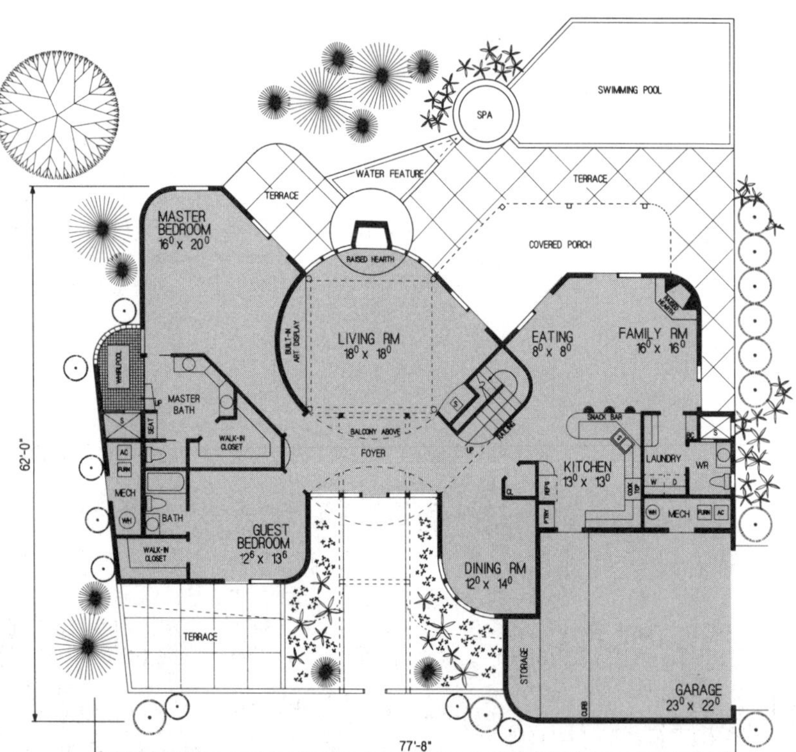

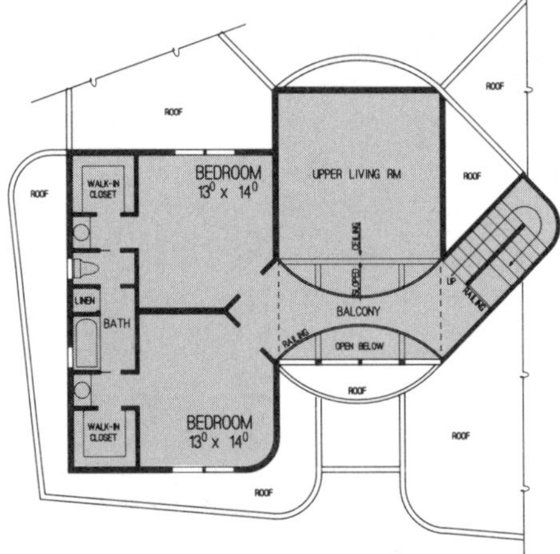

● There is no end to the distinctive features in this Southwestern contemporary. Formal living areas are concentrated in the center of the plan, perfect for entertaining. To the right of the plan, the kitchen and family room function well together as a working and living area. Also note the separate laundry room. The optional guest bedroom or den and the master bedroom are located to the left of the plan. Upstairs, the remaining two bedrooms are reached by a balcony overlooking the living room and share a bath with twin vanities.

Design P2926

First Floor: 1,570 square feet
Second Floor: 598 square feet; Lower Level: 1,080 square feet
Total: 2,650 square feet

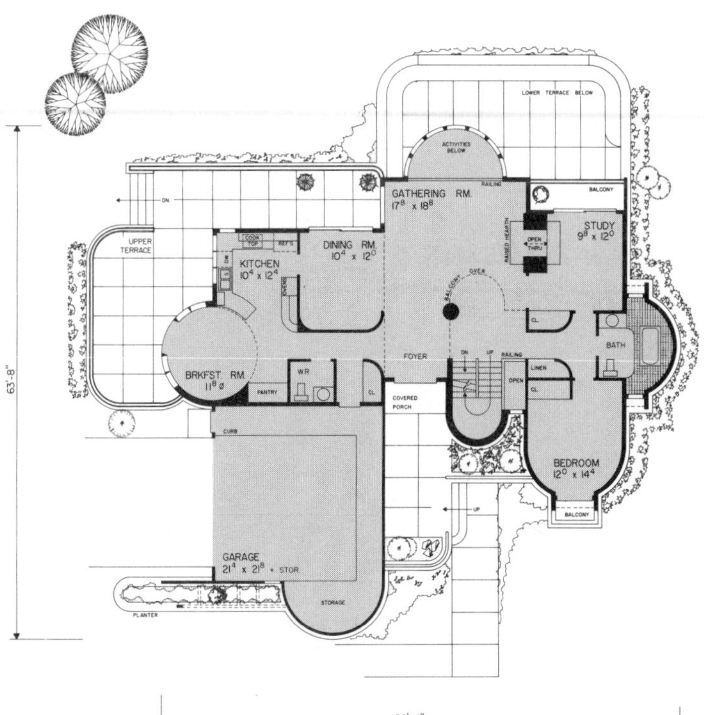

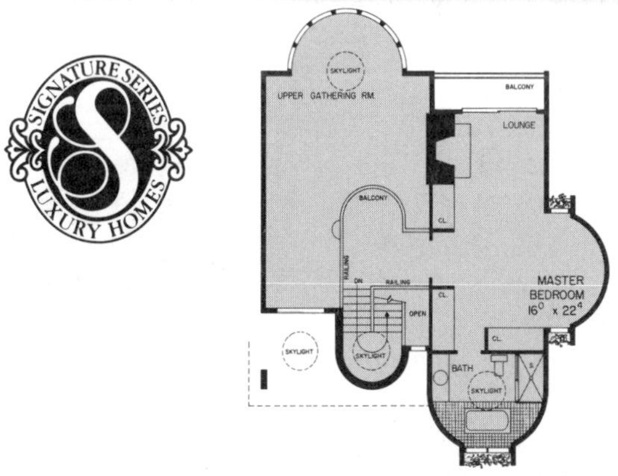

● This striking Contemporary design offers plenty of leisure living on three levels including an activities room with bar, exercise room with sauna, two gathering rooms, circular glass windows, and skylights. Note the outstanding master bedroom suite with skylight over the bath, adjoining lounge, and adjacent upper gathering room.

Design P2339 First Floor: 2,068 square feet; Second Floor: 589 square feet; Total: 2,657 square feet

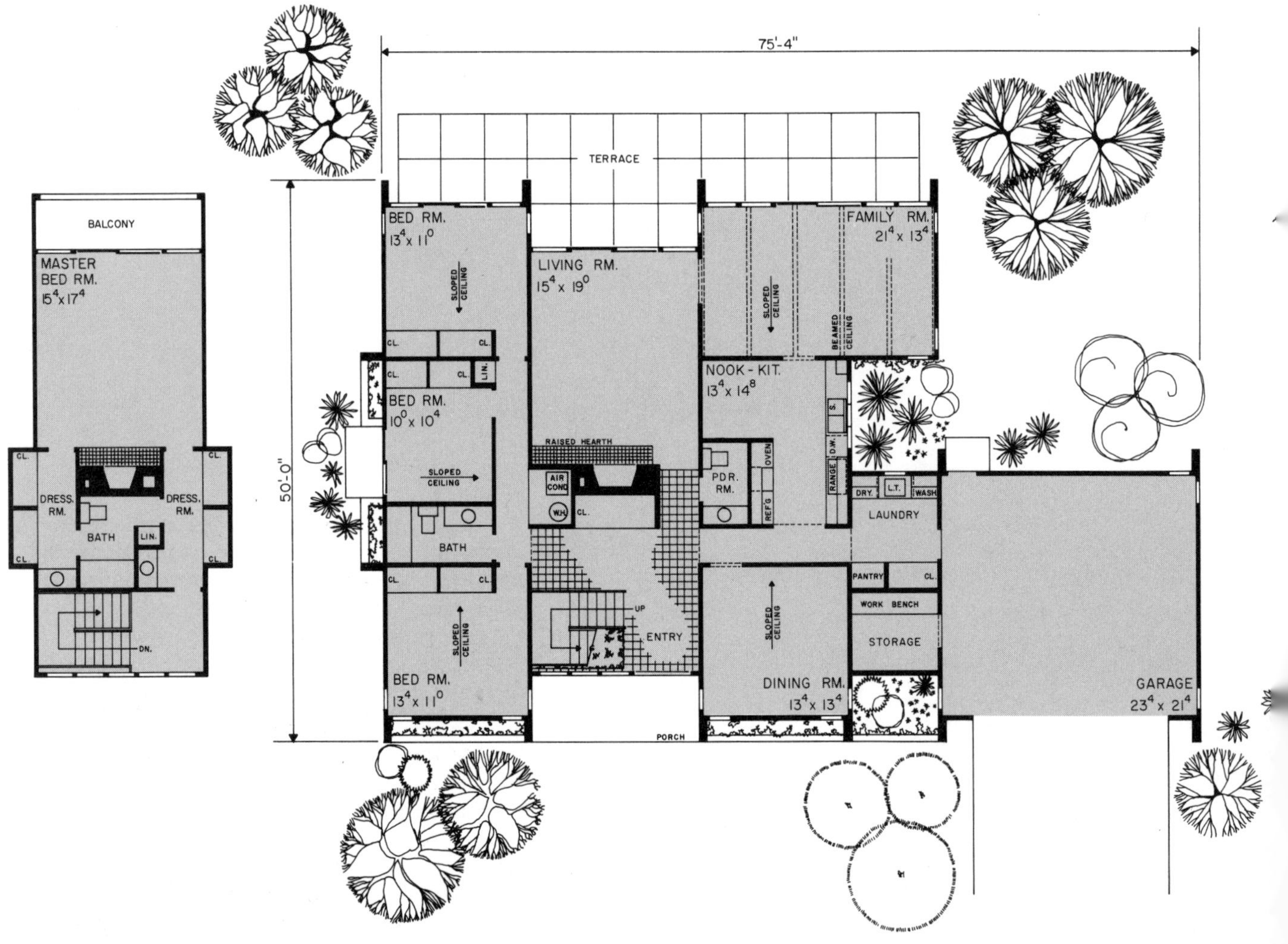

● Here, the influence of the Spanish Southwest comes into clear view. The smooth texture of the stucco exterior contrasts pleasingly with the roughness of the tile roofs. Contributing to the appeal of this contemporary design are the varying roof planes, the interesting angles and the blank wall masses punctuated by the glass areas. Whether called upon to function as a two-story home, or a one-story ranch with an attic studio, this design will deliver interesting and enjoyable living patterns. Sloping ceilings and generous glass areas foster a feeling of spaciousness. Traffic patterns are excellent and the numerous storage facilities are outstanding. Fireplaces are the focal point of the living room and the second floor master bedroom. Three more bedrooms are on the first floor.

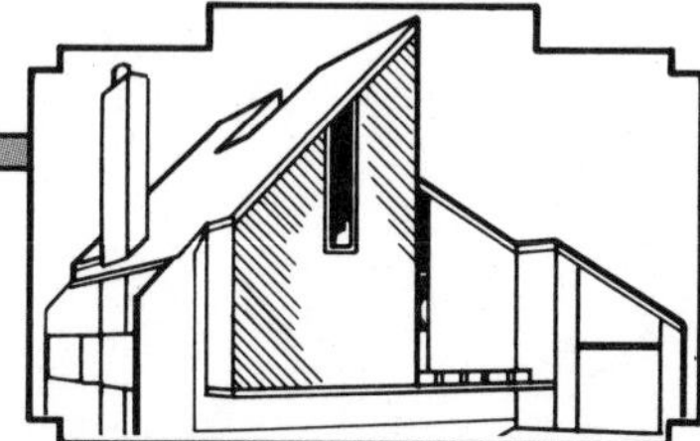

Pacific Wood Contemporary

The Pacific Wood Contemporary is one of the most recent developments in Western architecture. It has its roots in the early 1960s largely due to the design efforts of two notable architects— Charles Moore and Robert Venturi.

The most easily recognizable element of the Pacific Wood Contemporary home is its multi-directional shed roof, often used in conjunction with other roof types. The joining together of different angles and levels results in a juxtaposition of geometric shapes that gives these homes their contemporary appeal.

The forerunners to today's Pacific Wood Contemporaries were clad almost exclusively in wood shingles. However, modern variations use wood siding in either horizontal, vertical or diagonal patterns. Two or even all three patterns may be used on a home, further enhancing the feeling of counterpoint and shape collision. Brick or stonework veneer is also sometimes used for the entire facade or may be used as accent on a wood-clad facade.

The characteristic shed roof may either dominate the overall form of the exterior or may only be an architectural suggestion. There is usually little or no overhanging eave and roof/wall junctures are smooth and uncomplicated.

Windows and doors follow the contemporary mode. Windows may be small and placed high on walls or there may be extensive areas of fixed glass and window walls. Fenestration, or window placement, is often asymmetrical. The common entrance for this style of home is recessed either in a covered alcove or walled courtyard.

The Pacific Wood Contemporary lends itself well to a casual floor plan of multi-levels. Varying roof planes and an asymmetrical nature fit well with a hillside or split-foyer plan. Balconies are a natural result—both inside and out. They may overlook a gathering area from a second-story interior or act as a roof over a basement-level terrace. Wooden decks also extend the livability and blend with the rustic feel of these homes.

Further enhancing the indoor/outdoor lifestyle in the Pacific Wood Contemporary are such features as partially enclosed courtyards, atriums, solariums and greenhouses. They are designed to take advantage of dramatic natural views while providing open, useful living spaces.

Design P2925 First Floor: 1,128 square feet; Second Floor: 844 square feet; Total: 1,972 square feet

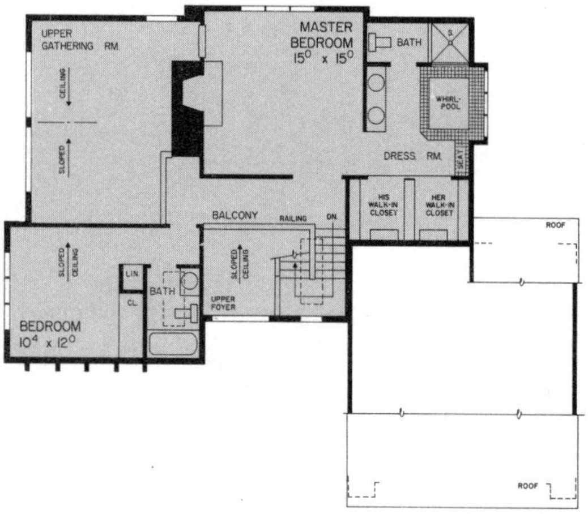

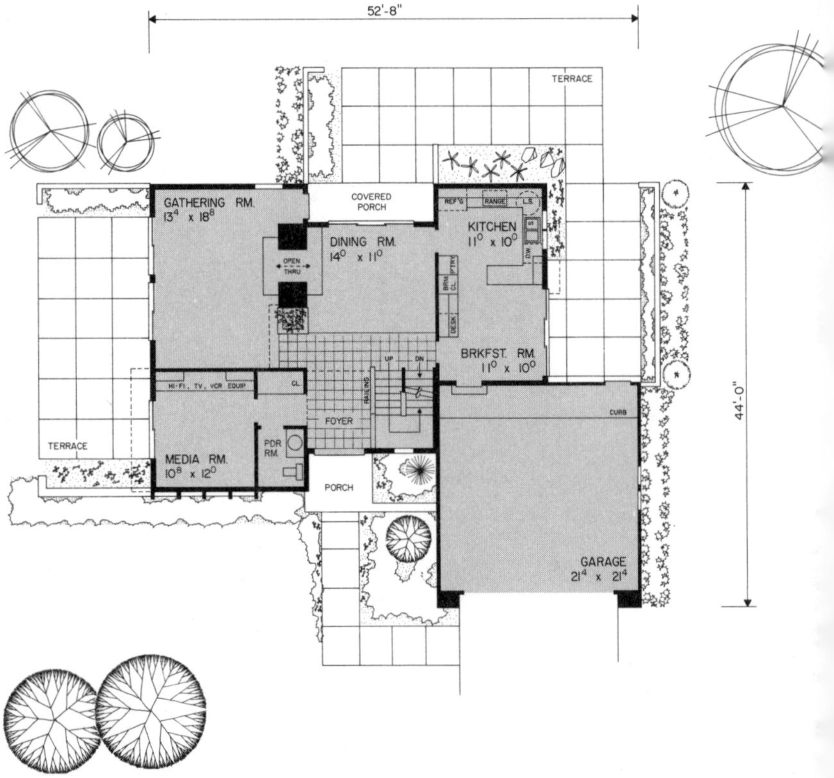

● What a refreshing and exciting two-story contemporary. The expansive wide-overhanging roofs make a distinctive design statement. This is also true of the effective uses of varying exterior materials and surface textures. The front entry area is noteworthy for its panelled double doors below the large radial head window. This window and the two vertical strips of glass to its right permit an abundance of natural light to flood the foyer and open staircases. While enjoying privacy from the street, the various rooms enjoy wonderful views of the rear and side yards. The cathedral ceiling of the gathering room and its windowed wall will make this the family's favorite area. A through-fireplace serves both the gathering and dining rooms at the same time. The corner kitchen serves both dining areas well. The media room will house all that hi-tech equipment. Upstairs, two bedrooms and baths.

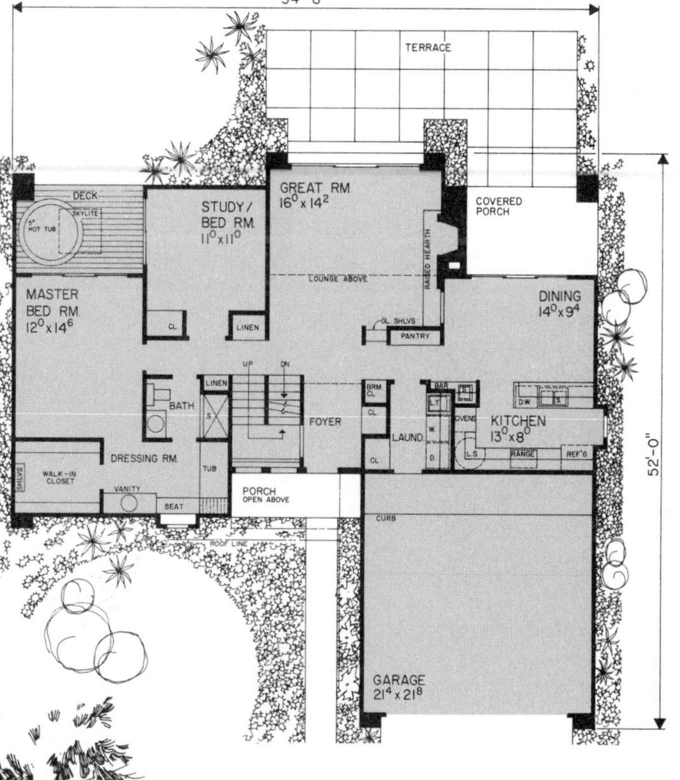

Design P2822

First Floor: 1,363 square feet
Second Floor: 351 square feet
Total: 1,714 square feet

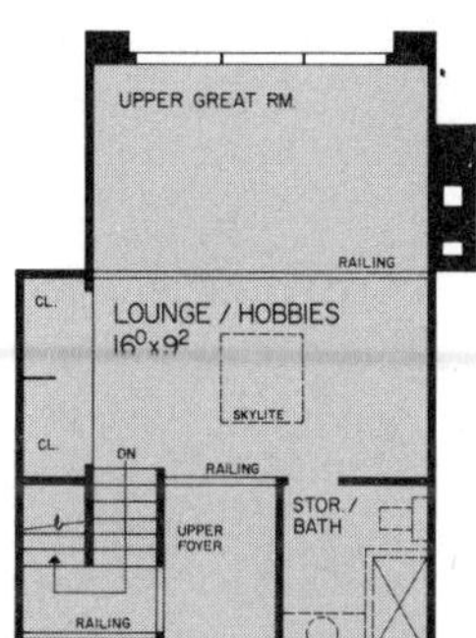

● Here is a truly unique house whose interior was designed with the current decade's economies, life-styles and demographics in mind. While functioning as a one-story home, the second floor provides an extra measure of livability when required. In addition, this two-story section adds to the dramatic appeal of both the exterior and the interior. Within only 1,363 square feet, this contemporary delivers refreshing and outstanding living patterns for those who are buying their first home, those who have raised their family and are looking for a smaller home and those in search of a retirement home.

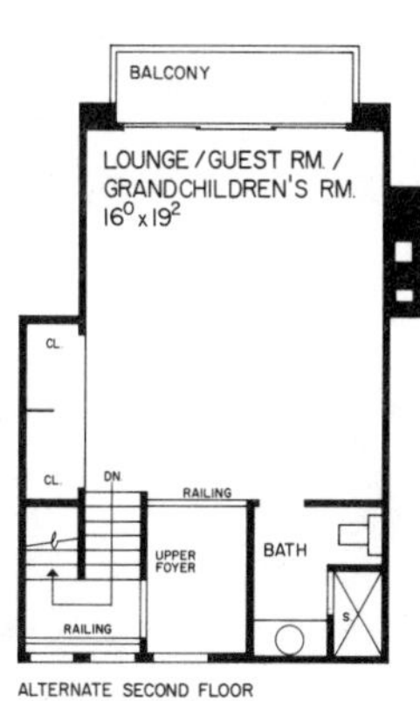

ALTERNATE SECOND FLOOR

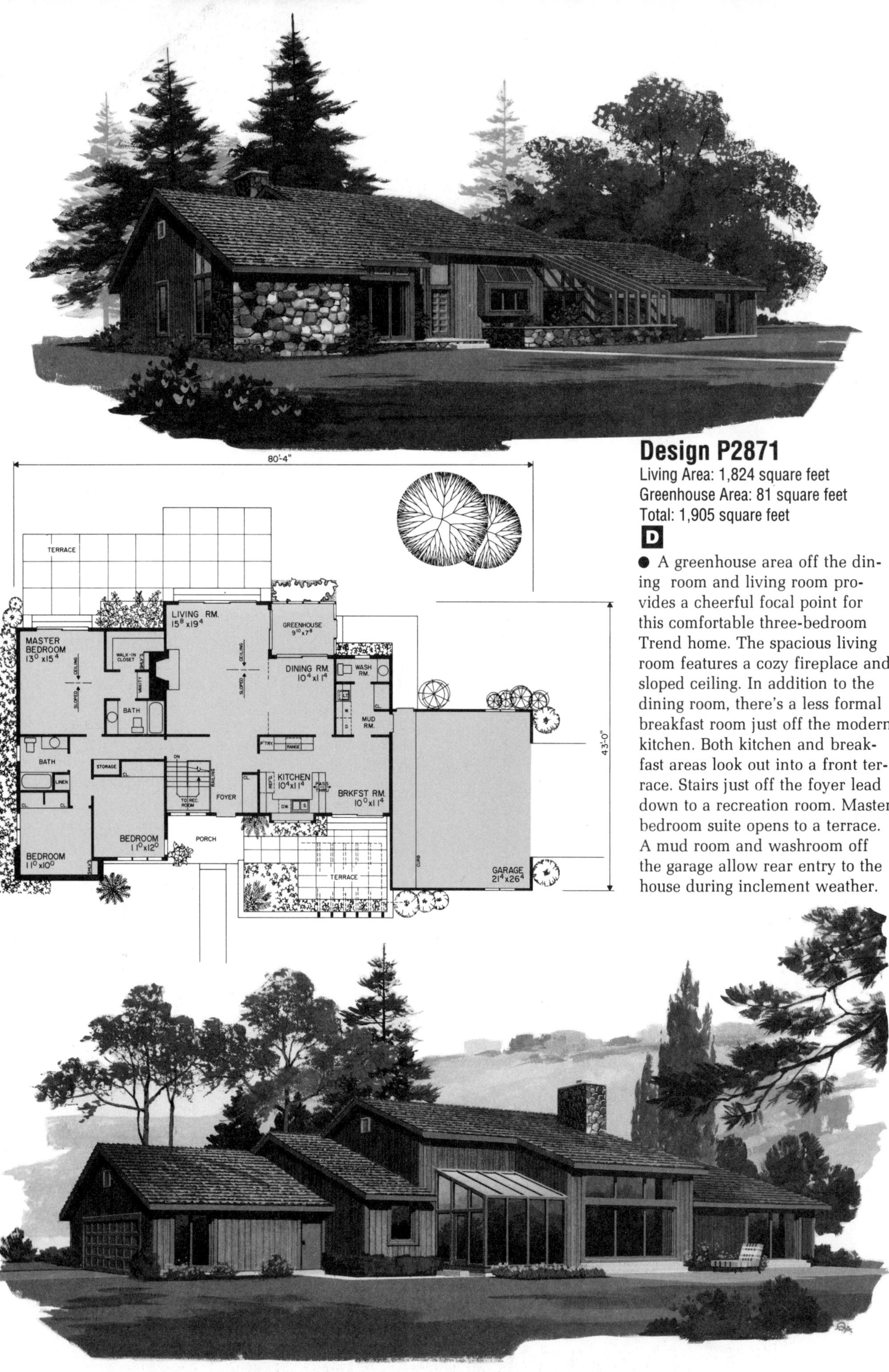

Design P2871

Living Area: 1,824 square feet
Greenhouse Area: 81 square feet
Total: 1,905 square feet

D

● A greenhouse area off the dining room and living room provides a cheerful focal point for this comfortable three-bedroom Trend home. The spacious living room features a cozy fireplace and sloped ceiling. In addition to the dining room, there's a less formal breakfast room just off the modern kitchen. Both kitchen and breakfast areas look out into a front terrace. Stairs just off the foyer lead down to a recreation room. Master bedroom suite opens to a terrace. A mud room and washroom off the garage allow rear entry to the house during inclement weather.

Design P2828

First Floor: 1,078 square feet
Second Floor: 1,066 square feet
Total: 2,144 square feet

● The first floor of this contemporary home features an interior kitchen with a snack bar, a living room with raised-hearth fireplace, and a dining room. The first-floor bedroom will make a great guest suite with nearby full bath and terrace access. Upstairs, a large master bedroom is joined by two family bedrooms, one of which could easily serve as a nursery, office or media room. Also notice the two balconies, three skylights and sewing/hobbies room upstairs. Storage space is available everywhere you look—hall closets on the second floor, in the first floor laundry room and garage, and in the basement plan.

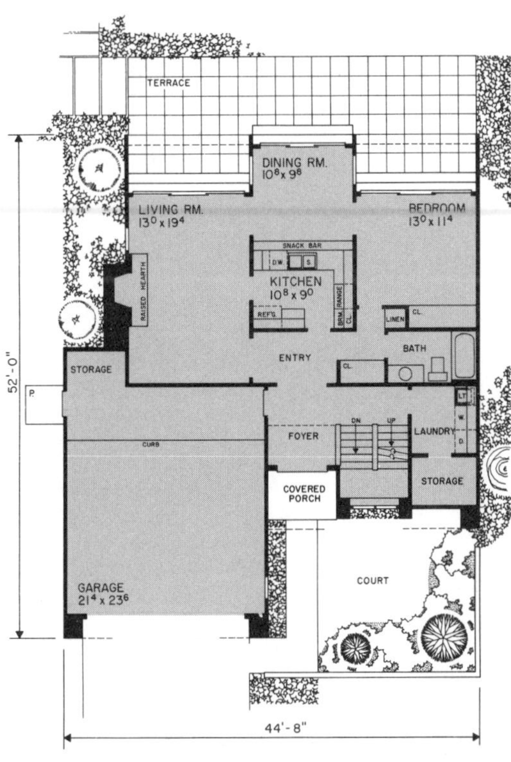

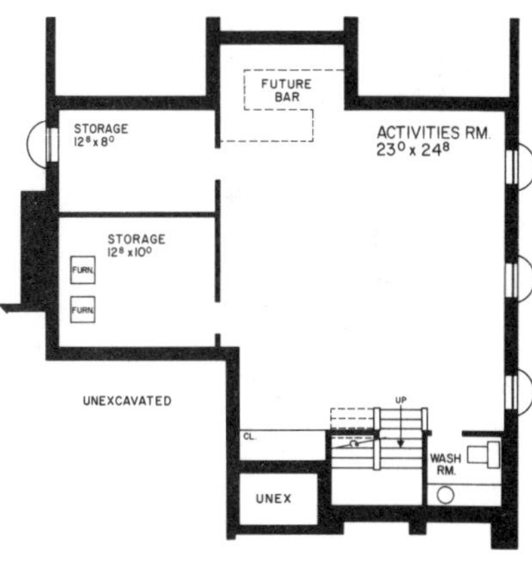

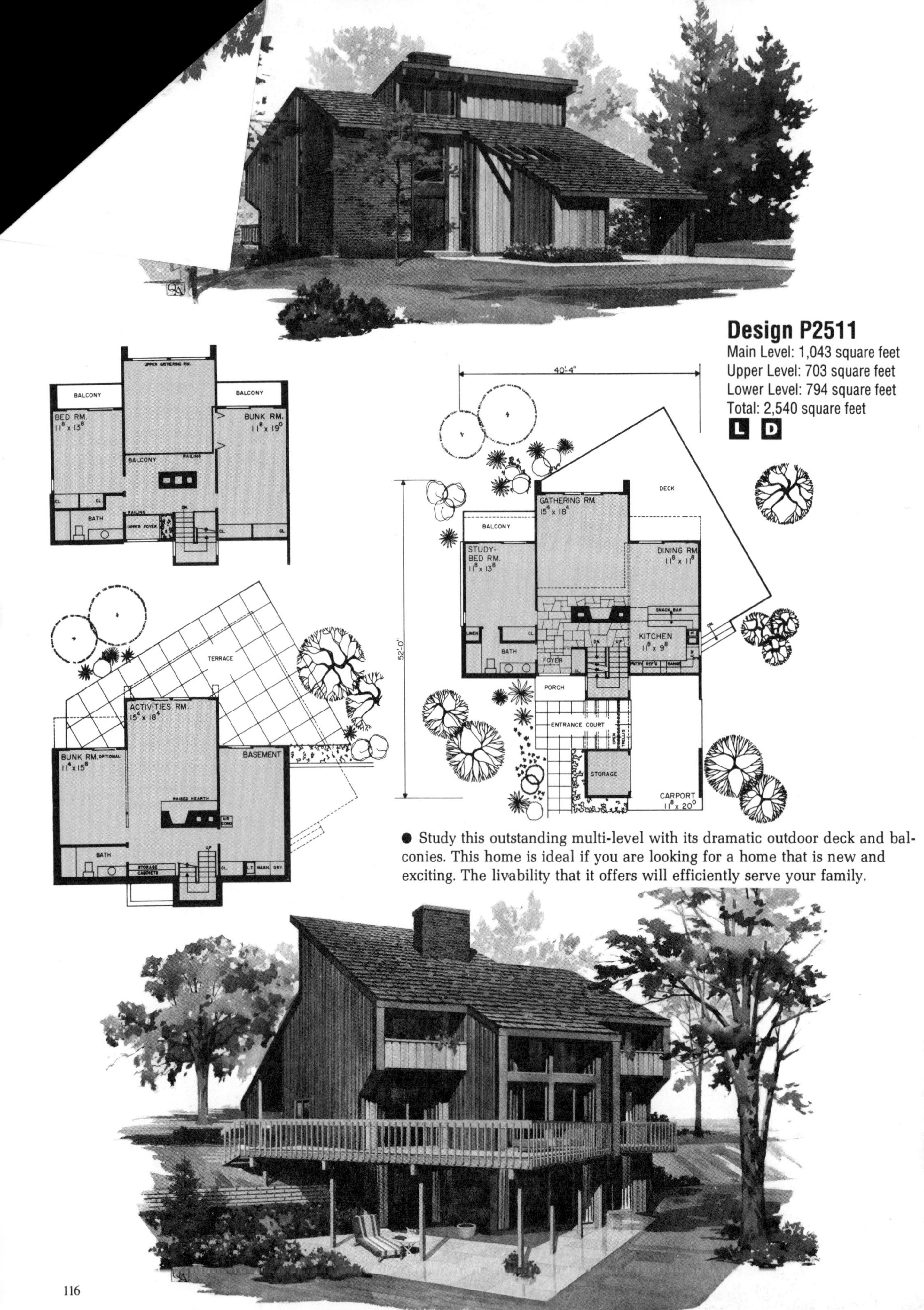

Design P2511

Main Level: 1,043 square feet
Upper Level: 703 square feet
Lower Level: 794 square feet
Total: 2,540 square feet

L D

● Study this outstanding multi-level with its dramatic outdoor deck and balconies. This home is ideal if you are looking for a home that is new and exciting. The livability that it offers will efficiently serve your family.

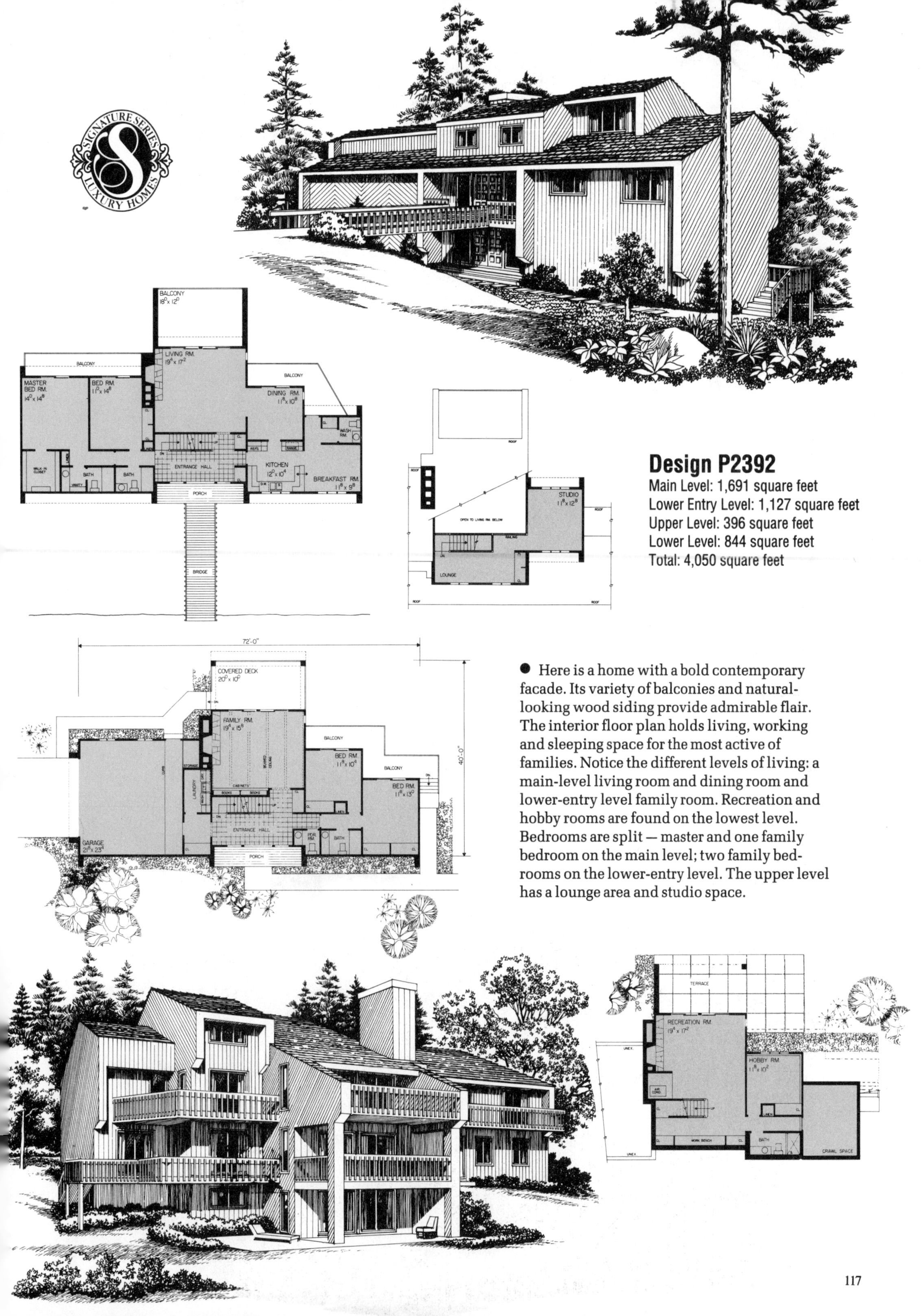

Design P2392

Main Level: 1,691 square feet
Lower Entry Level: 1,127 square feet
Upper Level: 396 square feet
Lower Level: 844 square feet
Total: 4,050 square feet

● Here is a home with a bold contemporary facade. Its variety of balconies and natural-looking wood siding provide admirable flair. The interior floor plan holds living, working and sleeping space for the most active of families. Notice the different levels of living: a main-level living room and dining room and lower-entry level family room. Recreation and hobby rooms are found on the lowest level. Bedrooms are split — master and one family bedroom on the main level; two family bedrooms on the lower-entry level. The upper level has a lounge area and studio space.

Design P2830

Main Level: 1,795 square feet
Lower Level: 1,546 square feet
Total: 3,341 square feet

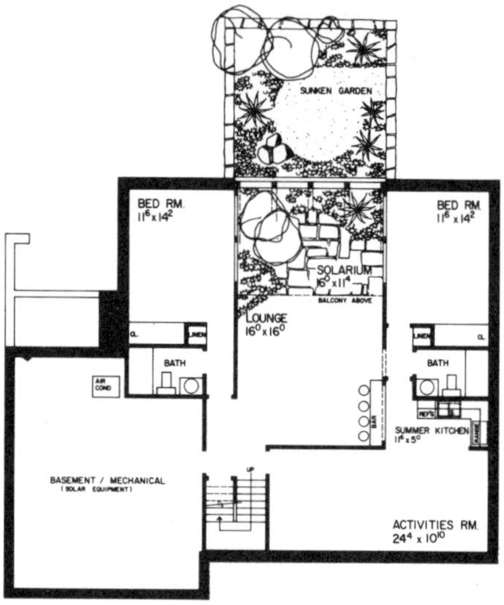

● This home has been created with the advantages of passive solar heating in mind. For optimum energy savings, this delightful design combines a passive solar device, the solarium, with optional active collectors. Included with the purchase of this design are four plot plans to assure that the solar collectors will face the south. Schematic details for solar application are also included.

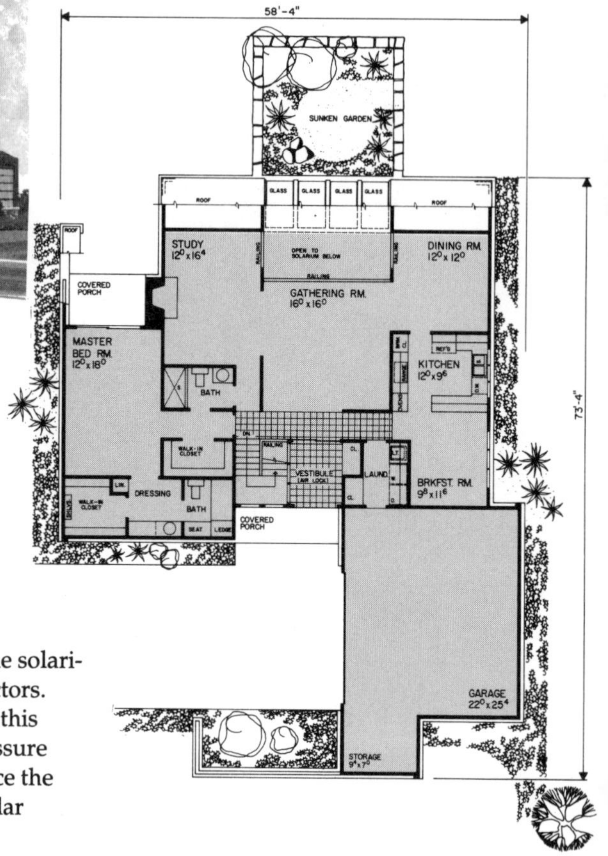

Design P2716

Main Level: 1,013 square feet
Upper Level: 885 square feet
Lower Level: 1,074 square feet
Total: 2,972 square feet

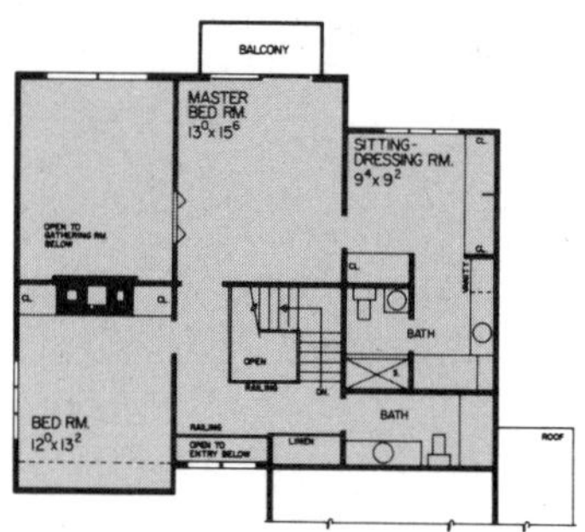

● This plan has a genuine master suite — overlooking the gathering room through shuttered windows. The gathering room has a raised-hearth fireplace, sloped ceiling and sliding glass doors onto the main balcony. A family room and study also have fireplaces. The kitchen features plenty of built-ins and a separate dining nook.

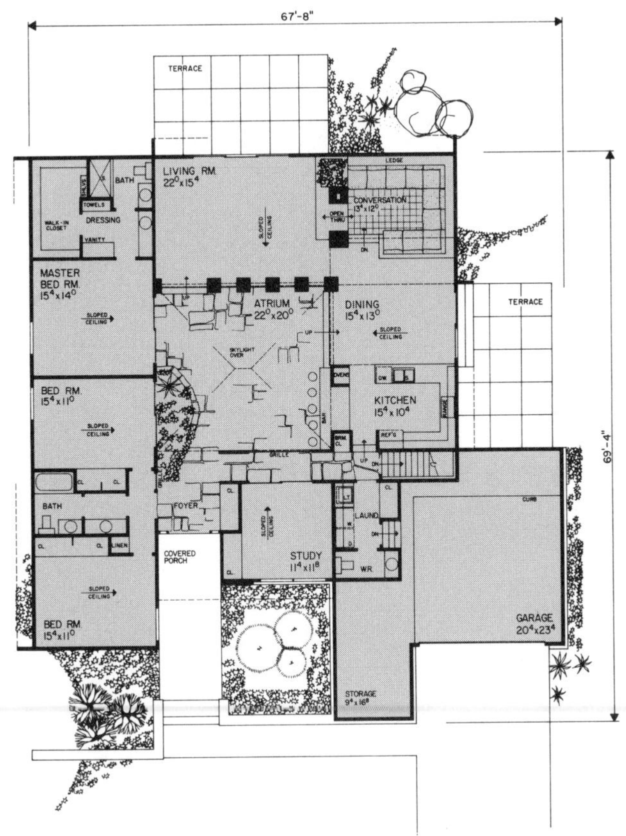

Design P2832

Square Footage: 2,805 (Excluding Atrium)

D

● The advantage of passive solar heating is a significant highlight of this contemporary design. The huge skylight over the atrium provides shelter during inclement weather, while permitting plenty of natural light to the atrium below and the surrounding areas. During the summer, shades afford protection from the sun. Sloping ceilings highlight each of the major rooms: three bedrooms, formal living and dining and study. The conversation area between the two formal areas will really be something to talk about. The broad expanses of roof can accommodate solar panels should an active system be desired.

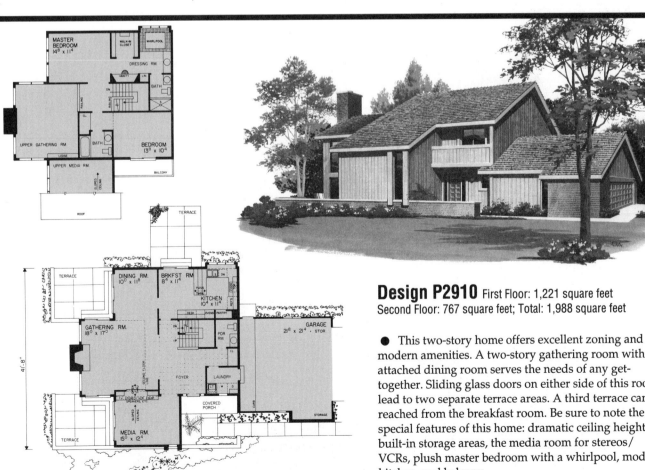

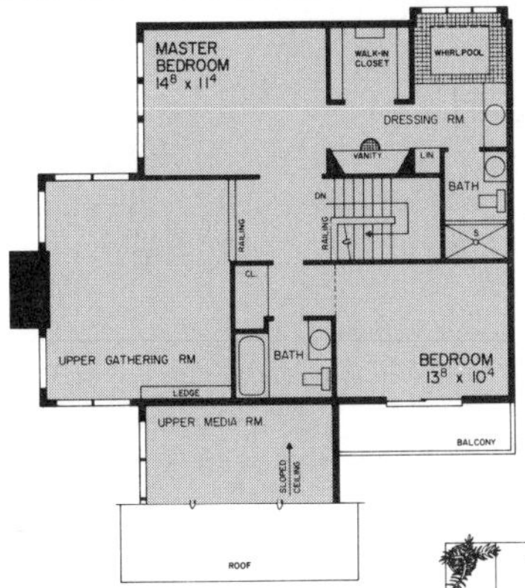

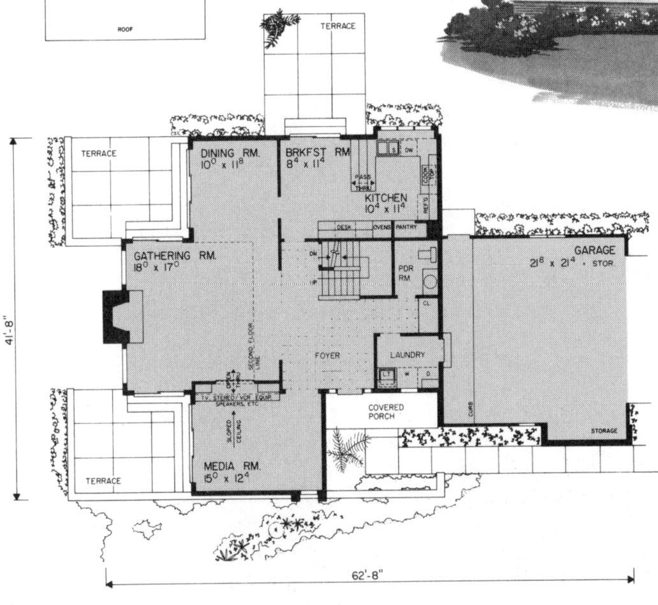

Design P2910

First Floor: 1,221 square feet
Second Floor: 767 square feet; Total: 1,988 square feet

● This two-story home offers excellent zoning and modern amenities. A two-story gathering room with attached dining room serves the needs of any get-together. Sliding glass doors on either side of this room lead to two separate terrace areas. A third terrace can be reached from the breakfast room. Be sure to note the special features of this home: dramatic ceiling heights, built-in storage areas, the media room for stereos/VCRs, plush master bedroom with a whirlpool, modern kitchen, and balcony.

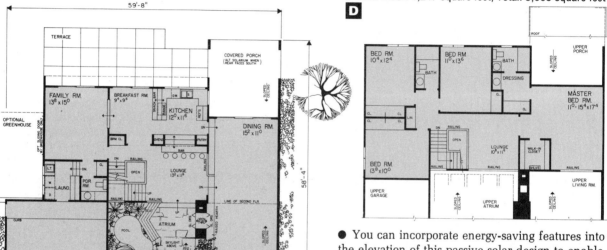

Design P2831 First Floor: 1,758 square feet
Second Floor: 1,247 square feet; Total: 3,005 square feet

D

59'-8"
58'-4"
TERRACE
COVERED PORCH (ALT. SOLARIUM WHEN REAR FACES SOUTH)
OPTIONAL GREENHOUSE
FAMILY RM. 13⁸ x 15⁰
BREAKFAST RM. 9⁴ x 9⁶
KITCHEN 12⁰ x 11⁶
DINING RM. 15² x 11⁰
LOUNGE 13⁸ x 11⁶
LAUND.
PDR. RM.
ATRIUM
POOL
SKYLIGHT ABOVE
LIVING RM. 15² x 22⁰
GARAGE 21⁸ x 21⁸
LINE OF SECOND FLR.
SLOPED CEILING
RAISED HEARTH

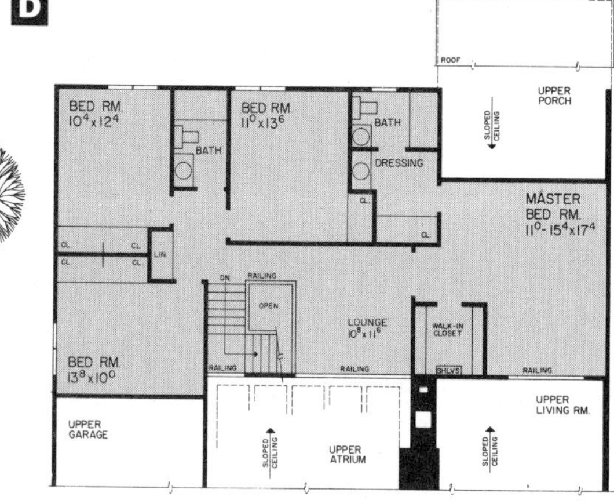

● You can incorporate energy-saving features into the elevation of this passive solar design to enable you to receive the most sunlight on your particular site. Multiple plot plans (included with the blueprints) illustrate which elevations should be solarized for different sites and which extra features can be incorporated. The features can include a greenhouse added to the family room, the back porch turned into a solarium or skylights installed over the entry.

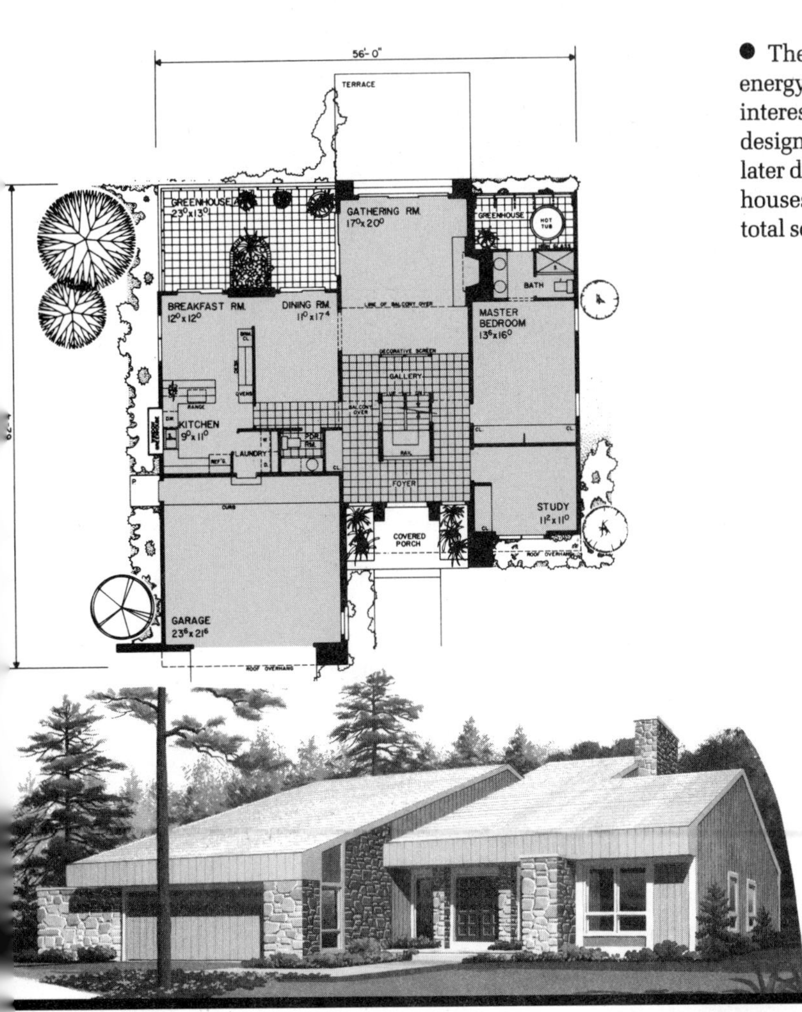

The greenhouses in this design enhance its energy-efficiency and allow for spacious and interesting living patterns. Being a 1½-story design, the second floor could be developed at a later date when the space is needed. The greenhouses add an additional 418 square feet to the total square footage.

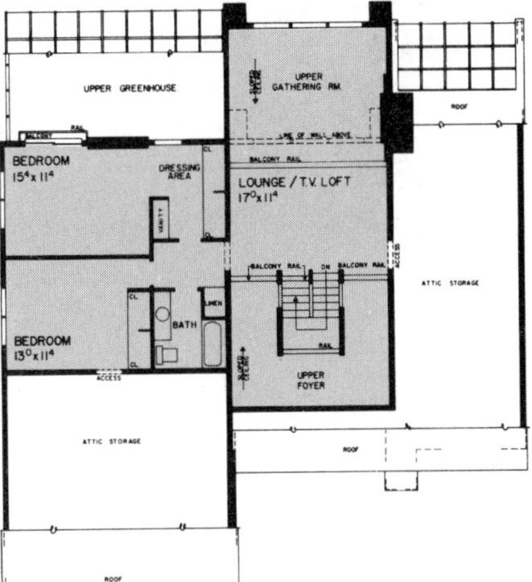

Design P2884

First Floor: 1,855 square feet
Second Floor: 837 square feet
Total: 2,692 square feet

Design P2759

Upper Level: 1,747 square feet
Lower Level: 1,513 square feet
Total: 3,260 square feet

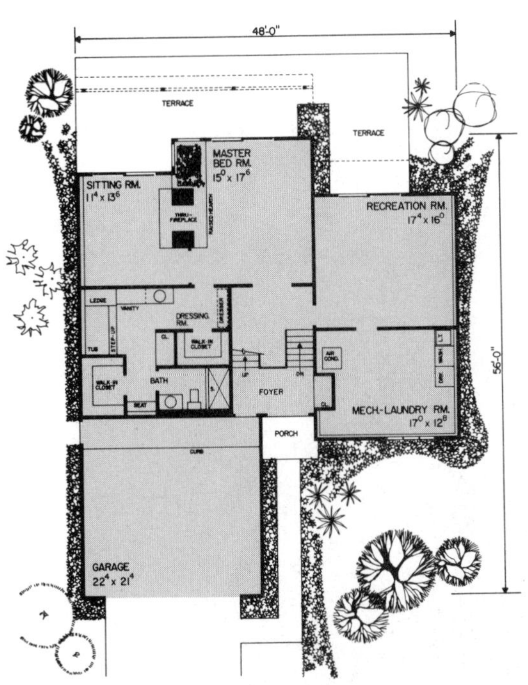

A contemporary bi-level with a large studio on a third level. The design also provides great indoor/outdoor living relationships with terraces and decks. The formal living/dining area has a sloped ceiling and built-in wet bar. The dramatic beauty of a raised-hearth fireplace and built-in planter will be enjoyed in the living room. Both have sliding glass doors to the rear deck. The breakfast area has ample space for a table plus a built-in snack bar. The lower level houses the recreation room, laundry and an outstanding master suite, including through-fireplace, sitting room, tub, shower and more.

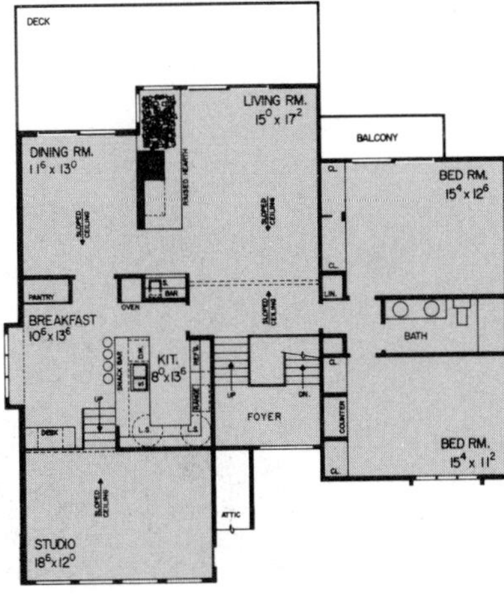

Design P2823

First Floor: 1,370 square feet
Second Floor: 927 square feet
Total: 2,297 square feet

L **D**

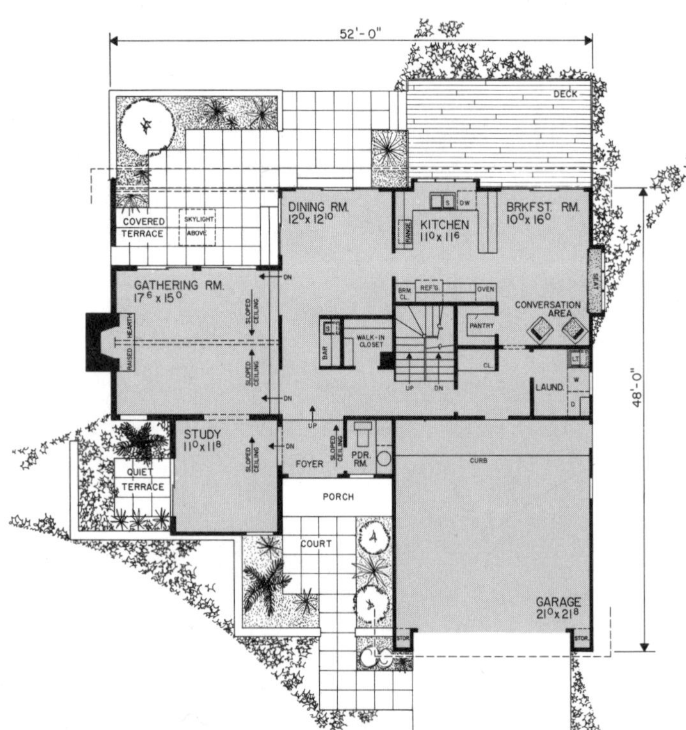

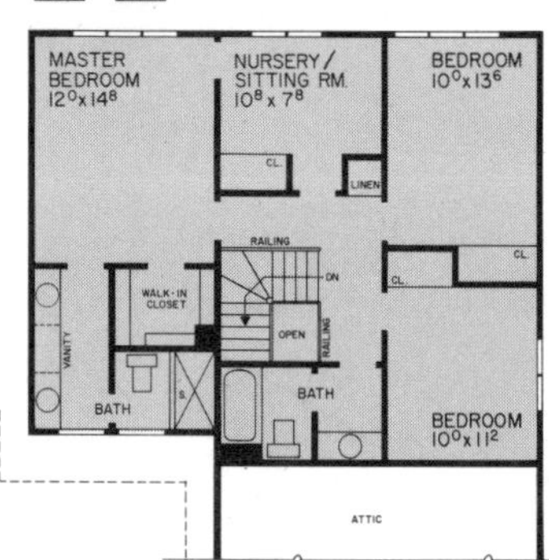

● The street view of this contemporary design features a small courtyard entrance as well as a private terrace off the study. Inside the livability will be outstanding. This design features spacious first-floor activity areas that flow smoothly into each other. In the gathering room a raised-hearth fireplace creates a dramatic focal point. An adjacent covered terrace, featuring a skylight, is ideal for outdoor dining and could be screened in later for an additional room.

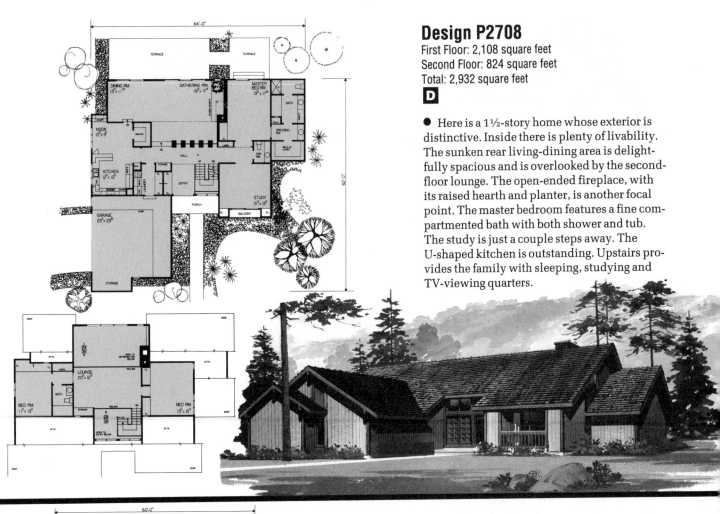

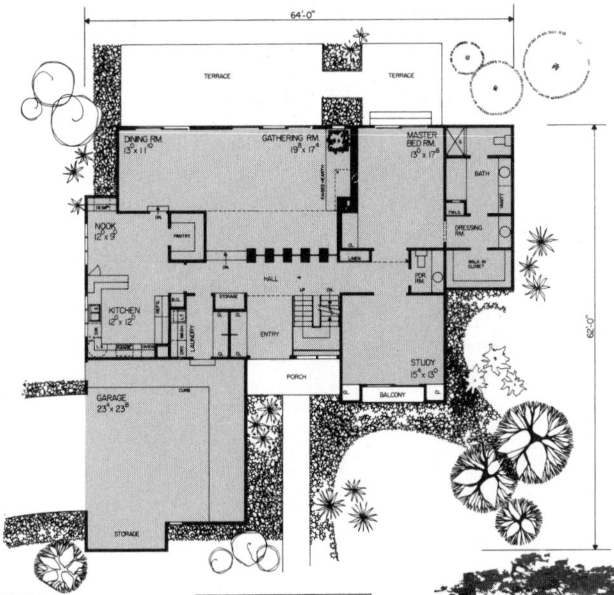

Design P2708

First Floor: 2,108 square feet
Second Floor: 824 square feet
Total: 2,932 square feet

D

● Here is a 1½-story home whose exterior is distinctive. Inside there is plenty of livability. The sunken rear living-dining area is delightfully spacious and is overlooked by the second-floor lounge. The open-ended fireplace, with its raised hearth and planter, is another focal point. The master bedroom features a fine compartmented bath with both shower and tub. The study is just a couple steps away. The U-shaped kitchen is outstanding. Upstairs provides the family with sleeping, studying and TV-viewing quarters.

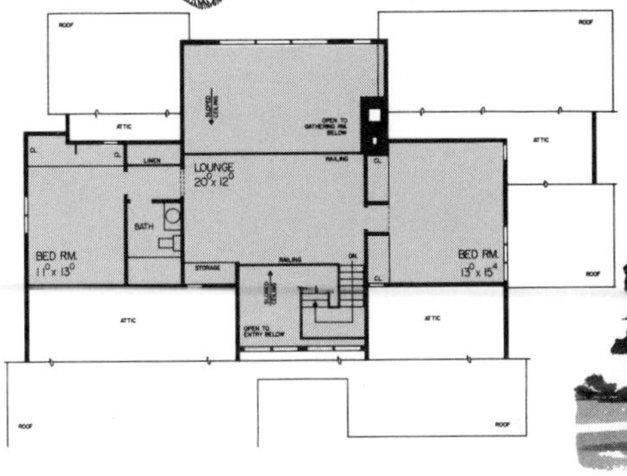

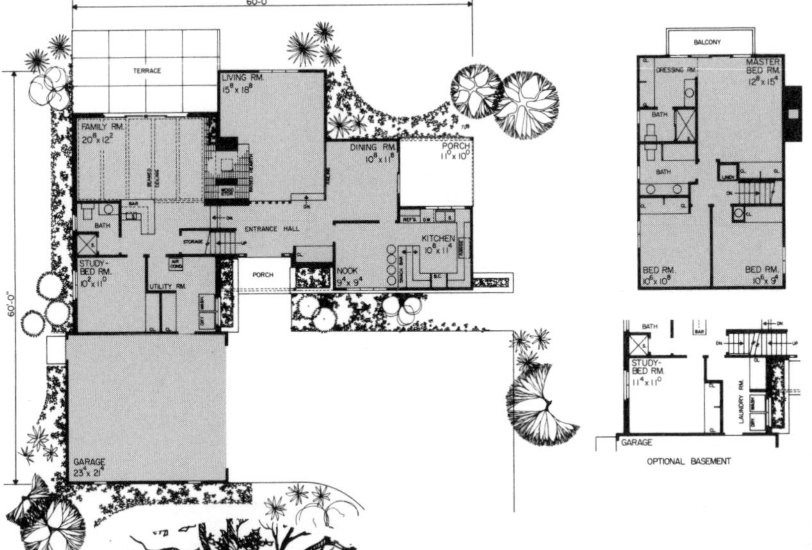

Design P2379

First Floor: 1,525 square feet
Second Floor: 748 square feet
Total: 2,273 square feet

L **D**

● This is one house that has it all. The living room and family room levels are sunken and share a dramatic through-fireplace. A beamed ceiling highlights the family room. Nearby is a full bath and a study which could be utilized as a fourth bedroom. The functional kitchen has a pass-through to the snack bar in the breakfast nook. The adjacent dining room overlooks the living room. Upstairs are three bedrooms, two baths and an outdoor balcony. Blueprints for this designs include optional basement details.

Design P2827

Upper Level: 1,618 square feet
Lower Level: 1,458 square feet
Total: 3,076 square feet

L

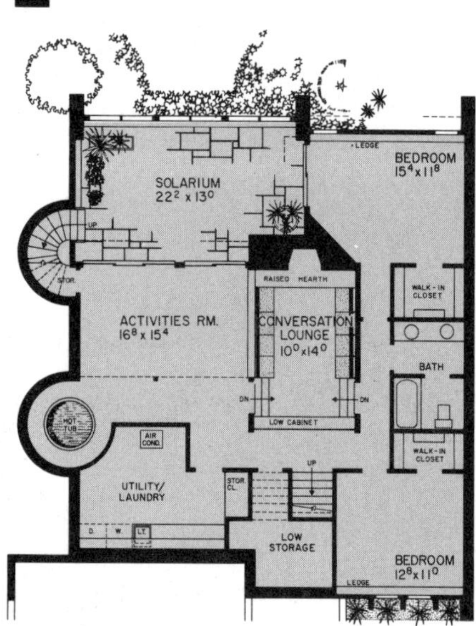

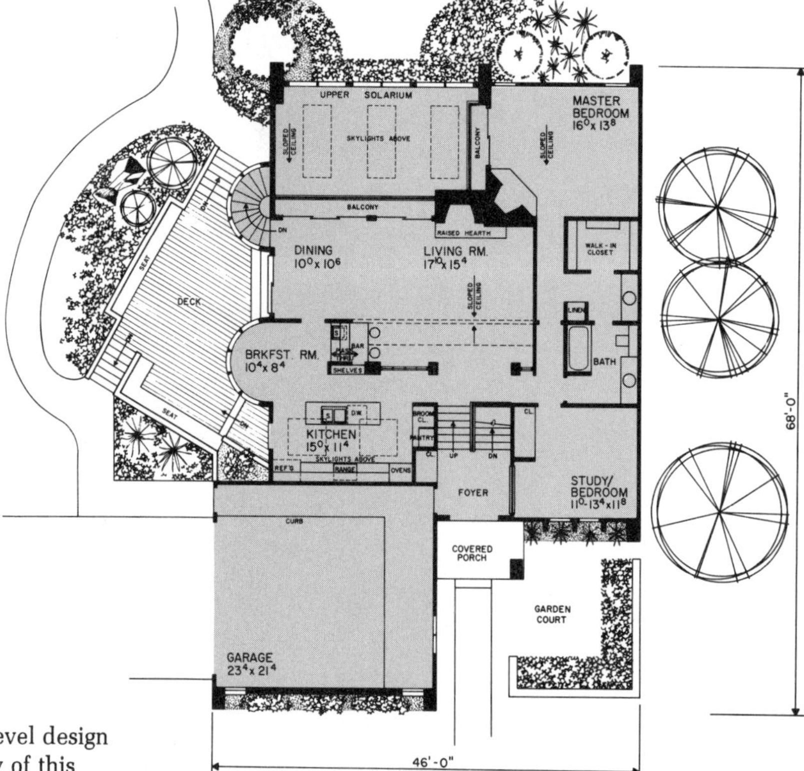

● The towering, two-story solarium in this bi-level design is its key to energy savings. Study the efficiency of this floor plan. The conversation lounge on the lower level is a unique focal point.

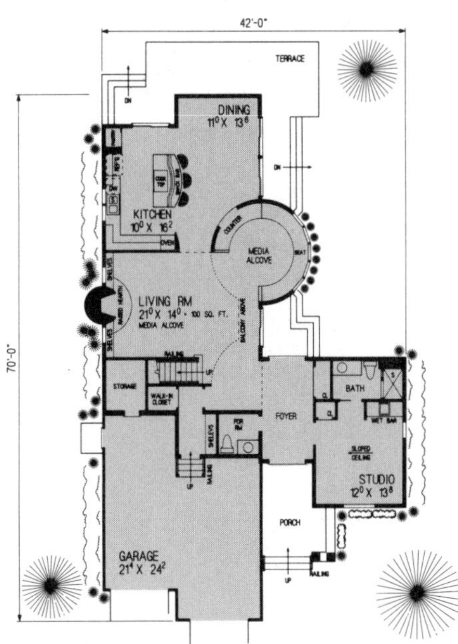

Design P3410

First Floor: 2,061 square feet
Second Floor: 997 square feet
Total: 3,058 square feet

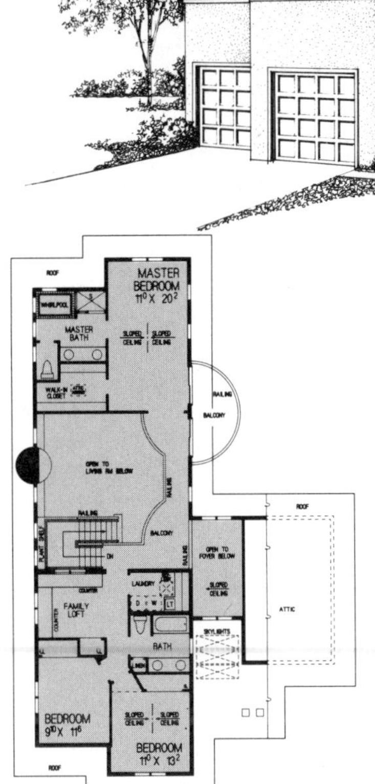

● Designed for a narrow lot, this home features a surprising amount of space. An obvious highlight on the first floor is the sophisticated circular media alcove. The living room features a raised-hearth fireplace with shelves on either side. The large kitchen with central cook top and a snack bar is adjacent to the dining room with sliding glass doors to a terrace. Also on the first floor is a studio with a wet bar and full bath, a perfect place for overnight guests. Upstairs, the master suite and curved balcony are separated from the other two family bedrooms.

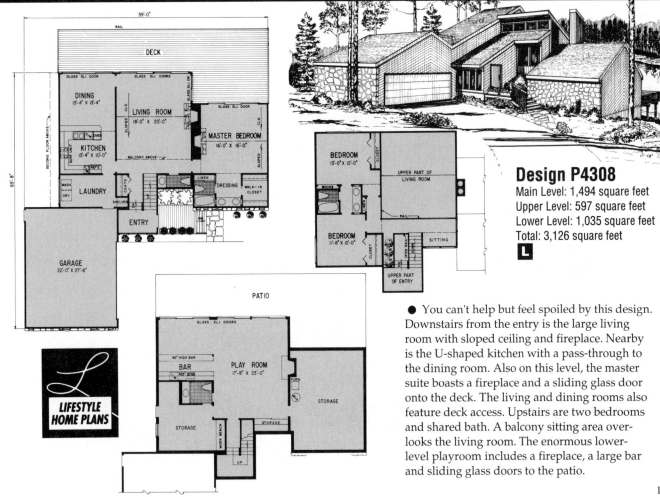

Design P4308

Main Level: 1,494 square feet
Upper Level: 597 square feet
Lower Level: 1,035 square feet
Total: 3,126 square feet
L

● You can't help but feel spoiled by this design. Downstairs from the entry is the large living room with sloped ceiling and fireplace. Nearby is the U-shaped kitchen with a pass-through to the dining room. Also on this level, the master suite boasts a fireplace and a sliding glass door onto the deck. The living and dining rooms also feature deck access. Upstairs are two bedrooms and shared bath. A balcony sitting area overlooks the living room. The enormous lower-level playroom includes a fireplace, a large bar and sliding glass doors to the patio.

Design P2835

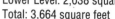

Main Level: 1,626 square feet
Lower Level: 2,038 square feet
Total: 3,664 square feet

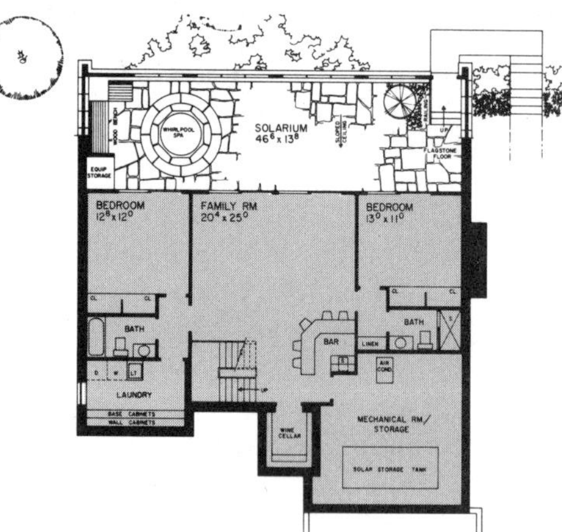

● Passive solar techniques and an active solar component heat and cool this striking contemporary design. The lower level solarium admits sunlight during the day. The earth berms on the three sides of the lower level help keep out the winter cold and summer heat. The active system uses collector panels to gather the sun's heat, which is circulated throughout the house by a heat exchanger. Note that where active solar collectors are a design OPTION, they must be contracted locally.

Design P2834

First Floor: 1,775 square feet
Second Floor: 1,041 square feet
Lower Level: 1,128 square feet
Total: 3,944 square feet

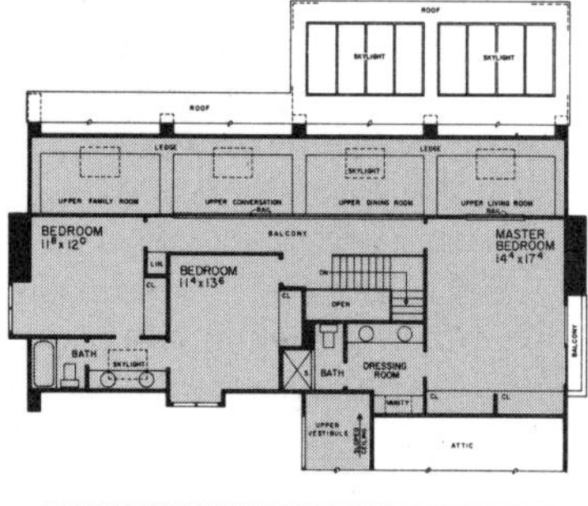

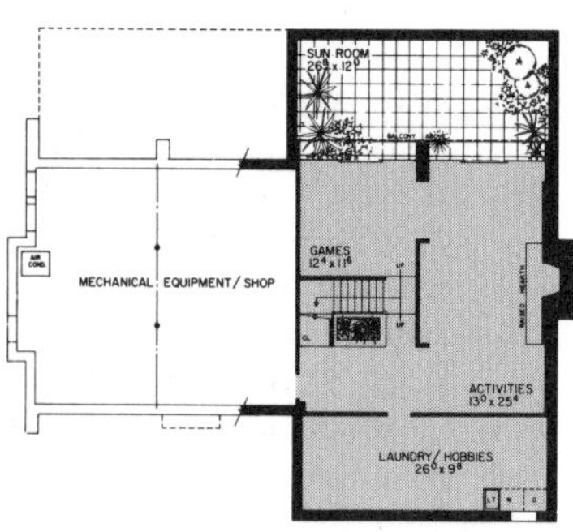

● This passive solar design offers 3,900 square feet of livability situated on three levels. The primary passive element will be the lower level sun room which admits sunlight for direct-gain heating. The solar warmth collected in the sun room will radiate into the rest of the house. During the warm summer months, shades are put over the skylight. Solar heating panels may be installed on the south-facing portion of the roof. An attic fan exhausts any hot air out of the house in the summer and circulates air in the winter.

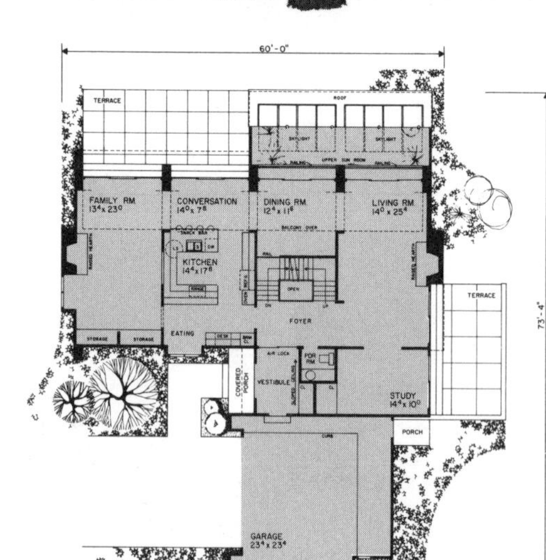

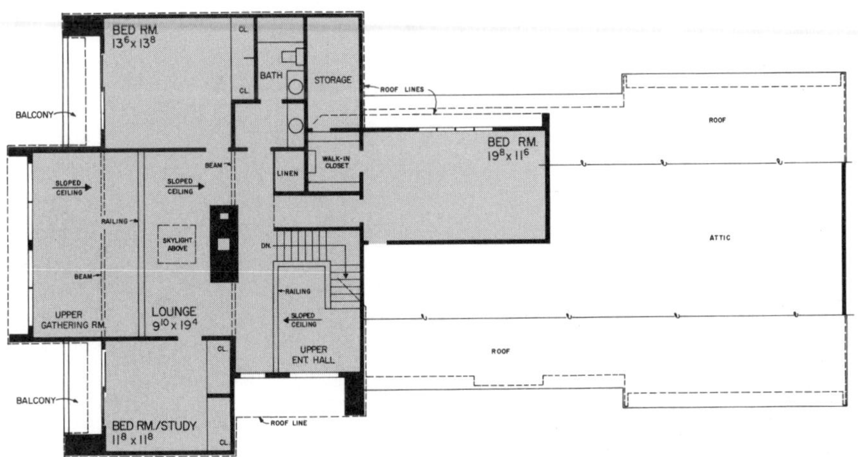

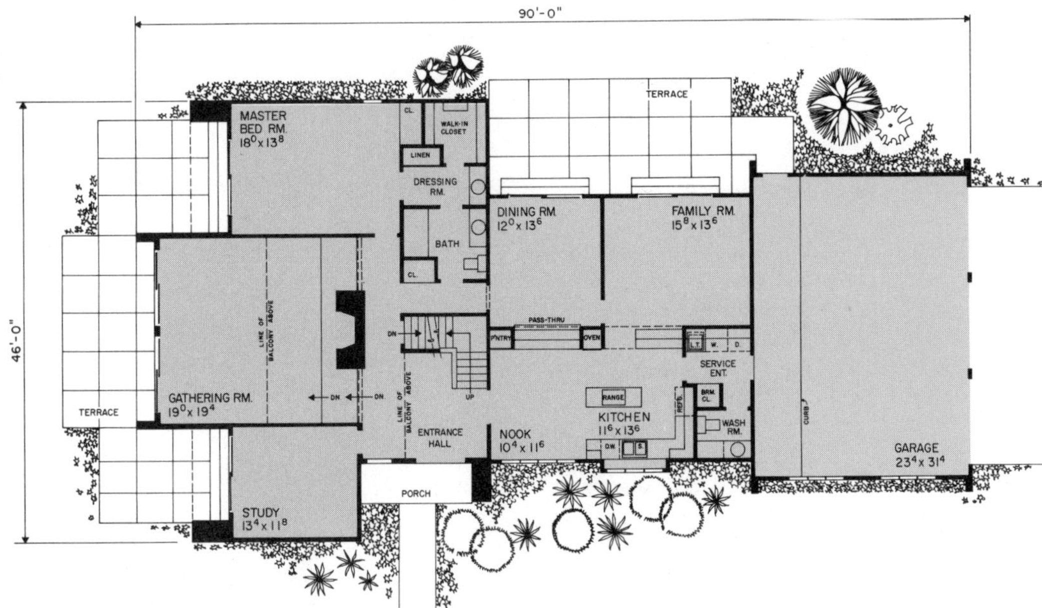

Design P2781

First Floor: 2,132 square feet
Second Floor: 1,156 square feet
Total: 3,288 square feet

● This beautifully designed two-story could be considered a dream house of a lifetime. The exterior is sure to catch the eye of anyone who takes sight of its unique construction. The front kitchen features an island range, adjacent breakfast nook and pass-thru to formal dining room. The master bedroom suite with its privacy and convenience on the first floor has a spacious walk-in closet and dressing room. The side terrace is accessible through sliding glass doors from the master bedroom, gathering room and study. The second floor has three bedrooms and storage space galore. Also notice the lounge which has a sloped ceiling and a skylight above. This delightful area looks down into the gathering room. The outdoor balconies overlook the wrap-around terrace. Surely an outstanding trend house for decades to come.

Design P2879 Living Area Including Atrium: 3,173 square feet
Upper Lounge/Balcony: 267 square feet
Total: 3,440 square feet

● This plush modern design seems to have it all, including an upper lounge, upper family room, and upper foyer. There's also an atrium with skylight centrally located downstairs. A modern kitchen with snack bar service to a breakfast room also enjoys its own greenhouse window. A deluxe master bedroom includes its own whirlpool and bay window. Three other bedrooms also are isolated at one end of the house downstairs to allow privacy and quiet. A spacious family room in the rear enjoys its own raised-hearth fireplace and view of a rear covered terrace. A front living room with its own fireplace looks out upon a side garden court and the central atrium. There's also a formal dining room situated between the kitchen and living room, plus a three-car garage, covered porches, and sizable laundry with washroom just off the garage.

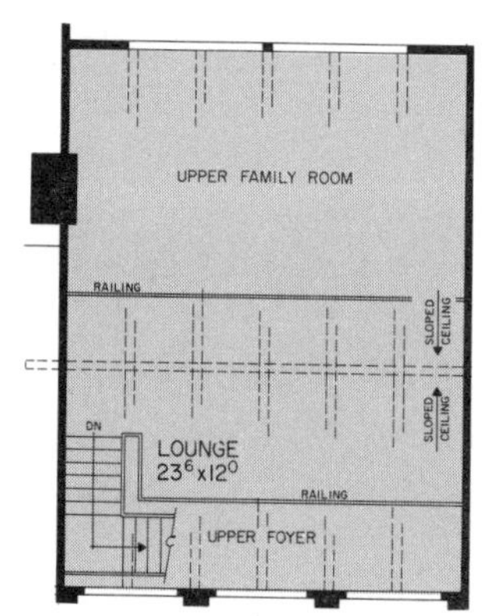

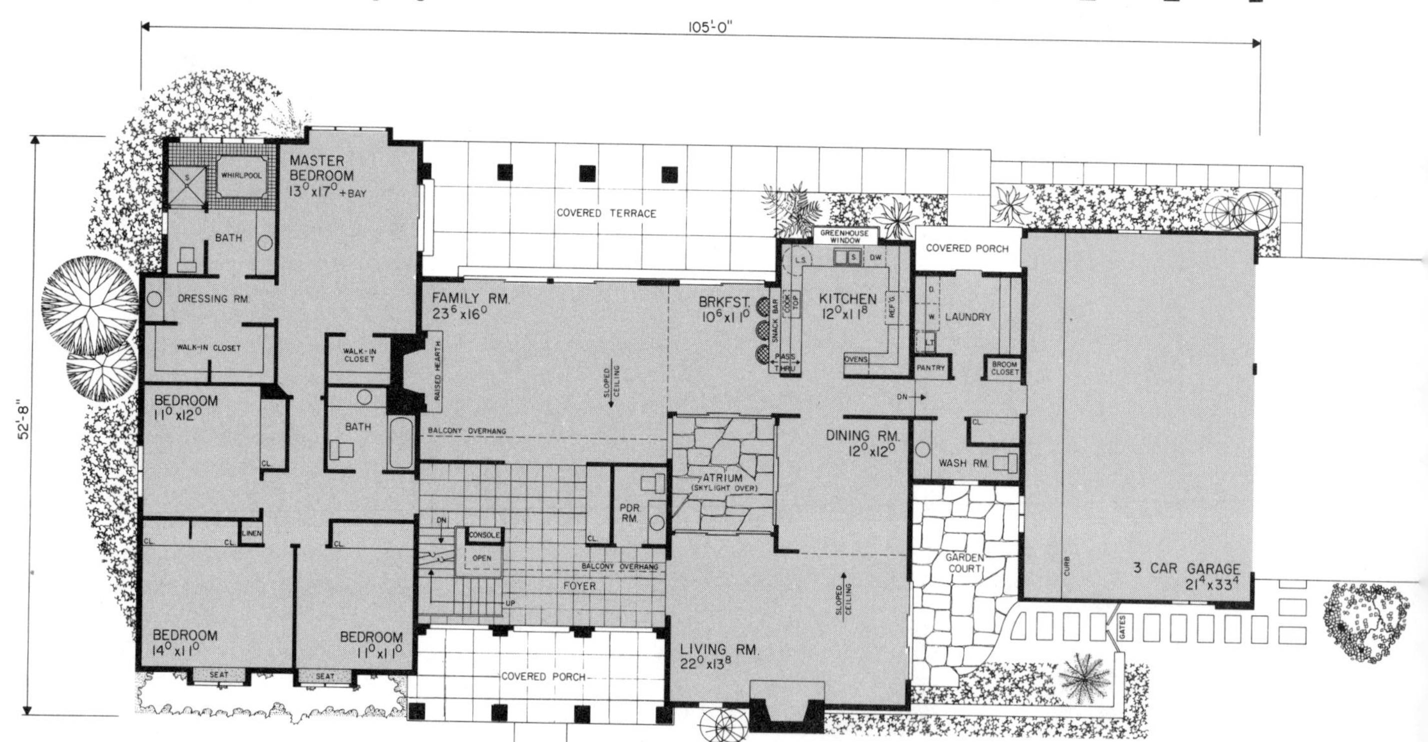

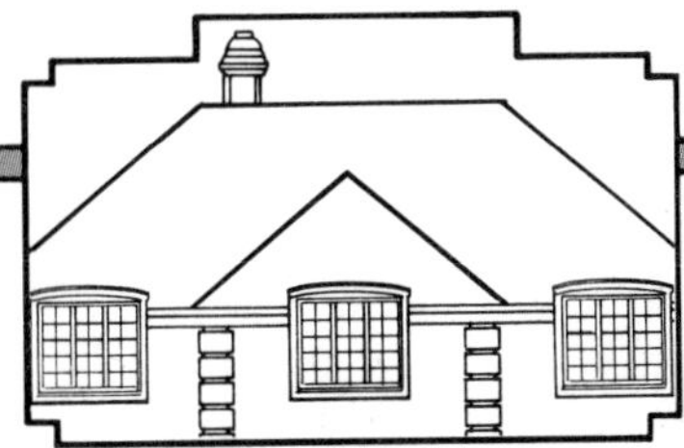

Northwest Chateau

By the late 1960s and early 1970s, housing styles began turning away from the modern elements that characterized the 1950s and early 1960s. Traditional forms and details once again began to appear, but with some new twists.

Of particular note are homes that are popular throughout the country but have predominance in Northern California and the Pacific Northwest—a style that is perhaps best identified as Northwest Chateau. The Northwest Chateau combines many of the same components as homes that are classified Neo-French or Neo-Tudor.

Neo-French homes were especially popular throughout the decade of the 1970s and copied some of the features of more classic French and Norman style. The most notable characteristics of Neo-French architecture are high hipped roof lines and dormers that break through the cornice. The tops of windows and doors are often arched or rounded and may extend up the full height of the facade. Both one- and two-story floor plans are common and their facades are usually asymmetrical.

Other dominant details include tall brick or stone chimney stacks, Palladian or circle-head windows and recessed entries with the suggestion of columns. The height of the roof line allows for floor plan features such as cathedral and sloped ceilings, volume living and sleeping areas, two-story foyers and second-floor balconies with overlooks.

Common exterior cladding includes brick and stone, often with wood trim and accents. Shake and shingle roofs are the norm.

Neo-Tudors are identified by imposing, steeply pitched front gables and decorative half-timbering details. Long, narrow windows, often grouped in fours, grace the facade. Diamond-panes are a classically derived detail sometimes seen. One-story ranches are probably the most common type of Neo-Tudor built, but 1½- and two-story adaptations have gained more popularity in recent years.

Additional features that adorn Neo-Tudors include bay and boxed windows, tall brick chimney stacks, recessed entries and, like traditional Tudors, mixtures of exterior building materials.

Northwest Chateaus have elements of both these extremely popular Neo-Eclectic styles and sprinkle in details borrowed from others — most notably Neo-Mediterranean style and Neoclassical Revival style. Pedimented front entries, small second-floor balconies and porch roofs supported by masonry columns are all beautiful details borrowed from a variety of styles.

Because the Northwest Chateau is a recent architectural development, it encompasses all the best in modern floor planning. Common are open living areas, grand master suites, excellent indoor/outdoor livability and appealing shapes and angles. This eclectic style may be the most complete combination of modern and classical elements yet devised.

Design P3450

First Floor: 1,801 square feet
Second Floor: 1,086 square feet
Total: 2,887 square feet

● A striking facade includes a covered front porch with four columns. To the left of the foyer is a large gathering room with a fireplace and bay window. The adjoining dining room leads to a covered side porch. The kitchen includes a snack bar, pantry, desk, and eating area. The first-floor master suite provides a spacious bath with walk-in closet, whirlpool and shower. Also on the first floor: a study and a garage workshop. Two bedrooms and a lavish guest suite share the second floor.

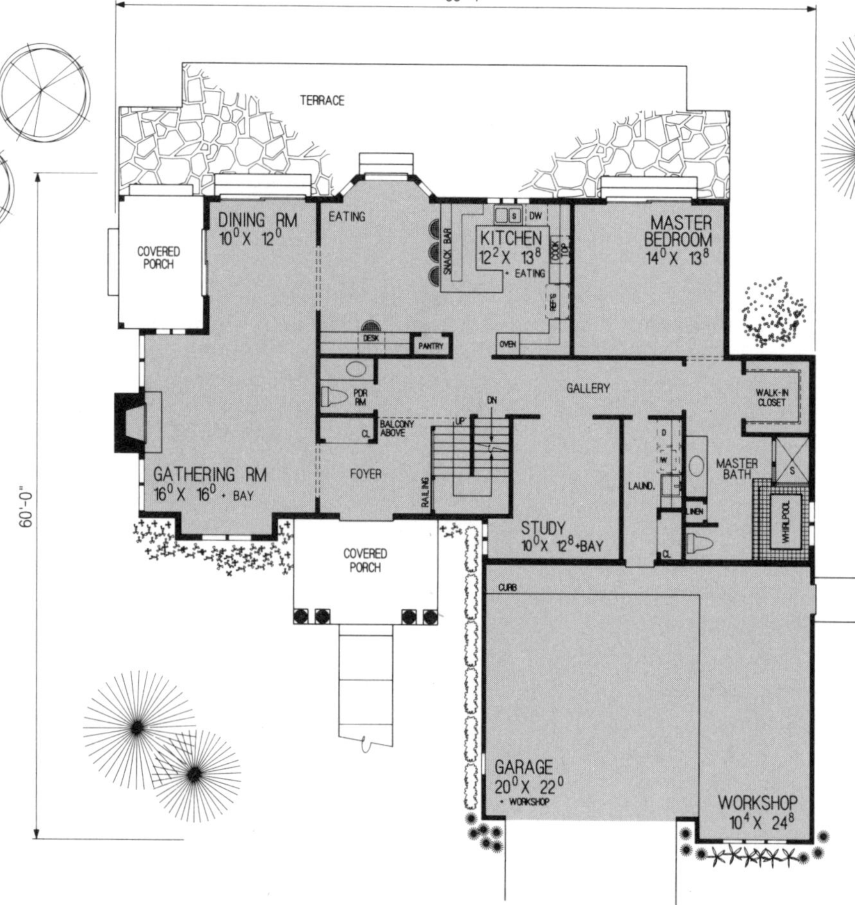

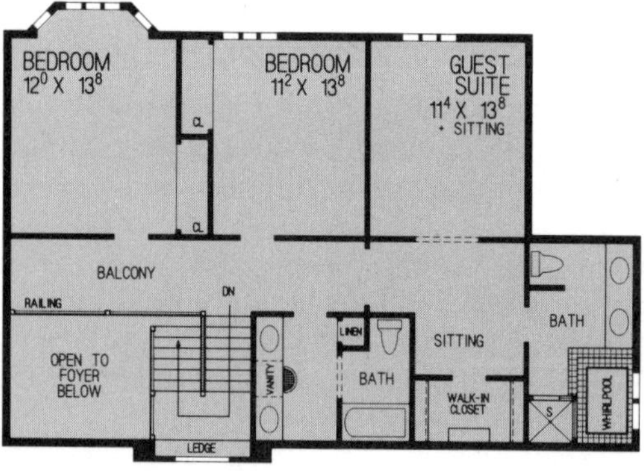

Custom Alterations? See page 203 for customizing this plan to your specifications.

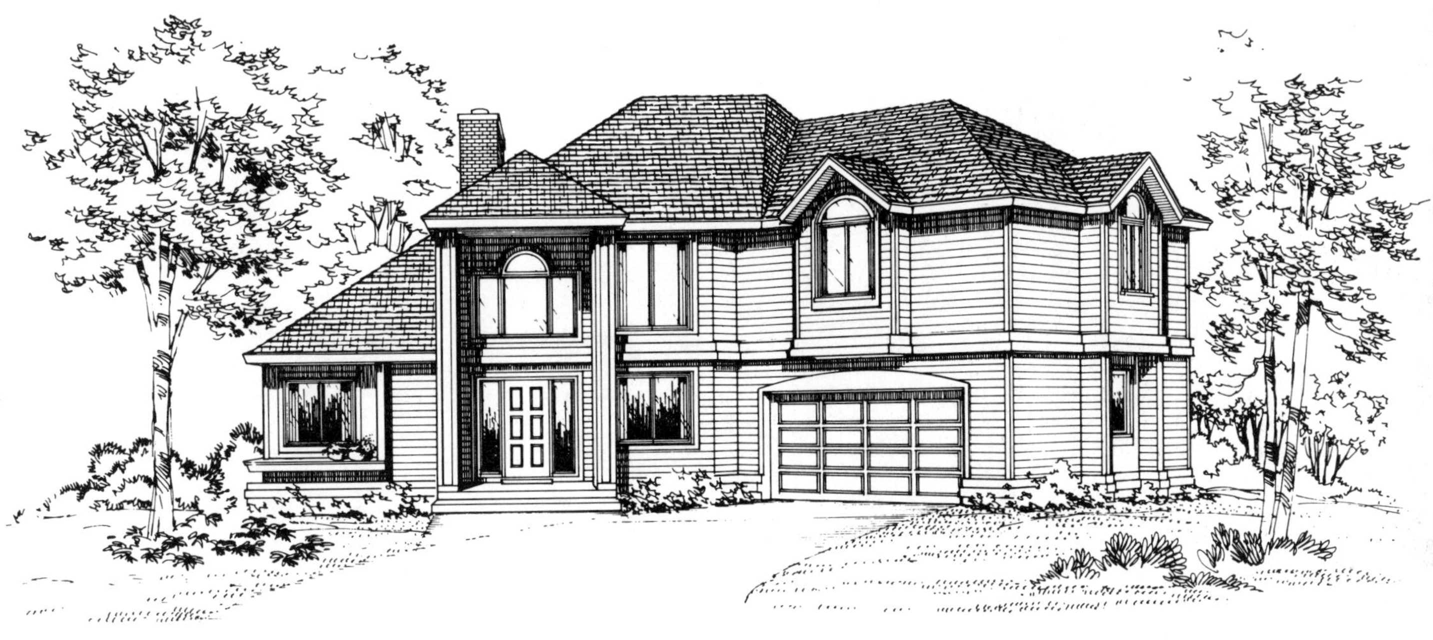

Design P3439

First Floor: 1,443 square feet
Second Floor: 937 square feet
Total: 2,380 square feet

● Featuring a facade of wood and window glass, this home presents a striking first impression. It's floor plan is equally as splendid. Formal living and dining areas flank the entry foyer—both are sunken a step down. Also sunken from the foyer is the family room with attached breakfast nook. A fireplace in this area sits adjacent to a built-in audiovisual center. A nearby study with adjacent full bath doubles as a guest room. Upstairs are three bedrooms including a master suite with whirlpool spa and walk-in closet. Plant shelves adorn the entire floor plan.

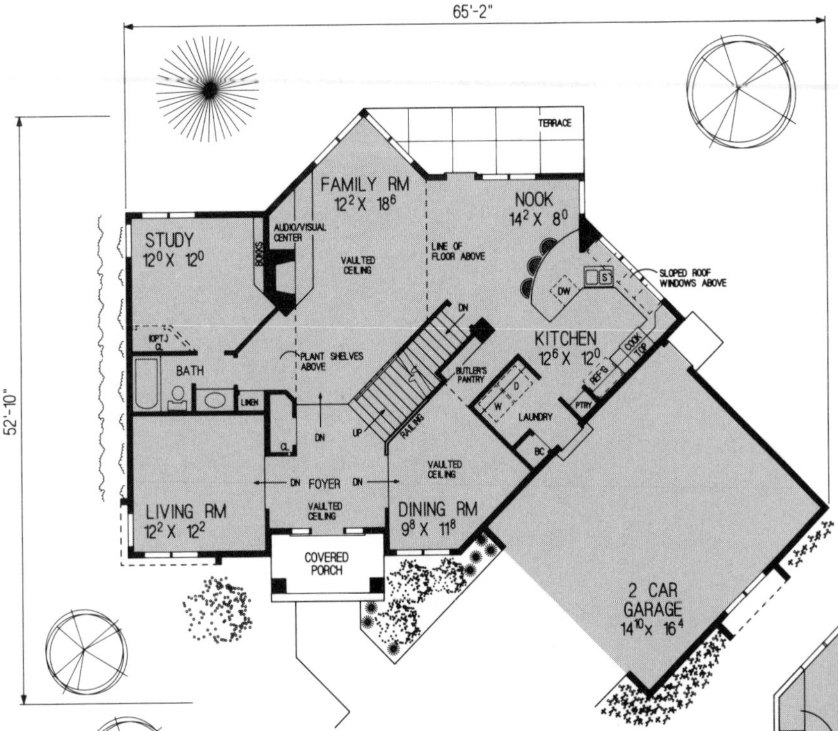

65'-2"
52'-10"
TERRACE
FAMILY RM
12^2 X 18^6
NOOK
14^2 X 8^0
STUDY
12^0 X 12^0
AUDIO/VISUAL CENTER
BOOKS
VAULTED CEILING
LINE OF FLOOR ABOVE
SLOPED ROOF WINDOWS ABOVE
DW
KITCHEN
12^6 X 12^0
COOK TOP
REF'G
BUTLER'S PANTRY
LAUNDRY
PTRY
BC
PLANT SHELVES ABOVE
BATH
LINEN
CL
UP
DN
RAILING
VAULTED CEILING
FOYER
LIVING RM
12^2 X 12^2
DINING RM
9^8 X 11^8
COVERED PORCH
2 CAR GARAGE
14^{10} X 16^4

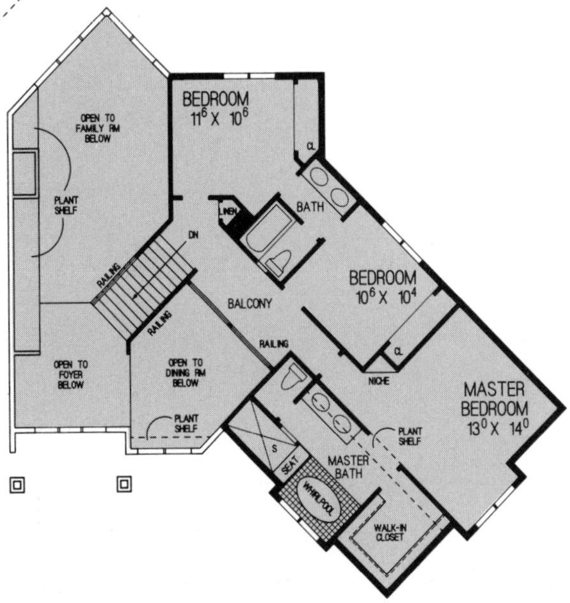

OPEN TO FAMILY RM BELOW
PLANT SHELF
BEDROOM
11^6 X 10^6
CL
BATH
LINEN
DN
BEDROOM
10^6 X 10^4
RAILING
BALCONY
RAILING
CL
NICHE
OPEN TO FOYER BELOW
OPEN TO DINING RM BELOW
PLANT SHELF
MASTER BEDROOM
13^0 X 14^0
PLANT SHELF
MASTER BATH
SEAT
WHIRLPOOL
WALK-IN CLOSET

CUSTOMIZABLE

Custom Alterations? See page 203 for customizing this plan to your specifications.

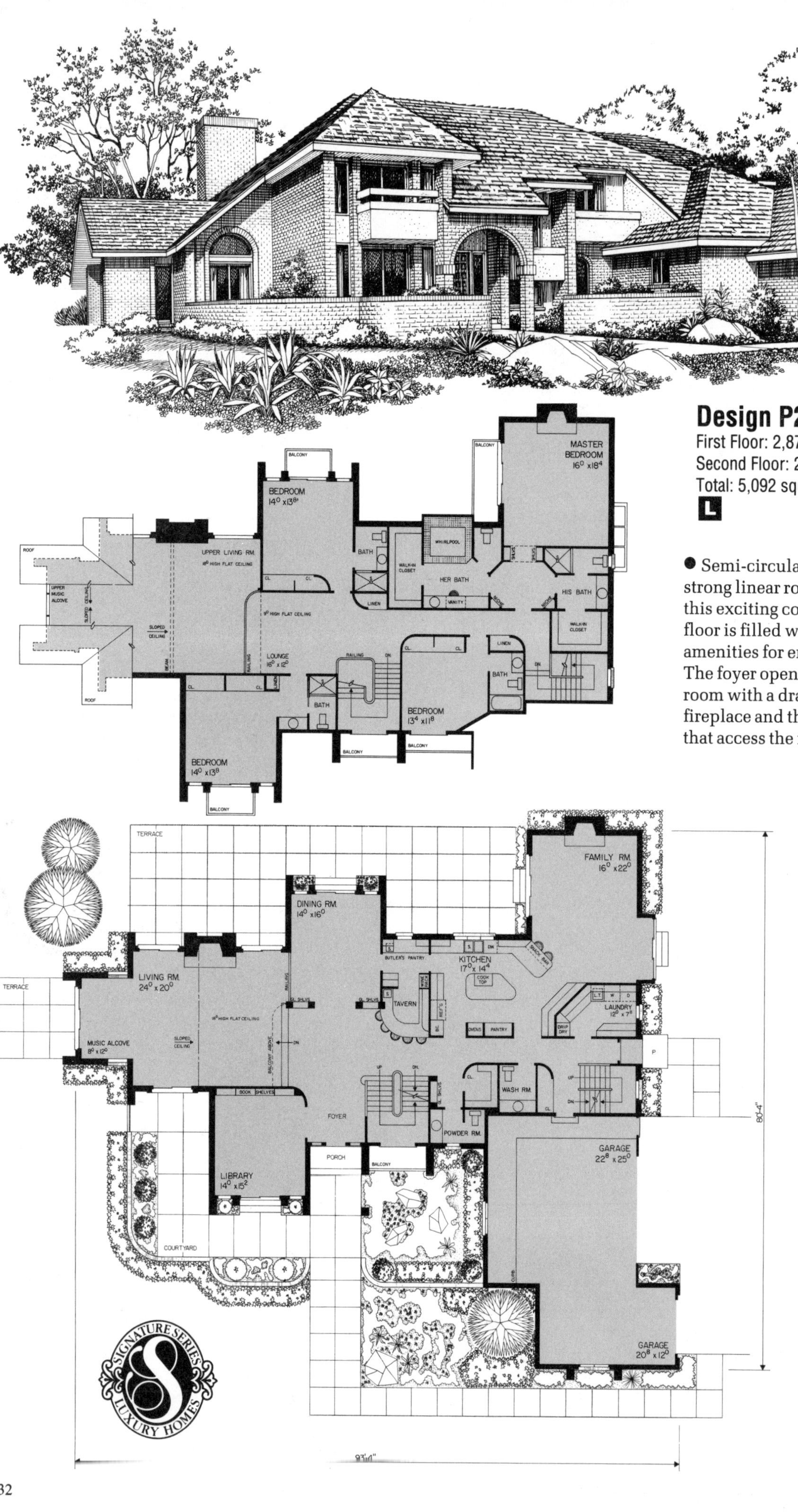

Design P2952

First Floor: 2,870 square feet
Second Floor: 2,222 square feet
Total: 5,092 square feet
L

● Semi-circular arches complement the strong linear roof lines and balconies of this exciting contemporary. The first floor is filled with well-planned amenities for entertaining and relaxing. The foyer opens to a step-down living room with a dramatic sloped ceiling, fireplace and three sliding glass doors that access the front courtyard and terrace. A tavern with built-in wine rack and an adjacent butler's pantry are ideal for entertaining. The family room features a fireplace, sliding glass door, and a handy snack bar. The kitchen allows meal preparation, cooking and storage within a step of the central work island. Three second-floor bedrooms, each with a private bath and balcony, are reached by either of two staircases. The master suite, with His and Hers baths and walk-in closets, whirlpool, and fireplace, adds the finishing touch to this memorable home.

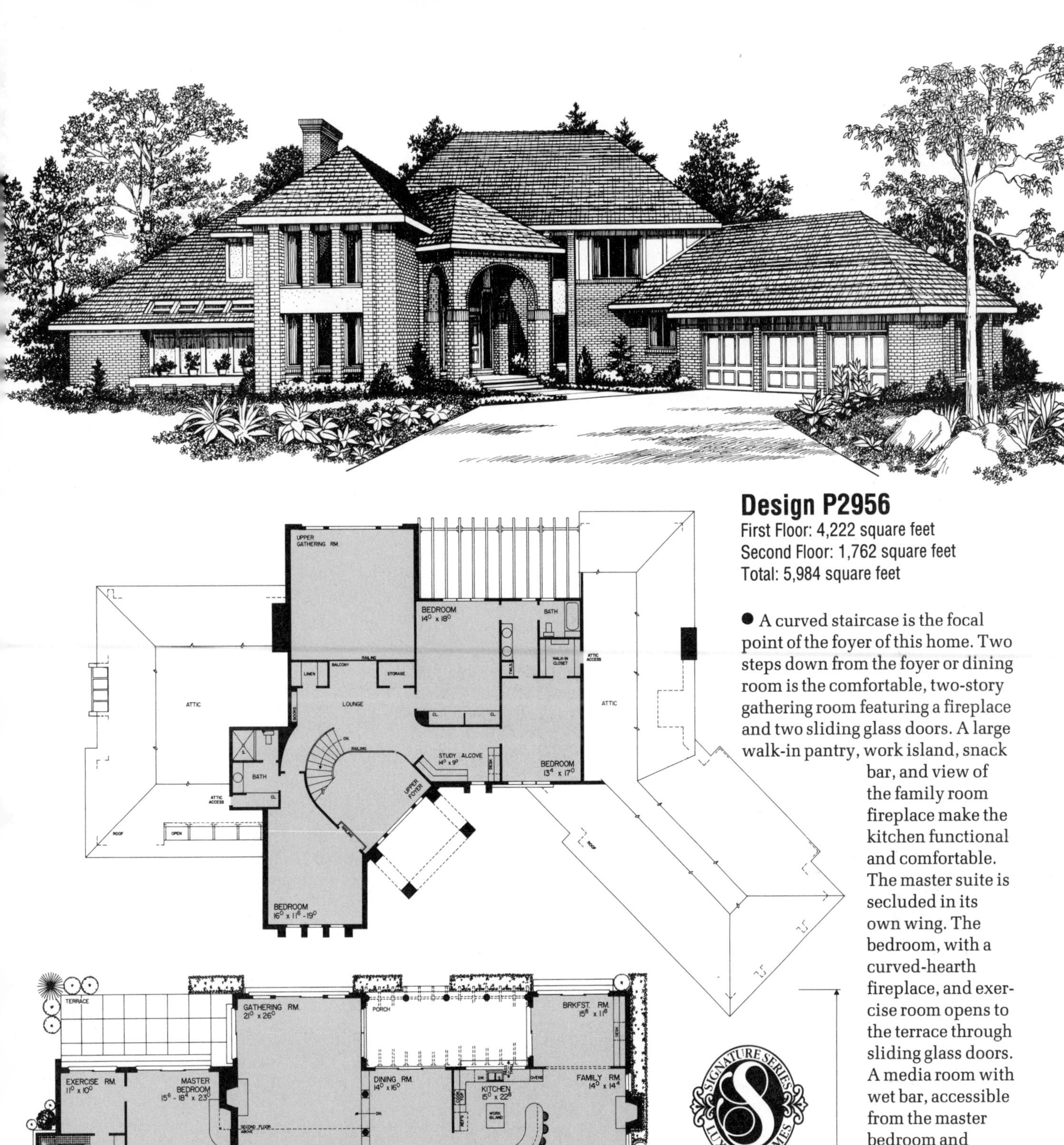

Design P2956

First Floor: 4,222 square feet
Second Floor: 1,762 square feet
Total: 5,984 square feet

● A curved staircase is the focal point of the foyer of this home. Two steps down from the foyer or dining room is the comfortable, two-story gathering room featuring a fireplace and two sliding glass doors. A large walk-in pantry, work island, snack bar, and view of the family room fireplace make the kitchen functional and comfortable. The master suite is secluded in its own wing. The bedroom, with a curved-hearth fireplace, and exercise room opens to the terrace through sliding glass doors. A media room with wet bar, accessible from the master bedroom and foyer, is the perfect place to relax. The second-floor stairs open to a lounge which overlooks the gathering room. Three additional bedrooms and a quiet study alcove on the second floor round out this gracious home.

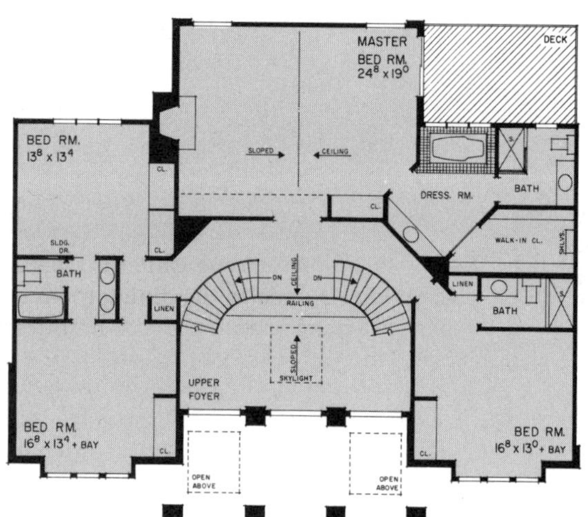

Design P3364

First Floor: 2,883 square feet
Second Floor: 1,919 square feet
Total: 4,802 square feet

● The impressive stonework facade of this contemporary home is as dramatic as it is practical — and it contains a grand floor plan. Notice the varying levels — a family room, living room, media room, and atrium are down a few steps from the elegant entry foyer. The large L-shaped kitchen is highlighted by an island work center and a pass-through snack bar. A double curved staircase leads to a second floor where four bedrooms and three full baths are found.

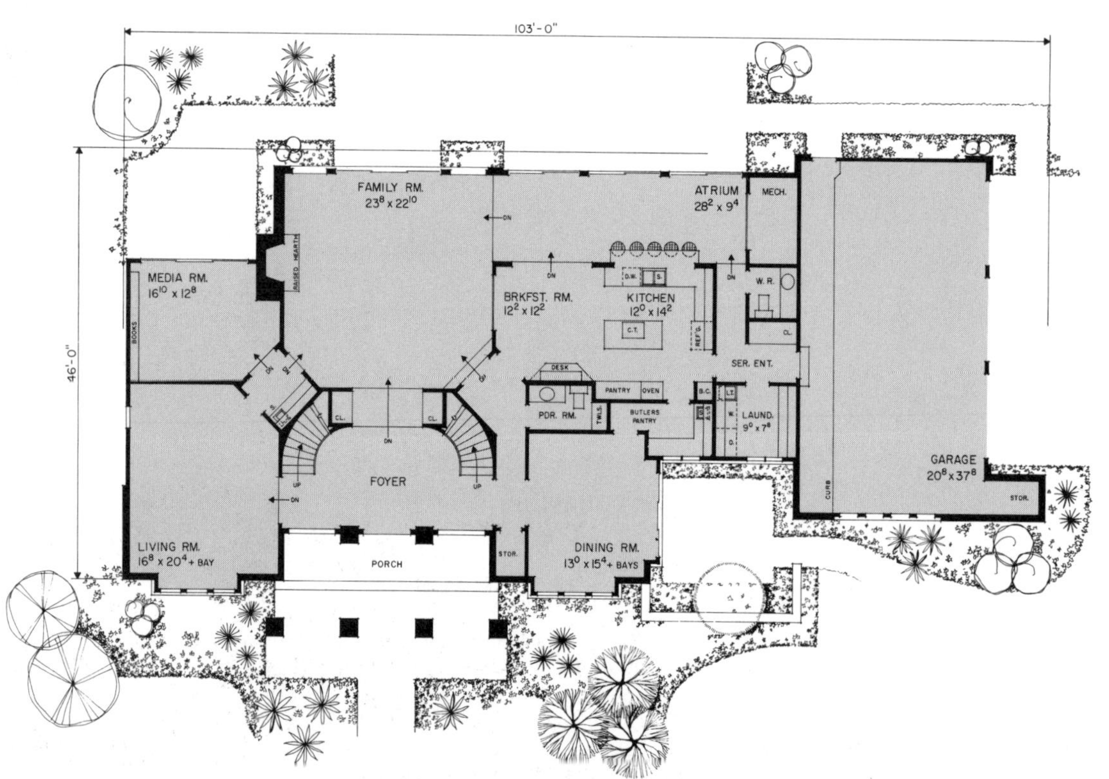

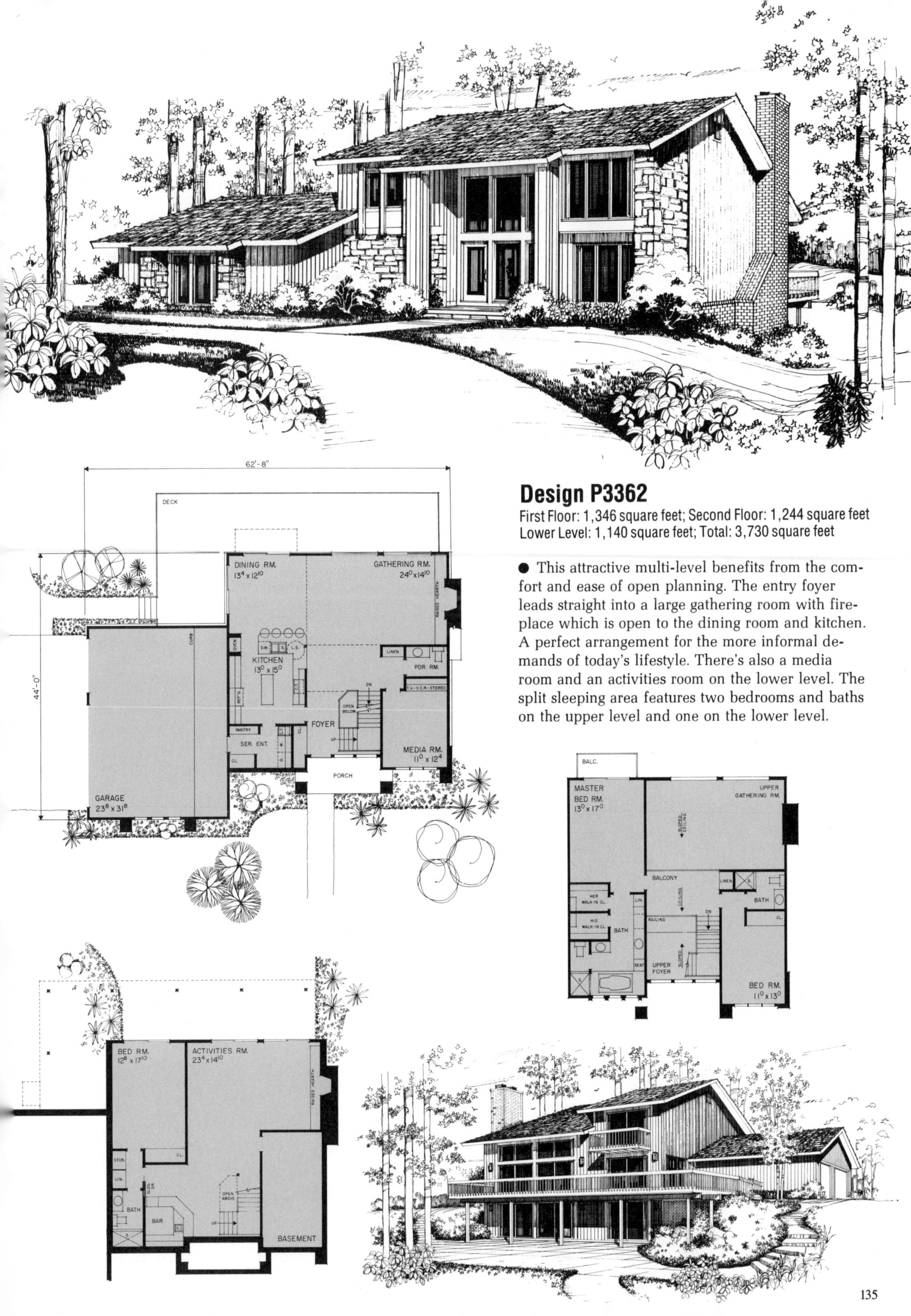

Design P3362

First Floor: 1,346 square feet; Second Floor: 1,244 square feet
Lower Level: 1,140 square feet; Total: 3,730 square feet

● This attractive multi-level benefits from the comfort and ease of open planning. The entry foyer leads straight into a large gathering room with fireplace which is open to the dining room and kitchen. A perfect arrangement for the more informal demands of today's lifestyle. There's also a media room and an activities room on the lower level. The split sleeping area features two bedrooms and baths on the upper level and one on the lower level.

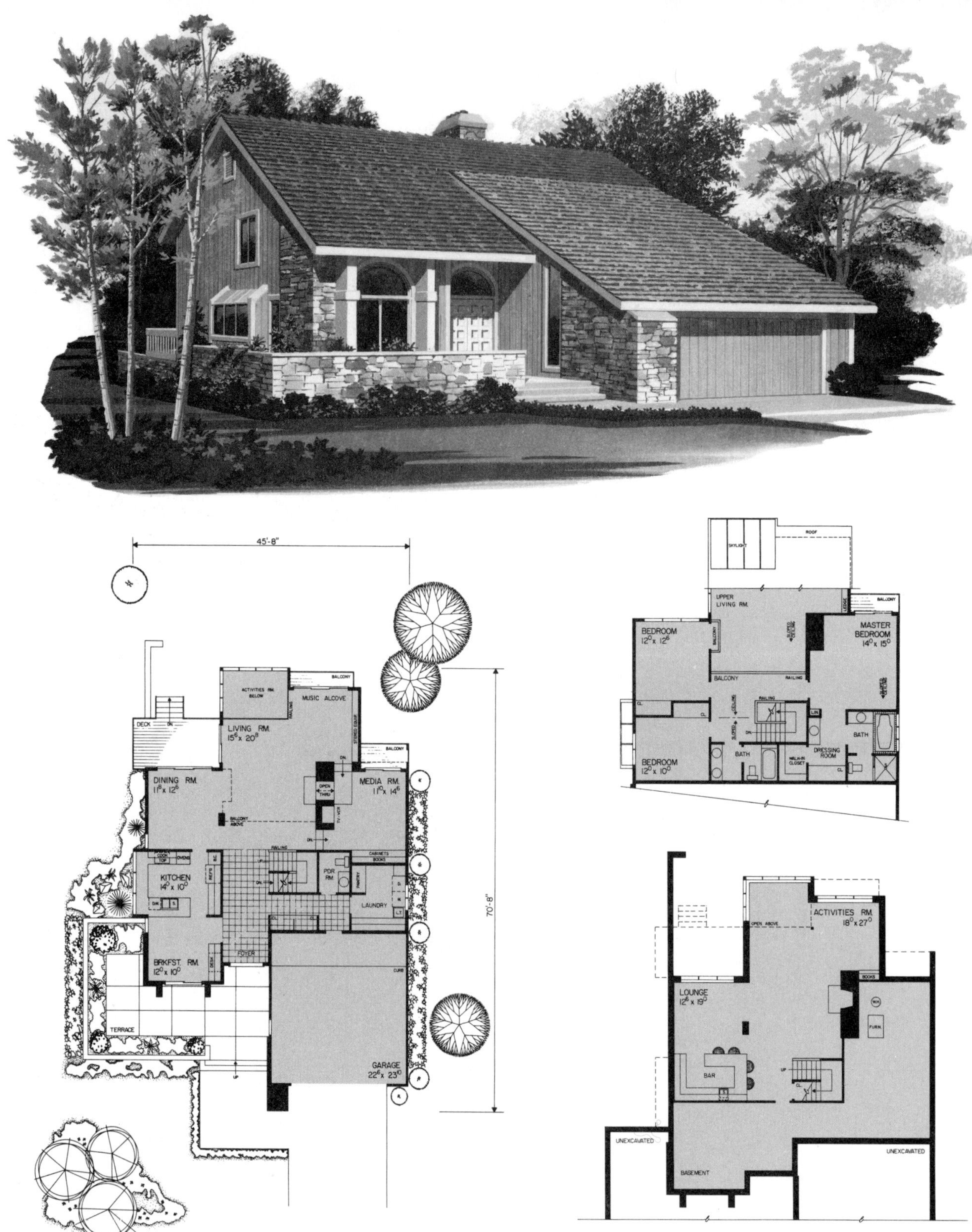

Design P2944 Main Level: 1,545 square feet; Upper Level: 977 square feet; Lower Level: 933 square feet; Total: 3,455 square feet

● This eye-catching contemporary features three stacked levels of livability. And what livability it will truly be! The main level has a fine U-shaped kitchen which is flanked by the informal breakfast room and formal dining room. The living room will be dramatic, indeed. Its sloping ceiling extends through the upper level. It overlooks the lower level activities room and has wonderfully expansive window areas for full enjoyment of surrounding vistas. A two-way fireplace can be viewed from dining, living and media rooms. A sizable deck and two cozy balconies provide for flexible outdoor living. Don't miss the music alcove with its wall for stereo equipment. Upstairs, the balcony overlooks the living room. It serves as the connecting link for the three bedrooms. The lower level offers more cheerful livability with the huge activities room plus lounge area. Note bar, fireplace.

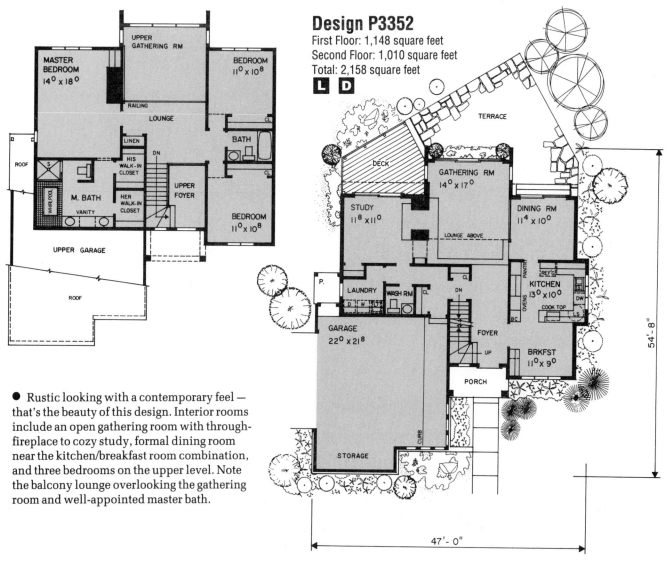

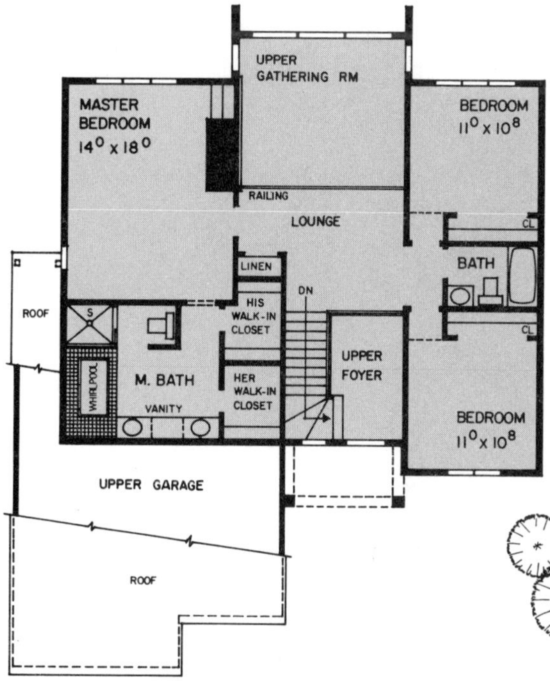

Design P3352

First Floor: 1,148 square feet
Second Floor: 1,010 square feet
Total: 2,158 square feet

L D

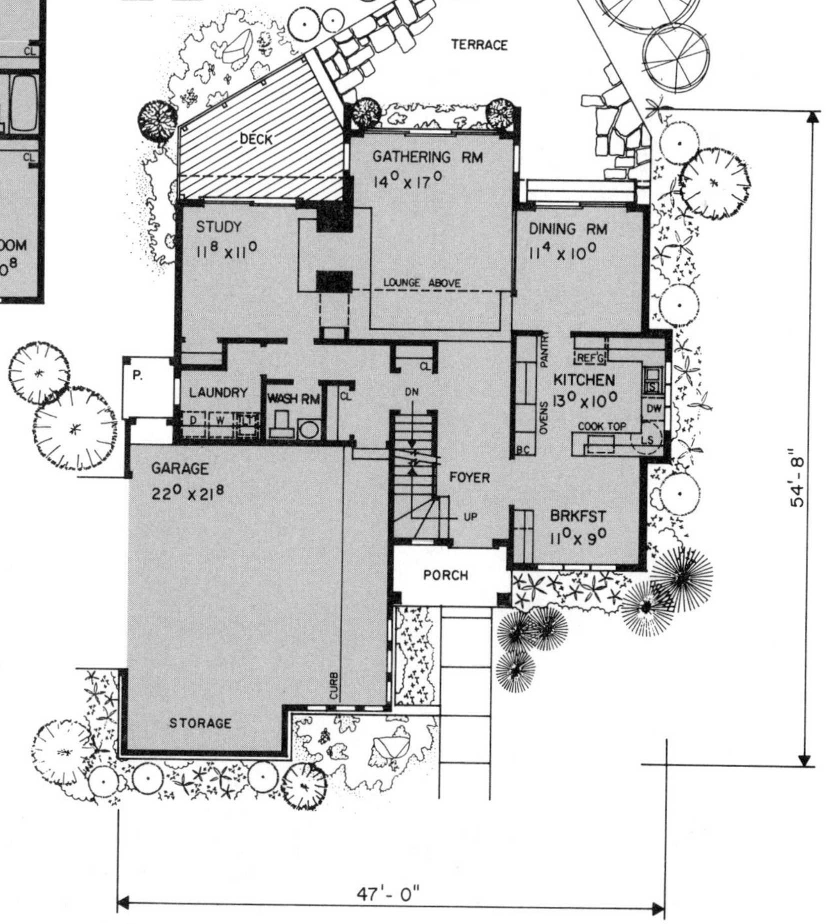

UPPER GATHERING RM
MASTER BEDROOM $14^0 \times 18^0$
BEDROOM $11^0 \times 10^8$
RAILING
LOUNGE
LINEN
BATH
CL
DN
HIS WALK-IN CLOSET
HER WALK-IN CLOSET
ROOF
S
WHIRLPOOL
M. BATH
VANITY
UPPER FOYER
BEDROOM $11^0 \times 10^8$
UPPER GARAGE
ROOF

TERRACE
DECK
GATHERING RM $14^0 \times 17^0$
STUDY $11^8 \times 11^0$
DINING RM $11^4 \times 10^0$
LOUNGE ABOVE
PANTRY
REF'G
KITCHEN $13^0 \times 10^0$
S
DW
OVENS
COOK TOP
LS
BC
P.
LAUNDRY
D W
WASH RM
CL
DN
GARAGE $22^0 \times 21^8$
FOYER
UP
BRKFST $11^0 \times 9^0$
PORCH
CURB
STORAGE
54'-8"
47'-0"

● Rustic looking with a contemporary feel — that's the beauty of this design. Interior rooms include an open gathering room with through-fireplace to cozy study, formal dining room near the kitchen/breakfast room combination, and three bedrooms on the upper level. Note the balcony lounge overlooking the gathering room and well-appointed master bath.

Design P2868

Upper Level: 1,203 square feet
Lower Level: 1,317 square feet; Total: 2,520 square feet

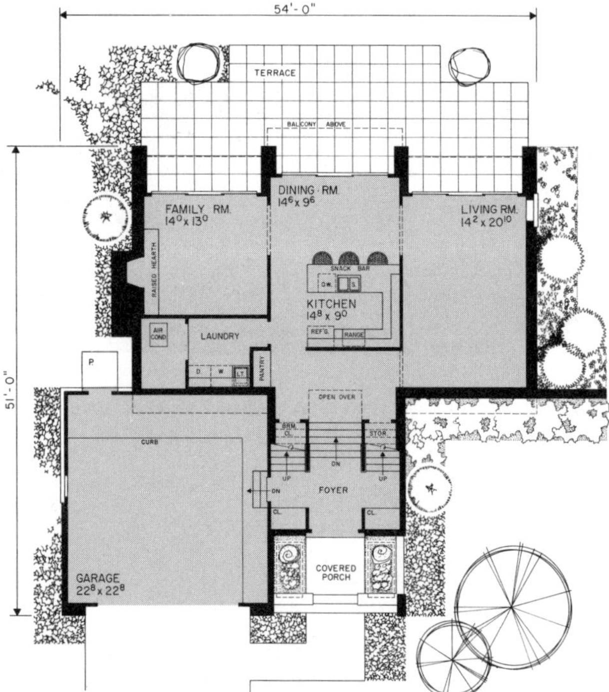

● Two couples sharing the expense of a house has got to be ideal and, of course, economical. The occupants of this house could do just that. The lower level, housing the kitchen, dining room, family and living rooms and the laundry facilities, is the common area to be shared by both couples. Centrally located, the kitchen and dining room act as a space divider to the living and family rooms so both couples can enjoy privacy.

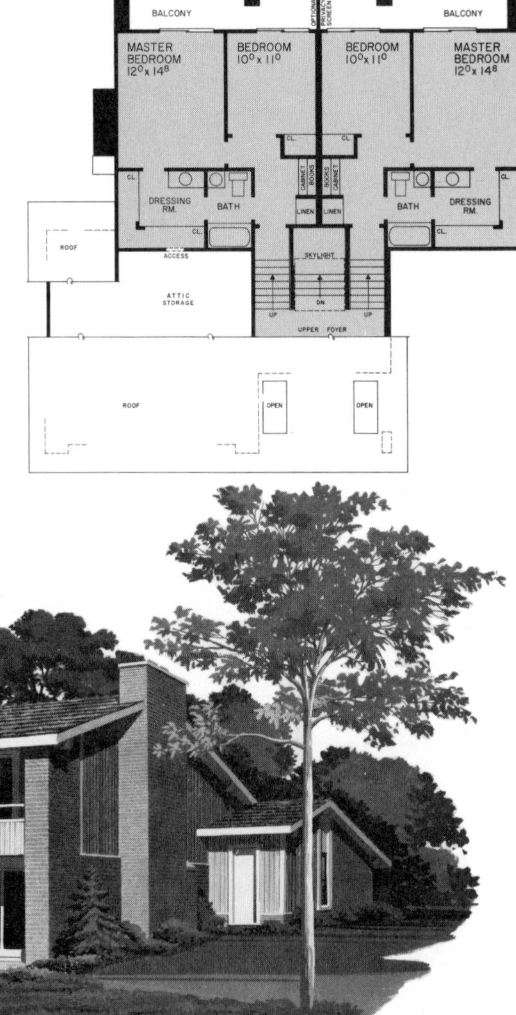

Separate stairways lead to the upper level from the skylit foyer. Each private area has two bedrooms, a dressing room and a full bath. Individual entrances can be locked for additional privacy. Sliding glass doors are in each of the rear rooms on both levels so the outdoors can be enjoyed to its fullest.

Design P2782

First Floor: 2,060 square feet
Second Floor: 897 square feet
Total: 2,957 square feet

D

● This plan includes great formal and informal living for the family or guests. The formal gathering room and informal family room share a dramatic raised-hearth fireplace. The kitchen has a snack bar, many built-ins, a pass-through to dining room and easy access to the large laundry/wash room. The master bedroom suite is located on the main level for added privacy. There's even a study with a built-in bar. The upper level has three more bedrooms, a bath and a lounge looking down into the gathering room.

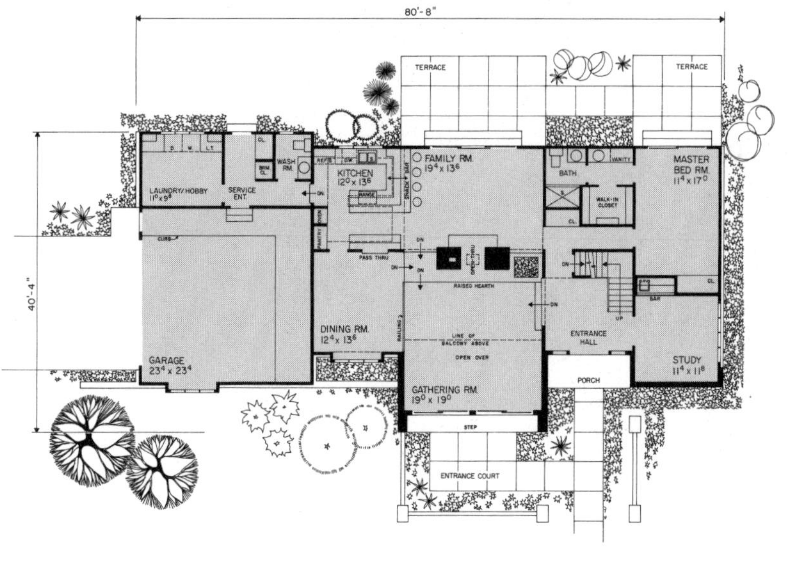

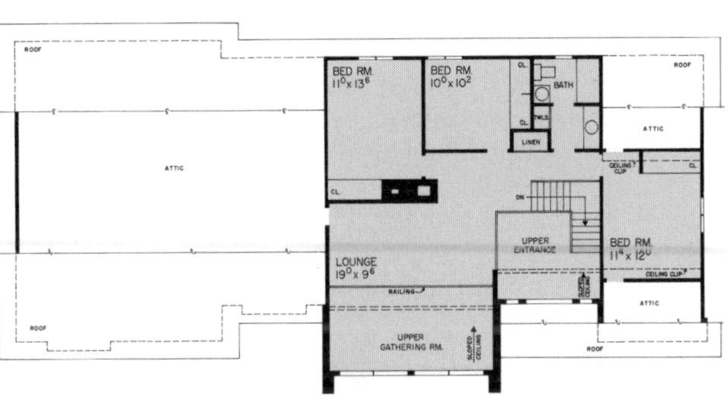

Design P2562

First Floor: 2,884 square feet
Second Floor: 864 square feet
Total: 3,748 square feet

D

● Here is an exciting contemporary design for the large, active family. It can function as either a four- or five-bedroom home. As a four-bedroom home the parents will enjoy a wonderful suite with study and exceptional bath facilities. Note stall shower, plus sunken tub. The upstairs features the children's bedrooms and a spacious balcony lounge which looks down to the floor below. The sunken gathering room has a sloped, beamed ceiling, dramatic raised-hearth fireplace and direct access to the rear terrace.

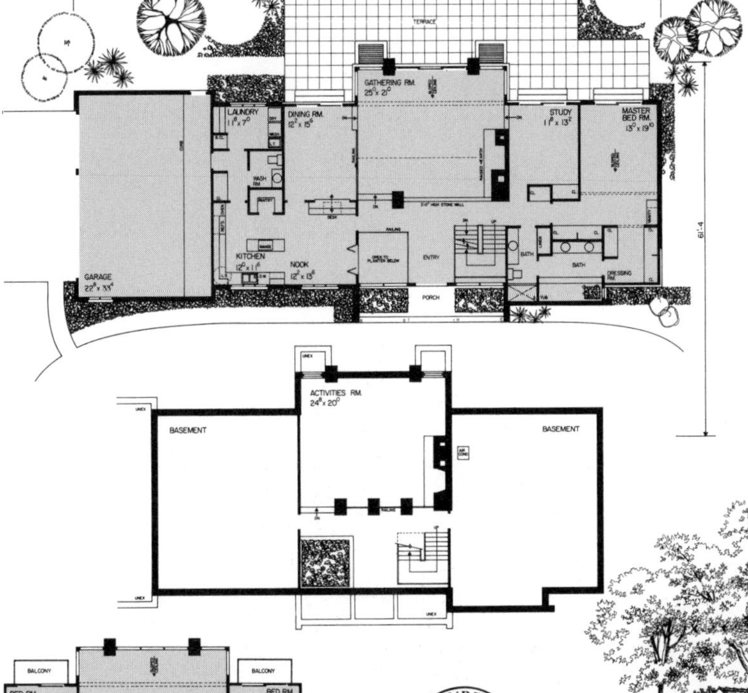

BALCONY
BALCONY
BED RM.
BED RM.
BALCONY LOUNGE $22^{0} \times 12^{0}$
BED RM. $12^{0} \times 12^{0}$
BATH

SIGNATURE SERIES LUXURY HOMES

Design P2780

First Floor: 2,006 square feet
Second Floor: 718 square feet
Total: 2,724 square feet

● This 1½-story contemporary has more fine features than one can imagine. The livability is outstanding and can be appreciated by the whole family. Note the fine indoor-outdoor living relationships.

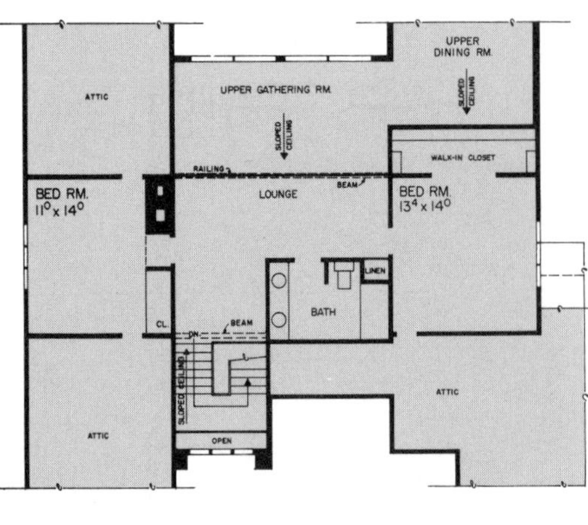

Design P2772

First Floor: 1,579 square feet
Second Floor: 1,240 square feet; Total: 2,819 square feet

● This four-bedroom two-story contemporary design is sure to suit your growing family needs. The rear U-shaped kitchen, flanked by the family and dining rooms, will be very efficient to the busy homemaker. Parents will enjoy all the convenience of the master bedroom suite.

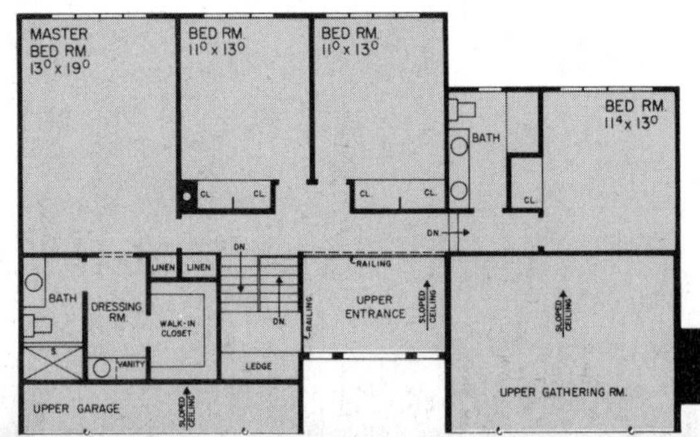

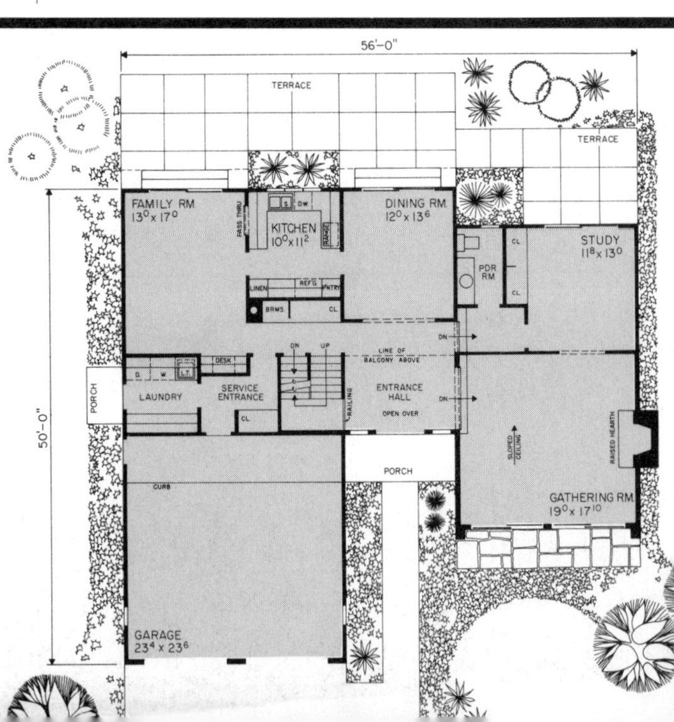

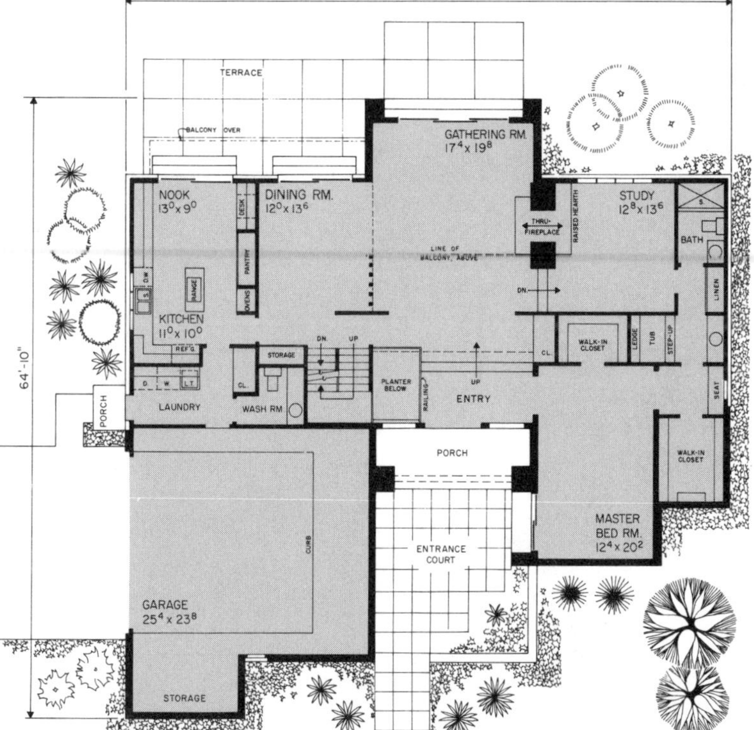

Design P2771

First Floor: 2,087 square feet
Second Floor: 816 square feet
Total: 2,903 square feet

● This design will provide an abundance of livability for your family. The second floor is highlighted by an open lounge which overlooks both the entry and the gathering room below.

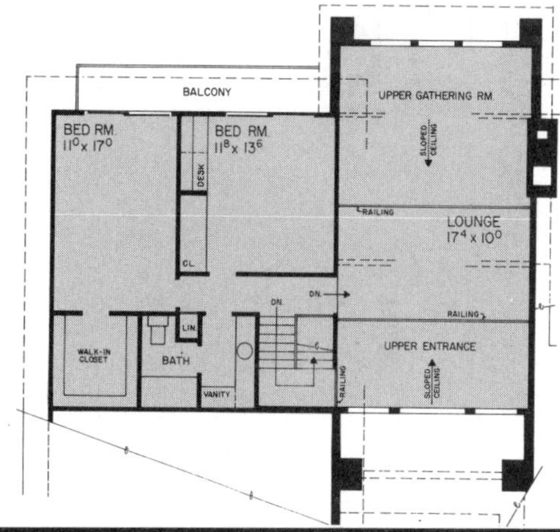

Design P3338

First Floor: 1,314 square feet
Second Floor: 970 square feet
Total: 2,284 square feet

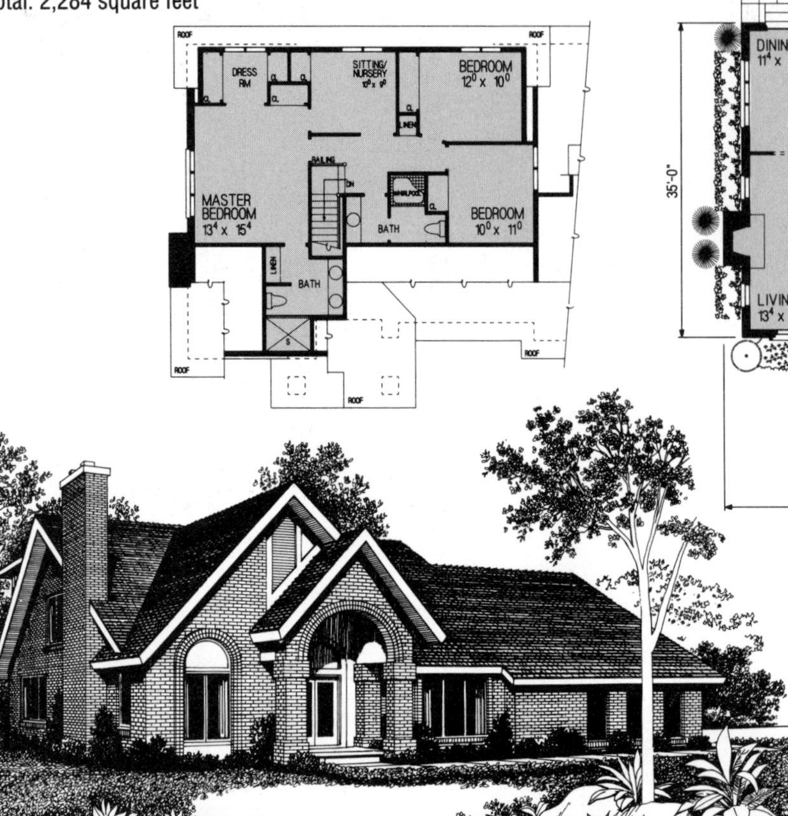

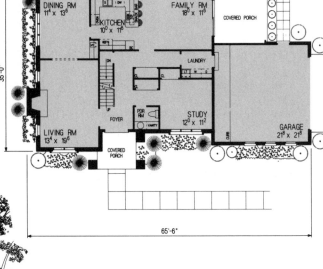

● For new parents or empty-nesters, this plan's master suite has an attached nursery or sitting room. Downstairs there's a formal living room and dining room and the more casual family room with snack-bar eating area. A front study is near the powder room.

Design P3347

First Floor: 1,915 square feet
Second Floor: 759 square feet
Total: 2,674 square feet

● Open living is the key to the abundant livability of this design. The gigantic gathering room/dining room area shares a through-fireplace with a unique sunken conversation area. An L-shaped kitchen has a pass-through snack bar to the breakfast room. On the second floor, two bedrooms are separated by a lounge with a balcony overlook.

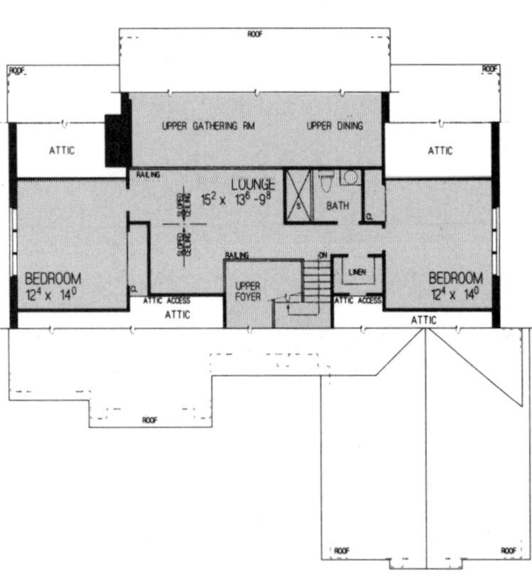

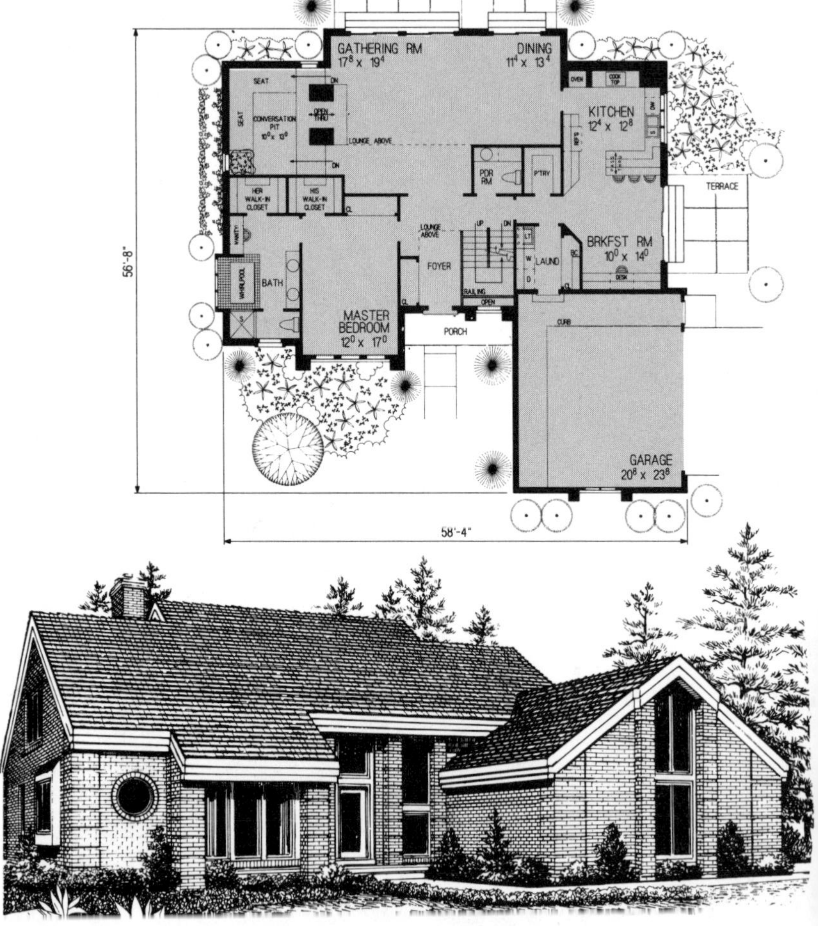

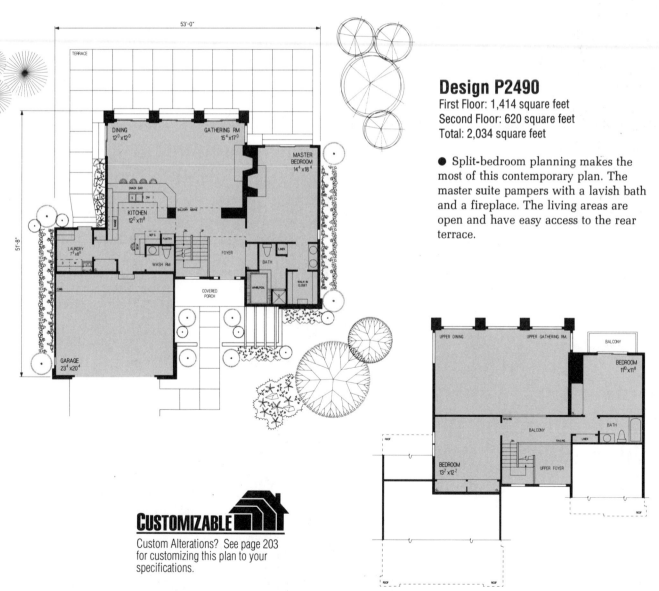

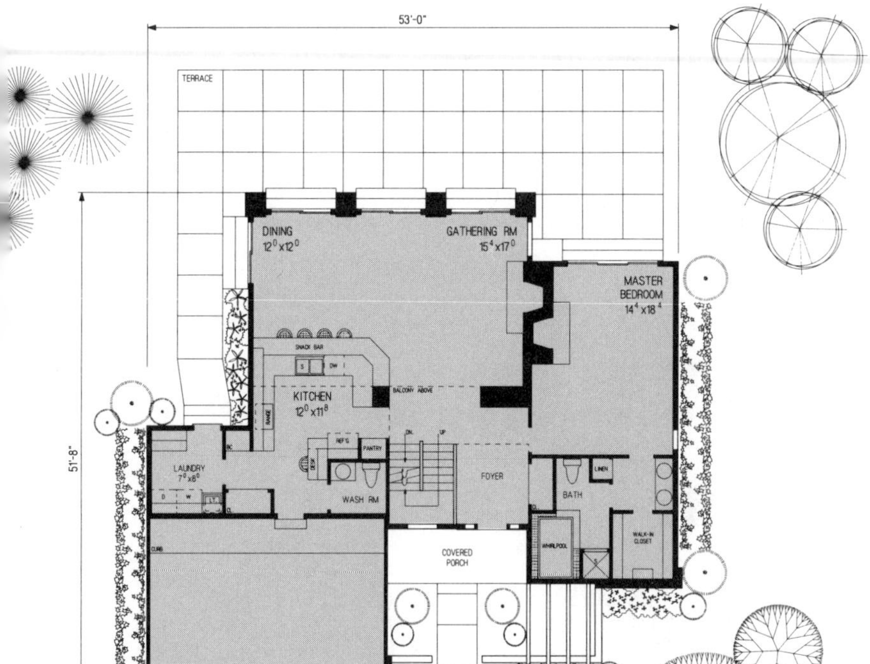

Design P2490

First Floor: 1,414 square feet
Second Floor: 620 square feet
Total: 2,034 square feet

● Split-bedroom planning makes the most of this contemporary plan. The master suite pampers with a lavish bath and a fireplace. The living areas are open and have easy access to the rear terrace.

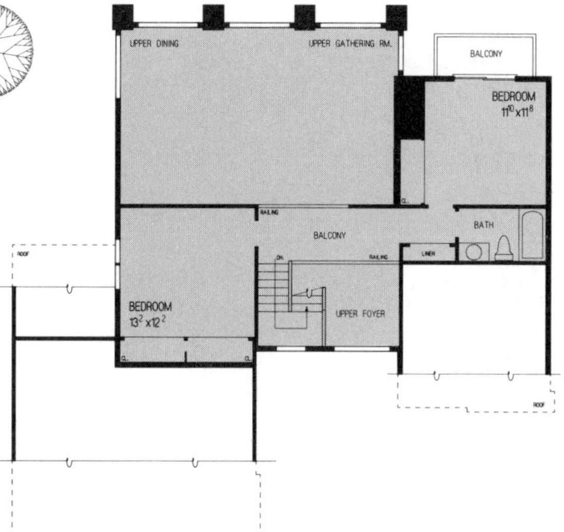

CUSTOMIZABLE

Custom Alterations? See page 203 for customizing this plan to your specifications.

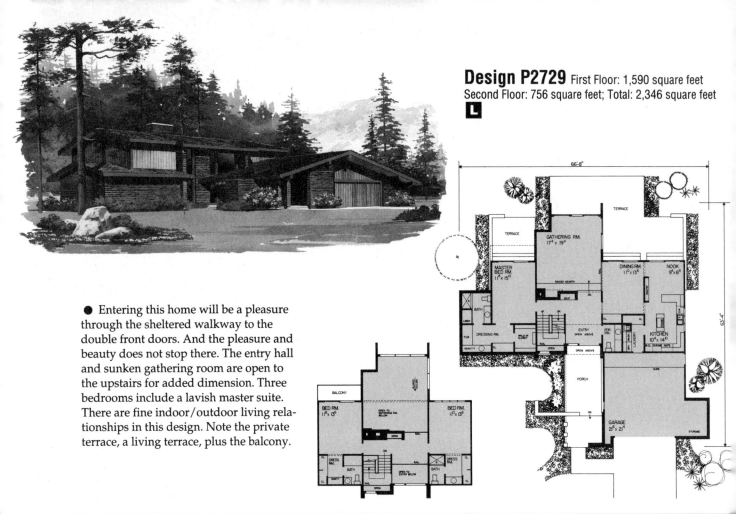

Design P2729 First Floor: 1,590 square feet
Second Floor: 756 square feet; Total: 2,346 square feet

L

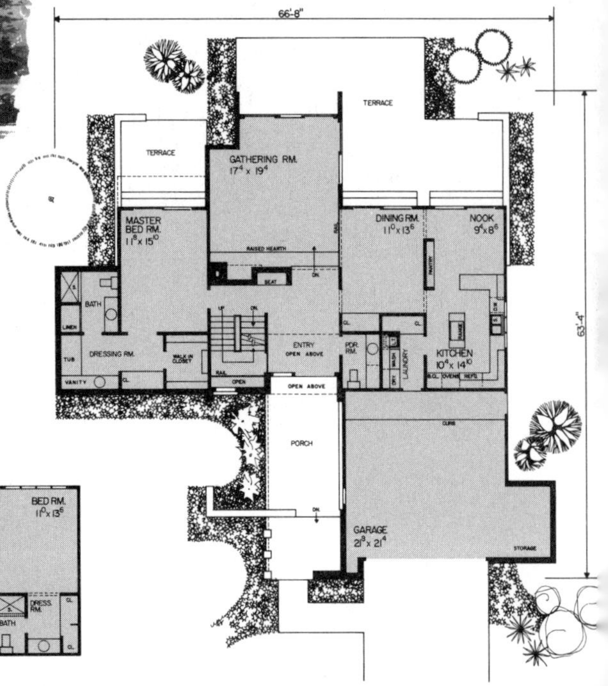

● Entering this home will be a pleasure through the sheltered walkway to the double front doors. And the pleasure and beauty does not stop there. The entry hall and sunken gathering room are open to the upstairs for added dimension. Three bedrooms include a lavish master suite. There are fine indoor/outdoor living relationships in this design. Note the private terrace, a living terrace, plus the balcony.

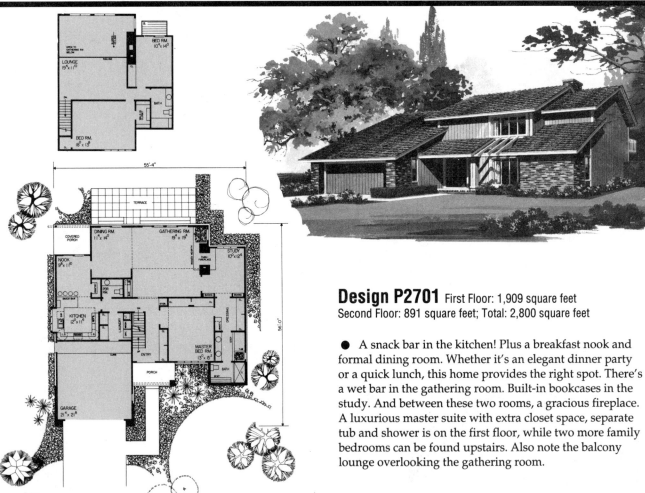

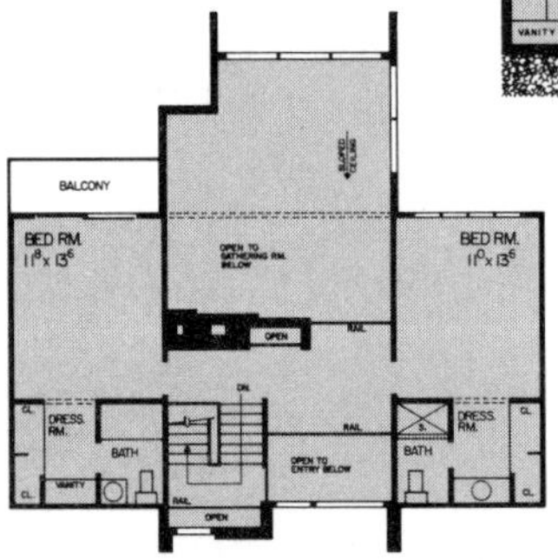

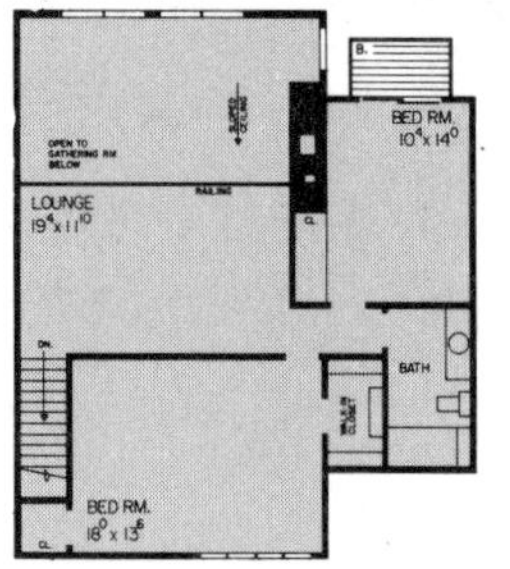

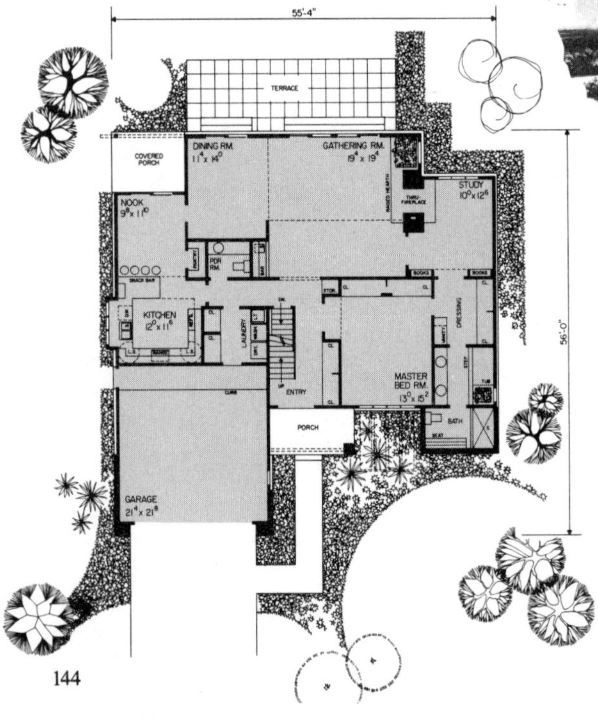

Design P2701 First Floor: 1,909 square feet
Second Floor: 891 square feet; Total: 2,800 square feet

● A snack bar in the kitchen! Plus a breakfast nook and formal dining room. Whether it's an elegant dinner party or a quick lunch, this home provides the right spot. There's a wet bar in the gathering room. Built-in bookcases in the study. And between these two rooms, a gracious fireplace. A luxurious master suite with extra closet space, separate tub and shower is on the first floor, while two more family bedrooms can be found upstairs. Also note the balcony lounge overlooking the gathering room.

Design P2748

First Floor: 1,232 square feet
Second Floor: 720 square feet
Total: 1,952 square feet

● This four bedroom contemporary will definitely have appeal for the entire family. The U-shaped kitchen/nook area with its built-in desk, adjacent laundry/wash room and service entrance will be very efficient for the busy kitchen activities. The family room with raised-hearth fireplace and the living room are both sunken one step.

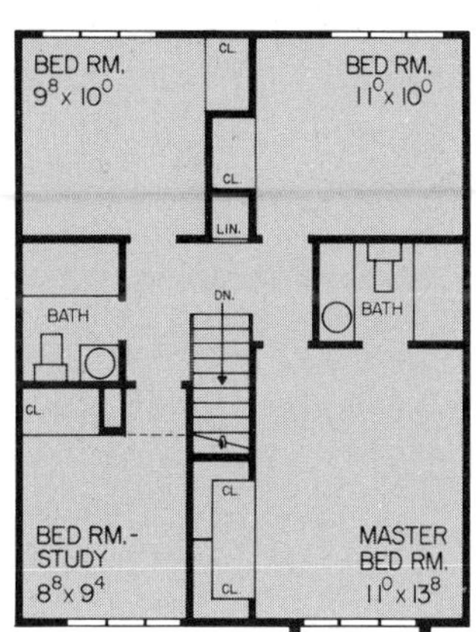

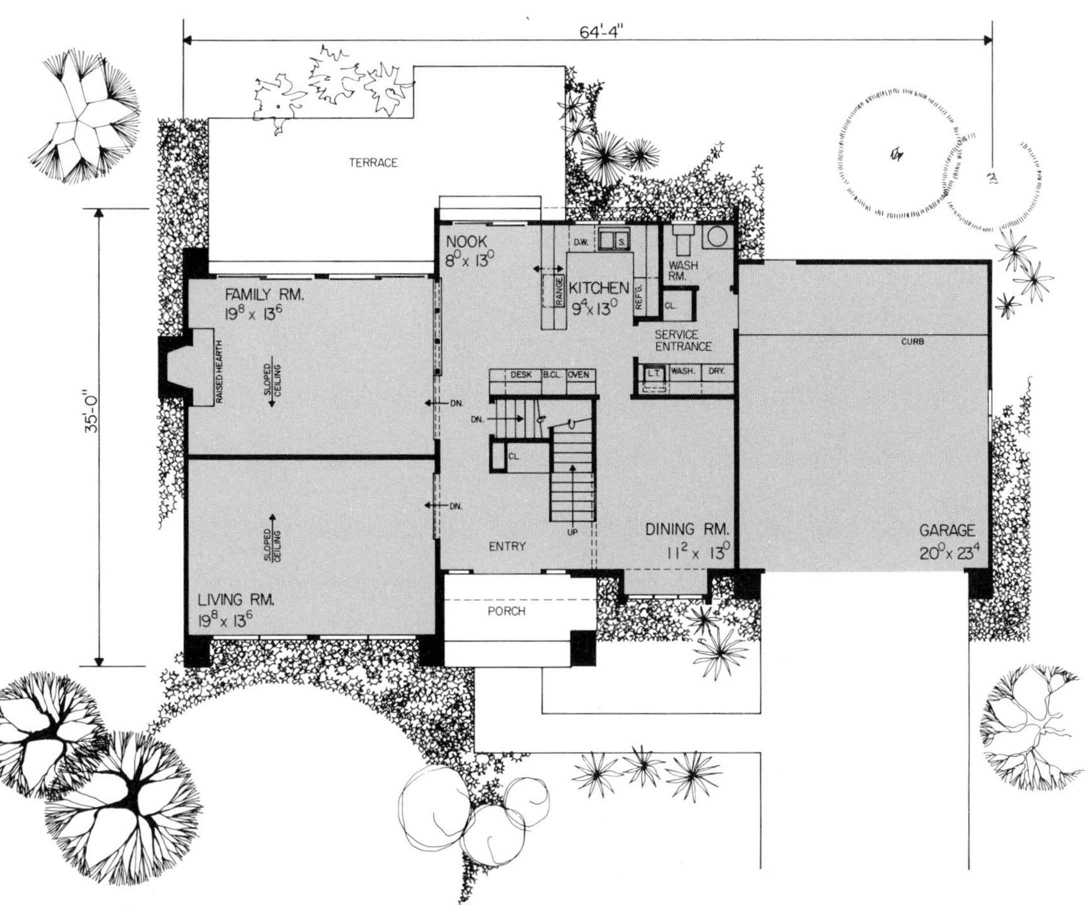

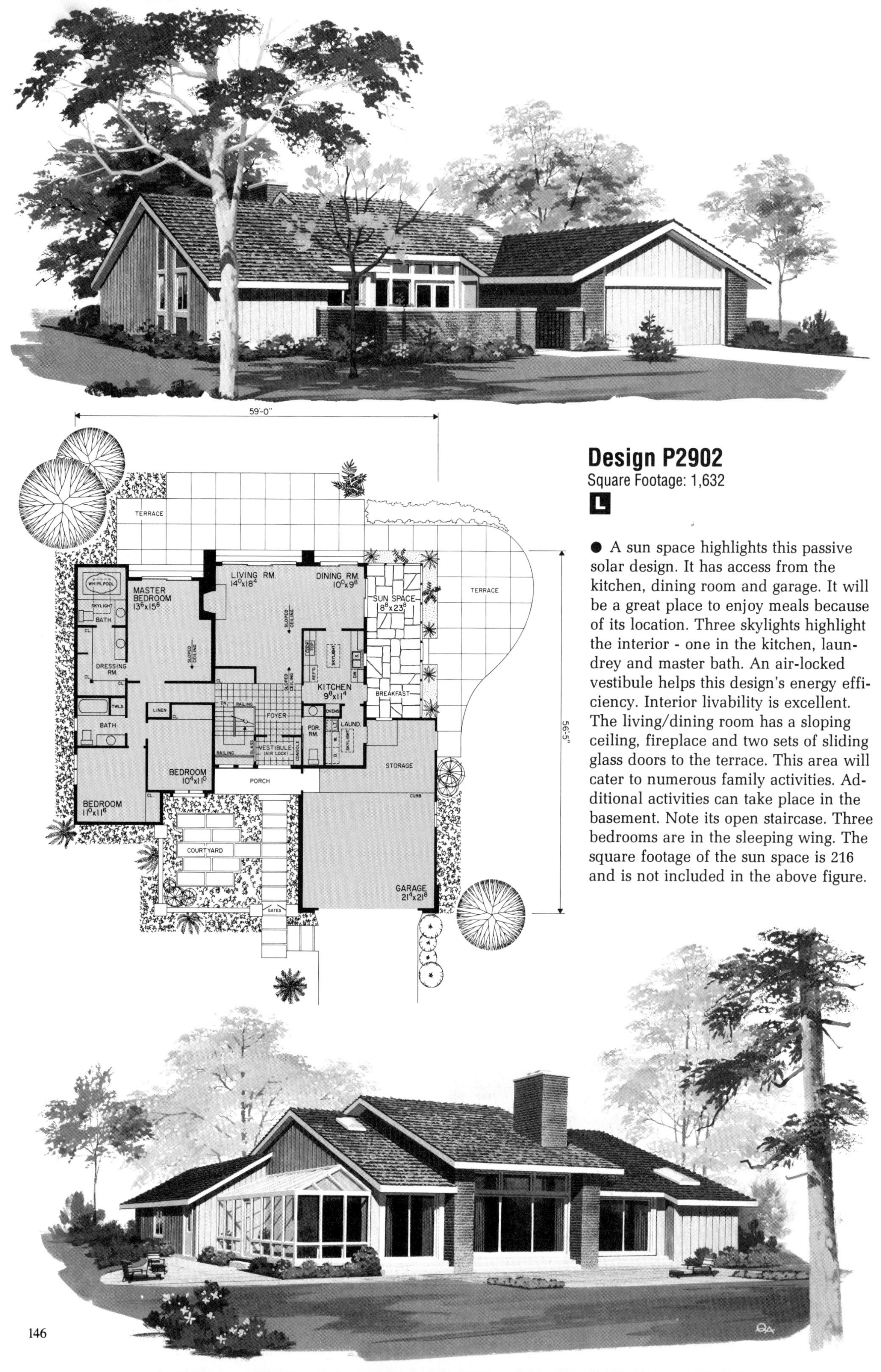

Design P2902

Square Footage: 1,632

L

● A sun space highlights this passive solar design. It has access from the kitchen, dining room and garage. It will be a great place to enjoy meals because of its location. Three skylights highlight the interior - one in the kitchen, laundrey and master bath. An air-locked vestibule helps this design's energy efficiency. Interior livability is excellent. The living/dining room has a sloping ceiling, fireplace and two sets of sliding glass doors to the terrace. This area will cater to numerous family activities. Additional activities can take place in the basement. Note its open staircase. Three bedrooms are in the sleeping wing. The square footage of the sun space is 216 and is not included in the above figure.

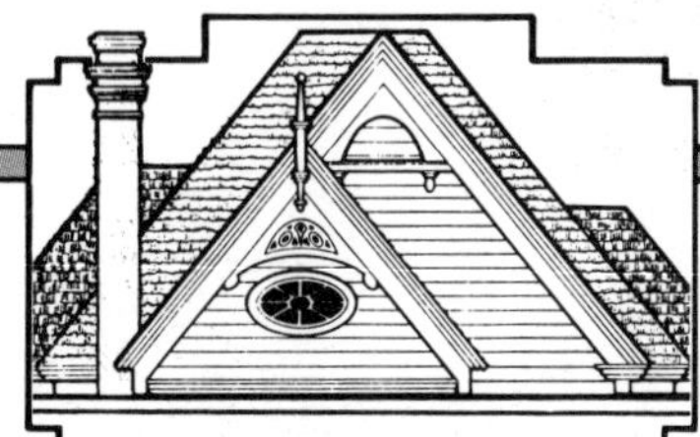

Victorian and Gothic

The Victorian architectural era saw its dominance in the last part of the reign of Queen Victoria from approximately 1860 to 1900. Advances in construction technology and an improved economic climate allowed for homes with intricate detail, complex shapes and a grand nature.

These homes grew from a boredom with earlier classical forms such as Greek Revival. Disdaining regular, symmetrical style, the early beginnings of Victorian Romanticism encompassed a style that is best described as Gothic Revival. Forms were freer and given to more experimentation. Though following the distinctive shapes of Medieval architecture, Gothic Revival added detailed gable trim, called vergeboard, which was cut into intricate patterns. This newly unrestrained style set the precedent for even more freedom in the elaborate Victorians.

Generally, Victorian homes share some basic elements. With roots in Medieval architecture, they are strongly asymmetrical, feature steeply pitched roofs and are replete with decorative detail. However, there are numerous variations to the Victorian theme, each with its own distinct characteristics.

Homes of the Second Empire are noted for their Mansard roof lines, dormer windows and decorative brackets below the eaves. They borrow from early Italianate styles combined with French stylizations.

Stick-style homes sport patterns of horizontal, diagonal or vertical boards, called stickwork, as decorative elements. Their roofs are generally gabled with occasional cross gables and have exposed rafter ends.

The most popular and most prevalent of the Victorian styles is the Queen Anne. Its steeply pitched roof lines take on highly irregular patterns though there is almost always a prominent front-facing gable. The detail work in Queen Anne homes is legendary— turned posts, spandrels, spindlework or gingerbread, decorative finials and corner brackets. Patterned shingles are common as are full-width or wrapping front porches, cut-away bay windows and towers.

The Shingle-style homes, as the name implies, feature wall and roof cladding of wood shingles. Like other Victorians, particularly Queen Annes, they have a steeply pitched roof with cross gables and extensive front porches. Their facades are asymmetrical and what little detail exists serves to highlight irregularity of shape.

The Richardson Romanesque, named for architect Henry Hobson Richardson, can be identified by its round-topped arches and towers with conical roofs. The facade of this unusual style is asymmetrical and the home itself is constructed with masonry walls, particularly stone.

Drawing on a simple style, the Folk Victorian gives the impression of being a ranch-style home that has been embellished with Victorian detailing. Among its quiet features are front porches and spindlework ornamentation at gable peaks and railings. Builders of the prototypes took advantage of pre-cut Victorian trim that had become widely available.

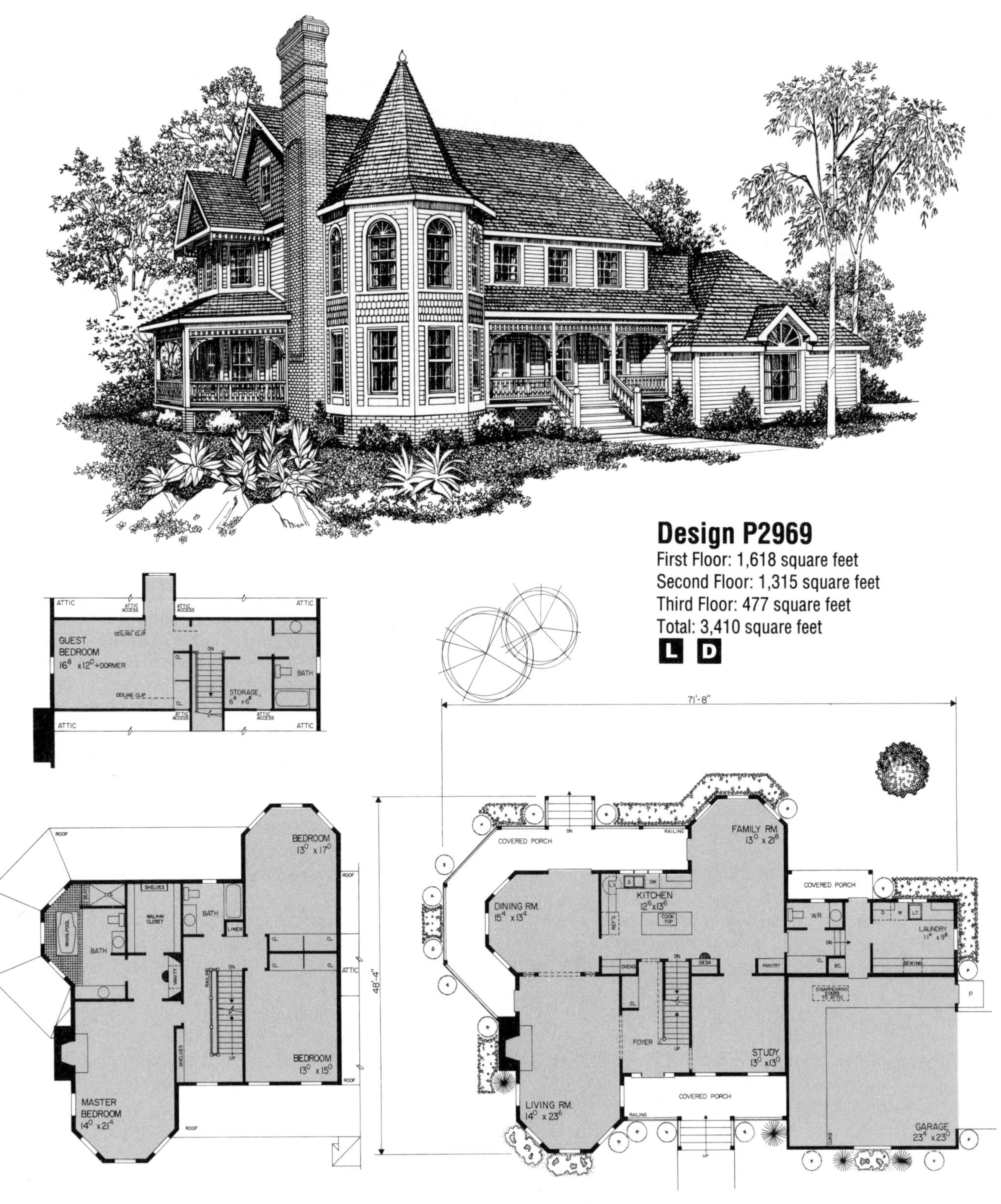

Design P2969

First Floor: 1,618 square feet
Second Floor: 1,315 square feet
Third Floor: 477 square feet
Total: 3,410 square feet
L **D**

● What could beat the charm of a turreted Victorian with covered porches to the front, side and rear? This delicately detailed exterior houses an outstanding family oriented floor plan. Projecting bays make their contribution to the exterior styling. In addition, they provide an extra measure of livability to the living, dining and family rooms, plus two of the bedrooms. The efficient kitchen, with its island cooking station, functions well with the dining and family rooms. A study provides a quiet first floor haven for the family's less active pursuits. Upstairs there are three big bedrooms and a fine master bath. The third floor provides a guest suite and huge bulk storage area (make it a cedar closet if you wish). This house has a basement for the development of further recreational and storage facilities. Don't miss the two fireplaces, large laundry and attached two-car garage. A great investment.

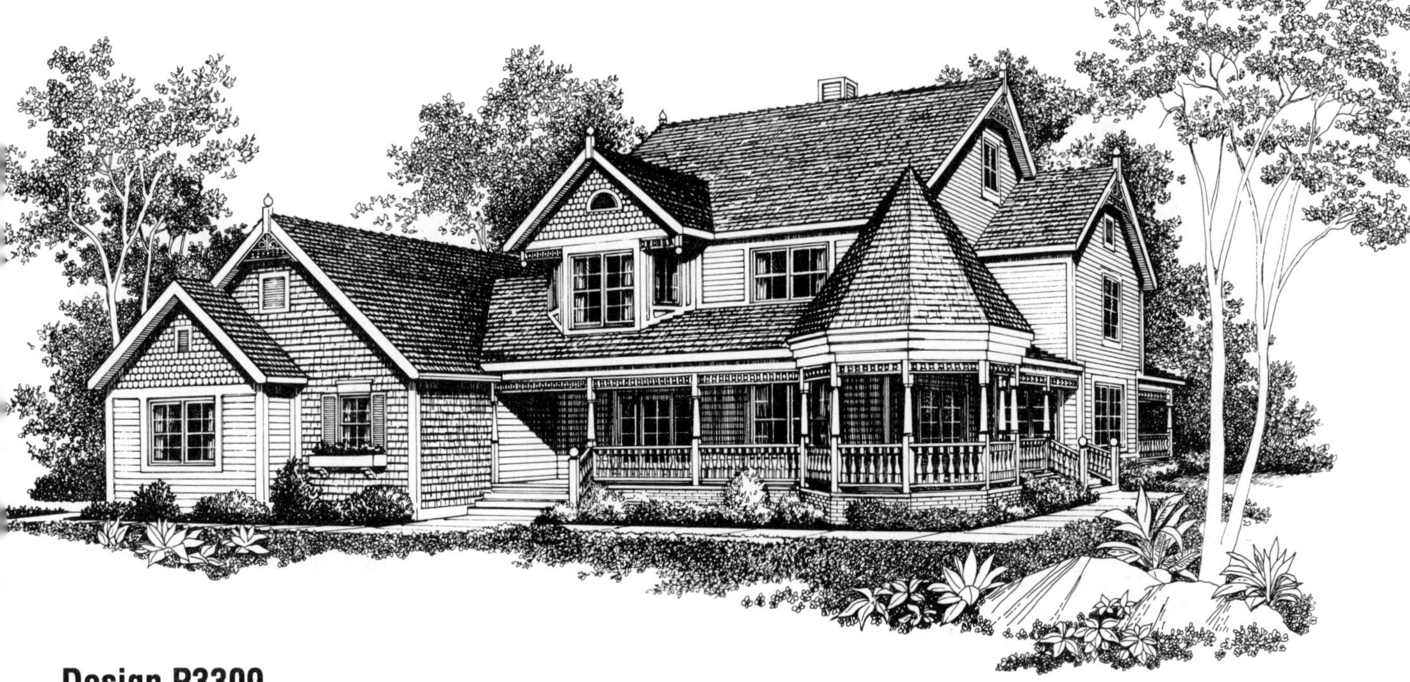

Design P3309

First Floor: 1,375 square feet
Second Floor: 1,016 square feet
Total: 2,391 square feet

● Covered porches, front and back, are a fine preview to the livable nature of this Victorian. Living areas are defined in a family room with fireplace, formal living and dining rooms, and a kitchen with breakfast room. An ample laundry room, garage with storage area, and powder room round out the first floor. Three second floor bedrooms are joined by a study and two full baths.

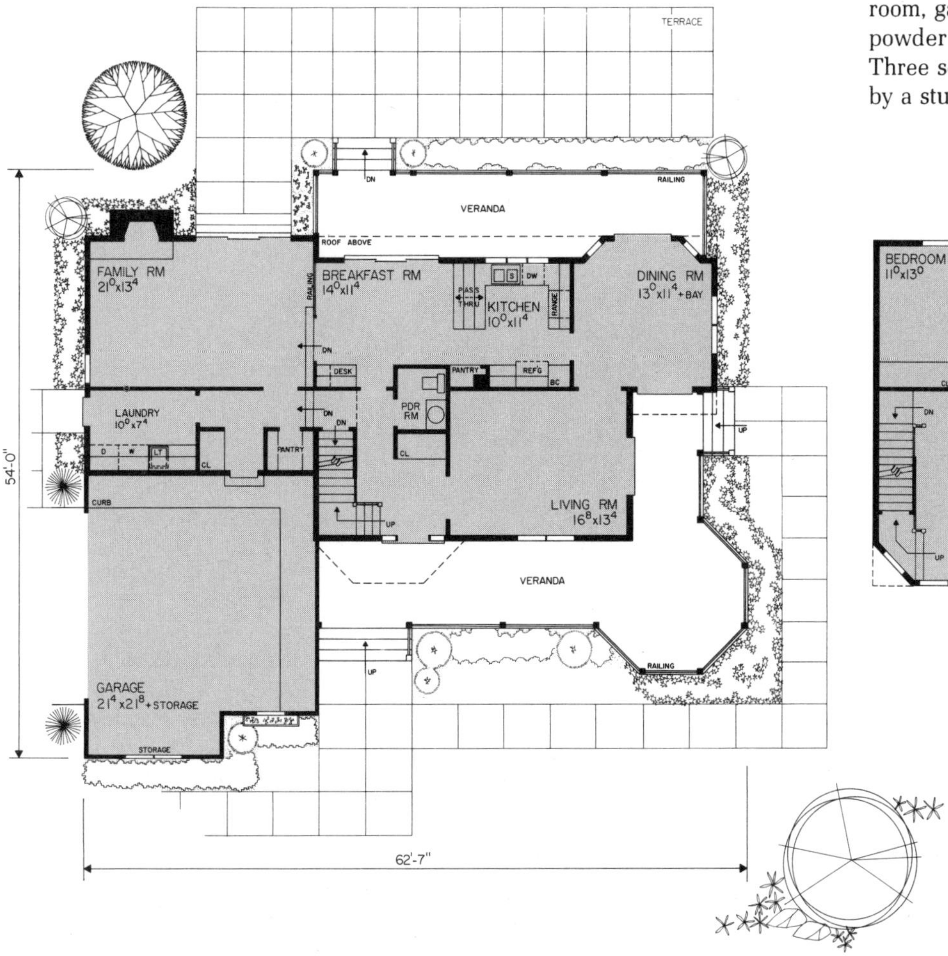

TERRACE
DN
RAILING
VERANDA
ROOF ABOVE
FAMILY RM
21^{0}x13^{4}
BREAKFAST RM
14^{0}x11^{4}
PASS THRU
KITCHEN
10^{0}x11^{4}
DW
RANGE
DINING RM
13^{0}x11^{4}+BAY
DESK
PANTRY
REF'G
BC
LAUNDRY
10^{0}x7^{4}
CL
PANTRY
PDR RM
CL
UP
LIVING RM
16^{8}x13^{4}
CURB
VERANDA
RAILING
GARAGE
21^{4}x21^{8}+STORAGE
STORAGE
54'-0"
62'-7"

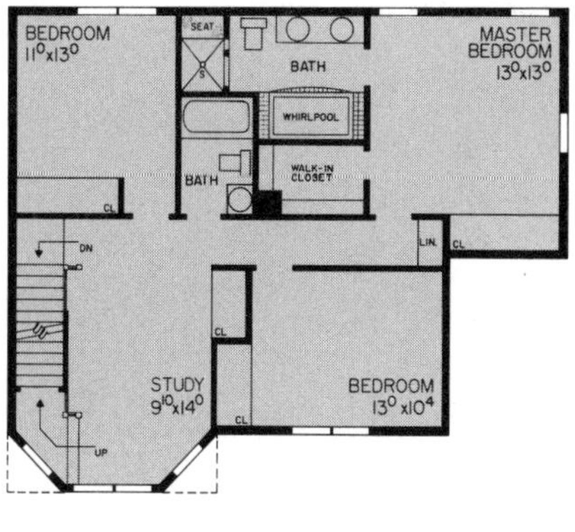

BEDROOM
11^{0}x13^{0}
SEAT
BATH
WHIRLPOOL
MASTER BEDROOM
13^{0}x13^{0}
BATH
WALK-IN CLOSET
CL
LIN.
CL
DN
STUDY
9^{10}x14^{0}
CL
CL
BEDROOM
13^{0}x10^{4}
UP

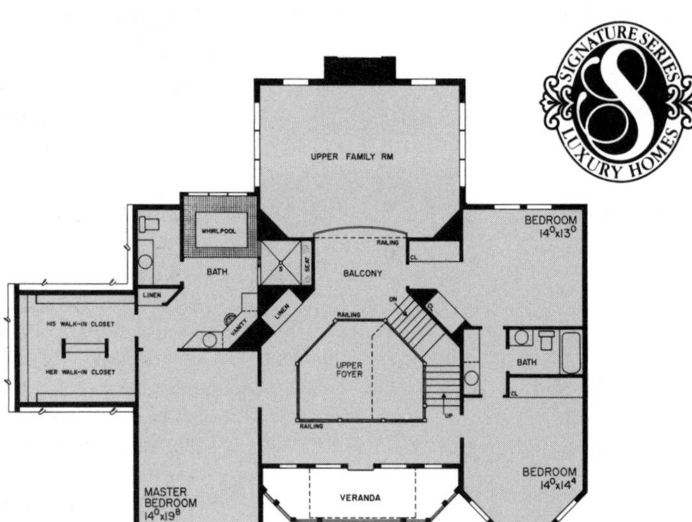

Design P3308

First Floor: 2,515 square feet
Second Floor: 1,708 square feet
Third Floor: 1,001 square feet
Total: 5,224 square feet

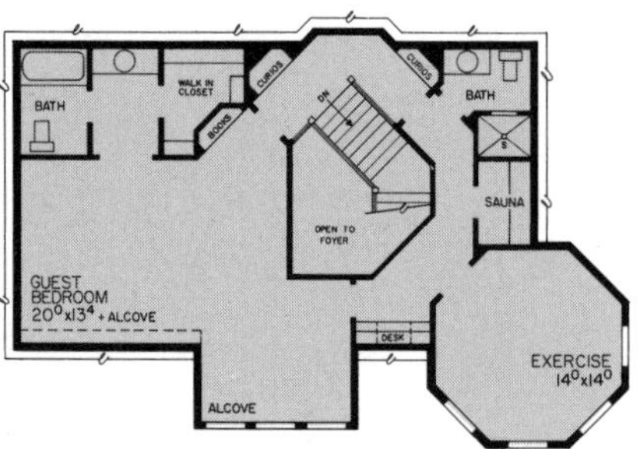

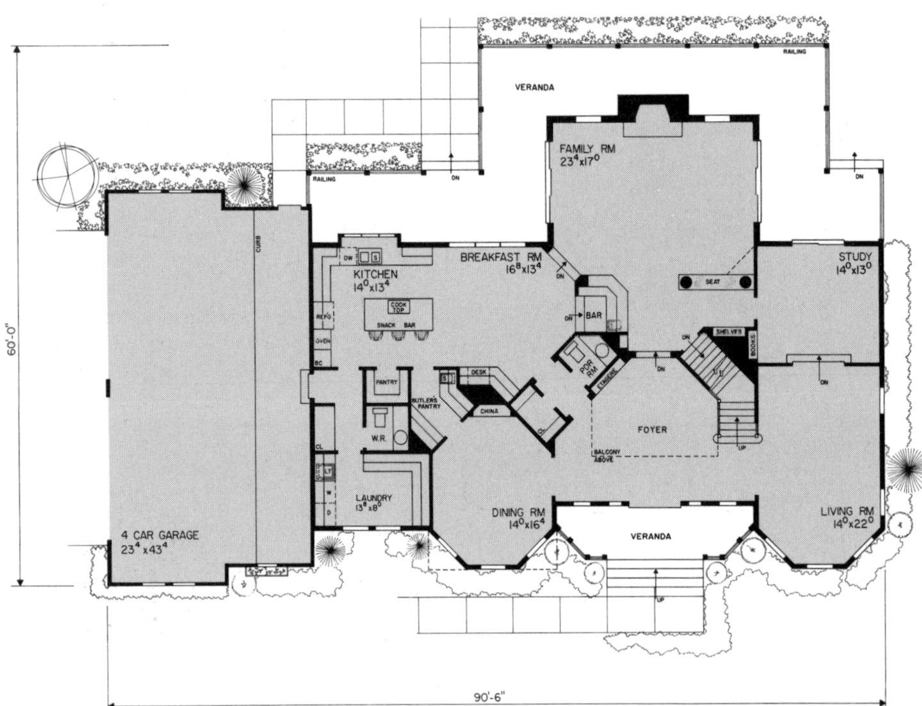

● Uniquely shaped rooms and a cache of amenities highlight this three-story beauty. Downstairs rooms accommodate both formal and informal entertaining and also provide a liberal share of work space in the kitchen and laundry. The second floor has two bedrooms and a full bath plus a master suite with His and Hers closets and whirlpool bath. An exercise room on the third floor has its own sauna and bath, while a guest room on this floor is complemented by a charming alcove and another full bath.

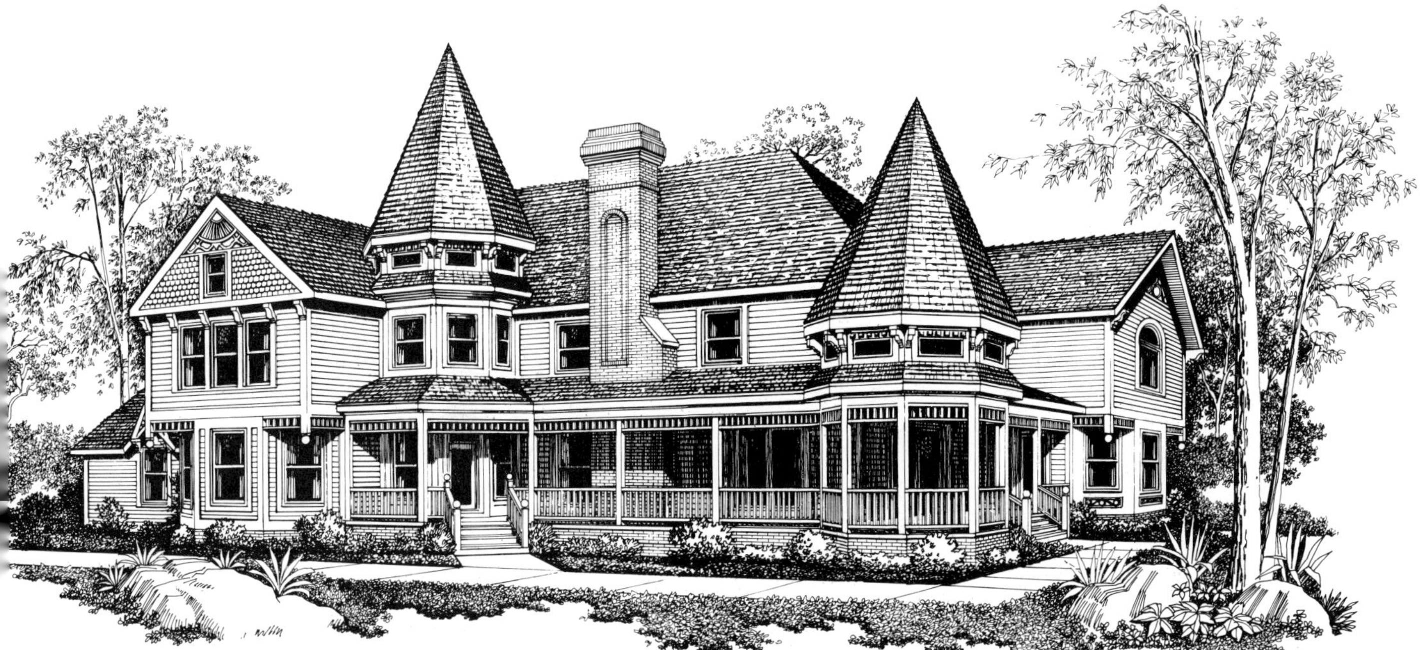

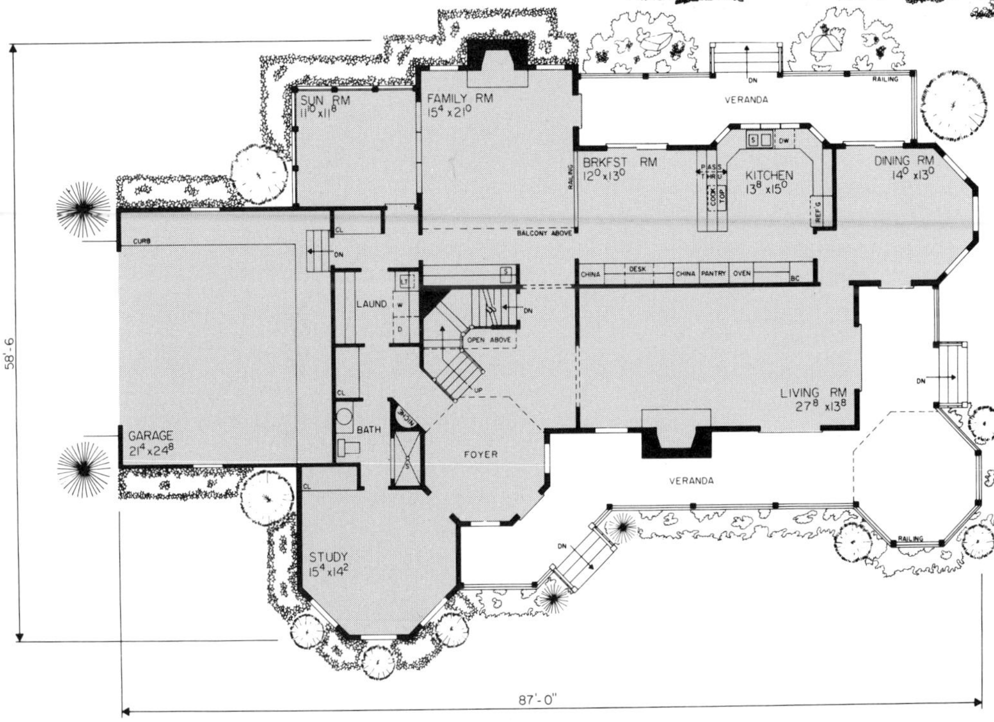

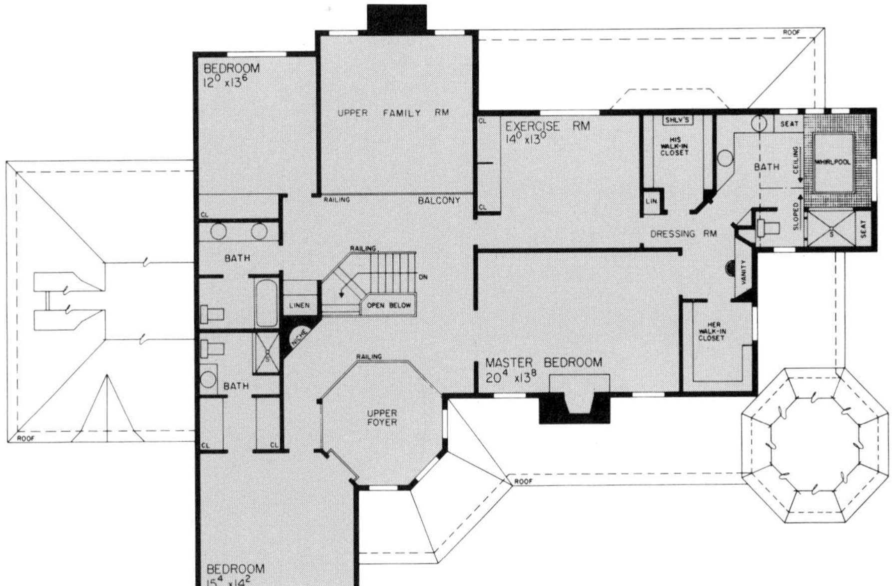

Design P3304

First Floor: 2,102 square feet
Second Floor: 1,971 square feet
Total: 4,073 square feet

● Victorian style is displayed in most exquisite proportions in this three-bedroom, four-bath home. From verandas, both front and rear, to the stately turrets and impressive chimney stack, this is a beauty. Inside is a great lay-out with many thoughtful amenities. Besides the large living room, formal dining room, and two-story family room, there is a cozy study for private time. A gourmet kitchen with built-ins has a pass-through counter to the breakfast room. The master suite on the second floor includes many special features: whirlpool spa, His and Hers walk-in closets, exercise room, and fireplace. There are two more bedrooms, each with a full bath, on the second floor.

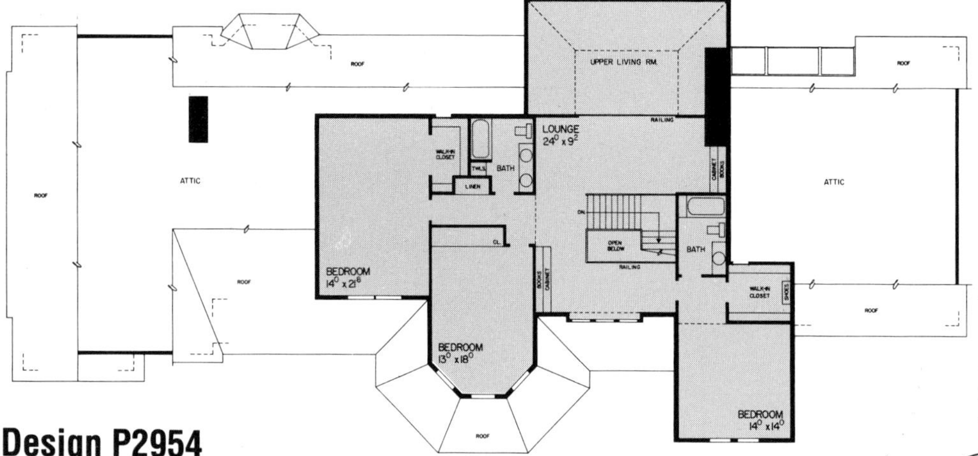

Design P2954

First Floor: 3,079 square feet
Second Floor: 1,461 square feet
Total: 4,540 square feet

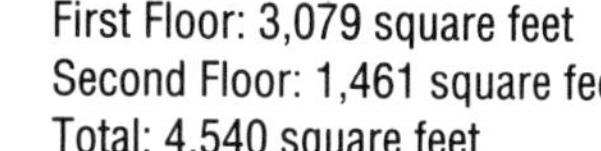

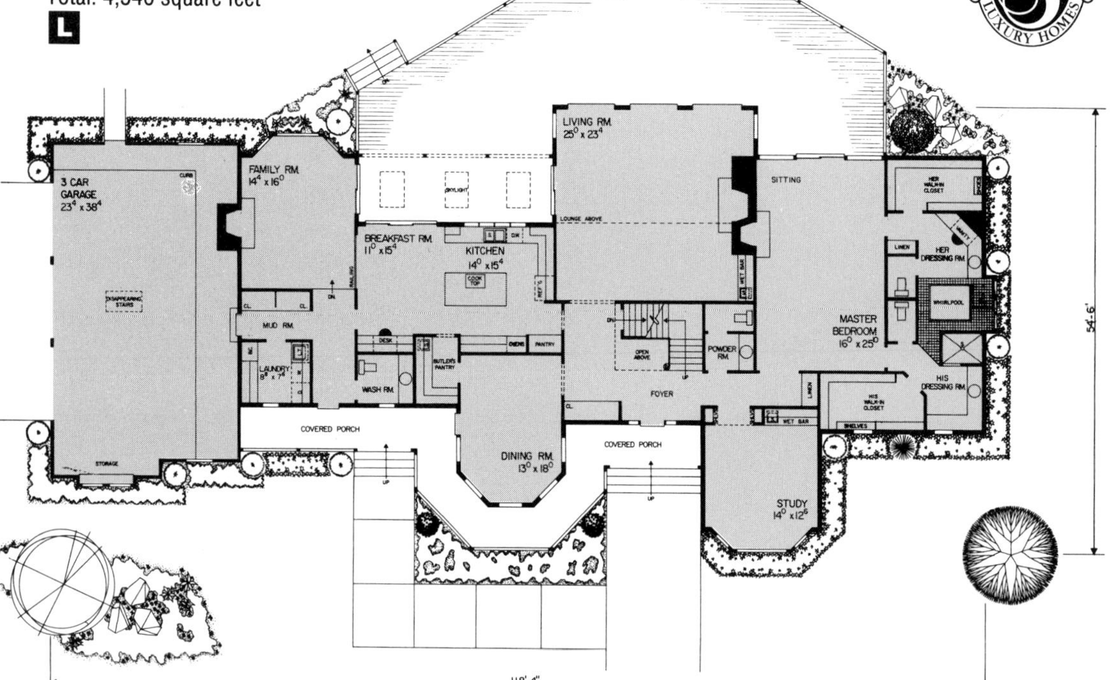

● This enchanting manor displays architectural elements typical of the Victorian Style: asymmetrical facade, decorative shingles and gables, and a covered porch. The two-story living room with fireplace and wet bar opens to the glass-enclosed rear porch with skylights. A spacious kitchen is filled with amenities, including an island cooktop, built-in desk, and butler's pantry connecting to the dining room. The master suite, adjacent to the study, opens to the rear deck. A cozy fireplace keeps the room warm on chilly evenings. Separate His and Hers dressing rooms are outfitted with vanities and walk-in closets, and a luxurious whirlpool tub connects the baths. The second floor opens to a large lounge with built-in cabinets and bookshelves. Three bedrooms and two full baths complete the second-floor livability. The three-car garage contains disappearing stairs to an attic storage area.

● A magnificent, finely wrought covered porch wraps around this impressive Victorian estate home. The gracious two-story foyer provides a direct view past the stylish bannister and into the great room with large central fireplace. To the left of the foyer is a bookshelf-lined library and to the right is a dramatic, octagonal-shaped dining room. The island cooktop completes a convenient work triangle in the kitchen, and a pass-through connects this room with the Victorian-style morning room. A butler's pantry, walk-in closet, and broom closet offer plenty of storage space. A luxurious master suite is located on the first floor and opens to the rear covered porch. A through-fireplace warms the bedroom, sitting room, and dressing room, which includes His and Hers walk-in closets. The step-up whirlpool tub is an elegant focal point to the master bath. Four uniquely designed bedrooms, three full baths, and a restful lounge with fireplace are located on the second floor. Who says you can't combine the absolute best of today's amenities with the quaint styling and comfortable warmth of the Victorian past!

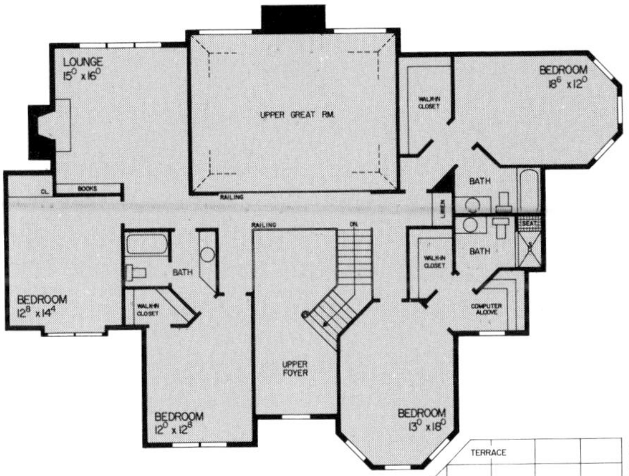

Design P2953

First Floor: 2,991 square feet
Second Floor: 1,802 square feet
Total: 4,793 square feet

L D

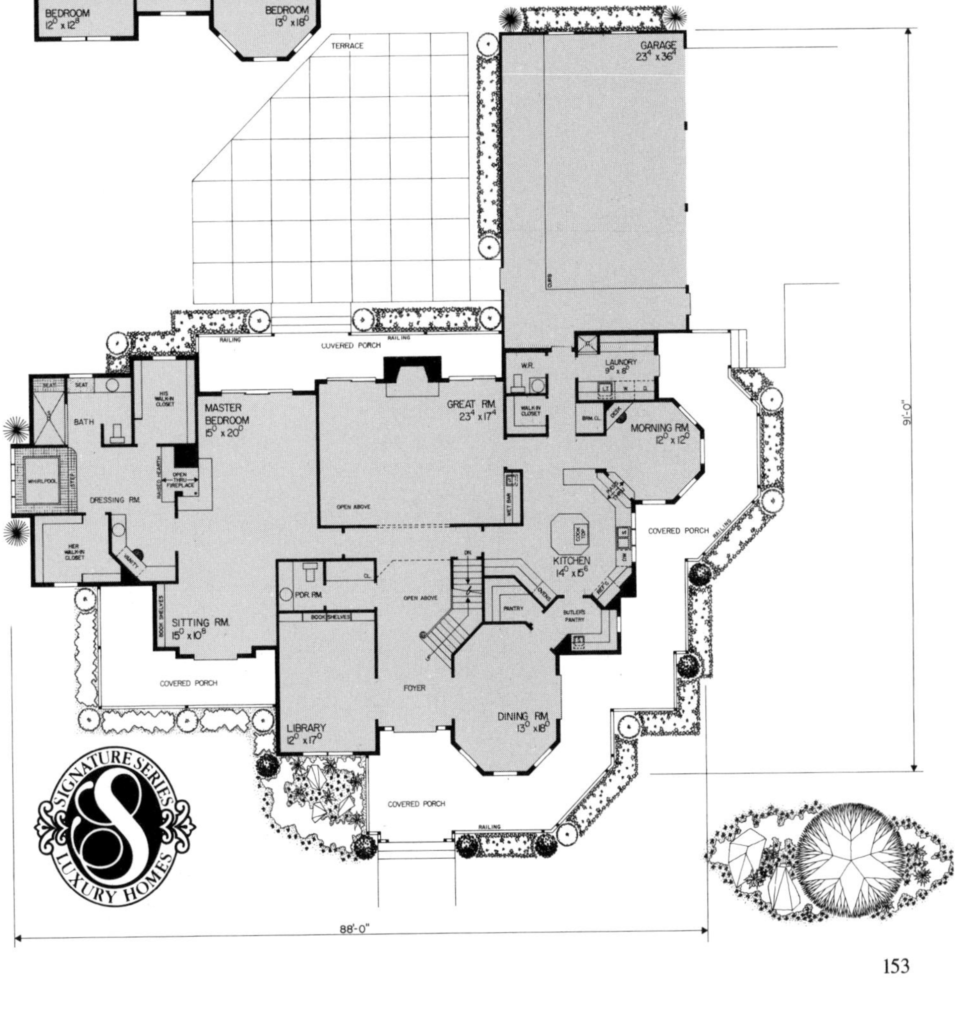

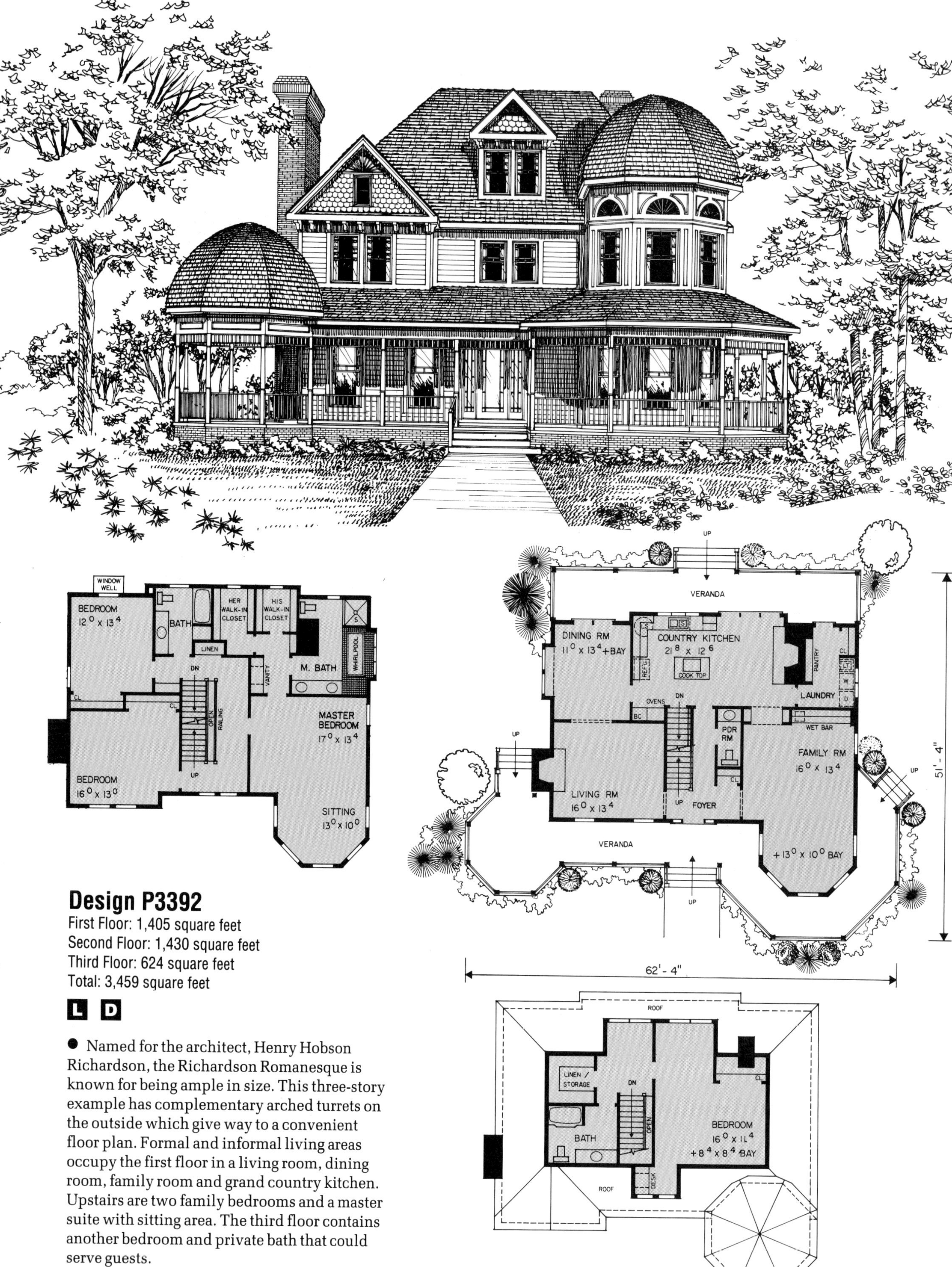

Design P3392

First Floor: 1,405 square feet
Second Floor: 1,430 square feet
Third Floor: 624 square feet
Total: 3,459 square feet

L **D**

● Named for the architect, Henry Hobson Richardson, the Richardson Romanesque is known for being ample in size. This three-story example has complementary arched turrets on the outside which give way to a convenient floor plan. Formal and informal living areas occupy the first floor in a living room, dining room, family room and grand country kitchen. Upstairs are two family bedrooms and a master suite with sitting area. The third floor contains another bedroom and private bath that could serve guests.

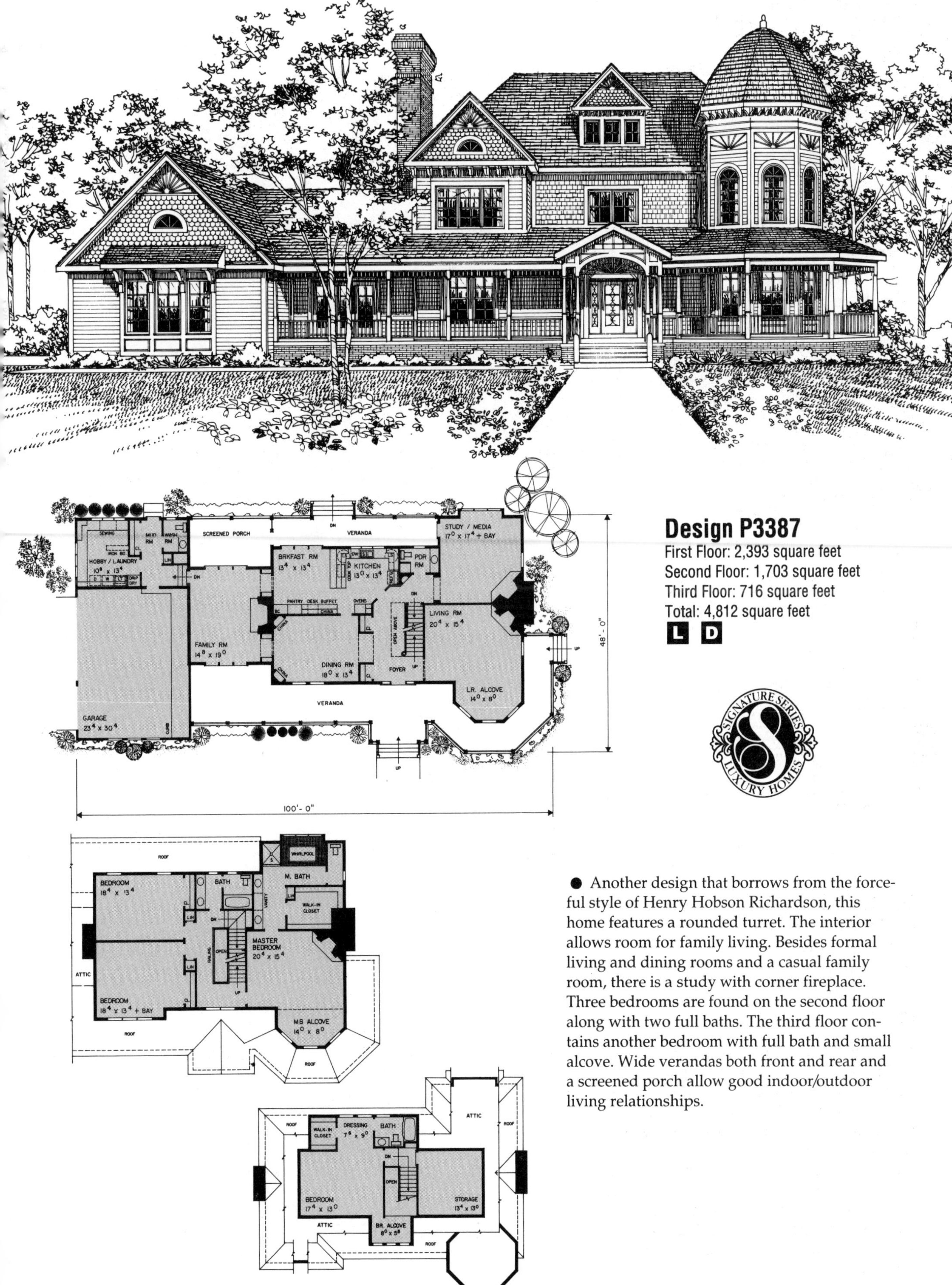

Design P3387

First Floor: 2,393 square feet
Second Floor: 1,703 square feet
Third Floor: 716 square feet
Total: 4,812 square feet

L **D**

● Another design that borrows from the forceful style of Henry Hobson Richardson, this home features a rounded turret. The interior allows room for family living. Besides formal living and dining rooms and a casual family room, there is a study with corner fireplace. Three bedrooms are found on the second floor along with two full baths. The third floor contains another bedroom with full bath and small alcove. Wide verandas both front and rear and a screened porch allow good indoor/outdoor living relationships.

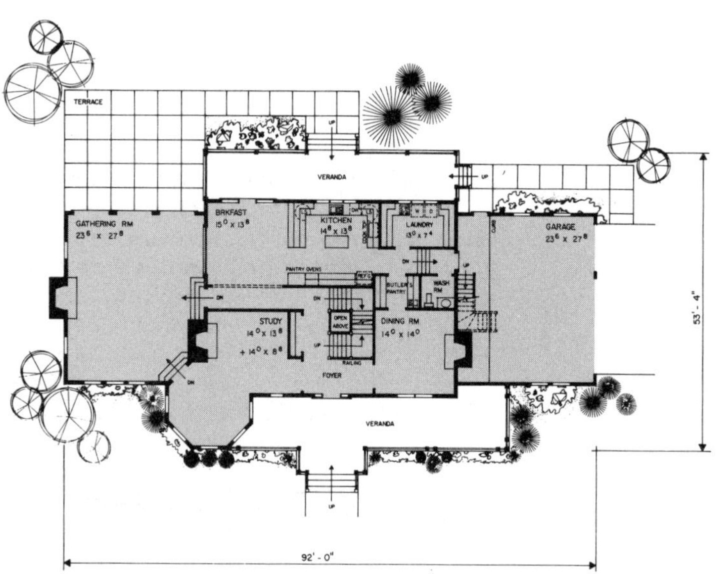

Design P3395

First Floor: 2,248 square feet
Second Floor: 2,020 square feet
Third Floor: 1,117 square feet
Total: 5,385 square feet

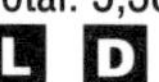

● This home is a lovely example of classic Queen Anne architecture. Its floor plan offers: a gathering room with fireplace, a study with an octagonal window area, a formal dining room and a kitchen with attached breakfast room. Bedrooms on the second floor include three family bedrooms and a grand master suite. On the third floor are a guest room with private bath and sitting room and a game room with attached library.

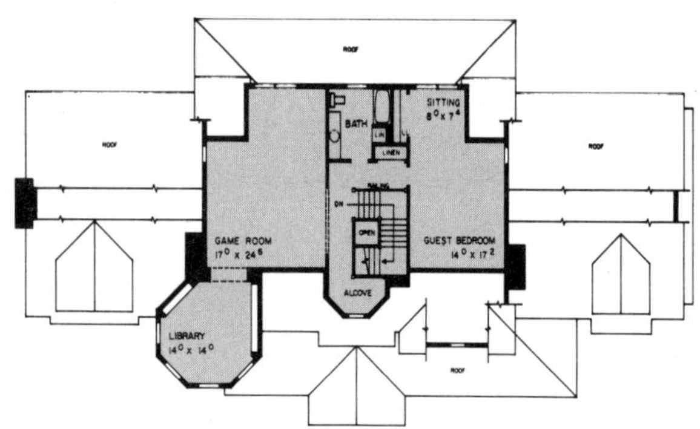

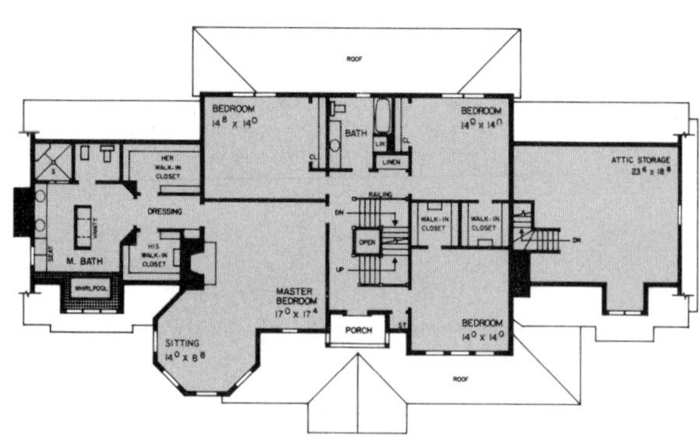

Design P3386

First Floor: 1,683 square feet
Second Floor: 1,388 square feet
Third Floor: 808 square feet
Total: 3,879 square feet

● This beautiful Folk Victorian has all the properties of others in its class. Living areas include a formal Victorian parlor, a private study and large gathering room. The formal dining room has its more casual counterpart in a bay-windowed breakfast room. Both are near the well-appointed kitchen. Five bedrooms serve family and guest needs handily. Three bedrooms on the second floor include a luxurious master suite. For outdoor entertaining, there is a covered rear porch leading to a terrace.

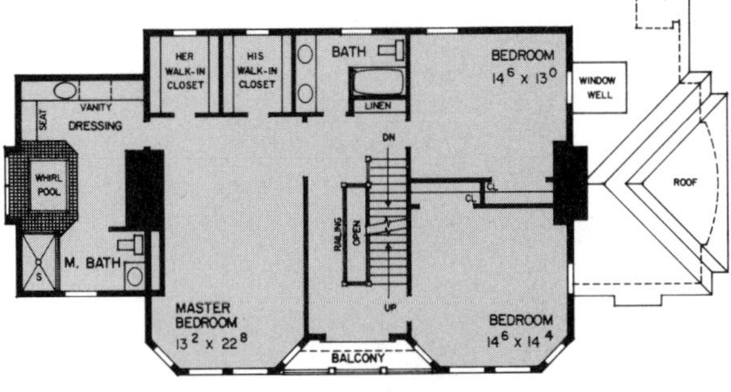

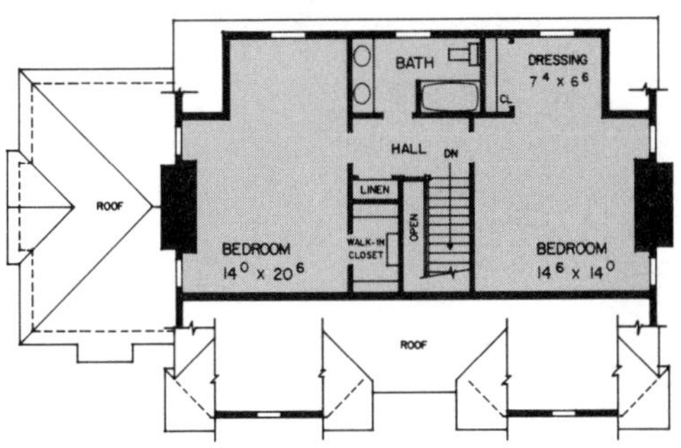

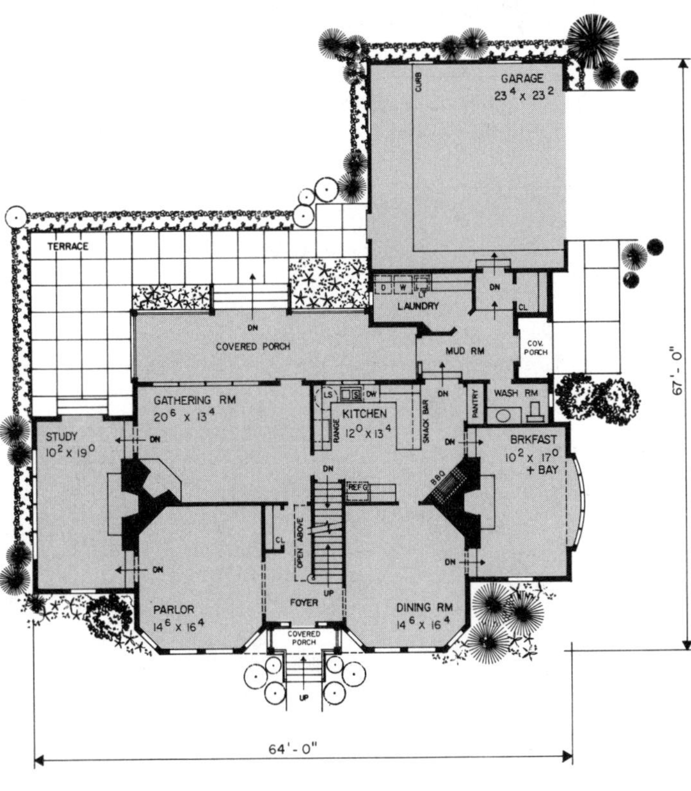

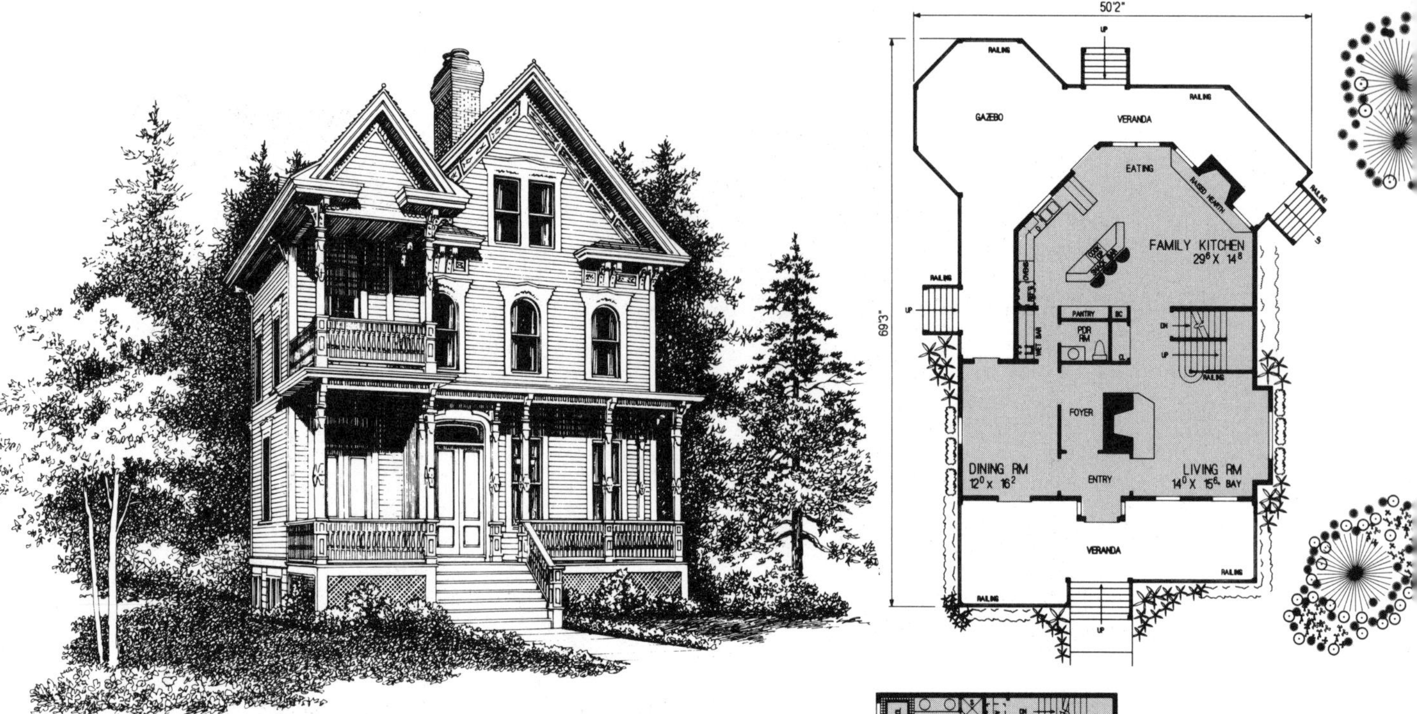

Design P3382

First Floor: 1,366 square feet
Second Floor: 837 square feet
Third Floor: 363 square feet
Total: 2,566 square feet

● A simple but charming Queen Anne Victorian, this home includes a living room with fireplace, large family kitchen with snack bar and a second fireplace, and a dining room with nearby wet bar. The second floor holds two bedrooms, one a master suite with grand bath. A tucked-away guest suite on the third floor has a private bath.

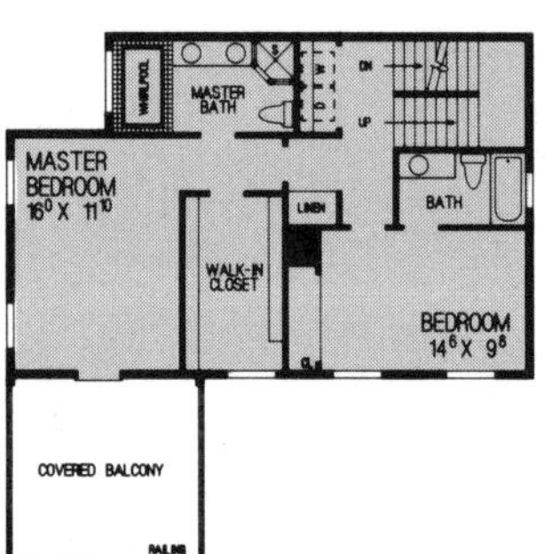

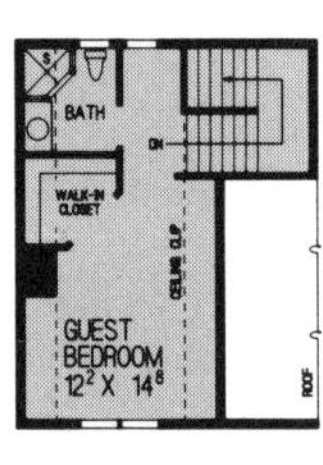

Design P2972

First Floor: 1,432 square feet
Second Floor: 1,108 square feet
Total: 2,540 square feet

L

● The spacious foyer of this Victorian is prelude to a practical and efficient interior. The formal living and dining area is located to one side of the plan. The more informal area of the plan includes the fine U-shaped kitchen which opens to the big family room. Just inside the entrance from the garage is the laundry; a closet and the powder room are a few steps away. The library will enjoy its full measure of privacy. Upstairs is the three-bedroom sleeping zone with a fireplace.

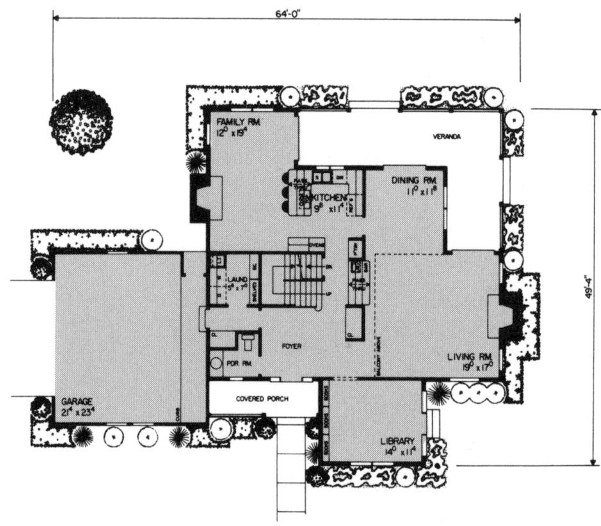

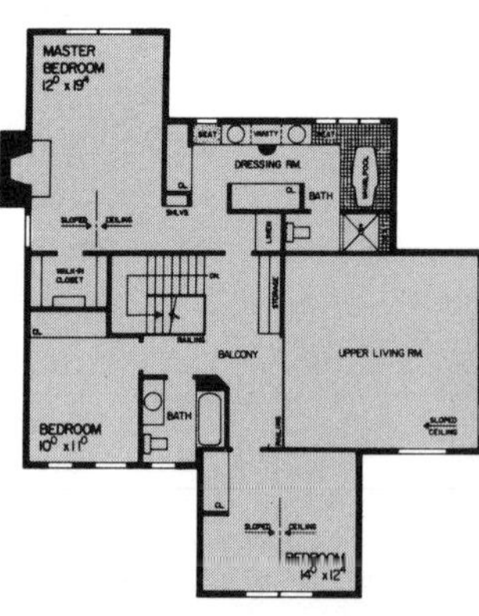

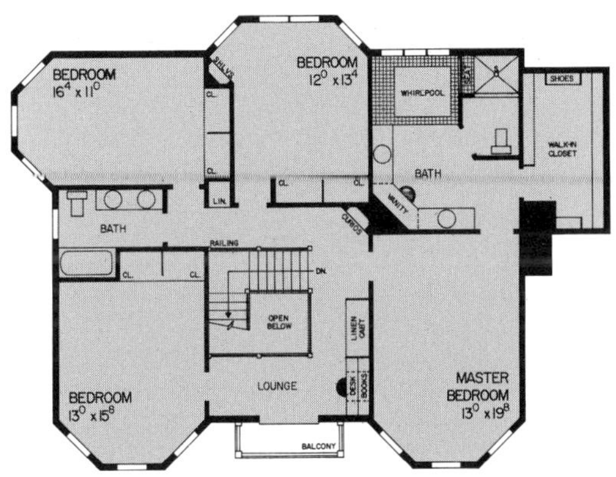

Design P2971 First Floor: 1,766 square feet
Second Floor: 1,519 square feet; Total: 3,285 square feet

L

● The stately proportions and the exquisite detailing of Victorian styling are exciting, indeed. Like so many Victorian houses, interesting roof lines set the character with this design. Observe the delightful mixture of gable roof, hip roof, and the dramatic turret. Horizontal siding, wood shingling, wide fascia, rake and corner boards make a strong statement. Of course, the delicate detailing of the windows, railings, cornices and front entry is most appealing to the eye. Inside, a great four-bedroom family living plan.

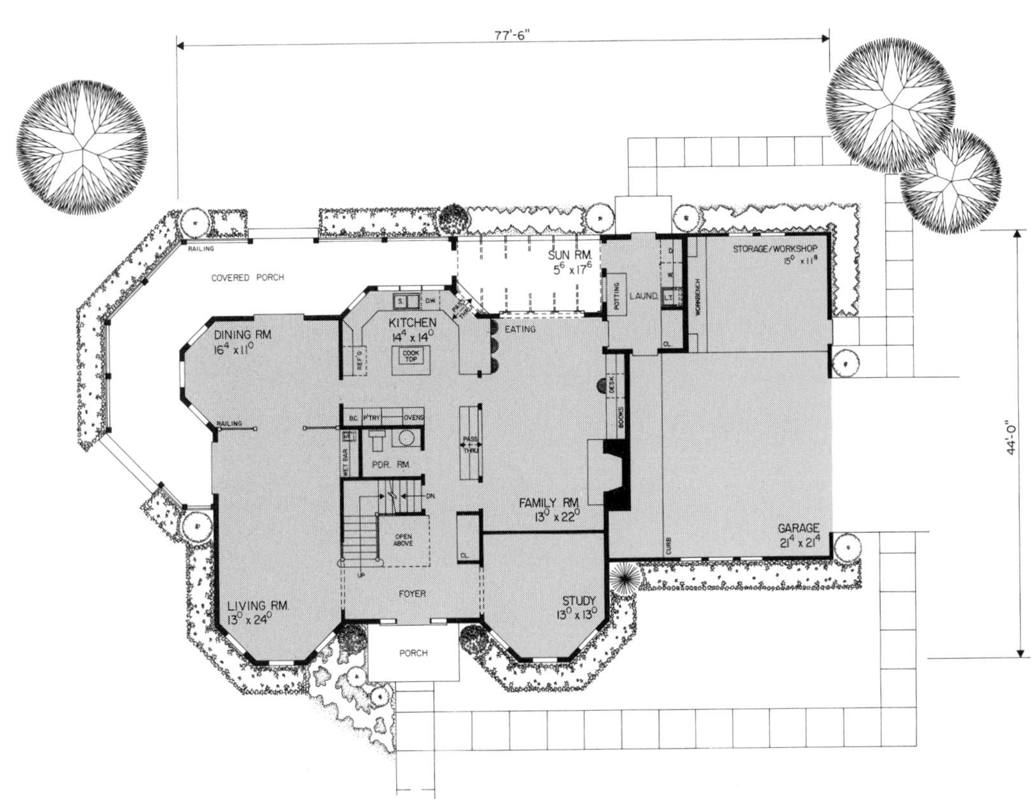

Design P3388

First Floor: 1,517 square feet
Second Floor: 1,267 square feet
Third Floor: 480 square feet
Total: 3,264 square feet

L **D**

● This delightful home offers the best in thoughtful floor planning. The home opens to a well-executed entry foyer. To the left is the casual family room with fireplace. To the right is the formal living room which connects to the formal dining area. The kitchen/breakfast room combination features an island cook top and large pantry. Second-floor bedrooms include a master suite and two family bedrooms served by a full bath. A guest room dominates the third floor.

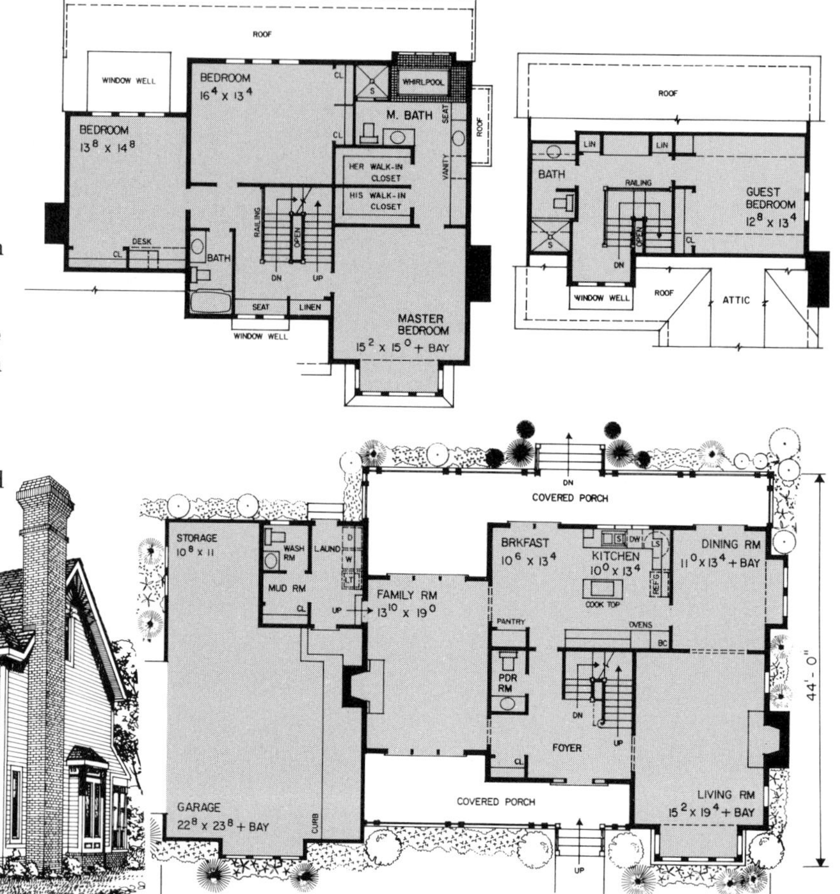

Design P3394

First Floor: 1,531 square feet
Second Floor: 1,307 square feet
Third Floor: 664 square feet
Total: 3,502 square feet

L **D**

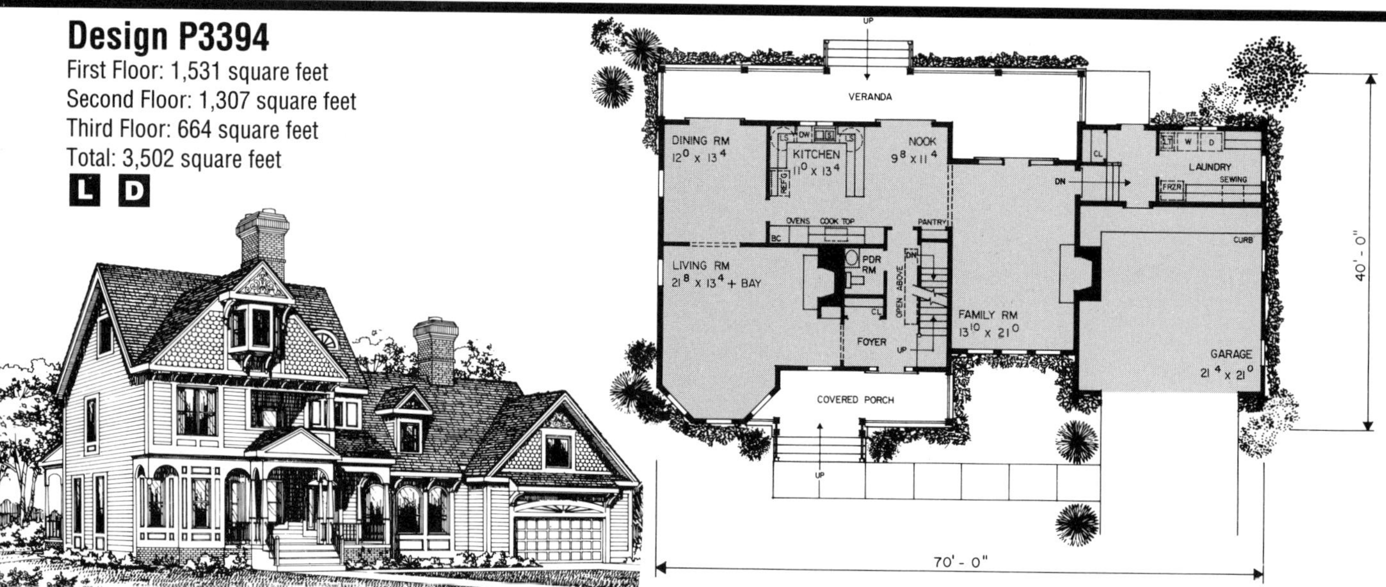

● The Folk Victorian is an important and delightful interpretation. And this version offers the finest in modern floor plans. The formal living areas are set off by a family room which connects the main house to the service areas. The second floor holds three bedrooms and two full baths. A sitting area in the master suite separates it from family bedrooms. On the third floor is a guest bedroom with gracious bath and large walk-in closet.

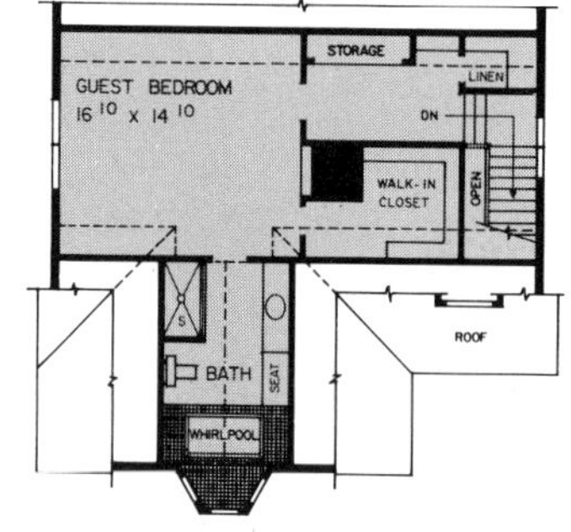

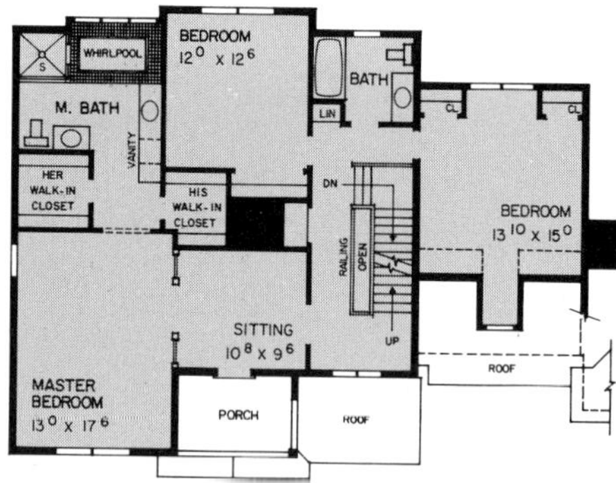

Design P2970 First Floor: 1,538 square feet

Second Floor: 1,526 square feet; Third Floor: 658 square feet
Total: 3,722 square feet

● A porch, is a porch, is a porch. But, when it wraps around to a side, or even two sides, of the house, we have called it a veranda. This charming Victorian features a covered outdoor living area on all four sides! It even ends at a screened porch which features a sun deck above. This interesting plan offers three floors of livability. And what livability it is! Plenty of formal and informal living facilities to go along with the potential of five bedrooms. The master suite is just that. It is adjacent to an interesting sitting room. It has a sun deck and excellent bath/personal care facilities. The third floor will make a wonderful haven for the family's student members.

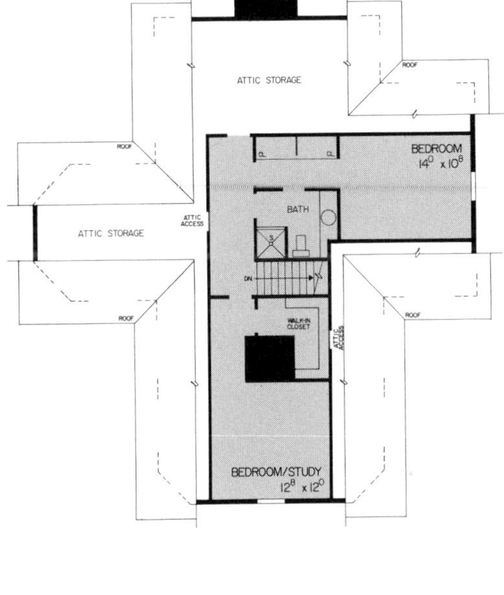

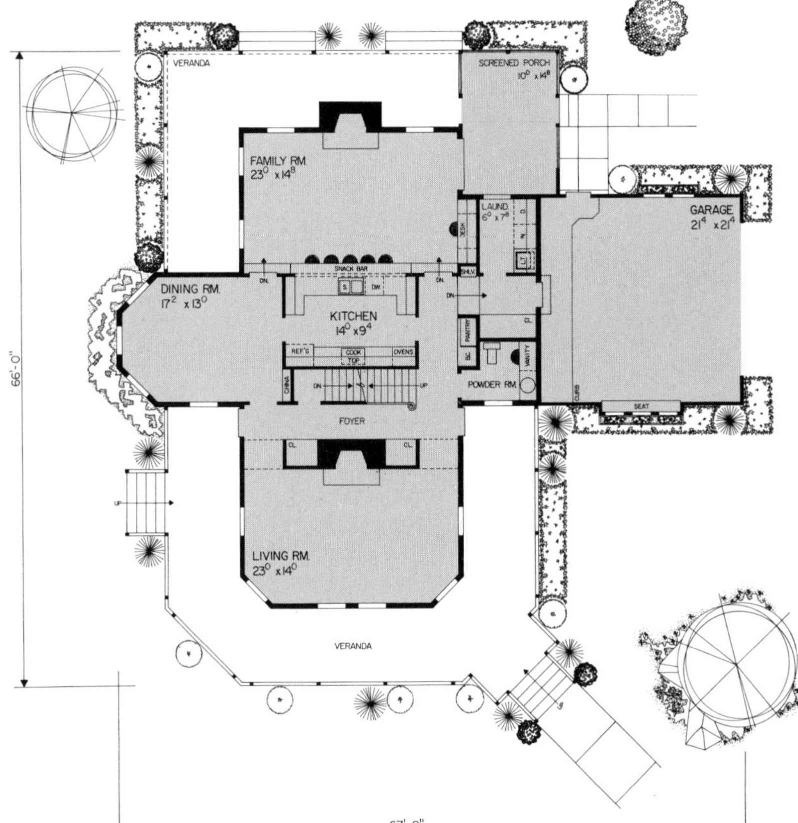

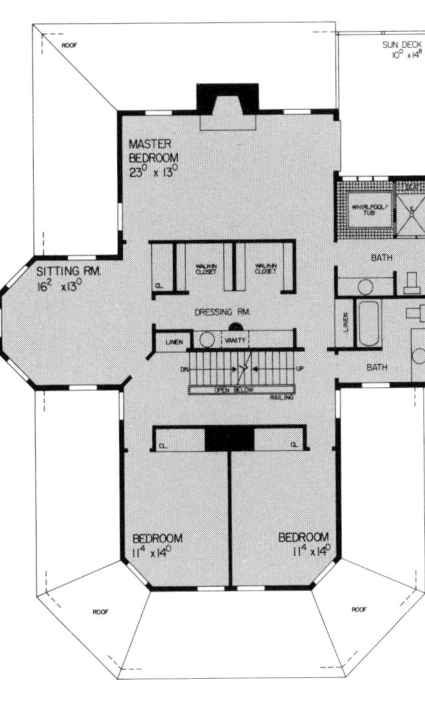

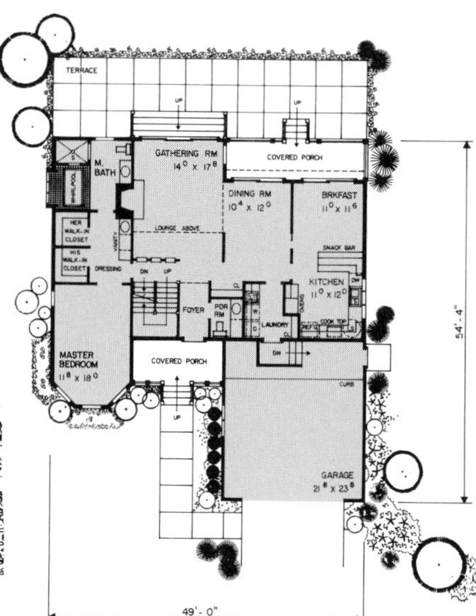

● A grand facade makes this Victorian stand out. Inside, guests and family are well accommodated: gathering room with terrace access, fireplace and attached formal dining room; split-bedroom sleeping arrangements. The master suite contains His and Hers walk-in closets, a separate shower and whirlpool tub and a delightful bay-windowed area. Upstairs there are three more bedrooms (one could serve as a study, one as a media room), a full bath and an open lounge area overlooking the gathering room.

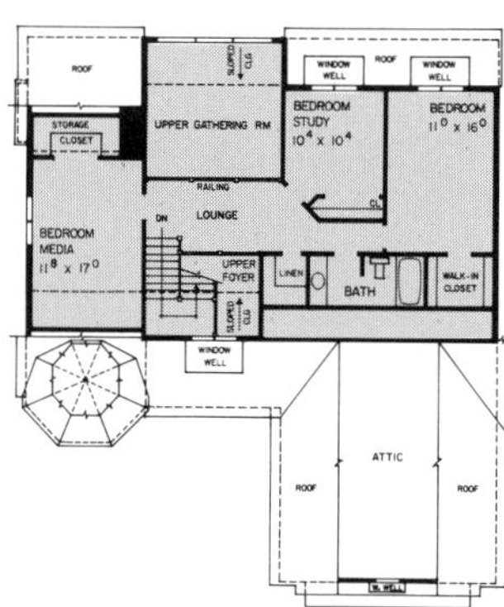

Design P3393

First Floor: 1,449 square feet
Second Floor: 902 square feet
Total: 2,351 square feet

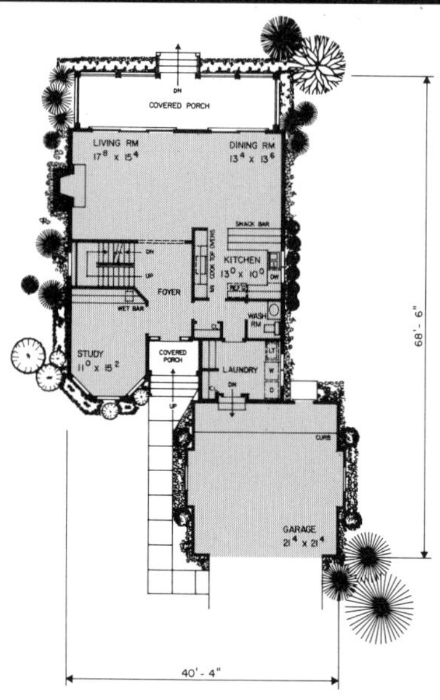

Design P3389

First Floor: 1,161 square feet
Second Floor: 1,090 square feet
Third Floor: 488 square feet
Total: 2,739 square feet

L D

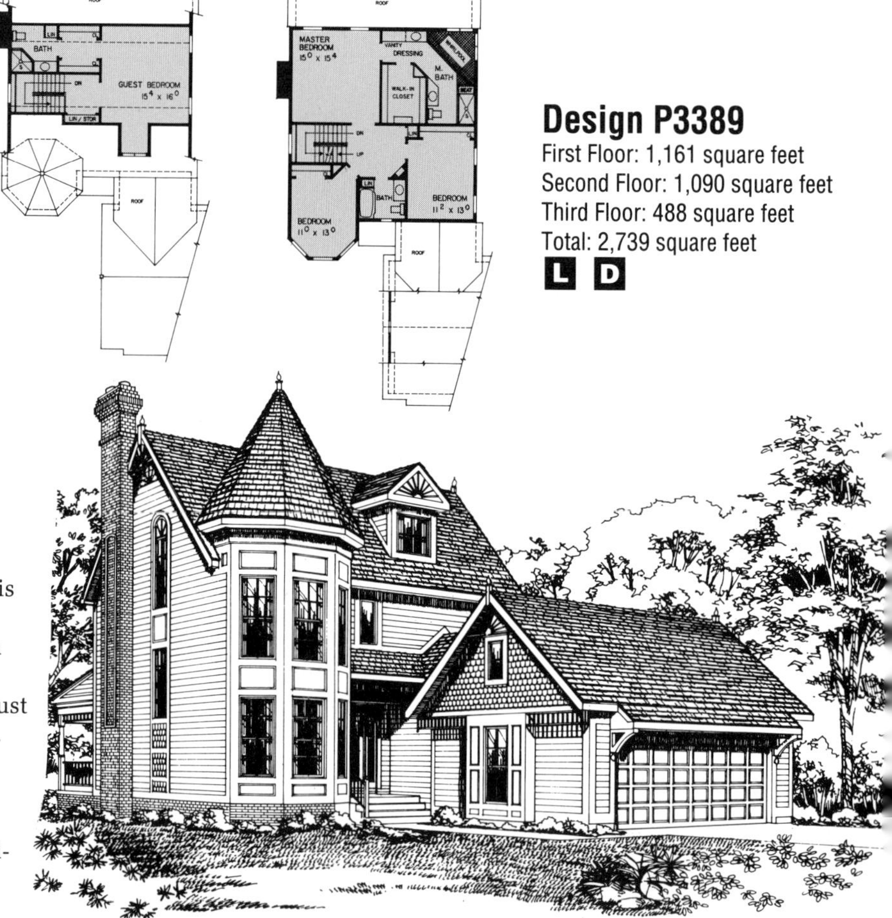

● A Victorian turret accents the facade of this compact three-story. Downstairs rooms include a grand-sized living room/dining room combination. The U-shaped kitchen has a snack-bar pass-through to the dining room. Just to the left of the entry foyer is a private study. On the second floor are three bedrooms and two full baths. The master bedroom has a whirlpool spa and large walk-in closet. The third floor is a perfect location for a guest bedroom with private bath.

Design P3391

First Floor: 1,230 square feet
Second Floor: 991 square feet
Total: 2,221 square feet

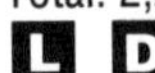

● Detailing is one of the characteristic features of Queen Anne Victorians and this home has no lack of it. Interior rooms add special living patterns. Features include a powder room for guests in the front hallway, a through-fireplace between the ample gathering room and cozy study, an efficient U-shaped kitchen with pantry, and a full-width terrace to the rear. On the second floor are three bedrooms — one a master suite with walk-in closet and amenity-filled bath. An open balcony overlooks the gathering room.

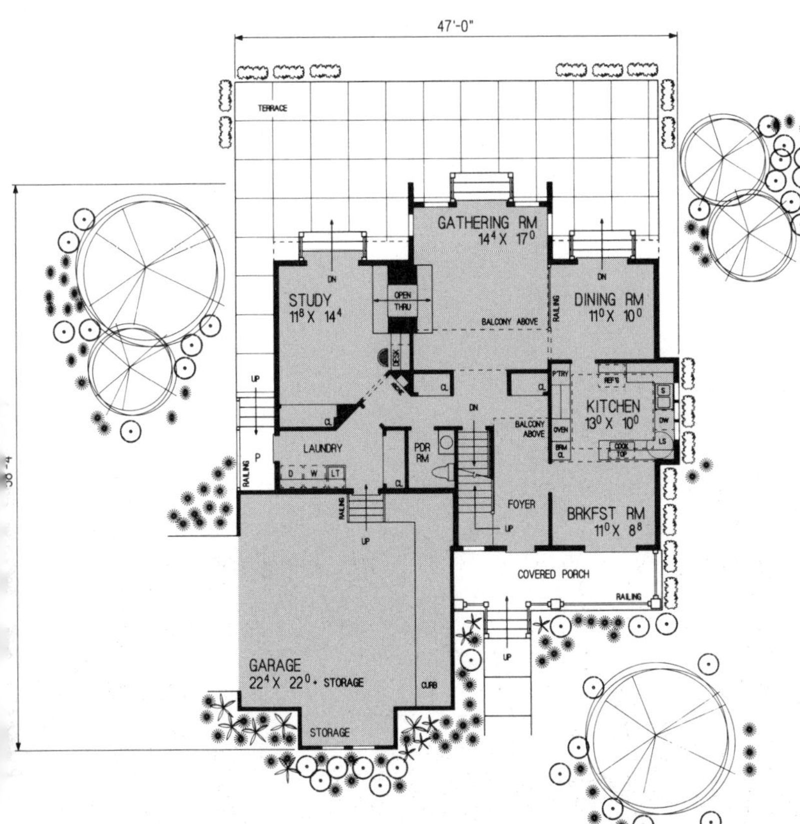

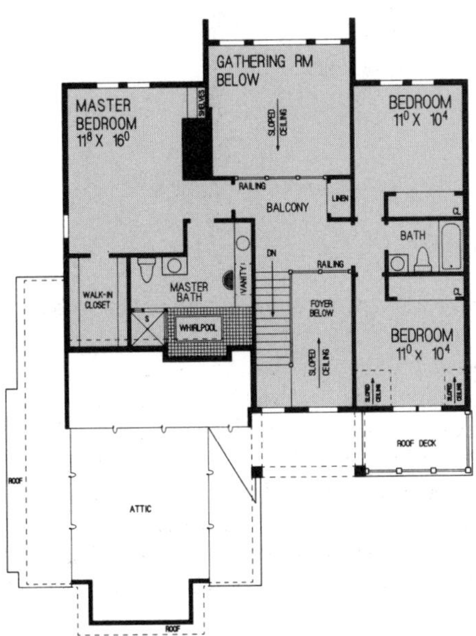

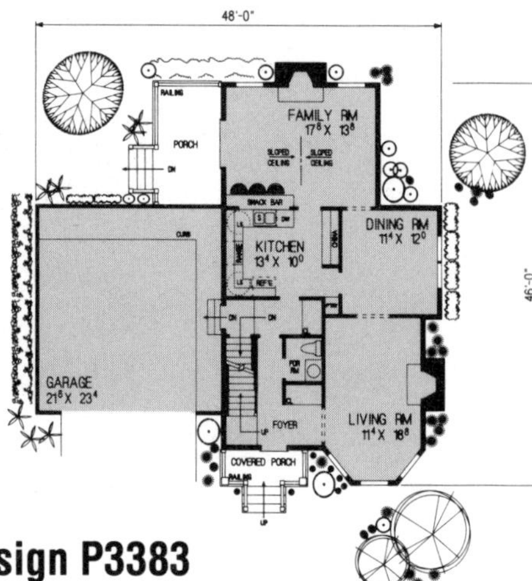

Design P3383

First Floor: 995 square feet
Second Floor: 1,064 square feet
Third Floor: 425 square feet
Total: 2,484 square feet

L **D**

STUDIO 23⁰ X 13⁶ + ALCOVE

ALCOVE

BEDROOM 14¹⁰ X 11⁴ + ALCOVE

BEDROOM 14⁴ X 11⁰

BATH

MASTER BEDROOM 11⁴ X 17⁴

COVERED PORCH

● This delightful Victorian cottage features exterior details that perfectly complement the convenient plan inside. Note the central placement of the kitchen, near to the dining room and the family room. Two fireplaces keep things warm and cozy. Three second-floor bedrooms include a master suite with bay window and two family bedrooms, one with an alcove and walk-in closet. Use the third-floor studio as a study, office or playroom for the children.

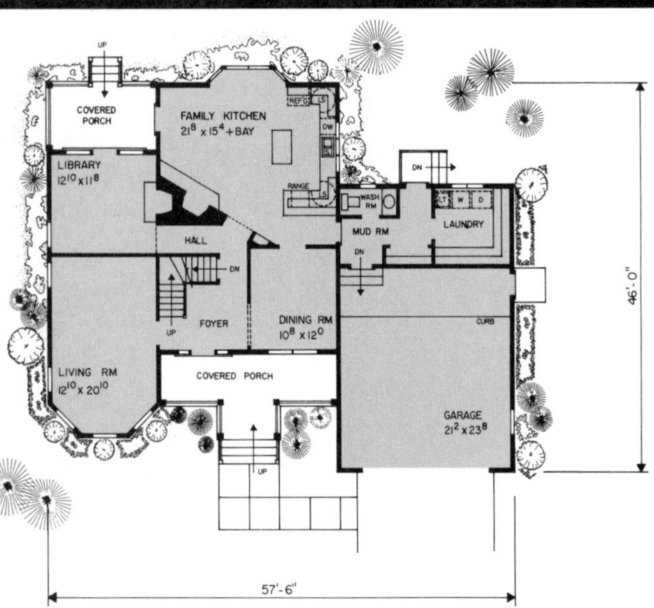

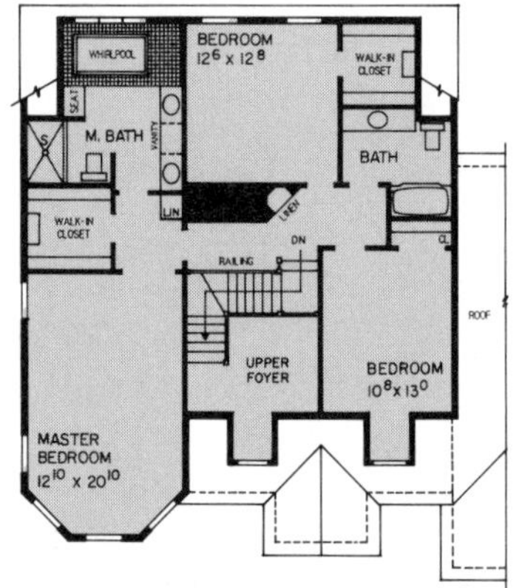

Design P3384

First Floor: 1,399 square feet
Second Floor: 1,123 square feet
Total: 2,522 square feet

L **D**

● Classic Victorian styling comes to the forefront in this Queen Anne. The interior boasts comfortable living quarters for the entire family. On opposite sides of the foyer are the formal dining and living rooms. To the rear is a country-style island kitchen with attached family room. A small library shares a covered porch with this informal gathering area and also has its own fireplace. Three bedrooms on the second floor include a master suite with grand bath. The two family bathrooms share a full bath.

● This two-story farmhouse will be a delight for those who work at home. The second floor has a secluded master bedroom and a studio. A U-shaped kitchen with snack bar and breakfast area with bay window are only the first of the eating areas, which extend to a formal dining room and a covered rear porch for dining al fresco. The two-story living room features a cozy fireplace. A versatile room to the back could serve as a media room or a third bedroom.

Design P3390

First Floor: 1,472 square feet
Second Floor: 1,116 square feet
Total: 2,588 square feet

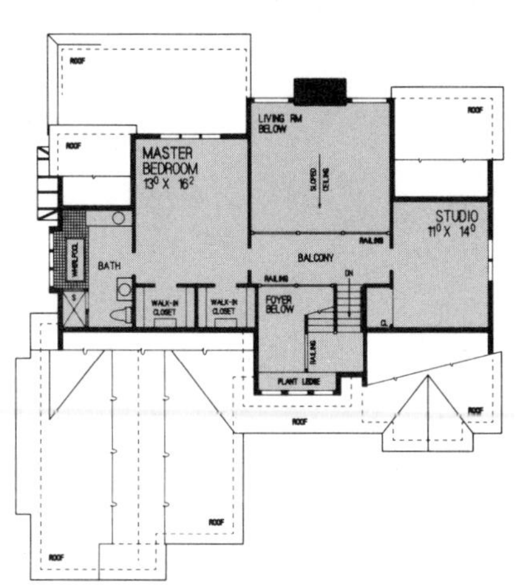

Design P3385

First Floor: 1,096 square feet
Second Floor: 900 square feet
Total: 1,996 square feet

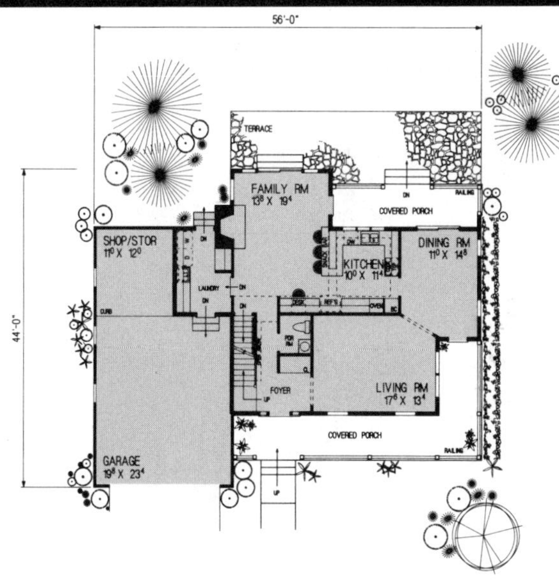

● Covered porches front and rear are complemented by a grand plan for family living. A formal living room and attached dining room provide space for entertaining guests. The large family room with fireplace is a gathering room for everyday use. Four bedrooms occupy the second floor. The master suite features two lavatories, a window seat and three closets. One of the family bedrooms has its own private balcony and could be used as a study.

Design P2829 First Floor: 2,044 square feet

Second Floor: 1,962 square feet; Total: 4,006 square feet

L **D**

● The architecture of this design is Post-Modern with a taste of Victorian styling. Detailed with gingerbread woodwork and a handsome double-width chimney, this two-story design is breathtaking. Enter this home to the large, tiled receiving hall and begin to explore this very livable floor plan. Formal areas consist of the front living room and the dining room. Each has features to make it memorable. The living room is spacious, has a fireplace and access to the covered porch; the dining room has a delightful bay window and is convenient to the kitchen for ease in meal serving. The library is tucked between these two formal areas. Now let's go to the informal area. The family room will welcome many an explorer. It will be a great place for many family activities. Note the L-shaped snack bar with cabinets below. Onward to the second floor, where the private area will be found. Start with the two bedrooms that have two full bathrooms joining them together. The older children will marvel at this area's efficiency and privacy. A third family bedroom is nearby. Then, there is the master bedroom suite. Its list of features is long, indeed. Begin with the "his" and "her" baths and see how many features you can list. A guest bedroom and bath are on the first floor.

Western Farmhouses

Despite the virtual demise of family farming in America, Farmhouse living continues to be as popular and widespread as ever. Showing up in all areas of the country, these rural traditionals are most evident in the midwest and the Great Plains states and are seen in the country, suburbs and city alike.

Predecessors of the modern Western Farmhouse had humble beginnings. Though today's Farmhouse ranges from moderate to giant proportions, early Farmhouses were usually quite small. Most farmers were members of a modest middle class and were neither able to afford nor desirous of much more than a utilitarian dwelling with the minimum requirements—living and sleeping areas plus a basic kitchen. More progressive Farmhouses may have included indoor plumbing, but more often than not, the half-mooned outhouse stood firm.

Architectural styles varied widely in the early Farmhouses, taking their detail points from local custom. However, some common aspects are evident. The home was the center of family life and as such, represented a common gathering point for the nucleus family as well as aunts, uncles, cousins, grandparents and other family members. The natural focus for these gatherings was the fireplace, symbol of hearth and home. In many cases, the hearth was actually part of the kitchen, a convention which set a precedent for the cozy country kitchens with hearths found in many modern Farmhouse designs.

Popular Western Farmhouses of today exhibit a number of charming features. The first aspect in evidence is a front porch or covered entry court where family and friends might gather to visit and relax. These outdoor areas may extend only across the front of the house or may wrap to one side or even on both sides. Porch roofs are usually supported by simple, squared posts. Railings and balustrades are plain and symmetrical with little or no ornamentation.

Dormer windows are most likely one of the more popular elements in the Western Farmhouse. It is not unusual to see four or more dormers extending out above the line of the porch roof. These dormers are offset by balanced rows of multi-paned windows on the first floor.

Because the Farmhouse is derived from such modest beginnings, it is usually not extravagantly adorned. Pediments above dormers, side-lighted front doors, lower-gabled wing extensions and twin chimney stacks all occur but not in opulent proportions. The Farmhouse represents a basic way of life, replete with traditional values, and consequently eschews architectural frivolity.

Fieldstone and brick are common exterior cladding for Farmhouses in many areas of the country, but the Western Farmhouse relies almost exclusively on horizontal wood siding. In a few more eclectic examples, vertical wood siding may be used, following the lead of Prairie-style houses.

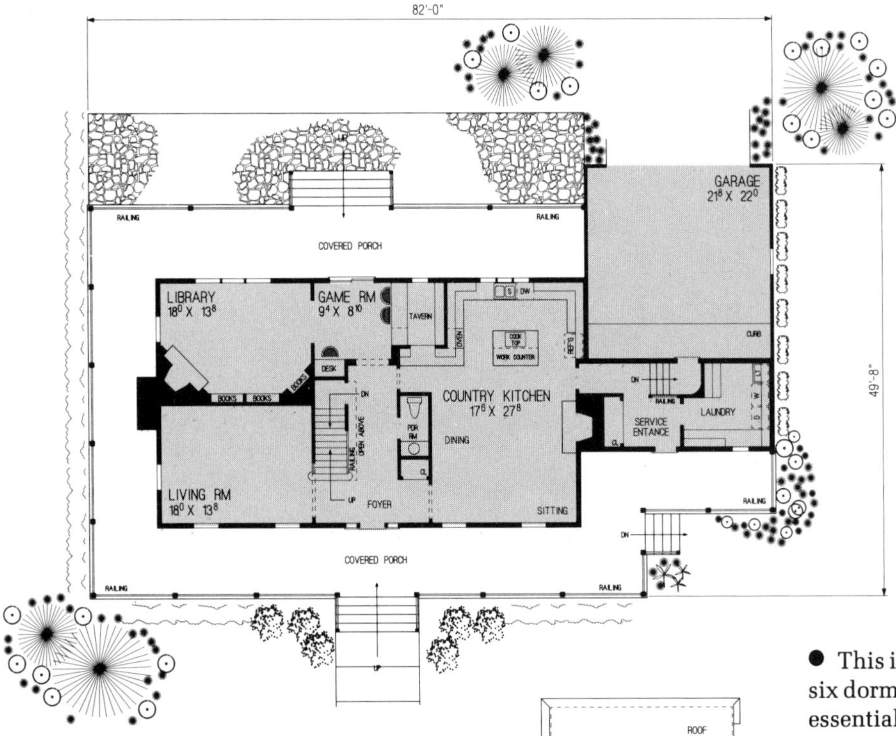

Design P3399

First Floor: 1,716 square feet
Second Floor: 2,102 square feet
Total: 3,818 square feet

L **D**

● This is the ultimate in farmhouse living — six dormer windows and a porch that stretches essentially around the entire house. Inside, the plan is open and inviting. Besides the large country kitchen with fireplace, there is a small game room with attached tavern, a library with built-in bookshelves and a fireplace, and a formal living room. The second floor has four bedrooms and three full baths. The service entrance features a laundry area conveniently just off the garage.

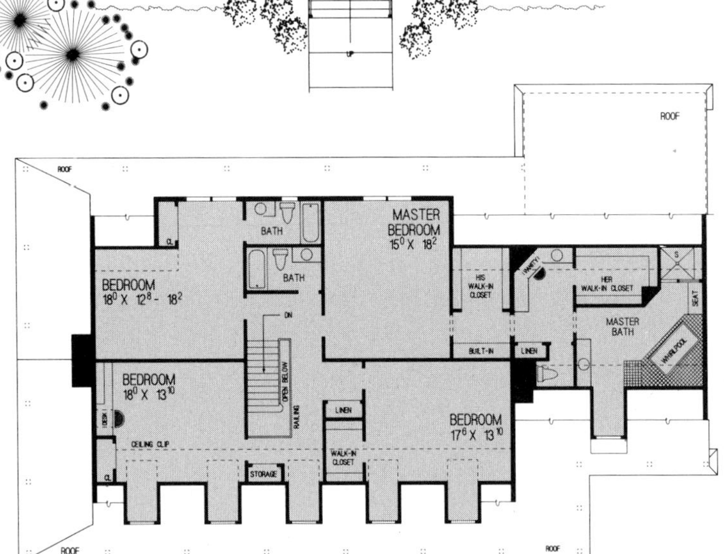

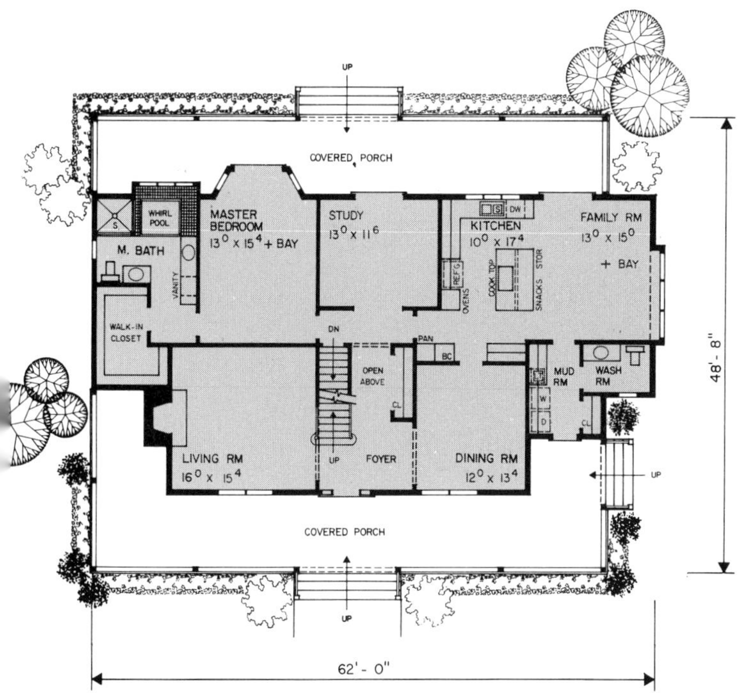

Design P3396

First Floor: 1,830 square feet
Second Floor: 1,012 square feet
Total: 2,842 square feet

L **D**

● Rustic charm abounds in this pleasant farmhouse rendition. Covered porches to the front and rear enclose living potential for the whole family. Flanking the entrance foyer are the living and dining rooms. To the rear is the L-shaped kitchen with island cook top and snack bar. A small family room/breakfast nook is attached. A private study is tucked away on this floor next to the master suite. On the second floor are three bedrooms and a full bath. Two of the bedrooms have charming dormer windows.

BEDROOM 13⁰ x 11⁰
CL
LIN
BATH
DRESSING
CL
DN
LIN
RAILING
OPEN
BEDROOM 13⁸ x 12⁰
CL
BEDROOM 14⁴ x 15⁰

Design P3397

First Floor: 1,855 square feet
Second Floor: 1,241 square feet
Total: 3,096 square feet

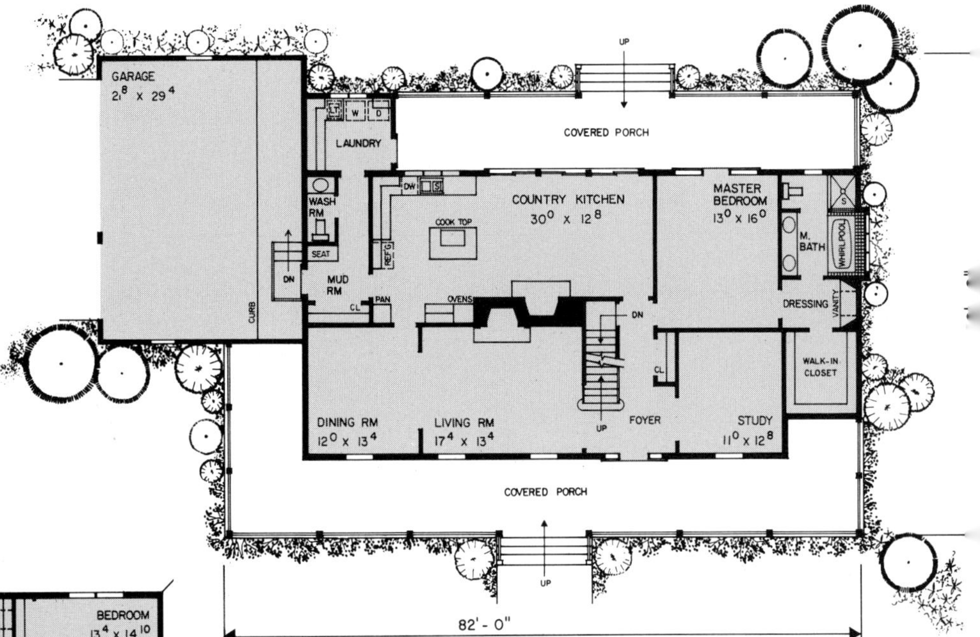

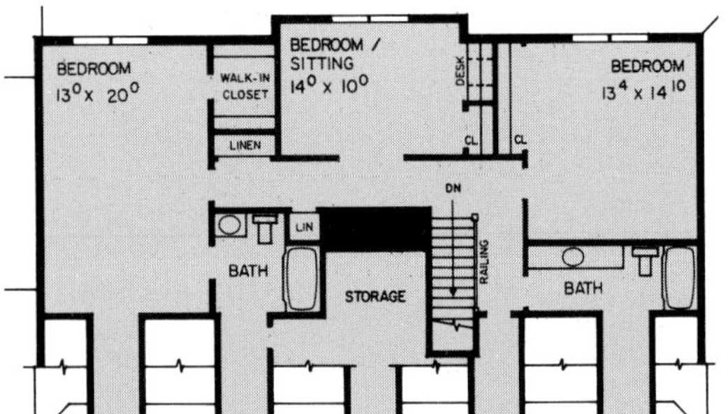

● Five second-story dormers and a wide covered front porch add to the charm of this farmhouse design. Inside, the entry foyer opens to the left to a formal living room with fireplace and attached dining room. To the right is a private study. The back of the plan is dominated by a huge country kitchen featuring an island cook top. On this floor is the master suite with a large walk-in closet. The second floor holds three bedrooms (or two and a sitting room) with two full baths.

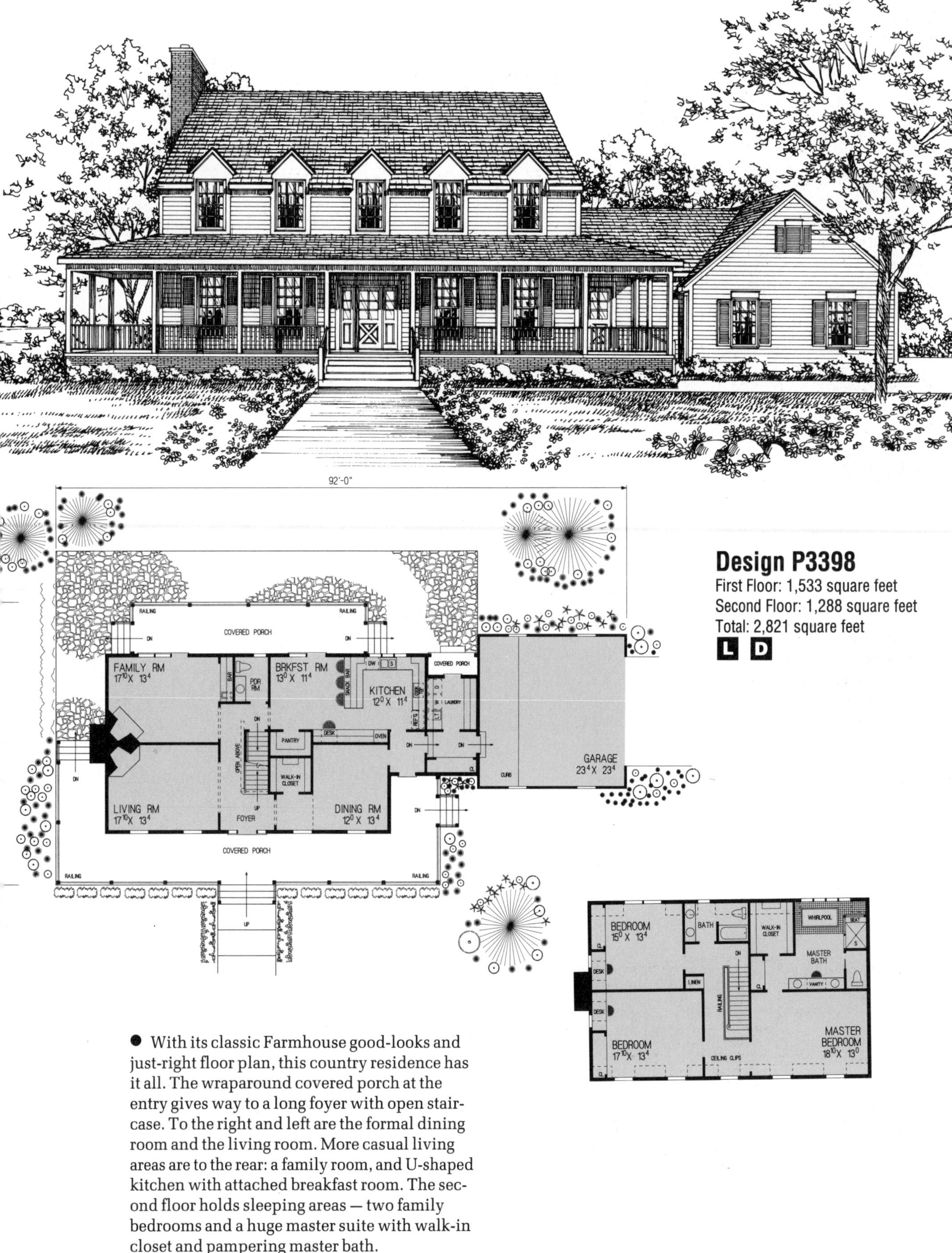

Design P3398

First Floor: 1,533 square feet
Second Floor: 1,288 square feet
Total: 2,821 square feet

L **D**

● With its classic Farmhouse good-looks and just-right floor plan, this country residence has it all. The wraparound covered porch at the entry gives way to a long foyer with open staircase. To the right and left are the formal dining room and the living room. More casual living areas are to the rear: a family room, and U-shaped kitchen with attached breakfast room. The second floor holds sleeping areas — two family bedrooms and a huge master suite with walk-in closet and pampering master bath.

Design P3438

First Floor: 1,489 square feet
Second Floor: 741 square feet
Total: 2,230 square feet

● A unique farmhouse plan which provides a grand floor plan, this home is comfortable in country or suburban settings. Formal entertaining areas share first-floor space with family gathering rooms and work and service areas. The master suite is also on this floor for convenience and privacy. Upstairs is a guest bedroom, private bath and loft area that makes a perfect studio. Special features make this a great place to come home to.

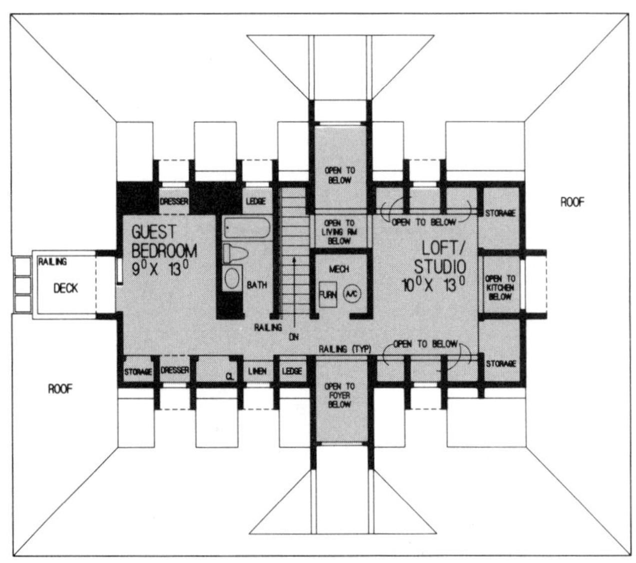

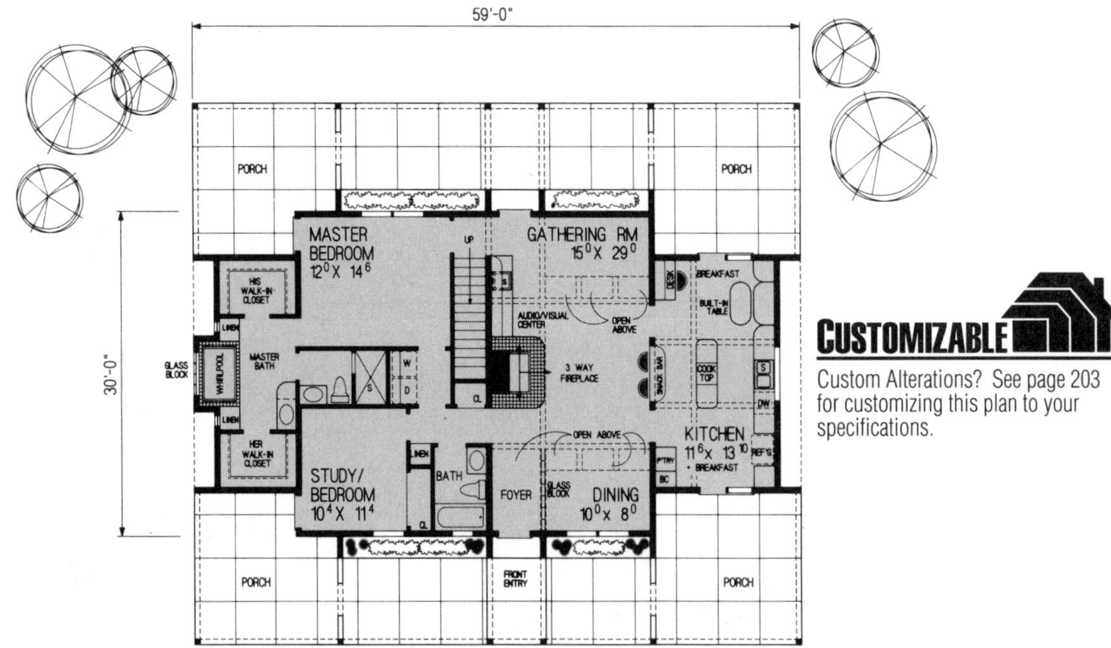

CUSTOMIZABLE

Custom Alterations? See page 203 for customizing this plan to your specifications.

FAMILY RM BELOW
RAILING
DN
DN
BALCONY
BATH
LINEN
WH
MECH
AC
RAILING
CL
OPEN TO FIRE PIT
CL
LEDGE
BEDROOM 13 X 11 • BAY
OPEN TO FOYER
BEDROOM 13 X 11 • BAY

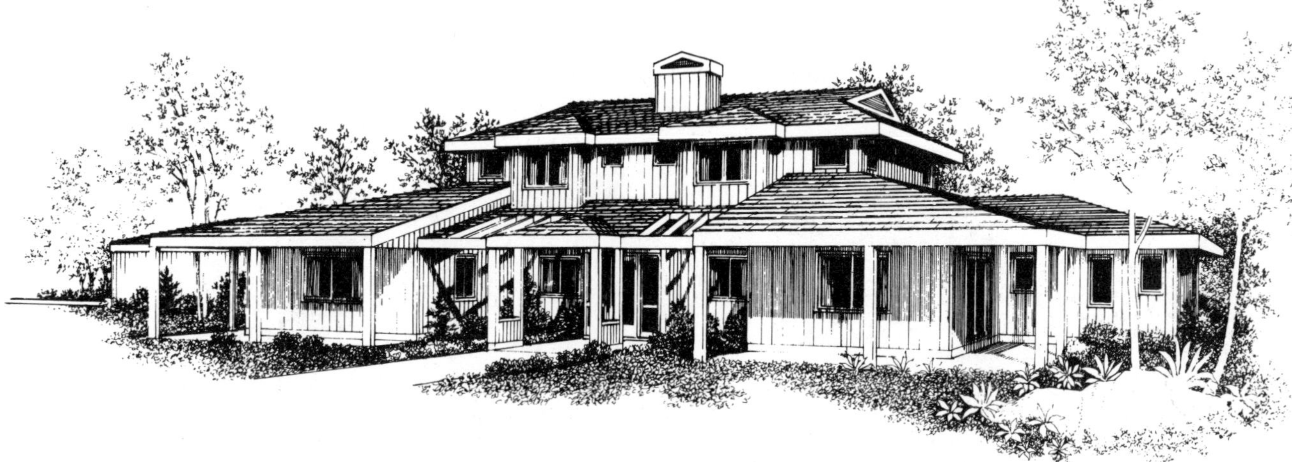

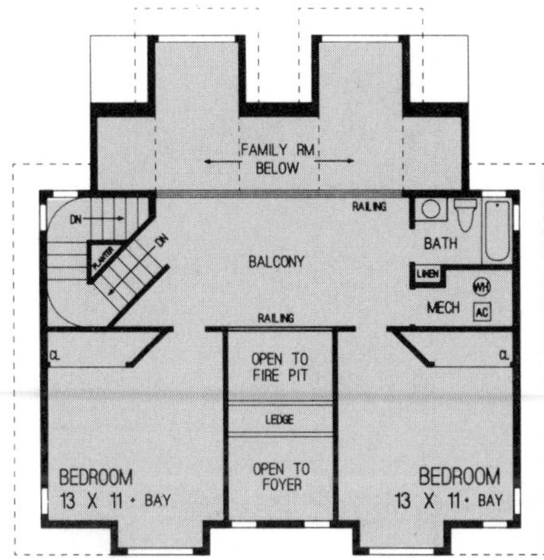

Design P3404

First Floor: 3,358 square feet
Second Floor: 868 square feet
Total: 4,226 square feet

L **D**

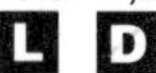

● Farmhouse design does a double take in this unusual and elegant rendition. Notice that most of the living takes place on the first floor: formal living room and dining room, gigantic family room with enormous firepit and porch access, guest bedroom or den and master bedroom suite. Upstairs there are two smaller bedrooms and a dramatic balcony overlook to the family room below.

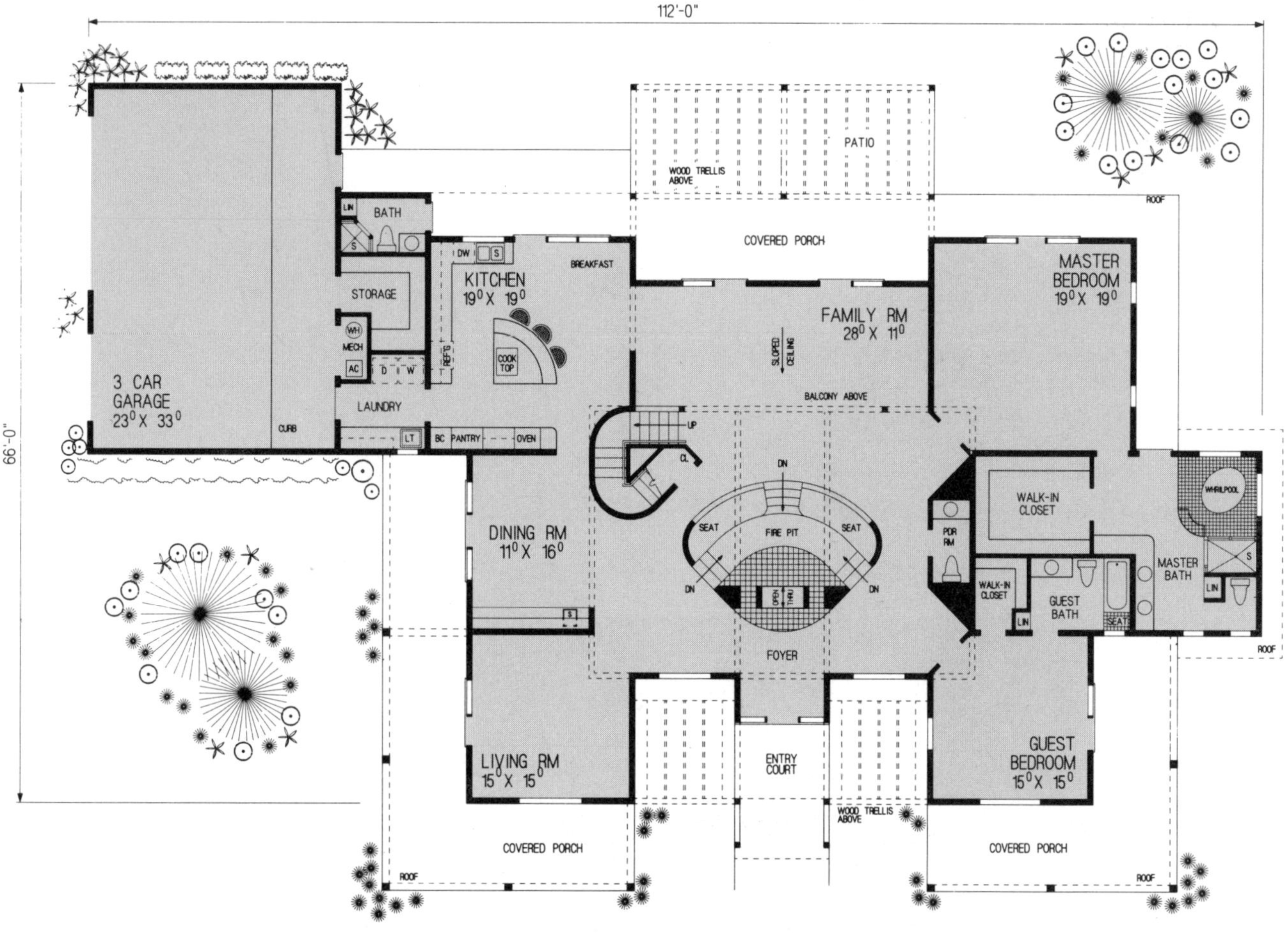

112'-0"
66'-0"
PATIO
WOOD TRELLIS ABOVE
ROOF
BATH
LIN
COVERED PORCH
DW
S
BREAKFAST
MASTER BEDROOM 19⁰ X 19⁰
KITCHEN 19⁰ X 19⁰
STORAGE
FAMILY RM 28⁰ X 11⁰
SLOPED CEILING
WH
MECH
AC
REF'G
COOK TOP
D W
3 CAR GARAGE 23⁰ X 33⁰
BALCONY ABOVE
LAUNDRY
CURB
LT
BC
PANTRY
OVEN
UP
CL
DN
WALK-IN CLOSET
WHIRLPOOL
DINING RM 11⁰ X 16⁰
SEAT
FIRE PIT
SEAT
PDR RM
MASTER BATH
WALK-IN CLOSET
S
DN
OPEN THRU
DN
GUEST BATH
LIN
SEAT
LIN
ROOF
FOYER
ENTRY COURT
LIVING RM 15⁰ X 15⁰
GUEST BEDROOM 15⁰ X 15⁰
WOOD TRELLIS ABOVE
COVERED PORCH
COVERED PORCH
ROOF
ROOF

Design P2775

First Floor: 1,317 square feet
Second Floor: 952 square feet
Total: 2,269 square feet

L

● This front-porch farmhouse adaptation is characteristic of those found in the rolling hills of Pennsylvania. The interior is quite impressive. Both the formal and informal areas are outstandingly spacious. There are two eating areas: the formal dining room and the nook with sliding glass doors to a dining terrace. Many built-ins will be found in the nook/kitchen area including a desk, pantry and more. Three family bedrooms, bath and master bedroom suite are on the second floor.

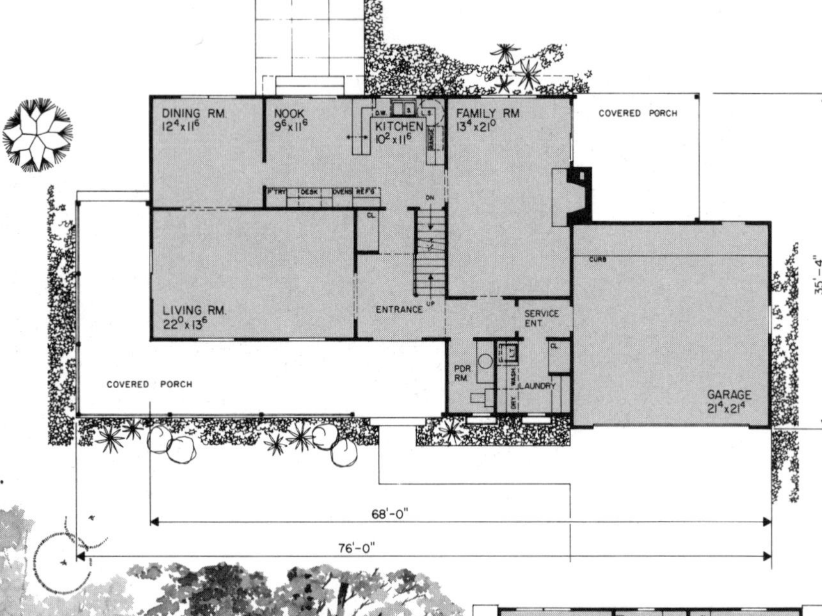

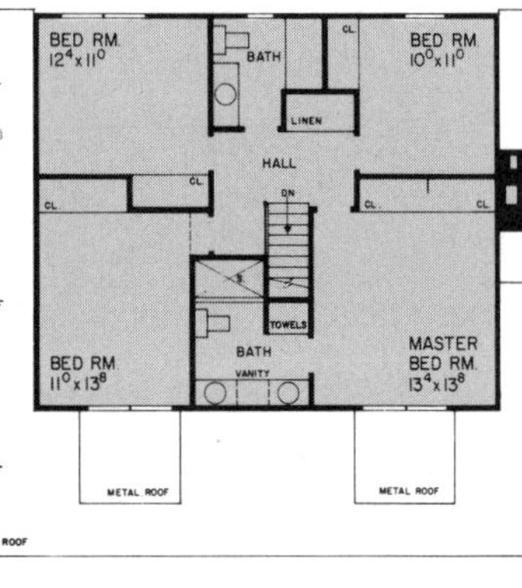

Design P2908

First Floor: 1,229 square feet
Second Floor: 1,153 square feet
Total: 2,382 square feet

L **D**

● This Early American farmhouse offers plenty of modern comfort with its covered front porch with pillars and rails, double chimneys, building attachment, and four upstairs bedrooms. The first-floor attachment includes a family room with bay window. The upstairs is accessible from stairs just off the front foyer. Included is a master bedroom suite. Downstairs is a modern kitchen with breakfast room, dining room, and front living room.

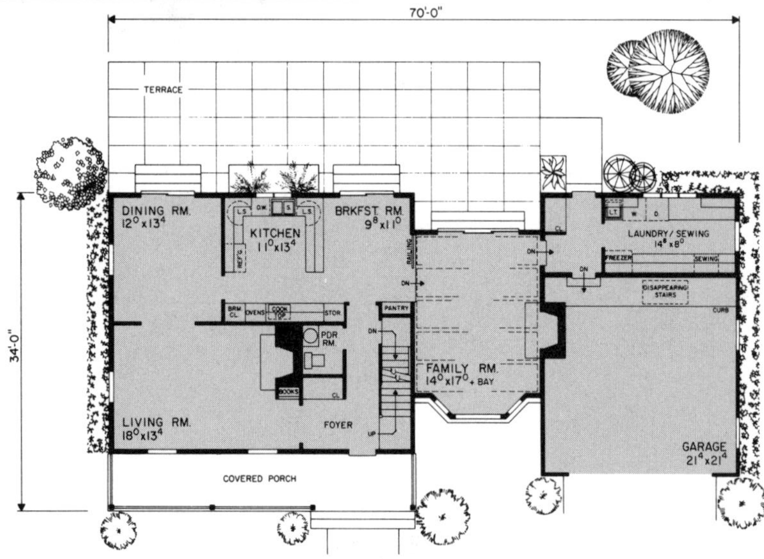

CUSTOMIZABLE

Custom Alterations? See page 203 for customizing this plan to your specifications.

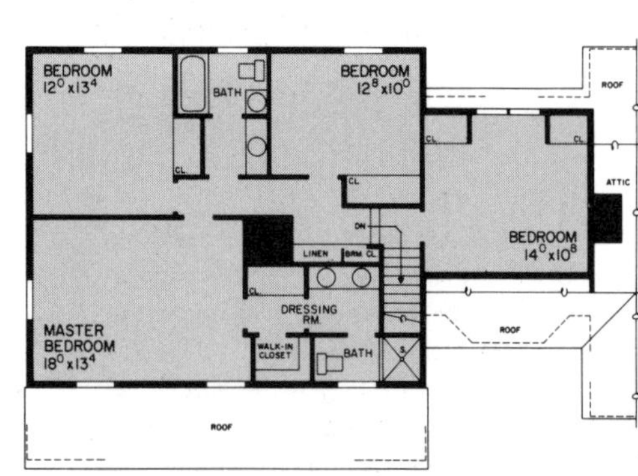

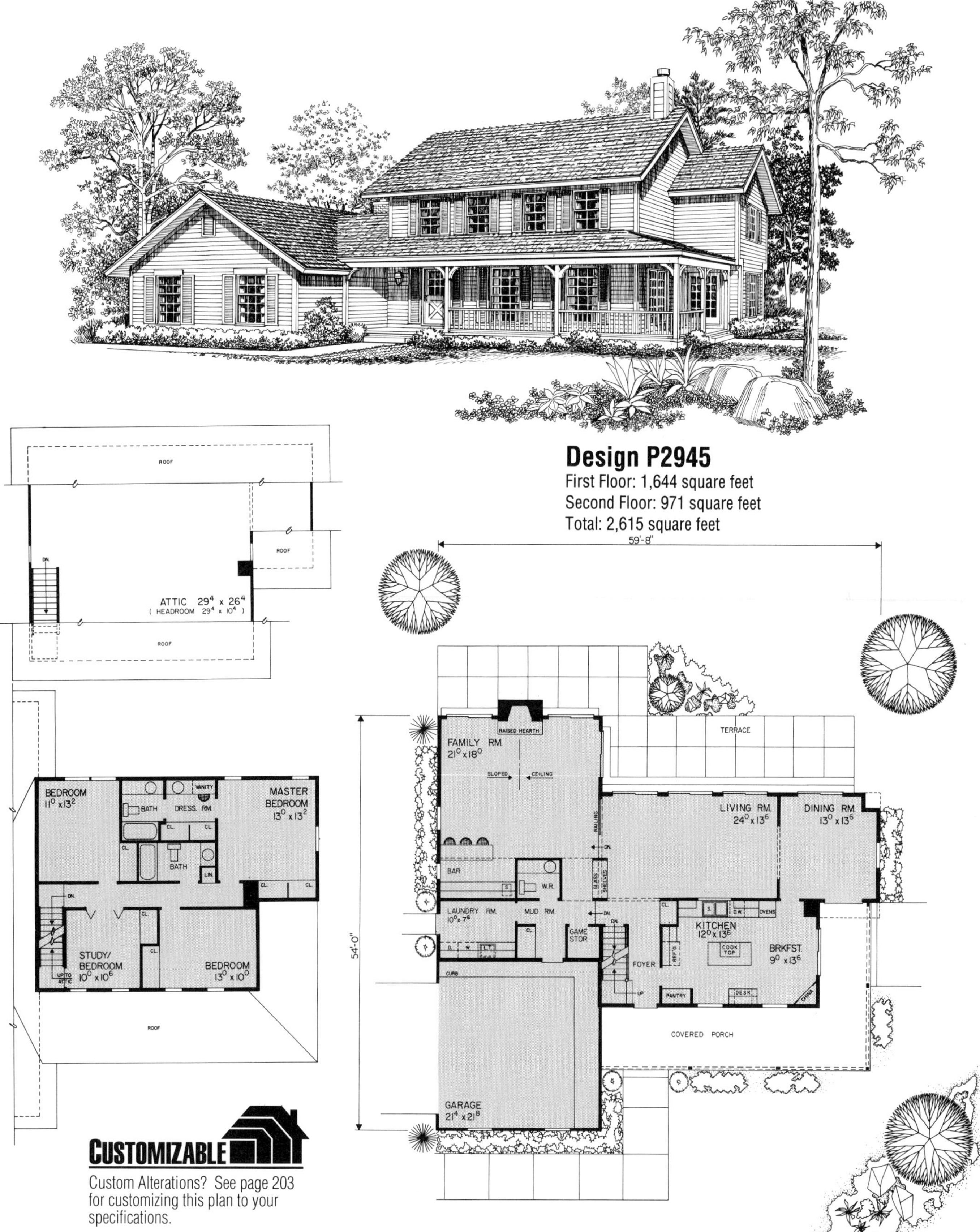

Design P2945

First Floor: 1,644 square feet
Second Floor: 971 square feet
Total: 2,615 square feet

CUSTOMIZABLE

Custom Alterations? See page 203 for customizing this plan to your specifications.

● Here is a new floor plan designed to go with the almost identical exterior of one of Home Planners' most popular houses. A masterfully affordable design, this plan manages to include all the basics - and then adds a little more. Note the wraparound covered porch, large family room with raised-hearth fireplace and wet bar, spacious kitchen with island cook top, formal dining room, rear terrace, and extra storage on the first floor. Upstairs, the plan's as flexible as they come: three or four bedrooms (the fourth could easily be a study or playroom) and lots of unfinished attic just waiting for you to transform it into living space. This could make a fine studio, sewing room, home office, or just a place for the safe, dry storage of the family's paraphernalia, Christmas decorations, etc.

Design P2776

First Floor: 1,134 square feet
Second Floor: 874 square feet
Total: 2,008 square feet

Custom Alterations? See page 203 for customizing this plan to your specifications.

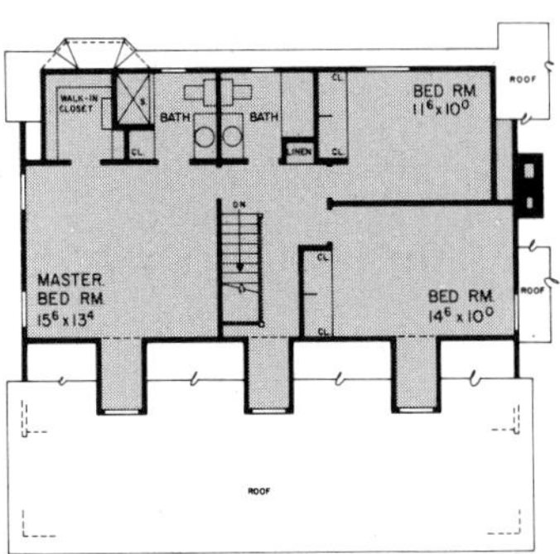

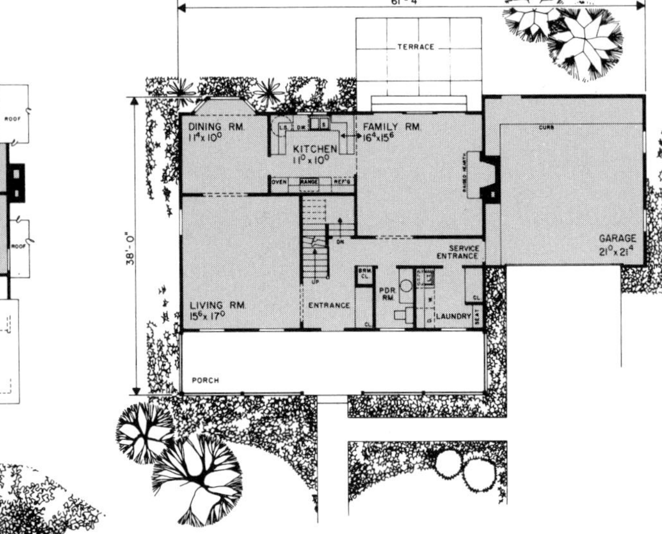

● This board-and-batten farmhouse design has all of the country charm of New England. Immediately off the front entrance is the delightful corner living room. The dining room with bay window is easily served by the U-shaped kitchen. Informal family living enjoyment resides in the family room which features a raised-hearth fireplace and sliding glass doors to the rear terrace. The second floor houses all of the sleeping facilities.

Design P2865

First Floor: 1,703 square feet
Second Floor: 1,044 square feet
Total: 2,747 square feet

● Here's a cozy traditional farmhouse with a big wraparound covered porch. Up front, flanking the entry foyer, are a living room with fireplace and formal dining room. To the rear are a study, that could be used as a guest room, and the family room with another fireplace. The kitchen/breakfast room combination is conveniently located near the service entrance off the garage. Note bedrooms with dormer windows upstairs.

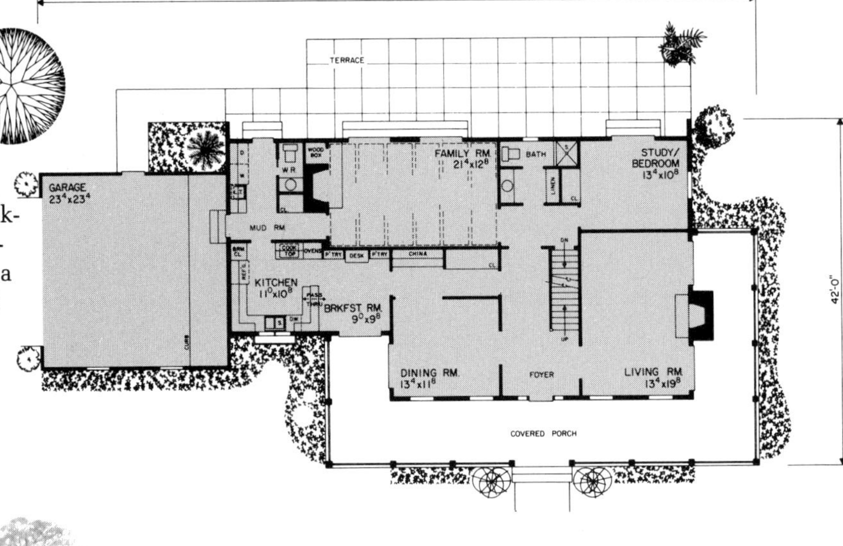

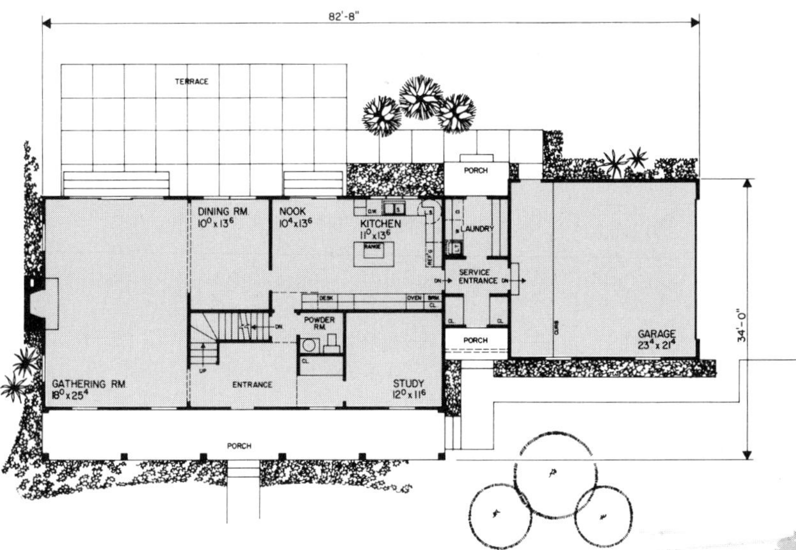

Design P2650

First Floor: 1,451 square feet
Second Floor: 1,091 square feet
Total: 2,542 square feet

L **D**

● The dormers and the covered porch with pillars introduce this house. Inside, the appeal is also outstanding. Note the size (18′ x 25′) of the gathering room which is open to the dining room. The kitchen/nook area is very spacious and features a cooking island, built-in desk and more. It's convenient having the laundry and the service area close to the kitchen. Make special note of the service entrance doors leading to both the front and back of the house.

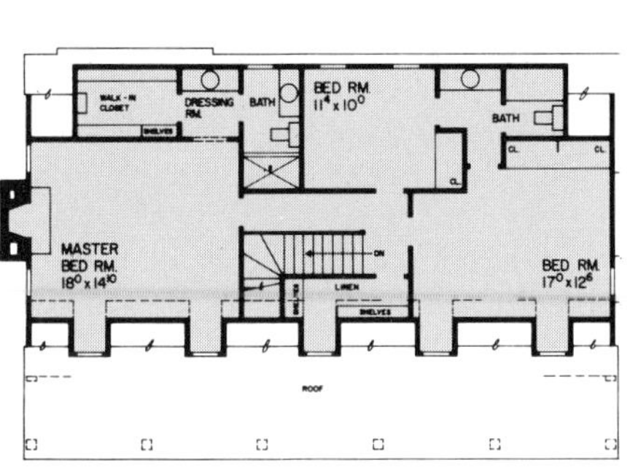

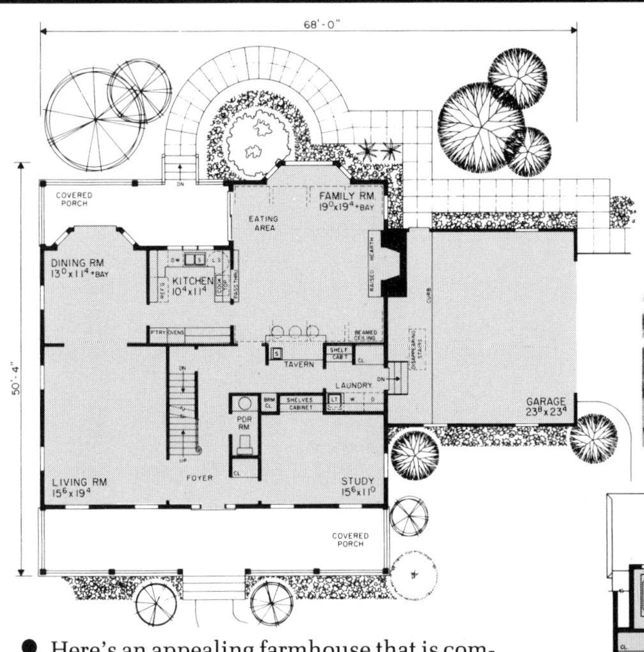

● Here's an appealing farmhouse that is complemented by an inviting front porch. Just inside is a nice-sized study to the right and a spacious living room to the left. The adjacent dining room has an attractive bay window. Just a step away is an efficient kitchen. Family activities will be enjoyed in the large family room. Upstairs you'll find a master bedroom suite featuring a bath with an oversized tub and shower and a dressing room. Also on this floor: two bedrooms, full bath and a large attic.

Design P2890

First Floor: 1,612 square feet
Second Floor: 1,356 square feet
Total: 2,968 square feet

D

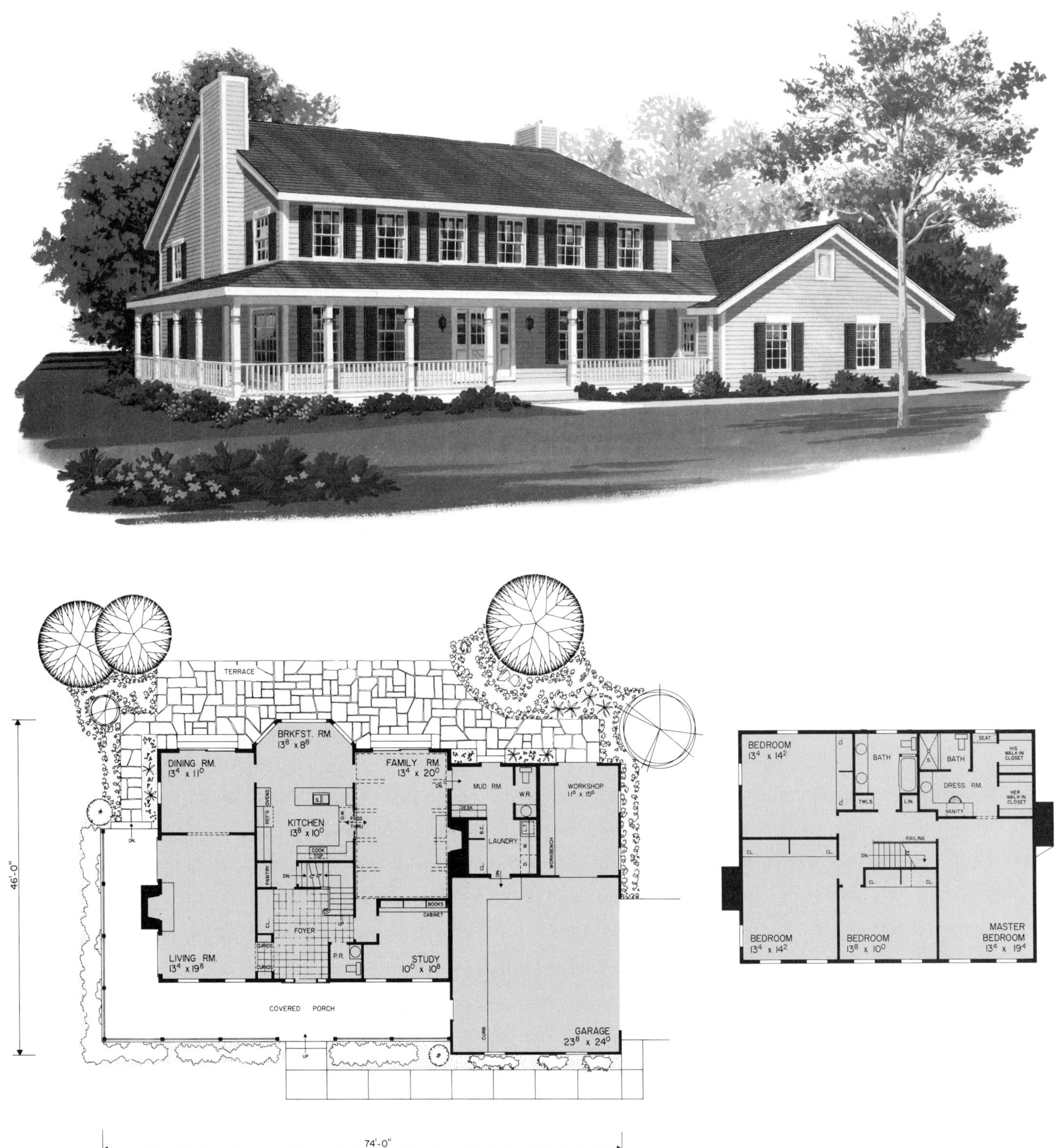

Design P2946 First Floor: 1,590 square feet; Second Floor: 1,344 square feet; Total: 2,934 square feet

L **D**

● Here's a traditional design that's made for down-home hospitality, the pleasures of casual conversation, and the good grace of pleasant company. The star attractions are the large covered porch and terrace, perfectly relaxing gathering points for family and friends. Inside, though, the design is truly a hard worker; separate living room and family room, each with its own fireplace; formal dining room; large kitchen and breakfast area with bay windows; separate study; workshop with plenty of room to maneuver; mud room; and four bedrooms up, including a master suite. Not to be overlooked are the curio niches, the powder room, the built-in bookshelves, the kitchen pass-through, the pantry, the planning desk, the workbench, and the stairs to the basement.

Western Vacation Homes

Nowhere in the country are the great outdoors revered and enjoyed as actively as in the West. From Rocky Mountain ski chalets to ocean-side deck houses, the Western Vacation home is a long-standing leisure-time favorite.

Vacation homes generally are smaller, less elaborate versions of permanent residences and consequently mimic many of the same styles from Tudor to Bungalow. One immensely popular style that was developed specifically for vacation living is the A-frame. The style actually was created as somewhat of a joke by architect Rudolph Schindler. He was to design a home for an exclusive area at Lake Arrowhead where housing restrictions specified "Norman style" only. Schindler, a one-time draftsman for Frank Lloyd Wright, knew he would never be able to create something in the modern style at which he was so adept and, therefore, designed the first A-frame which he declared "Norman style." It was never challenged and, in fact, has grown to become one of the most popular Vacation home styles since.

While there is no one consummate variety of Western Vacation home, there are some characteristics that are shared by all of these cozy get-aways.

Probably the most important factor in a Vacation home is that it be accommodating to leisure lifestyles. This does not necessarily mean large, but may mean larger-sized rooms with few interior walls—open living spaces. There might be no clear delineation, in fact, between living areas and dining areas and the kitchen may be open to both with only a snack counter as separation.

Sleeping areas take on different configurations as well. Instead of two or three large, private bedrooms, a Vacation home could function nicely with one private master suite and a large loft bunk area for children. Or there might be several smaller bedrooms that offer some degree of privacy but don't demand a great percentage of the overall square footage.

Great and abundant outdoor living areas are essential to a Vacation home. There are any number of choices: decks, patios, balconies and terraces to name a few. It is best to have several outdoor areas to satisfy different activities. A large main deck is a natural gathering place for general relaxation, dining and conversation, but a master suite terrace allows space for more private encounters and a children's deck provides an activity center for boisterous play.

There are other components to the perfect Vacation home that, though not essential, make these homes more inviting and comfortable. For example, a fireplace in the main living area cheers and warms the home on a cold winter evening and, in some cases, is necessary for the home to be used at all during several months of the year.

Other items such as built-in storage spaces that keep the home from becoming crowded and cluttered and a small laundry area for clean-ups after messy activities will be appreciated for their time- and space-saving assets.

As a final ingredient, add plenty of windows and skylights so that interior spaces are filled with light and the scenic views beyond!

Design P4061 First Floor: 1,008 square feet
Second Floor: 323 square feet; Total: 1,331 square feet

D

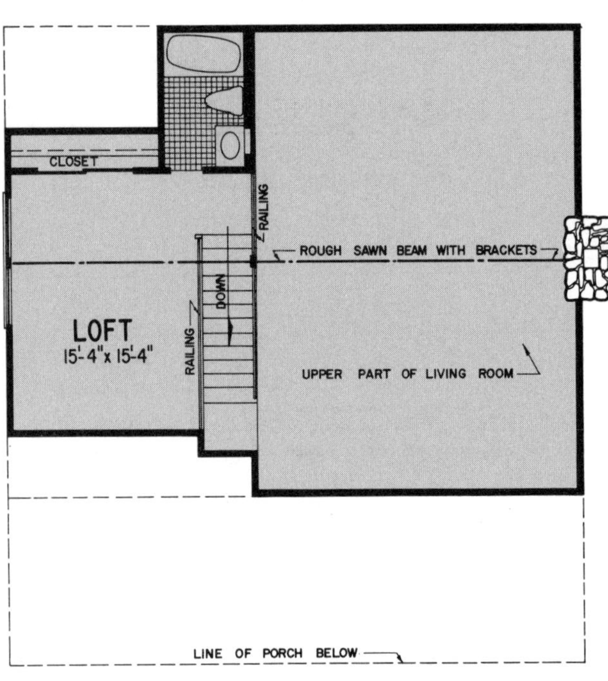

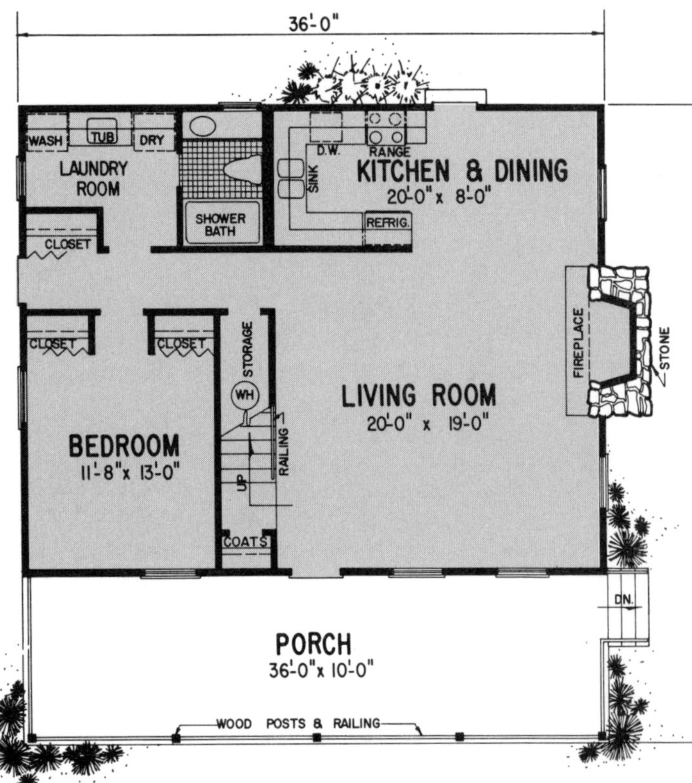

LIFESTYLE HOME PLANS

● This charming farmhouse design will be economical to build and a pleasure to occupy. Like most vacation homes, this design features an open plan. The large living area includes a living room and dining room and a massive stone fireplace. A partition separates the kitchen from the living room. Also downstairs are a bedroom, full bath, and laundry room. Upstairs is a spacious sleeping loft overlooking the living room. Don't miss the large front porch — this will be a favorite spot for relaxing.

Design P2488 First Floor: 1,113 square feet; Second Floor: 543 square feet; Total: 1,656 square feet

D

Custom Alterations? See page 203 for customizing this plan to your specifications.

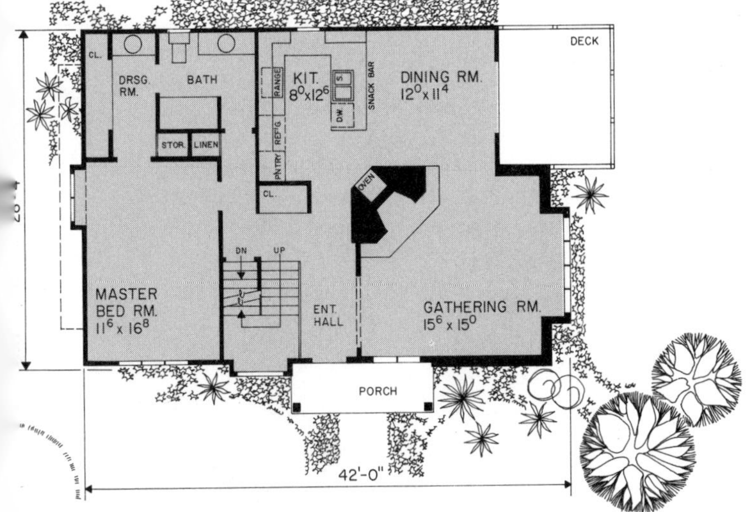

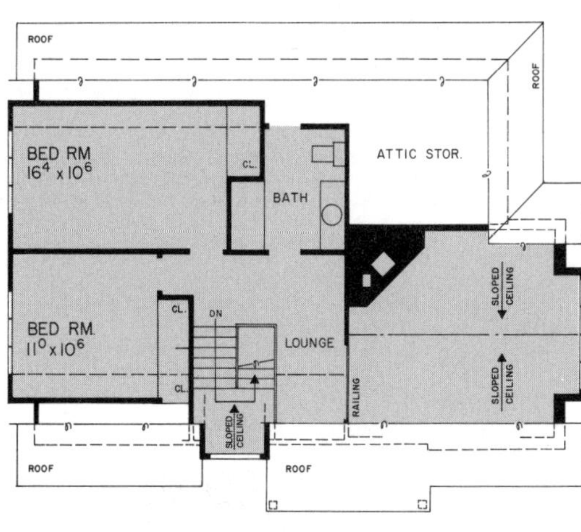

● A cozy cottage for the young at heart! Whether called upon to serve the young active family as a leisure-time retreat at the lake, or the retired couple as a quiet haven in later years, this charming design will perform well. As a year round second home, the upstairs with its two sizable bedrooms, full bath and lounge area looking down into the gathering room below, will ideally accommodate the younger generation. When called upon to function as a retirement home, the second floor will cater to the visiting family members and friends. Also, it will be available for use as a home office, study, sewing room, music area, the pursuit of hobbies, etc. Of course, as an efficient, economical home for the young, growing family, this design will function well.

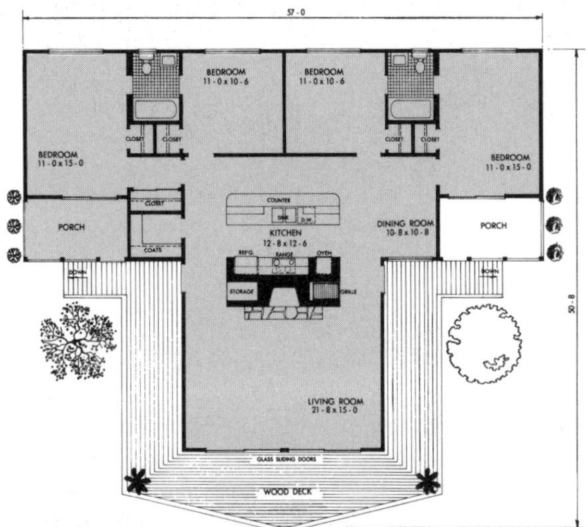

Design P4015

Square Footage: 1,420

● The perfect vacation home combines open, formal living spaces with lots of sleeping space. Study this plan carefully. The spacious living room has a warming fireplace and sliding glass doors onto the deck. Convenient to the dining room, the efficient kitchen is carefully placed so as not to interfere with the living room. Notice the four spacious bedrooms — there is plenty of room for accommodating guests. Two of the bedrooms boast private porches.

Design P4027

Square Footage: 1,232

● Good things come in small packages, too! The size and shape of this design will help hold down construction costs without sacrificing livability. The enormous great room is a multi-purpose living space with room for a dining area and several seating areas. Also notice the sloped ceilings. Sliding glass doors provide access to the wraparound deck and sweeping views of the outdoors. The well-equipped kitchen includes a pass-through and pantry. Two bedrooms, each with sloped ceiling and compartmented bath, round out the plan.

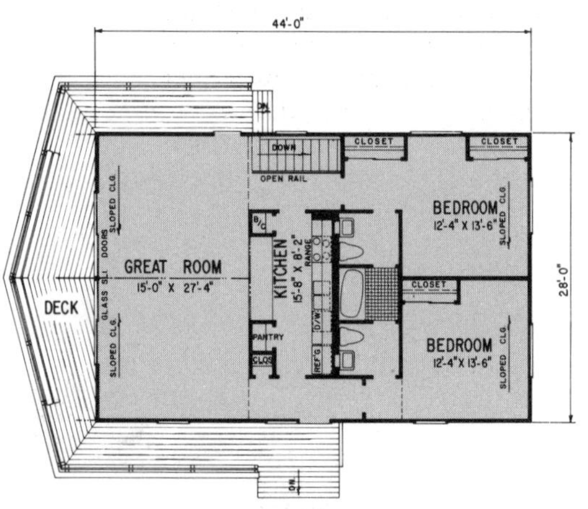

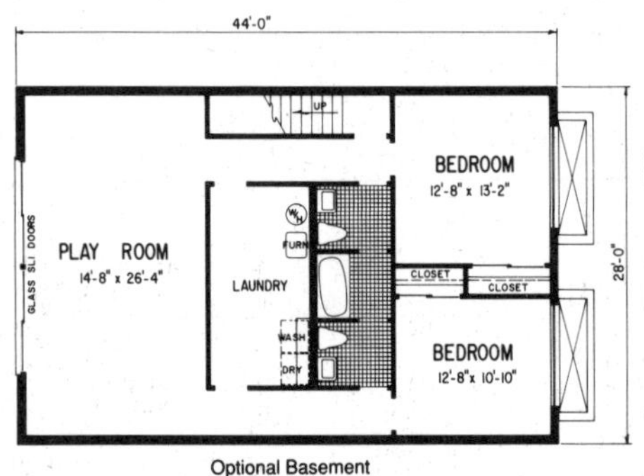

Optional Basement

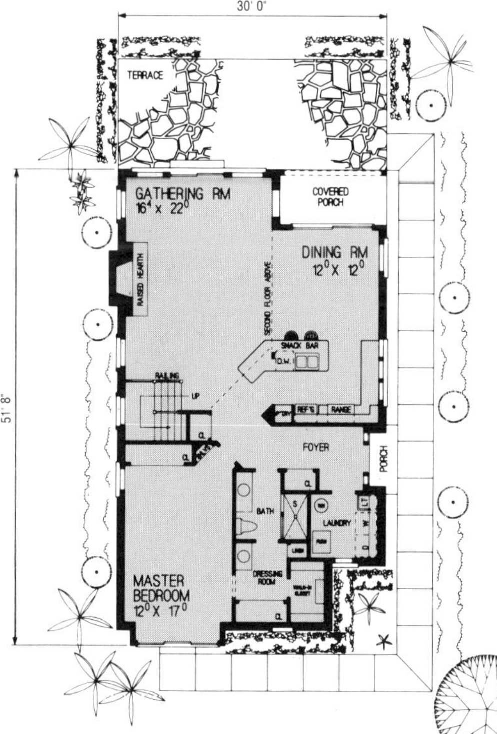

Design P2493

First Floor: 1,387 square feet
Second Floor: 929 square feet
Total: 2,316 square feet

● Perfect for a narrow lot, this shingle-and stone-sided Nantucket Cape caters to the casual lifestyle. The side entrance gives direct access to the wonderfully open living areas: gathering room with fireplace, kitchen with angled, pass-through snack bar, dining area with sliding glass doors to a covered eating area. Note also the large deck that further extends the living potential. Also on this floor is a large master suite. Upstairs is a convenient guest suite with private balcony. It is complemented by two smaller bedrooms.

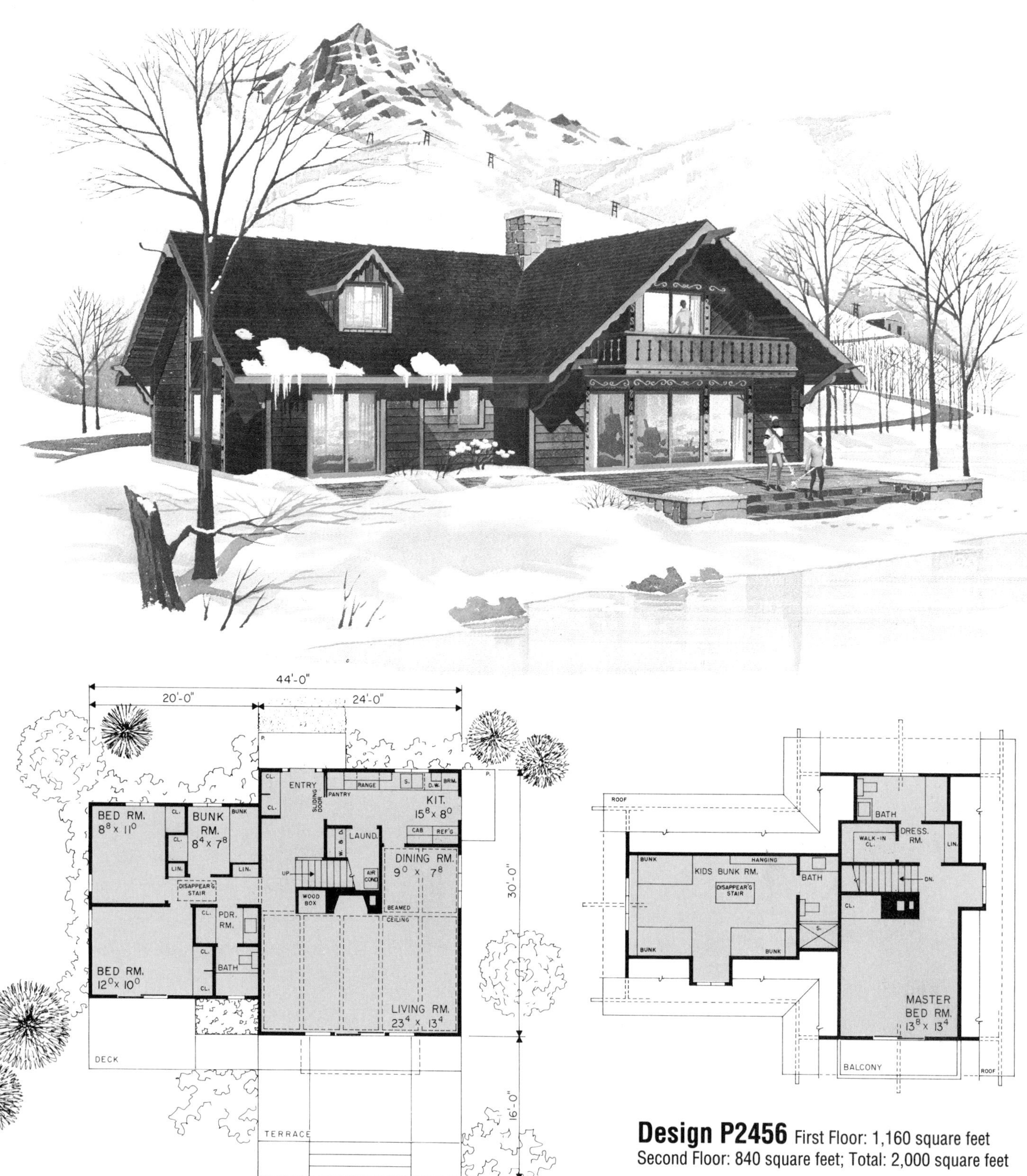

Design P2456

First Floor: 1,160 square feet
Second Floor: 840 square feet; Total: 2,000 square feet

● Here's how your Swiss chalet adaptation may look in the winter. Certainly an appealing design whatever the season. A delightful haven for skiers, fishermen and hunters alike. As for sleeping facilities, you'll really be able to pack 'em in. The first floor has two bedrooms plus a room which will take a double bunk. Across the hall is the compartment bath. A disappearing stair unit leads to the children's bunk room. The placement of single bunks or cots will permit the sleeping of three or four more. A bath with stall shower is nearby. The master bedroom suite is complete with walk-in closet, dressing room and private bath and opens onto the balcony. There is plenty of space in the L-shaped living-dining area with wood box and fireplace to accommodate the whole gang.

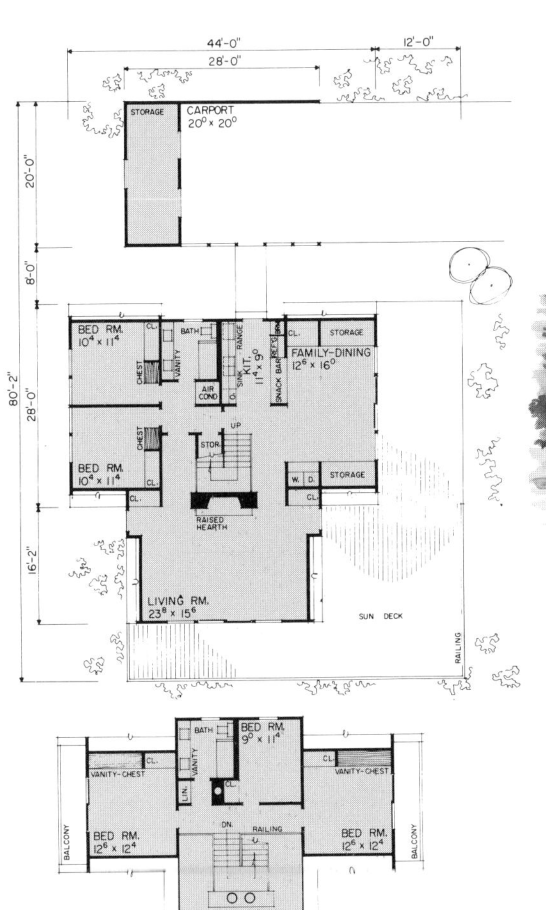

Design P1432 First Floor: 1,512 square feet

Second Floor: 678 square feet; Total: 2,190 square feet

● Perhaps more than any other design in recent years the A-frame has captured the imagination of the prospective vacation home builder. There is a gala air about its shape that fosters a holiday spirit whether the house be a summer retreat or a structure for year 'round living. This particular A-frame offers a lot of living with five bedrooms, two baths, and efficient kitchen, a family/dining area, and outstanding storage. As in most designs of this type, the living room with its great height and large glass area is extremely dramatic at first sight.

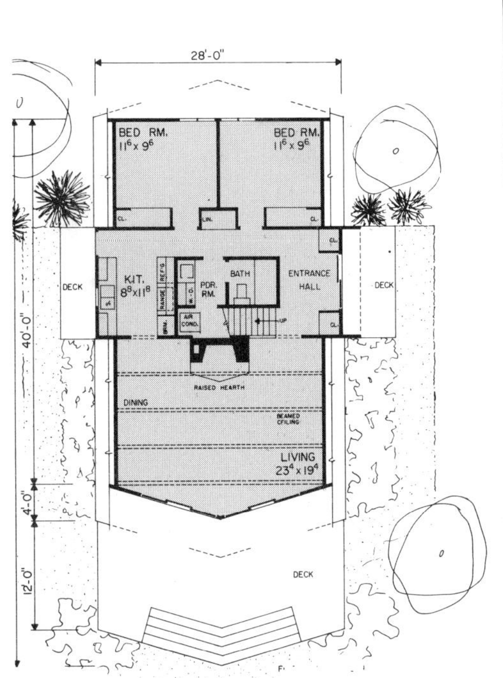

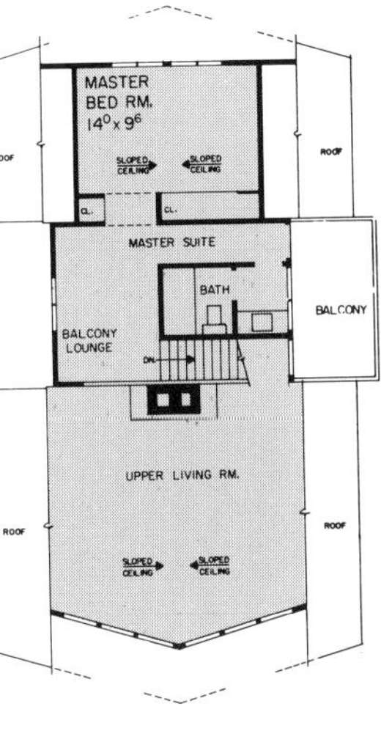

Design P2431

First Floor: 1,057 square feet
Second Floor: 406 square feet
Total: 1,463 square feet

● A favorite everywhere, the A-frame vacation home is easily recognizable. Inside, the beauty of architectural detailing is apparent. The living room sports a high ceiling which slopes and has exposed beams. The second-floor master suite has a private balcony, private bath and lounge. Don't miss the raised-hearth fireplace for cozy winter nights.

Design P2439

Square Footage: 1,312

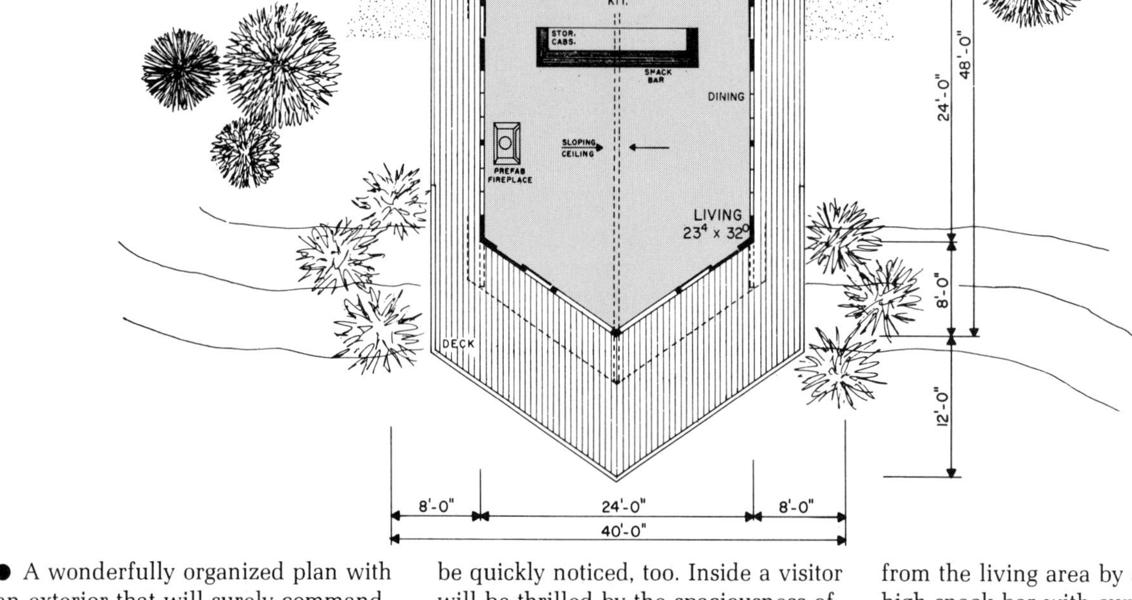

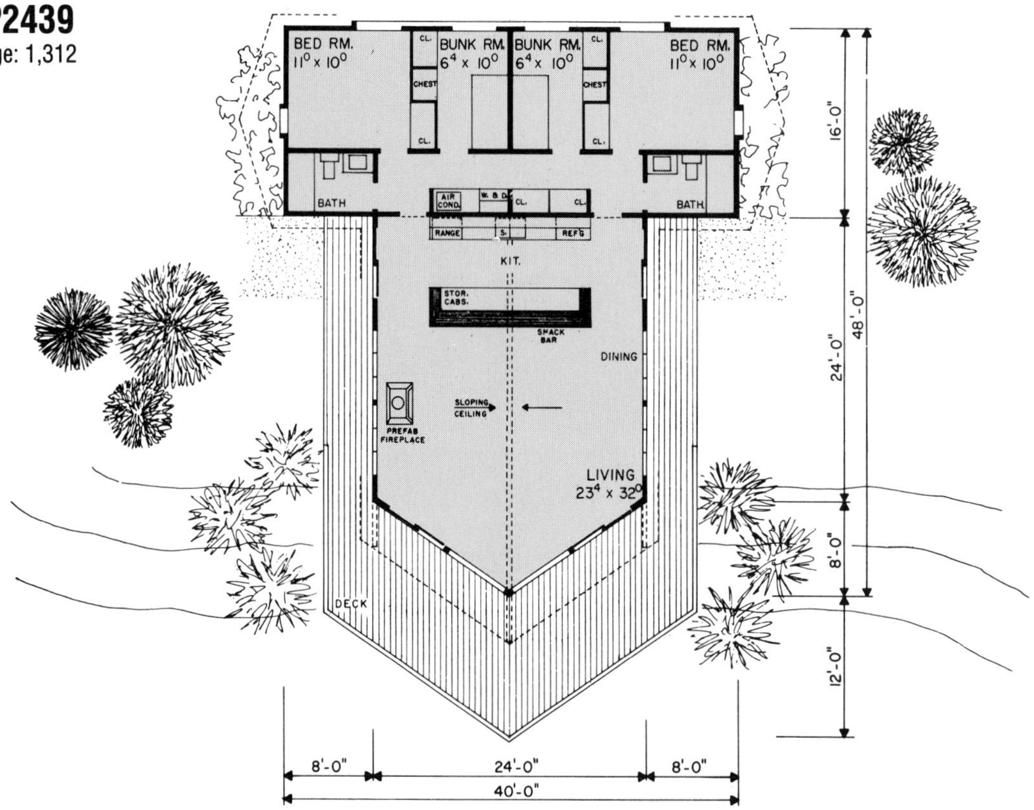

● A wonderfully organized plan with an exterior that will surely command the attention of each and every passer-by. And what will catch the eye? Certainly the roof lines and the pointed glass gable end wall will be noticed immediately. The delightful deck will be quickly noticed, too. Inside a visitor will be thrilled by the spaciousness of the huge living room. The ceilings slope upward to the exposed ridge beam. A free-standing fireplace will make its contribution to a cheerful atmosphere. The kitchen is separated from the living area by a three-foot-high snack bar with cupboards below servicing the kitchen. What could improve upon the sleeping zone when it has two bedrooms, two bunk rooms, two full baths, two built-in chests and fine closet space?

Design P1499 Main Level: 896 square feet; Upper Level: 298 square feet; Lower Level: 896 square feet; Total: 2,090 square feet

● Three level living results in family living patterns which will foster a delightful feeling of informality. Upon arrival at this charming second home, each family member will enthusiastically welcome the change in environment - both indoors and out. Whether looking down into the living room from the dormitory balcony, or walking through the sliding doors onto the huge deck, or participating in some family activity in the game room, everyone will count the hours spent here as relaxing ones. Study the plan carefully. Note the sleeping facilities on each of the three levels. Two bedrooms and a dormitory in all to sleep the family and friends comfortably. There are two full baths, a separate laundry room and plenty of storage. Don't miss the efficient U-shaped kitchen.

Blue prints show details for brick veneer and cavity wall construction.

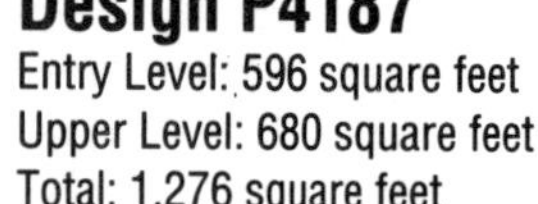

Design P4187

Entry Level: 596 square feet
Upper Level: 680 square feet
Total: 1,276 square feet

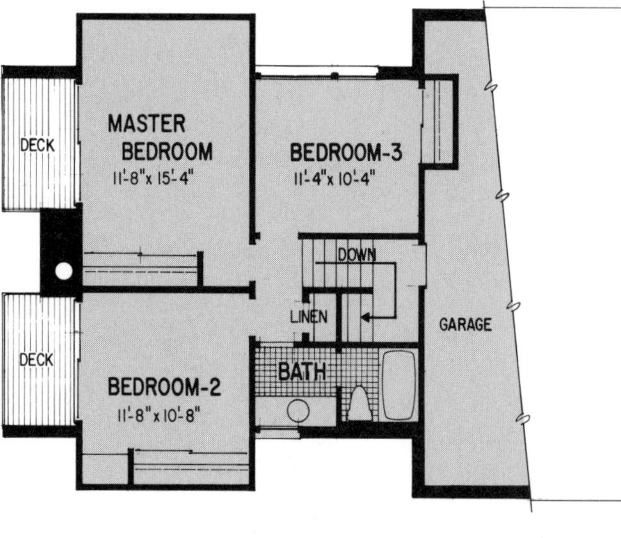

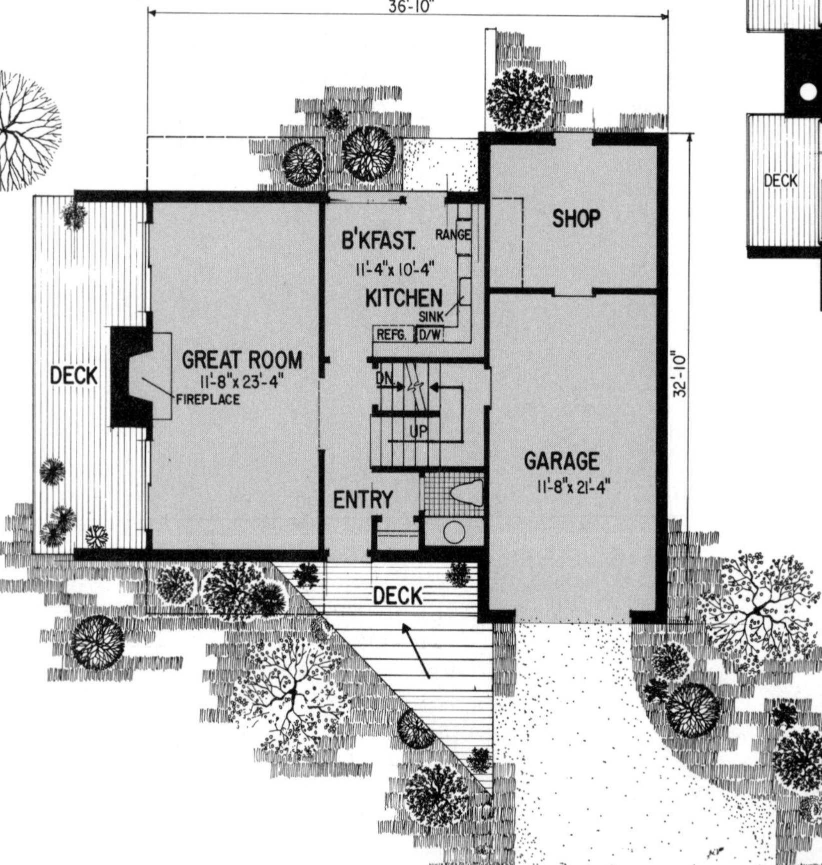

● Sloping rooflines and geometrical projections create a striking exterior for this home. The interior features all the relaxed informality of a vacation home. The enormous great room has enough space to accommodate a dining area, if desired, or several seating areas. An adjacent deck provides additional living space. The well-equipped kitchen includes a breakfast nook. Upstairs are three bedrooms and a shared bath. Two of the bedrooms feature private decks.

Design P4114

Main Level: 852 square feet
Upper Level: 146 square feet
Total: 998 square feet

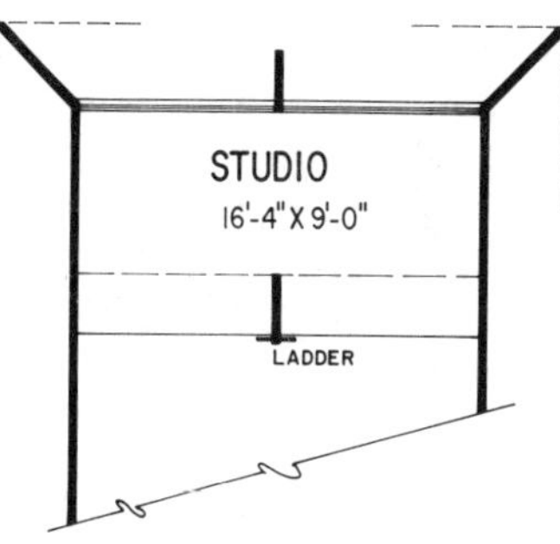

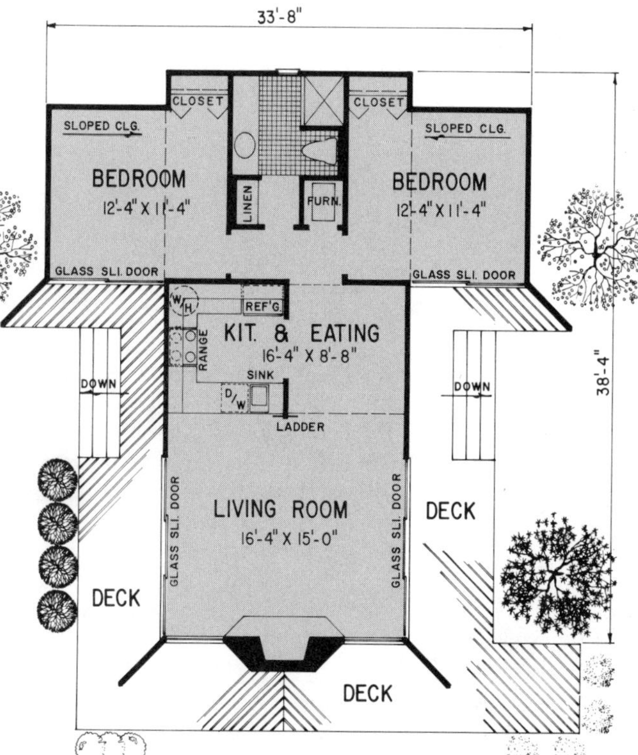

● This home was designed with the outdoors in mind. A large, wraparound deck provides ample space for sunning and relaxing. Huge windows and sliding glass doors open up the interior with lots of sunlight and great views — a must in a vacation home. Open planning makes for relaxed living patterns; the kitchen, living, and eating area flow together into one large working and living space. An upstairs loft provides added space for a lounge or an extra sleeping area.

When You're Ready To Order . . .

Let Us Show You Our Home Blueprint Package.

Building a home? Planning a home? Our Blueprint Package contains nearly everything you need to get the job done right, whether you're working on your own or with help from an architect, designer, builder or subcontractors. Each Blueprint Package is the result of many hours of work by licensed architects or professional designers.

QUALITY

Hundreds of hours of painstaking effort have gone into the development of your blueprint set. Each home has been quality-checked by professionals to insure accuracy and buildability.

VALUE

Because we sell in volume, you can buy professional-quality blueprints at a fraction of their development cost. With our plans, your dream home design costs only a few hundred dollars, not the thousands of dollars that custom architects charge.

SERVICE

Once you've chosen your favorite home plan, you'll receive fast efficient service whether you choose to mail your order to us or call us toll free at 1-800-521-6797.

SATISFACTION

Our years of service to satisfied home plan buyers provide us the experience and knowledge that guarantee your satisfaction with our product and performance.

ORDER TOLL FREE 1-800-521-6797

After you've studied our Blueprint Package and Important Extras on the following pages, simply mail the accompanying order form on page 205 or call toll free on our Blueprint Hotline: 1-800-521-6797. We're ready and eager to serve you.

Each set of blueprints is an interrelated collection of floor plans, interior and exterior elevations, dimensions, cross-sections, diagrams and notations showing precisely how your house is to be constructed.

Here's what you get:

Frontal Sheet
This artist's sketch of the exterior of the house, done in realistic perspective, gives you an idea of how the house will look when built and landscaped. Large ink-line floor plans show all levels of the house and provide a quick overview of your new home's livability, as well as a handy reference for studying furniture placement.

Foundation Plan
Drawn to 1/4-inch scale, this sheet shows the complete foundation layout including support

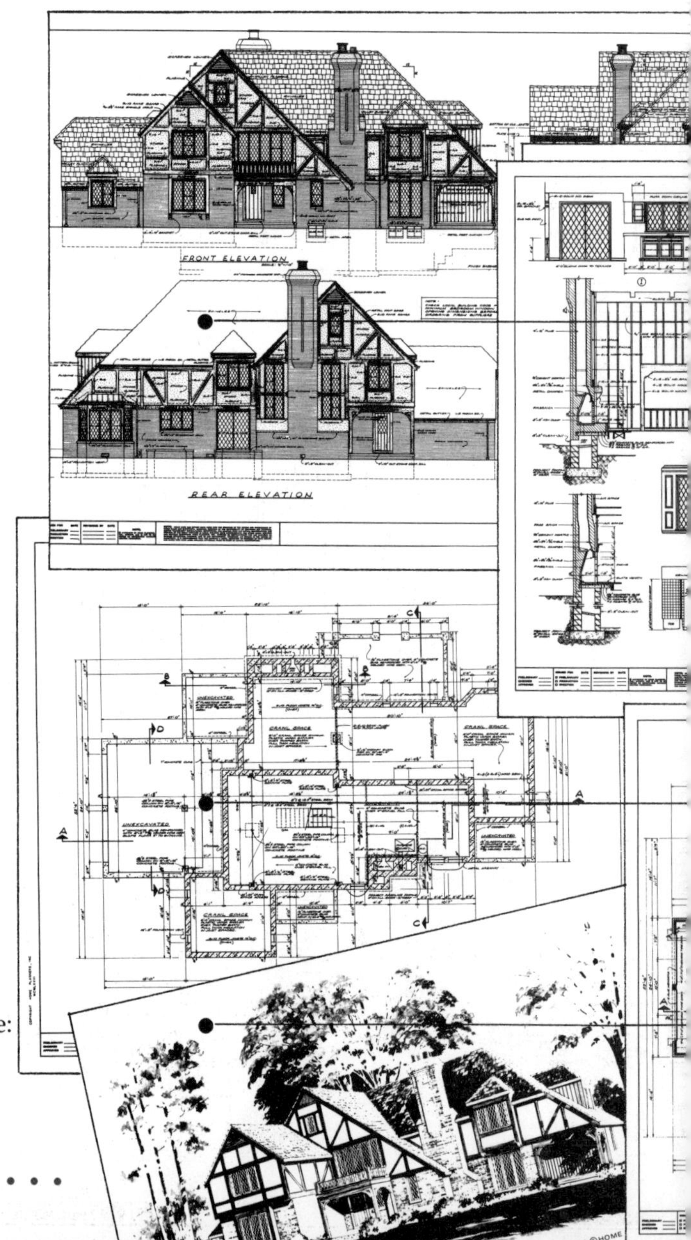

walls, excavated and unexcavated areas, if any, and foundation notes. If slab construction rather than basement, the plan shows footings and details for a monolithic slab. This page, or another in the set, also includes a sample plot plan for locating your house on a building site.

Detailed Floor Plans

Complete in 1/4-inch scale, these plans show the layout of each floor of the house. All rooms and interior spaces are carefully dimensioned and keys are provided for cross-section details given later in the plans. The positions of all electrical outlets and switches are clearly shown.

House Cross-Sections

Large-scale views, normally drawn at 3/8-inch equals 1 foot, show sections or cut-aways of the foundation, interior walls, exterior walls, floors, stairways and roof details. Additional cross-sections are given to show important changes in floor, ceiling or roof heights or the relationship of one level to another. Extremely valuable for construction, these sections show exactly how the various parts of the house fit together.

Interior Elevations

These large-scale drawings show the design and placement of kitchen and bathroom cabinets, laundry areas, fireplaces, bookcases and other built-ins. Little "extras," such as mantelpiece and wainscoting drawings, plus moulding sections, provide details that give your home that custom touch.

Exterior Elevations

Drawings in 1/4-inch scale show the front, rear and sides of your house and give necessary notes on exterior materials and finishes. Particular attention is given to cornice detail, brick and stone accents or other finish items that make your home distinctive.

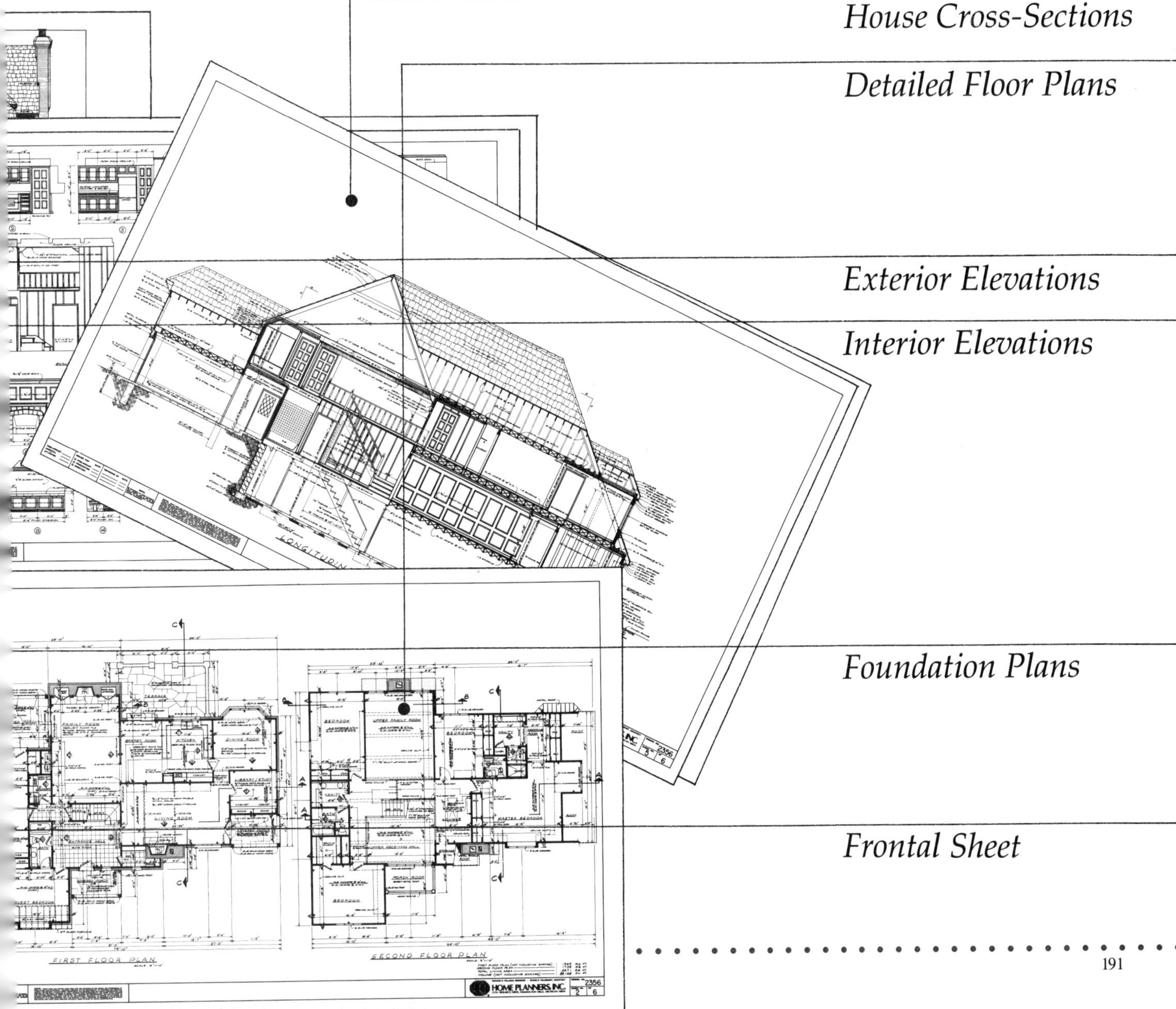

Important Extras To Do The Job Right!

Introducing six important planning and construction aids developed by our professionals to help you succeed in your home-building project.

To Order, Call Toll Free 1-800-521-6797

To add these important extras to your Blueprint Package, simply indicate your choices on the order form on page 205 or call us Toll Free 1-800-521-6797 and we'll tell you more about these exciting products.

MATERIALS LIST

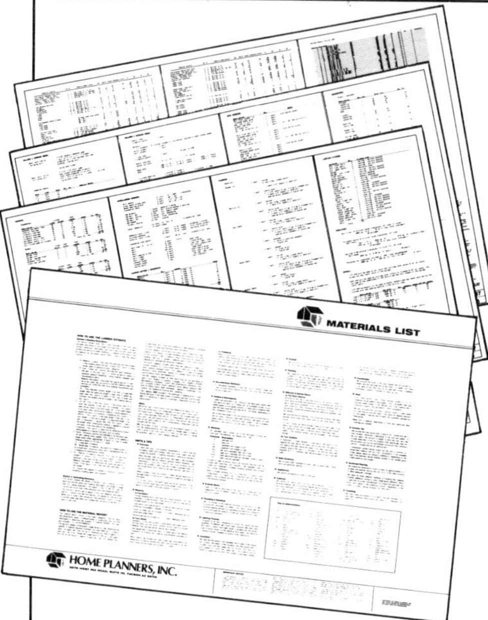

For many of the designs in our portfolio, we offer a customized materials take-off that is invaluable in planning and estimating the cost of your new home. This comprehensive list outlines the quantity, type and size of material needed to build your house (with the exception of mechanical system items). Included are:

- framing lumber
- roofing and sheet metal
- windows and doors
- exterior sheathing material and trim
- masonry, veneer and fireplace materials
- tile and flooring materials
- kitchen and bath cabinetry
- interior sheathing and trim
- rough and finish hardware
- many more items

(Note: Because of differing local codes, building methods, and availability of materials, our Materials Lists do not include mechanical materials. To obtain necessary take-offs and recommendations, consult heating, plumbing and electrical contractors. Materials Lists are not sold separately from the Blueprint Package.)

This handy list helps you or your builder cost out materials and serves as a ready reference sheet when you're compiling bids. It also provides a cross-check against the materials specified by your builder and helps coordinate the substitution of items you may need to meet local codes.

SPECIFICATION OUTLINE

This valuable 16-page document is critical to building your house correctly. Designed to be filled in by you or your builder, this booklet lists 166 stages or items crucial to the building process.

For the layman, it provides a comprehensive review of the construction process and helps in making the specific choices of materials, models and processes. For the builder, it serves as a guide to preparing a building quotation and forms the basis for the construction program.

Designed primarily as a reference for the homeowner, this Specification Outline can become a legally binding document. Once it is filled out and agreed upon by owner and builder, it becomes a complete Project Specification.

When combined with the blueprints, a signed contract and schedule, the Specification Outline becomes a legal document and record for the building of your home. Many home builders find it useful to order two of these outlines—one as a worksheet in formulating the specifications and another to be carefully completed as a legal document.

Detail Sheets

Because local codes and requirements vary greatly, we recommend that you obtain drawings and bids from licensed contractors to do your mechanical plans. However, if you want to know more about techniques — and deal more confidently with subcontractors — we offer these remarkably useful detail sheets. Each is an excellent tool that will enhance your understanding of these technical subjects.

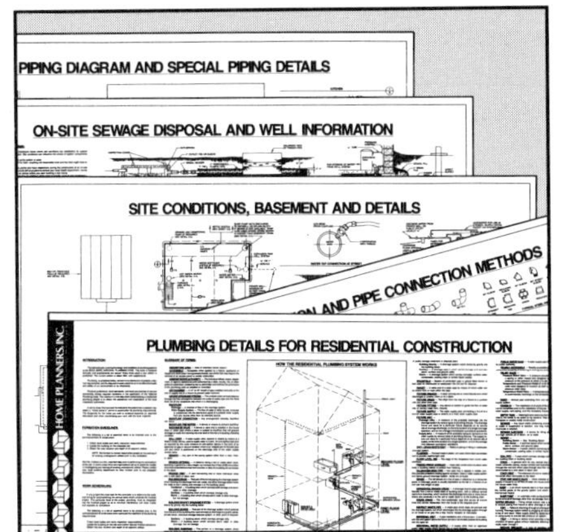

Plumbing

The Blueprint Package includes locations for all the plumbing fixtures in your new house, including sinks, lavatories, tubs, showers, toilets, laundry trays and water heaters. However, if you want to know more about the complete plumbing system, these 24x36-inch detail sheets will prove very useful. Prepared to meet requirements of the National Plumbing Code, these six fact-filled sheets give general information on pipe schedules, fittings, sump-pump details, water-softener hookups, septic system details and much more. Color-coded sheets include a glossary of terms.

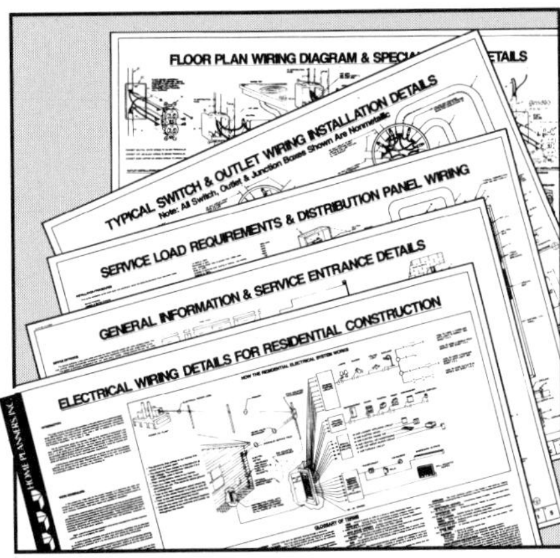

Electrical

The locations for every electrical switch, plug and outlet are shown in your Blueprint Package. However, these Electrical Details go further to take the mystery out of household electrical systems. Prepared to meet requirements of the National Electrical Code, these comprehensive 24x36-inch drawings come packed with helpful information, including wire sizing, switch-installation schematics, cable-routing details, appliance wattage, door-bell hookups, typical service panel circuitry and much more. Six sheets are bound together and color-coded for easy reference. A glossary of terms is also included.

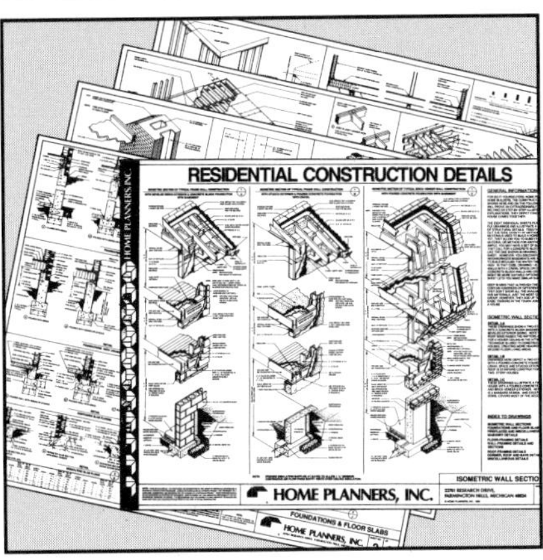

Construction

The Blueprint Package contains everything an experienced builder needs to construct a particular house. However, it doesn't show all the ways that houses can be built, nor does it explain alternate construction methods. To help you understand how your house will be built–and offer additional techniques–this set of drawings depicts the materials and methods used to build foundations, fireplaces, walls, floors and roofs. Where appropriate, the drawings show acceptable alternatives. These six sheets will answer questions for the advanced do-it-yourselfer or home planner.

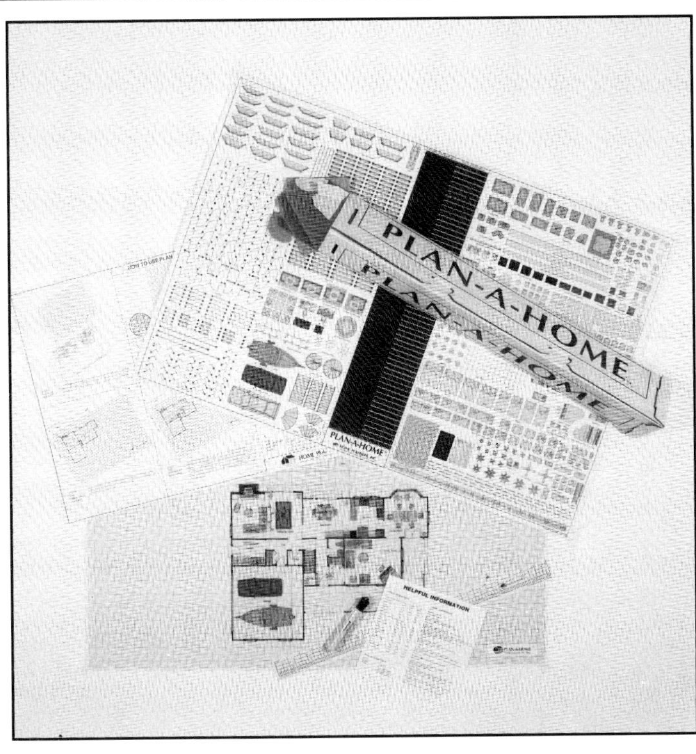

Plan-A-Home®

Plan-A-Home® is an easy-to-use tool that helps you design a new home, arrange furniture in a new or existing home, or plan a remodeling project. Each package contains:

- More than *700 peel-off planning symbols* on a self-stick vinyl sheet, including walls, windows, doors, all types of furniture, kitchen components, bath fixtures and many more. All are made of durable, peel-and-stick vinyl you can use over and over.
- A reusable, transparent, *1/4-inch scale planning grid* made of tough mylar that matches the scale of actual working drawings (1/4-inch equals 1 foot). This grid provides the basis for house layouts of up to 140x92 feet.
- *Tracing paper* and a protective sheet for copying or transferring your completed plan.
- A *felt-tip pen*, with water-soluble ink that wipes away quickly.

With Plan-A-Home®, you can make basic planning decisions for a new house or make modifications to an existing house. Use with your Blueprint Package to test modifications to rooms or to plan furniture arrangements before you build. Plan-A Home® lets you lay out areas as large as a 7,500 square foot, six-bedroom, seven-bath house.

D The Deck Blueprint Package

Many of the homes in this book can be enhanced with a professionally designed Home Planners' Deck Plan. Those home plans highlighted with a D have a matching or corresponding deck plan available which includes a Deck Plan Frontal Sheet, Deck Framing and Floor Plans, Deck Elevations and a Deck Materials List. A Standard Deck Details Package, also available, provides all the how-to information necessary for building *any* deck. Our plans and details are carefully prepared in an easy-to-understand format that will guide you through every stage of your deck-building project. See these pages for 25 different Deck layouts to match your favorite house.

SPLIT–LEVEL SUN DECK
Deck Plan D100

BI–LEVEL DECK WITH COVERED DINING
Deck Plan D101

FRESH–AIR CORNER DECK
Deck Plan D102

BACK–YARD EXTENDER DECK
Deck Plan D103

WRAP–AROUND FAMILY DECK
Deck Plan D104

DRAMATIC DECK WITH BARBECUE
Deck Plan D105

SPLIT–PLAN COUNTRY DECK
Deck Plan D106

DECK FOR DINING AND VIEWS
Deck Plan D107

BOLD, ANGLED CORNER DECK
Deck Plan D108

SPECTACULAR "RESORT–STYLE" DECK
Deck Plan D109

TREND–SETTER DECK
Deck Plan D110

TURN–OF–THE–CENTURY DECK
Deck Plan D111

WEEKEND ENTERTAINER DECK
Deck Plan D112

STRIKING "DELTA" DECK
Deck Plan D113

CENTER–VIEW DECK
Deck Plan D114

KITCHEN–EXTENDER DECK
Deck Plan D115

BI–LEVEL RETREAT DECK
Deck Plan D116

SPLIT–LEVEL ACTIVITY DECK
Deck Plan D117

OUTDOOR LIFESTYLE DECK
Deck Plan D118

TRI–LEVEL DECK WITH GRILL
Deck Plan D119

CONTEMPORARY LEISURE DECK
Deck Plan D120

ANGULAR WINGED DECK
Deck Plan D121

DECK FOR A SPLIT–LEVEL HOME
Deck Plan D122

GRACIOUS GARDEN DECK
Deck Plan D123

TERRACED DECK FOR ENTERTAINING
Deck Plan D124

For Deck Plan prices and ordering information, see pages 200-205.

Or call **Toll Free, 1-800-521-6797**.

The Landscape Blueprint Package

For the homes marked with an L in this book, Home Planners has created a front-yard landscape plan that matches or is complementary in design to the house plan. These comprehensive blueprint packages include a Frontal Sheet, Plan View, Regionalized Plant & Materials List, a sheet on Planting and Maintaining Your Landscape, Zone Maps and Plant Size and Description Guide. These plans will help you achieve professional results, adding value and enjoyment to your property for years to come. Each set of blueprints is a full 18" x 24" in size with clear, complete instructions and easy-to-read type. See the following pages for 40 different front-yard Landscape Plans to match your favorite house.

Regional Order Map

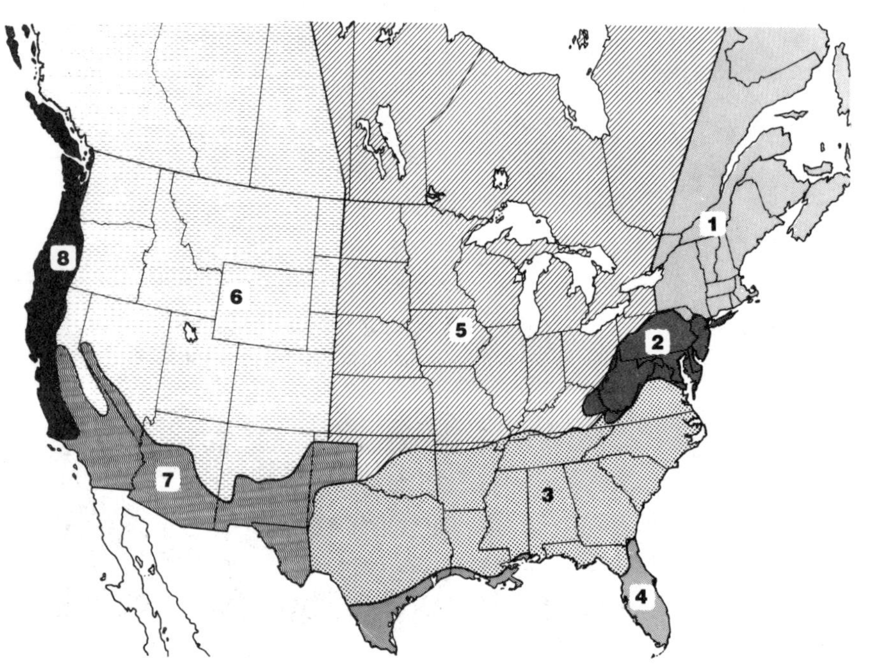

Most of the Landscape Plans shown on these pages are available with a Plant & Materials List adapted by horticultural experts to 8 different regions of the country. Please specify Geographic Region when ordering your plan. See pages 200-205 for prices, ordering information and regional availability.

Region	1	Northeast
Region	2	Mid-Atlantic
Region	3	Deep South
Region	4	Florida & Gulf Coast
Region	5	Midwest
Region	6	Rocky Mountains
Region	7	Southern California & Desert Southwest
Region	8	Northern California & Pacific Northwest

CAPE COD TRADITIONAL
Landscape Plan L200

WILLIAMSBURG CAPE
Landscape Plan L201

CAPE COD COTTAGE
Landscape Plan L202

GAMBREL-ROOF COLONIAL
Landscape Plan L203

CENTER-HALL COLONIAL
Landscape Plan L204

CLASSIC NEW ENGLAND COLONIAL
Landscape Plan L205

SOUTHERN COLONIAL
Landscape Plan L206

COUNTRY–STYLE FARMHOUSE
Landscape Plan L207

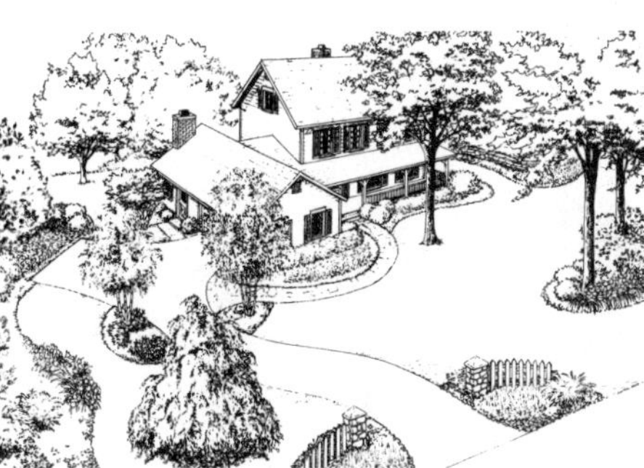

PENNSYLVANIA STONE FARMHOUSE
Landscape Plan L208

RAISED–PORCH FARMHOUSE
Landscape Plan L209

NEW ENGLAND BARN–STYLE HOUSE
Landscape Plan L210

NEW ENGLAND COUNTRY HOUSE
Landscape Plan L211

TRADITIONAL COUNTRY ESTATE
Landscape Plan L212

FRENCH PROVINCIAL ESTATE
Landscape Plan L213

GEORGIAN MANOR
Landscape Plan L214

GRAND–PORTICO GEORGIAN
Landscape Plan L215

BRICK FEDERAL
Landscape Plan L216

COUNTRY FRENCH RAMBLER
Landscape Plan L217

FRENCH MANOR HOUSE
Landscape Plan L218

ELIZABETHAN TUDOR
Landscape Plan L219

TUDOR ONE–STORY
Landscape Plan L220

ENGLISH–STYLE COTTAGE
Landscape Plan L221

MEDIEVAL GARRISON
Landscape Plan L222

QUEEN ANNE VICTORIAN
Landscape Plan L223

GOTHIC VICTORIAN
Landscape Plan L224

BASIC RANCH
Landscape Plan L225

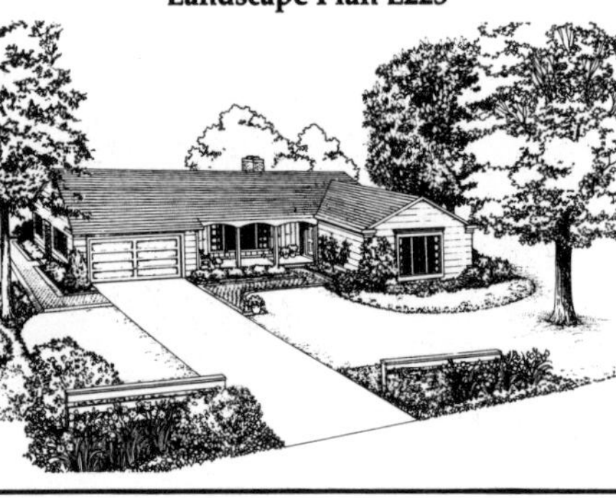

L–SHAPED RANCH
Landscape Plan L226

SPRAWLING RANCH
Landscape Plan L227

TRADITIONAL SPLIT–LEVEL
Landscape Plan L228

SHED–ROOF CONTEMPORARY
Landscape Plan L229

WOOD–SIDED CONTEMPORARY
Landscape Plan L230

HILLSIDE CONTEMPORARY
Landscape Plan L231

FLORIDA RAMBLER
Landscape Plan L232

CALIFORNIA STUCCO
Landscape Plan L233

LOW–GABLE CONTEMPORARY
Landscape Plan L234

NORTHERN BRICK CHATEAU
Landscape Plan L235

MISSION–TILE RANCH
Landscape Plan L236

ADOBE–BLOCK HACIENDA
Landscape Plan L237

COURTYARD PATIO HOME
Landscape Plan L238

CENTER–COURT CONTEMPORARY
Landscape Plan L239

For Landscape Plan prices and ordering information, see pages 200-205.

Or call **Toll Free,**
1-800-521-6797.

Price Schedule & Plans Index

House Blueprint Price Schedule

(Prices guaranteed through December 31, 1992)

	1-set Study Package	4-set Building Package	8-set Building Package	1-set Reproducible Sepias
Schedule A	$180	$240	$300	$360
Schedule B	$210	$270	$330	$420
Schedule C	$240	$300	$360	$480
Schedule D	$270	$330	$390	$540
Schedule E	$360	$420	$480	$600

Additional Identical Blueprints in same order.....$40 per set
Reverse Blueprints (Mirror Image).........................$40 per set
Specification Outlines...$5 each
Materials Lists:
Schedule A-D...$35
Schedule E..$45

Deck Plans Price Schedule

Price Group	Q	R	S
1 set	$25	$30	$35
3 sets	$40	$45	$50
6 sets	$55	$60	$65

Additional Identical Sets ....$10 each
Reverse Sets (Mirror Image) ....$10 each

Landscape Plans Price Schedule

Price Group	X	Y	Z
1 set	$35	$45	$55
3 sets	$50	$60	$70
6 sets	$65	$75	$85

Additional Identical Sets ....$10 each
Reverse Sets (Mirror Image) ....$10 each

These pages contain all the information you need to price your blueprints. In general the larger and more complicated the house, the more it costs to design and thus the higher the price we must charge for the blueprints. Remember, however, that these prices are far less than you would normally pay for the services of a licensed architect or professional designer.

Custom home designs and related architectural services often cost thousands of dollars, ranging from 5% to 15% of the cost of construction. By ordering our blueprints you are potentially saving enough money to afford a larger house, or to add those "extra" amenities such as a patio, deck, swimming pool or even an upgraded kitchen or luxurious master suite.

Index

To use the Index below, refer to the design number listed in numerical order (a helpful page reference is also given). Note the price index letter and refer to the House Blueprint Price Schedule above for the cost of one, four or eight sets of blueprints or the cost of a reproducible sepia. Additional prices are shown for identical and reverse blueprint sets, as well as a very useful Materials List for some of the plans. Also note in the Index below those plans that have matching or complementary Deck Plans or Landscape Plans. Refer to the schedules above for prices of these plans. Some of our plans can be customized through Home Planners' Home Customizer™ Service. These plans are indicated below with this symbol: . See page 203 for more information.

To Order: Fill in and send the order form on page 205—or call toll free 1-800-521-6797.

DESIGN	PRICE	PAGE	CUSTOMIZABLE	DECK	DECK PRICE	LANDSCAPE	LANDSCAPE PRICE	REGIONS
P1432	B	185						
P1499	B	187						
P1725	D	67						
P1726	B	69						
P1756	C	88						
P1928	D	85						
P1994	D	64						
P1997	D	66						
P2135	C	104						
P2143	B	65						
P2200	B	62						
P2214	D	70						
P2232	B	59						
P2236	C	6						
P2251	D	89						
P2252	C	58						
P2256	C	84						
P2258	C	87						
P2294	D	18				L236	Z	3,4,7
P2315	B	57						
P2317	D	87						
P2323	B	60						
P2335	C	22						
P2339	B	110						
P2379	B	123		D120	R	L212	Z	ALL
P2386	B	69				L238	Y	3,4,7,8
P2390	C	29		D101	R			
P2392	D	117						
P2431	A	185						
P2439	A	186						

DESIGN	PRICE	PAGE	CUSTOMIZABLE	DECK	DECK PRICE	LANDSCAPE	LANDSCAPE PRICE	REGIONS
P2456	B	184						
P2488	A	181	⌂	D102	Q			
P2490	A	143	⌂					
P2493	C	183						
P2502	C	91				L212	Z	ALL
P2504	C	90						
P2511	B	116		D108	R	L229	Y	ALL
P2517	C	60				L233	Y	3,4,7
P2534	D	84				L227	Z	ALL
P2549	C	94						
P2557	B	96						
P2562	D	139		D122	S			
P2566	C	61						
P2595	C	86						
P2650	B	177		D117	S	L201	Y	1-3,5,6,8
P2670	D	19		D105	R	L236	Z	3,4,7
P2677	B	62						
P2701	C	144						
P2708	C	123		D112	R			
P2710	D	92						
P2711	B	8	⌂	D105	R	L229	Y	ALL
P2716	C	118				L229	Y	ALL
P2720	D	86						
P2729	B	144				L234	Y	ALL
P2741	B	58		D114	R			
P2743	B	69						
P2748	A	145						
P2756	C	80		D101	R	L234	Y	ALL
P2759	C	121						
P2764	C	82						
P2765	D	82		D106	S			
P2771	C	141						
P2772	C	140						
P2774	B	15	⌂	D100	Q	L207	Z	1-6,8
P2775	B	174				L207	Z	1-6,8
P2776	B	176	⌂	D113	R	L207	Z	1-6,8
P2780	C	140						
P2781	C	127		D121	S	L230	Z	ALL
P2782	C	139		D101	R			
P2801	B	36		D105	R	L232	Y	4,7
P2804	B	62	⌂	D118	R	L232	Y	4,7
P2819	C	83		D113	R			
P2820	C	23		D124	S	L236	Z	3,4,7
P2822	A	113				L229	Y	ALL
P2823	B	122		D112	R	L229	Y	ALL
P2827	C	124				L229	Y	ALL
P2828	B	115						
P2829	D	166		D113	R	L219	Z	1-3,5,6,8
P2830	C	118						
P2831	C	120		D113	R			
P2832	C	119		D113	R			
P2834	D	126						
P2835	C	126						
P2843	C	20				L228	Y	ALL
P2846	C	7						
P2850	C	20		D122	S	L236	Z	3,4,7
P2856	C	105						
P2858	C	106						
P2865	C	176		D114	R			
P2866	C	81						
P2868	B	138						
P2871	B	114		D117	S			
P2875	B	23		D113	R	L236	Z	3,4,7
P2879	D	128						
P2881	C	106						
P2884	B	121						
P2890	C	177		D114	R			
P2893	C	104		D120	R			
P2894	C	107						
P2896	C	103						
P2902	B	146				L234	Y	ALL
P2906	C	78		D114	R			
P2908	B	174	⌂	D117	S	L205	Y	1-3,5,6,8
P2910	B	119						
P2912	B	79						
P2920	D	95		D104	S	L212	Z	ALL
P2922	D	21						
P2925	B	112						
P2926	D	109						
P2937	C	9				L229	Y	ALL
P2938	E	93						
P2944	C	136						
P2945	B	175	⌂					
P2946	C	178		D114	R	L207	Z	1-6,8
P2948	B	52	⌂					
P2949	C	73		D123	S			
P2950	C	29						
P2952	E	132				L235	Z	1-3,5,6,8
P2953	E	153		D111	S	L223	Z	1-3,5,6,8
P2954	E	152				L223	Z	1-3,5,6,8
P2956	E	133						
P2969	C	148		D110	R	L223	Z	1-3,5,6,8
P2970	D	161				L223	Z	1-3,5,6,8
P2971	C	159				L223	Z	1-3,5,6,8
P2972	B	158				L223	Z	1-3,5,6,8
P2973	B	12				L223	Z	1-3,5,6,8
P2974	A	13				L223	Z	1-3,5,6,8
P3304	E	151						
P3307	C	14		D111	S	L207	Z	1-6,8
P3308	E	150						
P3309	B	149						
P3311	D	63						
P3313	B	11						
P3314	B	10						
P3316	A	99						
P3318	B	98	⌂					

DESIGN	PRICE	PAGE	CUSTOMIZABLE	DECK	DECK PRICE	LANDSCAPE	LANDSCAPE PRICE	REGIONS
P3319	C	100	⌂					
P3321	C	101	⌂					
P3322	C	102	⌂					
P3323	C	26	⌂					
P3338	B	142						
P3344	D	38						
P3347	D	142						
P3352	B	137		D108	R	L229	Y	ALL
P3362	D	135						
P3364	D	134						
P3382	C	158		D110	R	L202	X	1-3,5,6,8
P3383	C	164		D111	S	L205	Y	1-3,5,6,8
P3384	C	164		D115	Q	L207	Z	1-6,8
P3385	C	165		D100	Q	L207	Z	1-6,8
P3386	E	157		D111	S	L216	Y	1-3,5,6,8
P3387	E	155		D110	R	L224	Y	1-3,5,6,8
P3388	D	160		D111	S	L207	Z	1-6,8
P3389	C	162		D115	Q	L205	Y	1-3,5,6,8
P3390	C	165		D106	S	L207	Z	1-6,8
P3391	C	163		D116	R	L207	Z	1-6,8
P3392	D	154		D110	R	L223	Z	1-3,5,6,8
P3393	C	162		D115	Q	L207	Z	1-6,8
P3394	D	160		D111	S	L207	Z	1-6,8
P3395	E	156		D111	S	L223	Z	1-3,5,6,8
P3396	C	169		D111	S	L207	Z	1-6,8
P3397	D	170		D110	R	L209	Y	1-6,8
P3398	C	171		D111	S	L224	Y	1-3,5,6,8
P3399	D	168		D110	R	L224	Y	1-3,5,6,8
P3400	C	54	⌂					
P3401	C	54	⌂					
P3402	D	55	⌂					
P3403	C	108		D115	Q	L237	Y	7
P3404	D	173		D106	S	L230	Z	1-8
P3405	D	74	⌂					
P3408	D	28						
P3409	C	27						
P3410	D	125						
P3411	C	46	⌂					
P3412	B	41	⌂					
P3413	C	40	⌂					
P3414	C	5	⌂					
P3415	C	47	⌂					
P3416	A	44	⌂					
P3417	A	49	⌂					
P3418	A	49	⌂					
P3419	B	44	⌂					
P3420	B	51	⌂					
P3421	B	42	⌂					
P3422	B	43	⌂					
P3423	C	45	⌂					
P3424	B	48	⌂					
P3425	C	30	⌂					
P3426	C	39	⌂					
P3427	C	50	⌂					
P3428	C	4	⌂					
P3430	C	41	⌂					
P3431	B	16	⌂					
P3432	C	75	⌂					
P3433	C	72	⌂					
P3434	D	76	⌂					
P3435	D	56	⌂					
P3436	C	34	⌂					
P3437	C	35	⌂					
P3438	C	172	⌂					
P3439	C	131	⌂					
P3440	C	32	⌂					
P3441	C	33	⌂					
P3447	D	25	⌂					
P3448	E	24	⌂					
P3449	C	31	⌂					
P3450	C	130	⌂					
P4027	A	182						
P4061	A	180		D115	Q			
P4114	A	189						
P4187	A	188						
P4308	C	125				L231	Z	ALL

Toll Free 1-800-521-6797

Normal Office Hours:
8:00 a.m. to 8:00 p.m.
Eastern Time
Monday through Friday
Our staff will gladly answer any questions during normal office hours. Our answering service can place orders after hours or on weekends.

If we receive your order by 5:00 p.m. Eastern Time, Monday through Friday, we'll process it the same day and ship it the following business day.

When ordering by phone, please have your charge card ready. We'll also ask you for the Order Form Key Number at the bottom of the coupon on page 205. Please use our Toll-Free number for blueprint and book orders only. For Customization orders call 1-800-322-6797, ext. 134.

By FAX: Copy the Order Form on page 205 and send it on our International FAX line: 1-602-297-6219.

For Customization: 1-800-322-6797, ext. 134

Canadian Customers
Order Toll-Free 1-800-848-2550

For faster, more economical service, Canadian customers may now call in orders on our Toll-Free line. Or, complete the order form on page 205, and mail with your check indicating U.S. funds to:

Home Planners, Inc.
3275 W. Ina Road, Suite 110
Tucson, AZ 85741

By FAX: Copy the Order Form on page 205 and send it on our International FAX line: 1-602-297-6219.

The Home Customizer™

Many of the plans in this book are customizable through our Home Customizer™ service. Look for this symbol on the pages of home designs. It indicates that the plan on that page is part of The Home Customizer™ service.

Some changes to customizable plans that can be made include:

- exterior elevation changes
- kitchen and bath modifications
- roof, wall and foundation changes
- room additions
- and much more!

If the plan you have chosen to build is one of our customizable homes, you can easily order the Home Customizer™ kit to start on the path to making your alterations. The kit, priced at only $19.95, may be ordered at the same time you order your blueprint package by calling on our toll-free number or using the order blank on page 319. Or you can wait until you receive your blueprints, spend some time studying them and then order the kit by phone, FAX or mail. If you then decide to proceed with the customizing service, the $19.95 price of the kit will be refunded to you after your customization order is received. The Home Customizer™ kit includes:

- instruction book with examples
- architectural scale
- clear acetate work film
- erasable red marker
- removable correction tape
- ¼" scale furniture cutouts
- 1 set of Customizable Drawings with floor plans and elevations

The service is easy, fast and *affordable*. Because we know and work with our plans and have them available on state-of-the-art computer systems, we can make the changes efficiently at prices much lower than those charged by architectural or drafting services. In addition, you'll be getting custom changes directly from Home Planners—the company whose dedication to excellence and long-standing professional experience are well recognized in the industry.

Call now to learn more about how simple it can be to have the *custom home* you've always wanted.

The Home Customizer™ kit contains everything you'll need to make your home a one of a kind.

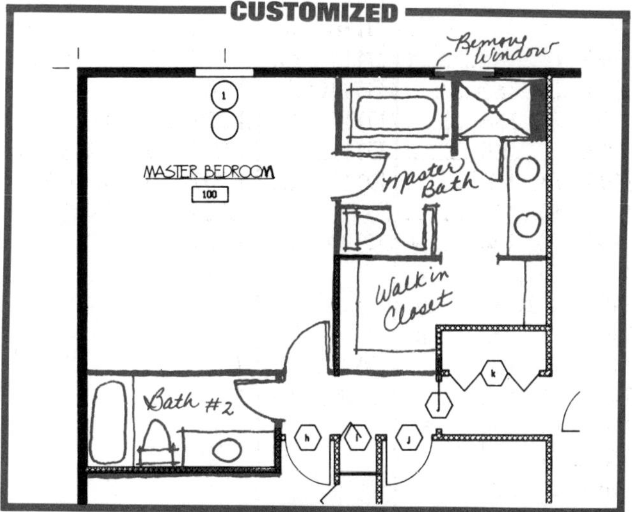

Making interior changes to the floor plan is simple and fun using the tools provided in The Home Customizer™ kit!

Look for this symbol next to Home Planners' designs that are customizable.

Custom Alterations? For information about how easily this plan can be altered — at rates surprisingly below standard architectural fees — call our Home Customizer Specialist at **1-800-322-6797.**

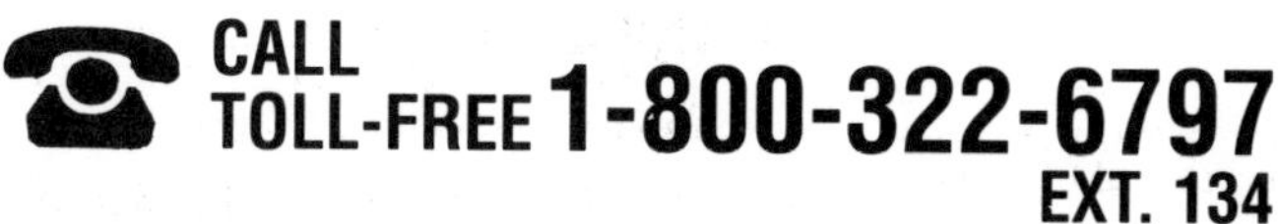

CALL
TOLL-FREE 1-800-322-6797
EXT. 134

Before You Order . . .

Before completing the coupon at right or calling us on our Toll-Free Blueprint Hotline, you may be interested to learn more about our service and products. Here's some information you will find helpful.

Quick Turnaround
We process and ship every blueprint order from our office within 48 hours. On most orders, we do even better. Normally, if we receive your order by 5 p.m. Eastern Time, we'll process it the same day and ship it the following day. Because of this quick turnaround, we won't send a formal notice acknowledging receipt of your order.

Our Exchange Policy
Since blueprints are printed in response to your order, we cannot honor requests for refunds. However, we will exchange your entire first order for an equal number of blueprints at a price of $20 for the first set and $10 for each additional set, plus the difference in cost if exchanging for a design in a higher price bracket. (Sepias are not exchangeable.) All sets from the first order must be returned before the exchange can take place. Please add $7 for postage and handling via UPS regular service; $10 via UPS 2nd Day Air.

About Reverse Blueprints
If you want to build in reverse of the plan as shown, we will include an extra set of reversed blueprints (mirror image) for an additional fee of $40. Although lettering and dimensions appear backward, reverses will be a useful visual aid if you decide to flop the plan. Right-reading reverses of Customizable Plans are available through our Customization Service. Call for more details.

Modifying or Customizing Our Plans
With such a great selection of homes, you are bound to find the one that suits you. However, if you need to make alterations to a design that is customizable, you need only order our Customizer™ kit or call our Customization representative at 1-800-322-6797, ext. 134, to get you started (see additional information on previous page).

If you decide to revise plans significantly that are not customizable through our service, we strongly suggest that you order reproducible sepias and consult a licensed architect or professional designer to help you redraw the plans.

Architectural and Engineering Seals
Some cities and states are now requiring that a licensed architect or engineer review and "seal" your blueprints prior to construction. This is often due to local or regional concerns over energy consumption, safety codes, seismic ratings, etc. For this reason, you may find it necessary to consult with a local professional to have your plans reviewed. This can normally be accomplished with minimum delays, for a nominal fee. In some cases, Home Planners can seal your plans through our Customization Service. Call for more details.

Compliance with Local Codes and Regulations
At the time of creation, our plans are drawn to specifications published by Building Officials Code Administrators (BOCA), the Southern Standard Building Code, or the Uniform Building Code and are designed to meet or exceed national building standards. Some states, counties and municipalities have their own codes, zoning requirements and building regulations. Before starting construction, consult with local building authorities and make sure you comply with local ordinances and codes, including obtaining any necessary permits or inspections as building progresses. In some cases, minor modifications to your plans by your builder, local architect or designer may be required to meet local conditions and requirements. Home Planners may be able to make these changes to Customizable Plans providing you supply all pertinent information from your local building authorities.

Foundation and Exterior Wall Changes
Most of our plans are drawn with either a full or partial basement foundation. Depending upon your specific climate or regional building practices, you may wish to convert this basement to a slab or crawlspace. Most professional contractors and builders can easily adapt your plans to alternate foundation types. Likewise, most can easily convert 2x4 wall construction to 2x6, or vice versa. If you need more guidance on these conversions, our handy Construction Detail Sheets, shown on page 193, describe how such conversions can be made. For Customizable Plans, Home Planners can easily provide the necessary changes for you.

How Many Blueprints Do You Need?
A single set of blueprints is sufficient to study a home in greater detail. However, if you are planning to obtain cost estimates from a contractor or subcontractors—or if you are planning to build immediately—you will need more sets. Because additional sets are cheaper when ordered in quantity with the original order, make sure you order enough blueprints to satisfy all requirements. The following checklist will help you determine how many you need:

_____Owner

_____Builder (generally requires at least three sets; one as a legal document, one to use during inspections, and at least one to give to subcontractors)

_____Local Building Department (often requires two sets)

_____Mortgage Lender (usually one set for a conventional loan; three sets for FHA or VA loans)

_____TOTAL NUMBER OF SETS

Toll Free 1-800-521-6797

Normal Office Hours:
8:00 a.m. to 8:00 p.m. Eastern Time
Monday through Friday
Our staff will gladly answer any questions during normal office hours. Our answering service can place orders after hours or on weekends.

If we receive your order by 5:00 p.m. Eastern Time, Monday through Friday, we'll process it the same day and ship it the following business day. When ordering by phone, please have your charge card ready. We'll also ask you for the Order Form Key Number at the bottom of the coupon. Please use our Toll-Free number for blueprint and book orders only.

For Customization orders call 1-800-322-6797, ext. 134.

By FAX: Copy the Order Form on the next page and send it on our International FAX line: 1-602-297-6219.

Canadian Customers
Order Toll-Free 1-800-848-2550
For faster, more economical service, Canadian customers may now call in orders on our Toll-Free line. Or, complete the order form at right, and mail with your check indicating U.S. funds to:

Home Planners, Inc.
3275 W. Ina Road, Suite 110
Tucson, AZ 85741

By FAX: Copy the Order Form on the next page and send it on our International FAX line: 1-602-297-6219.

ORDER FORM

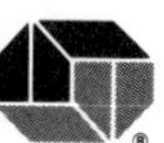

HOME PLANNERS, INC., 3275 WEST INA ROAD
SUITE 110, TUCSON, ARIZONA 85741

THE BASIC BLUEPRINT PACKAGE
Rush me the following (please refer to the Plans Index and Price Schedule in this section):

_____ Set(s) of blueprints for plan number(s) __________. $________
_____ Set(s) of sepias for plan number(s) __________. $________
_____ Additional identical blueprints in same order @ $40.00 per set. $________
_____ Reverse blueprints @ $40.00 per set. $________
_____ Home Customizer™ Kit(s) for Plan(s)__________ @ $19.95 per kit. $________

IMPORTANT EXTRAS
Rush me the following:

_____ Materials List @ $35 Schedule A-D; $45 Schedule E. $________
_____ Specification Outlines @ $5.00 each. $________
_____ Detail Sets @ $14.95 each; any two for $22.95; all three for $29.95 (save $14.90). $________
❑ Plumbing ❑ Electrical ❑ Construction
(These helpful details provide general construction advice and are not specific to any single plan.)

DECK BLUEPRINTS

_____ Set(s) of Deck Plan __________. $________
_____ Additional identical blueprints in same order @ $10.00 per set. $________
_____ Reverse blueprints @ $10.00 per set. $________
_____ Set of Standard Deck Details @ $14.95 per set. $________

LANDSCAPE BLUEPRINTS

_____ Set(s) of Landscape Plan __________. $________
_____ Additional identical blueprints in same order @ $10.00 per set. $________
_____ Reverse blueprints @ $10.00 per set. $________

Please indicate the appropriate region of the country for Plant & Material List. (See Map on page 196): Region ________

SUB-TOTAL $________
SALES TAX (Arizona residents add 5% sales tax; Michigan residents add 4% sales tax.) $________

POSTAGE AND HANDLING	1-3 sets	4 or more sets	
UPS DELIVERY (Requires street address - No P.O. Boxes)			
•UPS Regular Service Allow 4-5 days delivery	❑ $5.00	❑ $7.00	$________
•UPS 2nd Day Air Allow 2-3 days delivery	❑ $7.00	❑ $10.00	$________
•UPS Next Day Air Allow 1-2 days delivery	❑ $16.50	❑ $20.00	$________
POST OFFICE DELIVERY If no street address available. Allow 4-5 days delivery	❑ $7.00	❑ $10.00	$________
OVERSEAS AIR MAIL DELIVERY Note: All delivery times are from date Blueprint Package is shipped.	❑ $30.00	❑ $50.00	$________
	❑ Send COD		

TOTAL (Sub-total, tax, and postage) $________

YOUR ADDRESS (please print)
Name ____________________
Street ____________________
City ____________ State ________ Zip ________
Daytime telephone number (______) ____________

FOR CREDIT CARD ORDERS ONLY
Please fill in the information below:
Credit card number ____________________
Exp. Date: Month/Year ____________________
Check one: ❑ Visa ❑ MasterCard ❑ Discover Card

Signature ____________________
Please check appropriate box:
❑ Licensed Builder-Contractor
❑ Home Owner

Order Form Key
TB23

ORDER TOLL FREE
1-800-521-6797

ORDER FORM

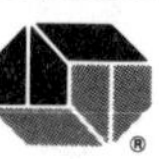

HOME PLANNERS, INC., 3275 WEST INA ROAD
SUITE 110, TUCSON, ARIZONA 85741

THE BASIC BLUEPRINT PACKAGE
Rush me the following (please refer to the Plans Index and Price Schedule in this section):

_____ Set(s) of blueprints for plan number(s) __________. $________
_____ Set(s) of sepias for plan number(s) __________. $________
_____ Additional identical blueprints in same order @ $40.00 per set. $________
_____ Reverse blueprints @ $40.00 per set. $________
_____ Home Customizer™ Kit(s) for Plan(s)__________ @ $19.95 per kit. $________

IMPORTANT EXTRAS
Rush me the following:

_____ Materials List @ $35 Schedule A-D; $45 Schedule E. $________
_____ Specification Outlines @ $5.00 each. $________
_____ Detail Sets @ $14.95 each; any two for $22.95; all three for $29.95 (save $14.90). $________
❑ Plumbing ❑ Electrical ❑ Construction
(These helpful details provide general construction advice and are not specific to any single plan.)

DECK BLUEPRINTS

_____ Set(s) of Deck Plan __________. $________
_____ Additional identical blueprints in same order @ $10.00 per set. $________
_____ Reverse blueprints @ $10.00 per set. $________
_____ Set of Standard Deck Details @ $14.95 per set. $________

LANDSCAPE BLUEPRINTS

_____ Set(s) of Landscape Plan __________. $________
_____ Additional identical blueprints in same order @ $10.00 per set. $________
_____ Reverse blueprints @ $10.00 per set. $________

Please indicate the appropriate region of the country for Plant & Material List. (See Map on page 196): Region ________

SUB-TOTAL $________
SALES TAX (Arizona residents add 5% sales tax; Michigan residents add 4% sales tax.) $________

POSTAGE AND HANDLING	1-3 sets	4 or more sets	
UPS DELIVERY (Requires street address - No P.O. Boxes)			
•UPS Regular Service Allow 4-5 days delivery	❑ $5.00	❑ $7.00	$________
•UPS 2nd Day Air Allow 2-3 days delivery	❑ $7.00	❑ $10.00	$________
•UPS Next Day Air Allow 1-2 days delivery	❑ $16.50	❑ $20.00	$________
POST OFFICE DELIVERY If no street address available. Allow 4-5 days delivery	❑ $7.00	❑ $10.00	$________
OVERSEAS AIR MAIL DELIVERY Note: All delivery times are from date Blueprint Package is shipped.	❑ $30.00	❑ $50.00	$________
	❑ Send COD		

TOTAL (Sub-total, tax, and postage) $________

YOUR ADDRESS (please print)
Name ____________________
Street ____________________
City ____________ State ________ Zip ________
Daytime telephone number (______) ____________

FOR CREDIT CARD ORDERS ONLY
Please fill in the information below:
Credit card number ____________________
Exp. Date: Month/Year ____________________
Check one: ❑ Visa ❑ MasterCard ❑ Discover Card

Signature ____________________
Please check appropriate box:
❑ Licensed Builder-Contractor
❑ Home Owner

Order Form Key
TB23

ORDER TOLL FREE
1-800-521-6797

Additional Plans Books

THE DESIGN CATEGORY SERIES

1.

ONE-STORY HOMES
A collection of 470 homes to suit a range of budgets in one-story living. All popular styles, including Cape Cod, Southwestern, Tudor and French. **384 pages. $8.95 ($10.95 Canada)**

2.

TWO-STORY HOMES
478 plans for all budgets in a wealth of styles: Tudors, Saltboxes, Farmhouses, Victorians, Georgians, Contemporaries and more. **416 pages. $8.95 ($10.95 Canada)**

3.

MULTI-LEVEL AND HILLSIDE HOMES 312 distinctive styles for both flat and sloping sites. Includes exposed lower levels, open staircases, balconies, decks and terraces. **320 pages. $6.95 ($8.95 Canada)**

4.

VACATION AND SECOND HOMES 258 ideal plans for a favorite vacation spot or perfec retirement or starter home. Includes cottages, chalets, and $1\frac{1}{2}$-, 2-, and multi-levels. **256 pages. $5.95 ($7.50 Canada)**

THE EXTERIOR STYLE SERIES

9.

330 EARLY AMERICAN HOME PLANS A heartwarming collection of the best in Early American architecture. Traces the style from Colonial structures to popular traditional versions. Includes a history of different styles. **304 pages. $9.95 ($11.95 Canada)**

10.

335 CONTEMPORARY HOME PLANS Required reading for anyone interested in the clean-lined elegance of Contemporary design. Features plans of all sizes and types, as well as a history of this style. **304 pages. $9.95 ($11.95 Canada)**

11.

COLONIAL HOUSES 161 history-inspired homes with up-to-date plans are featured along with 2-color interior illustrations and 4-color photographs. Included are many plans developed for *Colonial Homes'* History House Series. **208 pages. $10.95 ($12.95 Canada)**

12.

COUNTRY HOUSES Shows off 80 country homes in three eye-catching styles: Cape Cod Farmhouses and Center-Hall Colonials. Each features an architect's exterior rendering, artist's depiction of a furnishe interior room, large floor plan and planning tips. **208 pages. $10.95 ($12.95 Canada)**

PLAN PORTFOLIOS

MOST POPULAR HOME DESIGNS
Our customers' favorite plans, including one-story, $1\frac{1}{2}$-story, two-story, and multi-level homes in a variety of styles. Designs feature many of today's most popular amenities: lounges, clutter rooms, media rooms and more.

14. **272 pages. $8.95 ($10.95 Canada)**

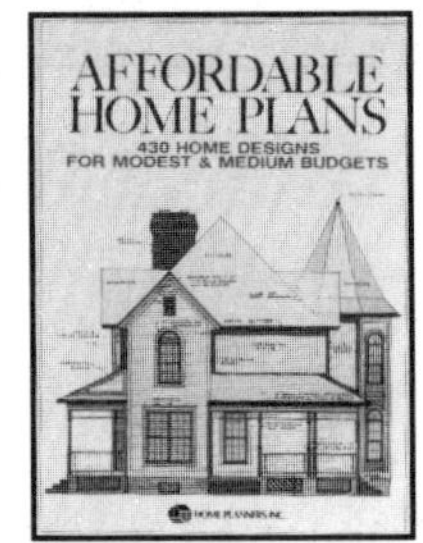

AFFORDABLE HOME PLANS For the prospective home builder with a modest or medium budget. Features 430 one-, $1\frac{1}{2}$-, two-story and multi-level homes in a wealth of styles. Included are cost saving ideas for the budget-conscious.

15. **320 pages. $8.95 ($10.95 Canada)**

LUXURY DREAM HOMES At last, the home you've waited A collection of 150 o best luxury home pl from seven of the m highly regarded designers and archit in the United States. dream come true for anyone interested in designing, building remodeling a luxury home.

16. **192 pages. $14.95 ($17.95 Canada)**

NEW FROM HOME PLANNERS

5.

WESTERN HOME PLANS Over 215 home plans from Spanish Mission and Monterey to Northwest Chateau and San Francisco Victorian. Historical notes trace the background and geographical incidence of each style. **208 pages. $8.95 ($10.95 Canada)**

6.

DECK PLANNER 25 practical plans and details for decks the do-it-yourselfer can actually build. How-to data and project starters for a variety of decks. Construction details available separately. **112 pages. $7.95 ($9.95 Canada)**

7.

THE HOME LANDSCAPER 55 fabulous front- and backyard plans that even the do-it-yourselfer can master. Complete construction blueprints and regionalized plant lists available for each design. **208 pages. $12.95 ($15.95 Canada)**

8.

BACKYARD LANDSCAPER Sequel to the popular *Home Landscaper*, contains 40 professionally designed plans for backyards to do yourself or contract out. Complete construction blueprints and regionalized plant lists available. **160 pages. $12.95 ($15.95 Canada)**

13.

/ICTORIAN DREAM HOMES 160 'ictorian and Farmhouse designs by hree master designers. Victorian style rom Second Empire homes through ıe Queen Anne and Folk Victorian ra. Beautifully drawn renderings ccompany the modern floor plans. **92 Pages. $12.95 ($15.95 Canada)**

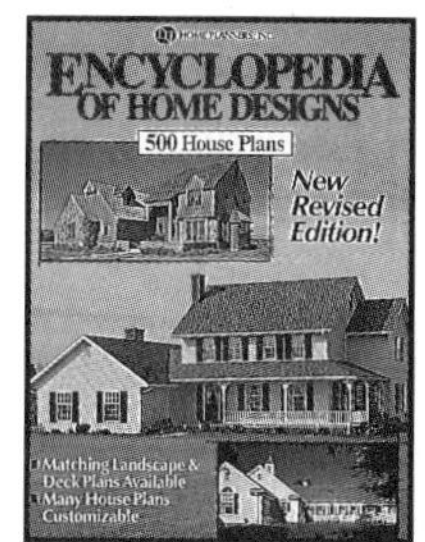

17.

EW ENCYCLOPEDIA OF HOME ESIGNS Our best collection of plans now bigger and better than ever! ver 500 plans organized by architecral category including all types and yles and 269 brand-new plans. The ost comprehensive plan book ever. **2 pages. $9.95 ($11.95 Canada)**

Please fill out the coupon below. We will process your order and ship it from our office within 48 hours. Send coupon and check for the total to:

HOME PLANNERS, INC.
3275 West Ina Road, Suite 110, Dept. BK
Tucson, Arizona 85741

THE DESIGN CATEGORY SERIES — A great series of books edited by design type. Complete collection features 1376 pages and 1273 home plans.

1. _____One-Story Homes @ $8.95 ($10.95 Canada) $ _____
2. _____Two-Story Homes @ $8.95 ($10.95 Canada) $ _____
3. _____Multi-Level & Hillside Homes @ $6.95 ($8.95 Canada) $ _____
4. _____Vacation & Second Homes @ $5.95 ($7.50 Canada) $ _____

NEW FROM HOME PLANNERS

5. _____Western Home Plans @ $8.95 ($10.95 Canada) $ _____
6. _____Deck Planner @ $7.95 ($9.95 Canada) $ _____
7. _____The Home Landscaper @ $12.95 ($15.95 Canada) $ _____
8. _____The Backyard Landscaper @ $12.95 ($15.95 Canada) $ _____

THE EXTERIOR STYLE SERIES

9. _____330 Early American Home Plans @ $9.95 ($11.95 Canada) $ _____
10. _____335 Contemporary Home Plans @ $9.95 ($11.95 Canada) $ _____
11. _____Colonial Houses @ $10.95 ($12.95 Canada) $ _____
12. _____Country Houses @ $10.95 ($12.95 Canada) $ _____
13. _____Victorian Dream Homes @ $12.95 ($15.95 Canada) $ _____

PLAN PORTFOLIOS

14. _____Most Popular Home Designs @ $8.95 ($10.95 Canada) $ _____
15. _____Affordable Home Plans @ $8.95 ($10.95 Canada) $ _____
16. _____Luxury Dream Homes @ $14.95 ($17.95 Canada) $ _____
17. _____New Encyclopedia of Home Designs @ $9.95 ($11.95 Canada) $ _____

Sub-Total $ _____
Arizona residents add 5% sales tax; Michigan residents add 4% sales tax $ _____
ADD Postage and Handling $ 3.00
TOTAL (Please enclose check) $ _____

Name (please print) _____________________
Address _____________________
City _____________ State _____________ Zip _____________

CANADIAN CUSTOMERS: Order books Toll-Free 1-800-848-2550. Or, complete the order form above, and mail with your check indicating U.S. funds to: Home Planners, Inc., 3275 W. Ina Road, Suite 110, Tucson, AZ 85741.

TO ORDER BOOKS BY PHONE CALL TOLL FREE 1-800-322-6797

TB23BK

INDEX